AQA

GCSE

History

AQA B Modern World History

John D Clare

David Ferriby Jim McCabe Alan Mendum Tony Hewitt

www.heinemann.co.uk
✓ Free online support
✓ Useful weblinks
✓ 24 hour online ordering

01865 888080

Heinemann

Part of Pearson

Heinemann is an imprint of Pearson Education Limited, a company incorporated in England and Wales, having its registered office at Edinburgh Gate, Harlow, Essex, CM20 2JE. Registered company number: 872828

www.pearsonschoolsandcolleges.co.uk

Heinemann is a registered trademark of Pearson Education Limited

Original text © David Ferriby, Jim McCabe, Tony Hewitt, Alan Mendum, Steve Waugh and Reed Educational and Professional Publishing Limited 2001, 2002

New material © Pearson Education Ltd 2009

First published 2009

12
10 9 8 7 6 5

British Library Cataloguing in Publication Data
A catalogue record for this book is available from the British Library

ISBN 978 043551041 1

Typeset by Tek-Art, Crawley Down, West Sussex
Original illustrations © Pearson Education Ltd, 2009
Cover photo/illustration © Getty Images/PhotoDisc
Photo research by Frances Topp
Printed and bound by Ashford Colour Press Ltd.

Acknowledgements
The author and publisher would like to thank the following individuals and organisations for permission to reproduce photographs:

Photo acknowledgements
Advertising archives, page 157
akg-images, pages 7, 14, 138, 142, 143, 149, 192, 193, 195 (Dachau), 202
akg-images/Jean-Pierre Verney, page 15
Alamy/Trinity Mirror/Mirrorpix, page 63
Aquarius Collection, page 159
Bridgeman Art Library, pages 11, 148, 161, 164, 208, 215
British Cartoon Archive, University of Kent, pages 12, 29 (Source F), 35, 44, 45, 48, 51, 53 (both), 55, 73, 75, 82, 85, 88, 91, 102, 105, 109, 265
Corbis, pages 25, 62, 99, 128 (Trotsky), 141, 144, 145, 150, 158, 175, 179, 182, 185, 190, 203, 209, 212, 214, 226, 245, 247, 249, 267, 275, 278, 280, 281
Corbis/Bettmann, page 128 (Winter Palace), 160, 166, 167, 222, 246, 272
David King, pages 124, 125, 127, 130, 132, 177, 178
Getty, pages 22, 123 (both), 147, 163 (Source Q), 195 (prisoners), 196, 200, 224, 228, 230, 231, 233, 239, 240, 244, 274, 277
Getty/Hulton Archive, pages 17, 122, 162
Kobal Collection/Universal, page 107
Krause, page 112
Mary Evans Picture Library, page 126, 129, 156
National Archives and Records Administration page 198
National Library of Wales, pages 64, 70, 86, 93
PA Photos AP, page 223, 225, 227, 242, 243, 276
Pacemaker Press, pages 254, 259, 260, 262, 264
Photodisc, page 94
Punch, page 28
Rex Features, page 49
RIA Novosti, pages 67, 120, 172, 176, 181, 183, 187
Science Photo Library/NASA, page 81
Topfoto, pages 18 (Source Q), 52, 84, 163, 165, 229, 255, 256, 257
Topfoto/Punch Limited, pages 13, 31, 33, 37, 47, 69
Unknown, pages 18 (Source P), 29 (Source G), 100, 104, 134, 186, 201, 211
Every effort has been made to contact copyright holders of material reproduced in this book. Any omissions will be rectified in subsequent printings if notice is given to the publishers.

Websites
The websites used in this book were correct and up-to-date at the time of publication. It is essential for tutors to preview each website before using it in class so as to ensure that the URL is still accurate, relevant and appropriate. We suggest that tutors bookmark useful websites and consider enabling students to access them through the school/college intranet.

Contents

Introduction

WELCOME TO GCSE MODERN WORLD HISTORY FOR AQA SPECIFICATION B

This book has been written specifically to support you during your AQA GCSE Modern World History for AQA Specification B.

The course includes a Modern World History student book with an ActiveBook and an ActiveTeach CD-ROM.

How to use this book

The AQA GCSE B Modern World History student book is divided into spreads that cover the material needed for individual lessons. Throughout the book are a number of features designed to help you clarify your understanding of the unit contents. These features include:

Sources

There are a lot of sources included throughout the book to allow you to practise your historical skills.

Historiography

This feature summarises clearly some of the major historiographical issues in each unit's content, presenting some alternative explanations and theories that are current or have been expressed in the past. This feature appears at the start of each chapter in Section 1.

Voice your opinion

There are many important historical debates that you need to be familiar with for your GCSE. We have flagged up some examples throughout the text for you to discuss and form an opinion on. These appear throughout Section 1.

Be a historian

There just isn't enough room to include all of the facts in this book so you are going to have to be a detective and find out some for yourself! This feature will encourage you to find out more or put together your own views. These appear throughout Section 1.

What was going on?

This feature briefly outlines the main themes and issues of the time period and identifies the key points you need to know to understand the period. It appears throughout Section 2A and is designed to help answer an 'inference' question.

Summary

This feature reviews a key issue of the spread and provides a 'for' and 'against' argument for a specific issue. It appears throughout Section 2B and provides exam support for answering this form of question.

Grade Studio

Grade Studio has been designed for you to improve your chances of achieving the best possible grades. Grade Studio appears as a section at the end of each chapter, where exam answers are broken down and the points where marks are awarded are clearly identified.

The student answers in the Grade Studio examples would achieve the highest marks. The comments on the right show where an examiner might award marks. The marks are not cumulative, but to achieve the highest grades you should aim to cover all the highlighted points.

You will find 28 Grade Studio activities throughout the student book on the CD-ROM. Look for this logo to see where activities will be on the CD-ROM.

Exam Café

Exam Café is to be used when revising and preparing for exams. Exam Café could be used in revision classes after school or in revision lessons.

Exam Cafe will help you prepare for the final exam. Like Grade Studio, Exam Café is in the student book with additional resources on the CD-ROM. From the CD-ROM you will be able to access a number of useful resources which will help you to organise your revision, practise exam questions, access sample mark schemes and locate extra resources to stretch yourself. Look for this logo to see where activities will be on the CD-ROM.

How to use this ActiveBook CD-ROM

In the back of your copy of the student book you will find an ActiveBook CD-ROM. This is for individual use and includes a copy of the book on screen, Grade Studio activities which have been designed for individual student use and the whole Exam Café resource.

ActiveTeach CD-ROM for teachers

To use the AQA GCSE Modern World History Specification B ActiveBook CD-ROM in a whole class environment your school needs to purchase the ActiveTeach CD-ROM. The ActiveTeach CD-ROM provides the book on screen to be used for whole class teaching and allows you to add your own resources to the Resource Bank and use annotation tools. The Zoom feature helps to examine sources and focus the class. The CD-ROM also includes interactive activities to be used on the whiteboard to engage your class as well as additional video resources.

You will see logos throughout the student book lessons to indicate where additional teaching resources appear on the ActiveTeach CD-ROM. There are 109 interactive activities and 10 video clips, plus all the teaching notes and worksheets from the teacher guide on the ActiveTeach CD-ROM which are all helpfully divided into lessons to ease your planning.

Interactive activities

Here you will find interactive activities that can be used as whole-class teaching tools. Activities range from review triangles to interactive maps and decision-making activities. All activities are also accompanied by teacher notes with learning objectives and AfL opportunities.

Video clips

From here you can launch video clips to support the student book and specification content. All video clips are accompanied by teacher notes.

International Relations: Conflict and Peace in the 20th Century

How should I study the main events of the 20th century?

The title of Unit 1 in the AQA History Specification B GCSE is International Relations: Conflict and Peace in the 20th Century. The unit is divided into six topics:

1. The origins of the First World War
2. Peacemaking 1918–1919 and the League of Nations
3. Hitler's foreign policy and the origins of the Second World War
4. The origins of the Cold War 1945–1955
5. Crises of the Cold War 1955–1970
6. The failure of Détente and the collapse of communism, 1970–1991

Your teacher will be asking you to study three or maybe four topics from this list.

You will notice that the list does not include the two world wars. The world wars are studied in Unit 3. The focus of Unit 1 is **diplomacy** during the 20th century. It explores how countries around the world dealt with one another. It also examines the aims and actions of the leading figures in international politics.

Unit 1 is assessed by means of a written exam. The exam paper (Paper 1) contains six questions – one for each topic. You must answer three questions. Each is worth 20 marks. Each question has three parts:

1. A 'Describe' question (4 marks)

For this part of the question, you just have to DESCRIBE a key event. The Grade Studio section at the end of each chapter lists all the events covered in that chapter. One way to prepare for the exam is to learn all the facts about these events off by heart.

You must know about these events – not only for the 'Describe' question, which is worth 4 marks, but also for the 'Either-Or' question.

2. An 'Interpretations' question (6 marks)

For this part of a question, you are given a quotation or a cartoon that offers a particular **interpretation** of events. You are then asked if you agree with its interpretation. Usually, it is more difficult to answer a cartoon question than a quotation question.

Analysing a particular interpretation of events – often the point of view of someone who was there at the time – is an important skill for a historian.

You can prepare for the exam by choosing any of the sources in Unit 1 and answering these questions:

a. 'DO I AGREE with this interpretation of events?'

b. 'Looking at the content and **provenance** of the source, WHY do I agree (or disagree) with it?'

3. An 'Either-Or' question (10 marks)

As you learn about the First World War, you will come to realise that a number of events can be seen as CAUSES of the war. In the 'Either-Or' part of the exam question, you are given two events that were among the causes of a major development in international relations.

You are then asked to consider which of the two was the more important cause. You have to DESCRIBE each event, EXPLAIN HOW each one was a cause of the major development and ASSESS which one was the more important cause. This is the highest-scoring question. It is worth 50 per cent of the marks on the paper.

How do I approach a 'Describe' question?

Each question in Paper 1 begins by asking you to describe an event or issue. Here is an example:

In 1946 Winston Churchill claimed that Europe had been divided by an 'Iron Curtain'. Describe how Europe became divided in the years 1945–1946.

These questions often start with some prompt information to try to jog your memory:

In 1946 Winston Churchill claimed that Europe had been divided by an 'Iron Curtain'.

But you need to focus on the part that actually tells you what to do:

Describe how Europe became divided in the years 1945–1946.

How to approach the question

Begin by making an opening statement that answers the question in general terms. For our example question, here are three possible opening statements. Which do you think is the best?

A	B	C
In 1945–46 an 'Iron Curtain' came down which, as Winston Churchill said, divided Europe into two opposing camps.	After the Second World War, the Soviet army stayed on in the countries of eastern Europe, and Stalin made sure that pro-Soviet communist regimes took power.	In 1945–46 communist regimes started to come to power in eastern European countries, which were different to the democratic governments of western Europe.

B or C would do fine for this opening statement. A is not a good answer as it just repeats the prompt information provided in the question.

However, to improve your answer, you need to ADD DETAIL to your description. One way of adding detail is to GO DEEPER by providing at least TWO EXTRA FACTS about the event mentioned in the question. Another way of adding detail is to GO BROADER by providing at least TWO EXTRA FACTS about the historical context of the event mentioned in the question.

Here are a few examples of extra facts about the Iron Curtain that would improve your answer:

a. At the Yalta Conference (and again at Potsdam), Stalin agreed with Britain and the USA that Germany would be divided into four 'sectors'.

b. At Yalta, Stalin agreed that Poland would be governed by both communists and non-communists. However, he then arrested non-communists, and the communists took over.

c. During the war, Stalin had given exiled communist governments training in how to take over their countries once the war had ended. After 1945 the exiled communists carried out this training. They returned to all the countries of eastern Europe, took control of the police and the radio and tried to win elections.

d. By 1946, Stalinist regimes had seized power in Albania, Bulgaria and Poland, and Stalinists were part of left-wing coalitions in Romania, Hungary and Czechoslovakia.

GradeStudio

Watch out for DATES!

The question specifies 1945–46, so you must not talk about communist takeovers in Romania, Hungary or Czechoslovakia. Those countries did not become communist until 1947.

BE A HISTORIAN!

- Choose an opening statement and two extra details from those given on this page. Write them out in your own words as though you were answering the example 'Describe' question in an exam.
- Choose some other events you have studied and practise writing 'Describe' answers for them.

How do I approach an 'Interpretations' question?

In the second part of each Paper 1 question you will be given a source and then asked whether you agree with its interpretation of events. Here is an example:

Source D

The Marshall Plan was seen as the Americans wanting to impose their influence over the countries to which they gave Marshall Aid. We saw it as an act of aggression by the Americans. This is why it was never accepted by the Soviet Union.

A Soviet view of the Marshall Plan, written in 1988 by Dimitri Sukhanov.

Sukhanov had been a senior Soviet politician when the Marshall Plan began in 1947.

Source D suggests reasons why the Americans introduced the Marshall Plan. Do you agree that these were the main reasons for the introduction of the Marshall Plan? Explain your answer by referring to the purpose of the source, as well as using its content and your knowledge.

How to approach the question

To answer this question you need to address TWO issues:

1. The provenance

The first issue is the provenance of the source – where it comes from. Who wrote it, drew it or said it? Is that person a reliable witness whose opinions you might wish to respect?

- In a basic answer, you would need to point out the basic significance of the source's provenance. In this example, because Sukhanov was a leading Soviet at the time, his testimony might be unreliable. Sukhanov was not an unbiased observer of American actions.

- In a more advanced answer, you would also need to add more DETAIL. You would need to EXPLAIN HOW the witness's personal situation or role in events might make his or her testimony either MORE RELIABLE (in this case, for example, Sukhanov might have inside information on how Stalin was thinking) or LESS RELIABLE (here, Sukhanov might be trying to justify Stalin's refusal to allow Marshall Aid to reach communist countries).

- To decide why the provenance of a source might be important, you will need to think especially about its purpose – why was it produced? What was the person who produced it trying to achieve?

2. The content

The second issue is the source's content. What historical event or situation is the source showing or describing? Is the source truthful? To decide how truthful it is, you will need to use your own knowledge of what happened.

- In a basic answer, you would need to connect the source to your general knowledge of events at the time. In this example, Sukhanov might be right; the purpose of Marshall Aid was to try to prevent the countries of Europe from becoming communist.

- In a more advanced answer, you would need to show a greater knowledge of specific facts and a greater understanding of events. You would need to EXPLAIN WHETHER you agree with the opinion given in the source. In this case, for example, you might find some truth in Sukhanov's statement – you could support your argument with details about the ambitions of the Truman Doctrine to 'contain communism' or details about the large proportion of Marshall Aid that was spent buying weapons and goods from the USA.

Watch out for DATES!

A source's date is an important aspect of its provenance. Sukhanov made this statement in 1988. The Cold War had not yet come to an end, and he may have been trying to make himself and Stalin look good or to blame the USA. Alternatively, long after the events he was describing, Sukhanov may have been looking back with 'rose-tinted spectacles'.

BE A HISTORIAN!

Using the ideas given on these pages, write a two-paragraph answer to the 'Interpretation' question.

- In the first paragraph, explain how the provenance makes you trust or distrust the source.

- In the second paragraph, explain whether your knowledge of the situation in 1947 leads you to agree or disagree with the source.

How do I approach an 'Either-Or' question?

In the third part of each Paper 1 question you will be given two events. You will be asked which of them you think was the more important cause of a major international development. Here is an example:

Which was the more important cause of Great Britain's entry into the First World War:

- The naval race with Germany 1906–14
- The Schlieffen Plan?

You must refer to both causes when giving your answer.

This question is about the EFFECTS of two particular events. However, before you start answering, you must look at the first part of the question. The question is not just about the general effects of the naval race and the Schlieffen Plan... it is about a specific effect of these events. HOW did the naval race and the Schlieffen Plan lead to Britain's entry into the First World War?

How to approach the question

To fully answer this question, you will need to **D**escribe – **E**xplain – **A**ssess – **C**ompare.

1. **Describe**
   You already know how to answer a 'Describe' question – you give a general description and add detail by mentioning two extra facts (see page 4). Start the 'Either-or' question by simply treating it as two 'Describe' questions. In this example, you would write a description first of the naval race and then a description of the Schlieffen Plan.

2. **Explain**
   Simple descriptions of the two events, of course, do not answer the question of which was the more important cause of Britain's entry into the war. So you now need to EXPLAIN HOW each of these events pushed Britain into the war.

3. **Assess**
   The question does not ask you just to explain how the two events led Britain to go to war with Germany. It asks you which was the more important event. So you now need to ASSESS HOW IMPORTANT these events were in pushing Britain into the war. Part of the way to do this is by looking at the RESULTS of both events.

4. **Compare**
   The final step is to compare the importance of one event with the importance of the other. You will need to write a write a final conclusion that EXPLAINS WHY one event is, in your opinion, more important than the other.

GradeStudio

MAKE UP YOUR MIND!

In your conclusion, don't just say that both events were important. And don't just repeat points you have already made. CHOOSE one of the two events, and think of a reason WHY you have chosen it as the more important one.

One good tip is to look at the DATES – the event that came later was probably the more important one.

BE A HISTORIAN!

1. Using the ideas given on these pages, DESCRIBE, then EXPLAIN, then ASSESS the Schlieffen Plan. Do the same for the naval race.

2. Finally, write a paragraph in which you COMPARE the importance of the naval race with the importance of the Schlieffen Plan. Decide which was the more important – and explain why you made that decision.

1.1 The Origins of the First World War

Overview

The world changed in 1871

Up until 1871, Germany had been not a single country but a collection of many states, some of them tiny. In 1871 the biggest of the German states, Prussia, defeated France in a war. The two French provinces of Alsace and Lorraine became part of the new German **Empire**, which was declared in the Palace of Versailles, near Paris.

In the 19th century, international relations had been dominated by two forces – **nationalism** (the belief in 'my nation, right or wrong') and **imperialism** (the belief that nations had the right to conquer other lands and build up an empire).

The British, who truly believed that 'Britannia ruled the waves', had an empire which covered one-fifth of the globe. The French, too, had a huge **colonial** empire. The French longed to take revenge on Germany for Alsace-Lorraine. Russia ruled an empire that stretched across all of Asia.

Even so, during the 19th century these nations believed that they ought to work together to keep the peace. The presence of huge areas of the globe which they could easily conquer, especially in Africa, gave them an alternative outlet for their military ambitions.

The arrival of Germany on the world stage **destabilised** international relations. The new nation was an economic and military superpower. Its strength frightened other nations.

One way in which the other nations responded was by forming **alliances** – defensive agreements with other

HISTORIOGRAPHY

In 1919 the Treaty of Versailles explicitly blamed Germany for causing the First World War. During the 1920s, however, when Germany was regaining international respectability, the American historian Sydney Bradshaw Fay argued that no specific country or person had been to blame for the war. Fay claimed that general forces – such as nationalism, imperialism, militarism and the formation of alliances – had dragged the world inevitably into war 'like mountain climbers tied to the same rope'.

The events of the Second World War, particularly the actions of Hitler, made historians less forgiving towards Germany. The British historian A.J.P. Taylor blamed a German 'bid for continental supremacy' for bringing on the First World War (The Struggle for Mastery, 1954). In the 1960s the German historian Fritz Fischer argued that there had been a 'will to war' amongst Germany's leaders (Germany's Aims in the First World War, 1961).

More recently, some historians have blamed Austria-Hungary for causing the First World War, and others have blamed Russia. It is even possible to blame the British, who were openly hostile towards Germany.

TIMELINE

1871	1882	1894	1902	1904	1905	1907	1908
Germany becomes a single country	Triple Alliance	France makes an alliance with Russia	Anglo-Japanese naval agreement	Entente Cordiale	First Moroccan crisis; Schlieffen Plan completed	Triple Entente	Bosnia annexed Austria-Hungary

countries. A nation would join an alliance in order to protect itself from attack. The idea was that a hostile power would not dare to attack a member of an alliance for fear of retaliation by all of its allies.

A second idea behind alliances was **militarism**, the belief that it was important for a country to have a strong and well-prepared fighting force that it could call on at any time.

In the years up to 1914, tensions increased

- Germany resented Britain's navy and its empire. In the years after 1898, Germany built up a powerful navy in order to challenge Britain and give Germany – in the words of the German emperor, Kaiser Wilhelm II – 'a place in the sun'.

- In 1905 and again in 1911, France and Germany clashed in Morocco. On both occasions, the alliance system worked, and Germany was forced to back down.

- A greater worry, however, was the Balkan Peninsula, an area in south-east Europe which had been conquered by the Turks. By 1878 the Turkish Empire had become too weak to keep control in the Balkans, and new Slav nation–states, such as Serbia, Bulgaria, and Romania, had seized independence there.

- The rulers of Austria-Hungary, who had many Slav peoples among their subjects, were greatly alarmed by the emergence in the region of independent Slav nations – especially Serbia. Austro-Hungarian generals regularly argued for war.

Looking back, what seems remarkable is not that war broke out in 1914, but that it had not broken out sooner. The years 1870–1914 saw resentments and tensions steadily increasing in Europe. It was as though a fireworks manufacturer were stuffing a rocket with gunpowder. By 1914 all that was needed was a small spark to light the blue touch-paper.

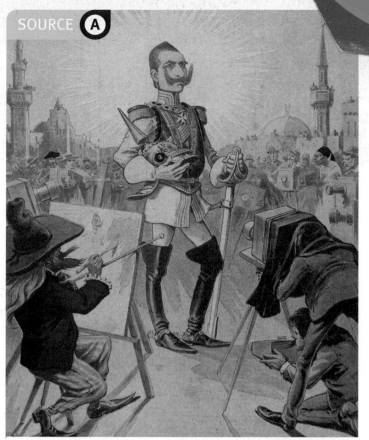

SOURCE Ⓐ

This cartoon was drawn by a French artist. It picks up on Kaiser Wilhelm II's famous declaration, made in 1901, that he wanted Germany to have 'a place in the sun'. In the cartoon, a haughty Wilhelm is dressed in military uniform and is being cheered, photographed and painted. The cartoonist ridicules Wilhelm's physical appearance, including his withered left arm (a deformity he had had since birth).

The cartoonist suggests that Wilhelm was a ridiculous, militaristic megalomaniac.

BE A HISTORIAN!

How many different possible causes of the First World War can you find on this double-page spread?

		5 July 1914 German 'blank cheque' to Austria	30 July 1914 Russia mobilises	3 August 1914 Germany declares war on France
11	**1912–13** **1914**			
Agadir crisis	Balkan Wars	28 June 1914 Assassination of Archduke Franz Ferdinand	23 July 1914 Austrian ultimatum to Serbia	1 August 1914 Germany declares war on Russia	4 August 1914 Britain declares war on Germany

1.1a Why were there two armed camps in Europe in 1914?

Wilhelm II's *Weltpolitik*

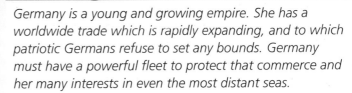

Weltpolitik (literally, 'world politics') is the term used to describe the foreign policy of Wilhelm II, who became the Kaiser (emperor) of Germany in 1888.

The new nation of Germany was the strongest industrial country in Europe. Its army was the most powerful in the world. However, because it was a new country, it did not have an empire. Many Germans felt that, as a result, their country was undervalued by the other countries of Europe.

The aim of *Weltpolitik* was to win Germany the respect it deserved from the world. Kaiser Wilhelm wanted his nation to emerge from the shadows and take its 'place in the sun'. He sought to achieve this goal with an aggressive foreign policy.

One of Wilhelm's ambitions was to turn Germany into a huge trading nation. In order to do so, the country would need an African empire. To become an imperial power, Germany would need a strong navy – as strong as Britain's. At that time, the British Empire covered one-fifth of the globe. Wilhelm's ambition alarmed the British.

Meanwhile, in Germany an organisation called the **Pan-German League** looked forward to the creation of 'Mitteleuropa' – a strong state encompassing all of central Europe that would be dominated by Germany and would include all people of Germanic race.

Wilhelm's aggressive foreign policy spread fear among many European countries, especially Britain, France and Russia. British fears intensified in 1908, when, in an interview he gave to the *Daily Telegraph* newspaper, Wilhelm declared that the English were 'as mad as March hares' and admitted that the German people disliked Britain.

VOICE YOUR OPINION!

Looking at Sources B–D, construct an argument that Germany was to blame for the First World War.

SOURCE B

Germany is a young and growing empire. She has a worldwide trade which is rapidly expanding, and to which patriotic Germans refuse to set any bounds. Germany must have a powerful fleet to protect that commerce and her many interests in even the most distant seas.

This comment was made by Kaiser Wilhelm to a *Daily Telegraph* reporter in 1908 and suggests that Germany wanted to become a dominant world power. The article was submitted to the German foreign office, which agreed that it could be published.

SOURCE C

Germany's foreign policy was based on a wish for growth. Sometimes it was friendly and based on reaching agreement. At other times it was aggressive. The final aim was always to expand German power and land.

This was written by the respected German historian Fritz Fischer in 1966.

SOURCE D

The aim is security for the German Reich ['realm'] for all imaginable time. France must be so weakened as to make her revival as a great power impossible for all time. Russia must be pushed back as far as possible from Germany's eastern frontier…

Furthermore: a commercial treaty which secures the French market for our exports and makes it possible to exclude British trade from France…

We must establish Germany's economic dominance over Mitteleuropa…

The question of colonial acquisitions, where the first aim is the creation of a Central African colonial empire…

Extracts from a list of war aims written by the German chancellor Theobald von Bethmann-Hollweg in September 1914.

The Alliance System, 1900–14

The division of the Great Powers of Europe (the British Empire, France, the Russian Empire, Germany, Austria-Hungary and Italy) into rival alliances is often seen as a major cause of the First World War.

- In 1882 Germany had formed an alliance with Austria-Hungary and Italy. Under this agreement, known as the **Triple Alliance**, the three powers undertook to help one another if they were attacked by an enemy power.

- Germany also had a **treaty** with Russia, but in 1890 Wilhelm let this treaty lapse.

- Soon after, in 1894, Russia formed an alliance with France. Under this agreement the two countries agreed to help each other if Germany attacked either of them.

In the 19th century, Britain had tried to remain in 'splendid isolation' by keeping out of global politics and concentrating only on its empire. However, fear of Germany's growing navy pulled Britain into the Alliance System after 1900.

- In 1902 Britain made a naval agreement with Japan.

- In 1904 Britain signed the **Entente Cordiale** (Friendly Agreement) with France. The two countries agreed to remain on good terms and not to quarrel over the ownership of colonies.

- In 1907 Britain also reached a friendly agreement with Russia. The Entente Cordiale became the **Triple Entente**.

The Great Powers of Europe were now divided into two opposing alliances. At the time, no one thought that this division might cause a war. In fact, people thought the formation of alliances would prevent war. After all, the treaties were defensive: a country agreed to help its ally only if its ally was attacked.

So why is the Alliance System seen as a cause of the First World War? The answer is that in a number of ways the system increased the atmosphere of suspicion and mistrust in Europe.

- The treaties the allies signed were secret. Therefore, a country had no way of knowing that its rivals were forming an alliance purely as a defensive measure and suspected instead that its rivals were making an aggressive move.

- As relations between rival powers worsened, each power would look for the support of its allies. In this way, the Alliance System turned local disputes into wider hostility.

- The Great Powers were also involved in a race to build up their arms and navies. Therefore, at the same time as becoming more aggressive, the rival alliances grew militarily stronger.

- Each alliance tried to get the better of the other in a series of conflicts between 1900 and 1914. These conflicts increased the tension between the powers, strengthened the alliances and created a highly volatile situation in which one incident could spark a war. The assassination in 1914 of Archduke Franz Ferdinand of Austria-Hungary was just such an incident.

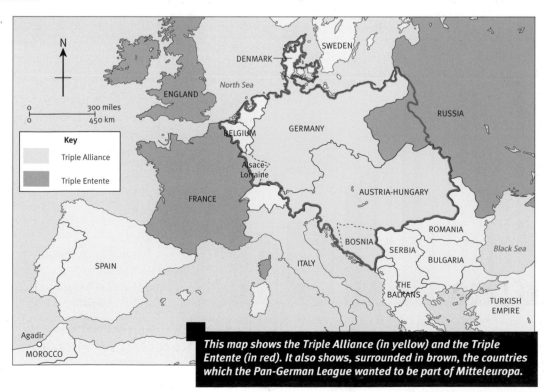

This map shows the Triple Alliance (in yellow) and the Triple Entente (in red). It also shows, surrounded in brown, the countries which the Pan-German League wanted to be part of Mitteleuropa.

The Arms Race

The build-up of armies, 1900–14

The existence of large armies in Europe was another threat to peace. Military leaders argued that the only way to ensure peace was to have an army strong enough to deter another country from invading. This view was supported by the manufacturers of arms, who made vast profits from the **arms race**.

All of the Great Powers, except for Britain, increased the size of their army during this period (see diagram, below).

- In 1913 the French raised the period of **conscription** (compulsory military service) from two years to three. The Russians raised theirs from three to three and a half years. This change of policy gave both countries more trained soldiers.

- By 1913 the German army was very powerful. Only Russia had more soldiers.

- Britain was the only power that had not introduced conscription by 1914.

Though the Russian army was the largest, it was badly equipped and far inferior to Germany's army. The Germans took pride in their armed forces. This military pride was encouraged by the Kaiser, who enjoyed being photographed in military uniform (see Source A on page 7).

(see Source A on page 7)

SOURCE

General von Moltke said: 'I believe war is unavoidable; war the sooner the better.' The Kaiser supported this. Tirpitz said that the navy would prefer to see the postponement of the great fight for one and a half years.

Notes made by the German naval commander Karl von Müller, who had attended a 'naval war cabinet' meeting with the Kaiser in December 1912. Moltke was head of the army, Tirpitz was head of the navy. This source suggests that the German military actively wanted war.

VOICE YOUR OPINION!

'Don't blame Germany. Britain and France were the aggressors – Germany was just defending itself.'
Are there ANY facts which support this opinion?

SOURCE E

The build-up of armies in Europe, 1900–14.

Key
- 1900
- 1910
- 1914

(Bar chart showing army sizes for Russia, Germany, France, Britain, Italy, Austria–Hungary, with vertical axis from 0 to 1,500,000.)

GradeStudio

A 'Describe' answer involves giving a general opening statement about the issue, and then writing about two or three aspects in detail. For instance, if you were asked to describe 'The Arms Race', you could describe it in general terms, before writing in detail about conscription in the French army, the growth in numbers of the different armies from 1900 to 1914, and the Dreadnought crisis of 1909.

The naval arms race, 1906–14

As an island nation with a large overseas empire, Britain needed a powerful navy. Since the British army was very small, Britain relied even more heavily on naval power. At the end of the 19th century, Britain had the largest navy in the world.

In 1898 Kaiser Wilhelm ordered Admiral Tirpitz, the head of the German navy, to build up Germany's navy rapidly so that it could rival Britain's. The British saw this development as a direct challenge to their nation and empire. The alliances Britain made with France and Russia were prompted in part by fears about Germany's naval buildup.

The German navy became a real threat to Britain after 1906, when both sides began building **Dreadnoughts**. This new kind of battleship was easily able to destroy the older types of battleships. Britain's naval supremacy depended on the older ships. So Britain and Germany began a race to build the most Dreadnoughts.

The naval race reached a peak in 1909. The government in Britain had planned to build only four Dreadnoughts in 1909–10. The Germans refused to limit the number of Dreadnoughts they would build. Many people in Britain saw the German naval buildup as a serious threat to British naval superiority. Public pressure on the government mounted, and there was a campaign for the government to spend more money building Dreadnoughts. The campaign's slogan was 'we want eight and we won't wait'. The government gave way and increased its spending on the British fleet in order to maintain Britain's naval superiority over Germany.

The naval race did much to make the British resent and fear the Germans and to lead Britain into a better relationship with France. However, the naval race was not the main cause of Britain's decision to go to war in 1914 – by then Britain had far more Dreadnoughts than the Germans.

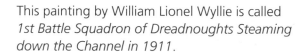

SOURCE G

Number of Dreadnoughts completed

	Great Britain	Germany
1907	1	–
1908	3	–
1909	3	4
1910	3	1
1911	4	6
1912	11	5
1913	2	1
1914	7	5
Total	34	22

This table shows how many Dreadnoughts Britain and Germany built during their naval race.

VOICE YOUR OPINION!

'The nations of Europe thought they were avoiding war, but everything they did only brought war closer'.

Do the facts support this view?

SOURCE H

This painting by William Lionel Wyllie is called *1st Battle Squadron of Dreadnoughts Steaming down the Channel in 1911*.

Wyllie was a British artist and a sailor. What image does this painting present?

SOURCE H

1.1b Why did war break out in 1914?

Murder at Sarajevo

The Black Hand

The **Black Hand**, a terrorist group formed in 1910, wanted to unite all Serbs living in the Balkans into a single 'Greater Serbia'. The group was led by a Serb colonel by the name of Dragutin Dimitrijevic (codenamed Apis). The Black Hand organised groups of bandits and trained **assassins**.
In 1911 the group attempted to assassinate the Austrian Emperor Franz Josef.

In 1914 the Black Hand decided to assassinate Archduke Franz Ferdinand, the heir to the throne of Austria-Hungary. The group wanted to destabilise the Austro-Hungarian empire and to make public their opposition to Austria-Hungary's annexation of Bosnia. Ironically, Franz Ferdinand was known to favour increased civil rights for Slavs. The Black Hand feared that if Franz Ferdinand succeeded in granting Serbs greater freedoms, they would be happy to remain under Austro-Hungarian rule, and support for a Greater Serbia would weaken.

This artist's impression of the assassination of Franz Ferdinand was drawn in 1914 by Felix Schwormstaedt and published in the German magazine **Illustrierte Zeitung**.

HISTORIOGRAPHY

In 1969, in his book *War by Timetable*, the British historian A.J.P. Taylor argued that railway timetables caused the First World War. He argued that the plans for calling up millions of soldiers – in particular working out the train timetables involved – were so complicated that once **mobilisation** had begun, plans could not be altered to suit the changing situation.

In 1914 the Germans had to implement the Schlieffen Plan. It was the only plan they had. Yet the war was not unolding as the plan had predicted it would. In fact, the plan had envisaged a radically different scenario.

German trains therefore took troops towards France according to the prearranged plan – even though the Germans really wanted to confront Russia. Similarly, the Schlieffen Plan forced the German army to go through Belgium – even though they knew this action would provoke Britain into war. And when Kaiser Wilhelm tried to pause the German mobilisation to give Russia time to back down, his generals told him that he could not. A total of 11,000 trains were on the move, and mobilisation could not be stopped.

SOURCE **K**

We muddled into war… The nations slithered over the brink into the boiling cauldron of war without any trace of apprehension or dismay… not one of them wanted war; certainly not on this scale.

A statement from David Lloyd George's *War Memoirs*, written in 1934. Lloyd George was a British government minister in 1914 and became prime minister during the war.

Death in Sarajevo

On 28 June 1914 Franz Ferdinand visited the Bosnian capital, Sarajevo. The Black Hand made two attempts to kill him. In the first, a bomb was thrown at the Archduke, but he deflected it so that it fell behind his car, where it exploded and injured several people in the following car.

The archduke cancelled his tour but insisted on visiting the injured in hospital. The driver of the royal car took a wrong turning. As he stopped to reverse, one of the assassins, Gavrilo Princip, fired two shots. The first one hit the archduke, and the second hit his wife. His wife died immediately. Franz Ferdinand died on the way to hospital.

Austria attacks Serbia

Such a murder would normally have been a matter for only the two countries involved. But relations between the alliances of Great Powers were so strained in 1914 that this event led to the outbreak of the First World War.

Some politicians in Austria-Hungary saw the assassination as an excuse for attacking Serbia and solving the problem of nationalist Serbs living within the Austro-Hungarian Empire (see page 13). The Austrians had no proof that the Serbian government had anything to do with the assassination. Nevertheless, on 23 July the Austrians issued an ultimatum to Serbia to comply with ten conditions or face war. The conditions demanded that the Serbians suppress all anti-Austrian activity in Serbia.

The Serbian reply to the Austrian ultimatum indicated that Serbia did not want a war. In fact, Serbia agreed to all the conditions except one (the sixth): it could not allow delegates from Austria-Hungary to be involved in the inquiry into the assassination. The Serbian government promised to hold an inquiry but could not accept Austro-Hungarian involvement. It felt that allowing the Serbian courts to be influenced by a foreign country would be a threat to Serb independence.

Although the Serbian government did not agree to this condition, it stressed that it was prepared to refer the dispute to an international court if Austria-Hungary was not satisfied with its reply.

Serbia's long-term aim remained the same: to unite all the Serbs living within the Austro-Hungarian empire into a Greater Serbia. However, in 1914 Serbia was recovering from the Balkan Wars, which had been fought in 1912 and 1913. It did not want to plunge into war with Austria-Hungary.

The Serb government had no official links whatsoever to the Black Hand Group, which was responsible for the assassination of Franz Ferdinand. Therefore, Serbia could see no justification for Austria-Hungary's declaration of war in 1914.

SOURCE **L**

An unjust war has been declared on a weak country. The anger in Russia shared fully by me is enormous. I foresee that very soon I shall be overwhelmed by the pressure forced upon me and be forced to take extreme measures which will lead to war. To try and avoid such a calamity as a European war I beg you in the name of our old friendship to do what you can to stop your allies from going too far. Nicky.

This telegram was sent from Tsar Nicolas to his cousin, Kaiser Wilhelm, on 29 July – the day before Russia announced mobilisation.

SOURCE **M**

I no longer have any doubt that Britain, Russia and France have agreed among themselves to wage war to destroy us. The encirclement of Germany has already been achieved.

Kaiser Wilhelm, speaking in 1914 before the outbreak of war.

SOURCE **N**

A cartoon of 1914, showing Germany's Kaiser Wilhelm terrified by the approaching Russian armies.

The cartoon's message is that Germany is terrified by Russia's mobilisation.

The Slide to War

Russia mobilises against Austria-Hungary

Although the Serbs had accepted most of the Austrian ultimatum, a number of leading figures in Austria-Hungary were determined to deal with Serbia militarily. On 28 July Austria-Hungary rejected the Serb response to its ultimatum and declared war. The Austro-Hungarian declaration of war on Serbia was the first step towards general war in 1914.

During the Bosnian crisis of 1908–9, Russia had let down its Slav allies in the Balkans. Tsar Nicholas II was determined not to fail Serbia again. The Russians first confirmed that they had the support of France. Then, on 30 July, they mobilised their army and made preparations for war.

Austria-Hungary, however, had not acted alone. On 5 July Austrian delegates had visited Germany to find out where the Kaiser stood on the Serbian question. They had received an assurance that Germany would support Austria-Hungary. Historians have called this assurance the 'blank cheque' – Germany promised to support Austria-Hungary *whatever the cost*.

Now that Russia was mobilising, the Austro-Hungarians expected Germany's help. Furthermore, Germany argued that allowing your neighbour to mobilise against you was like letting an enemy put a gun to your head. By the end of July, the Germans had decided to go to war.

Germany plans for war

Since the Franco-Russian Treaty of 1894 (see page 9), Germany had faced the problem of a possible war with France and Russia at the same time.

The German head of general staff was Count Alfred von Schlieffen. Von Schlieffen believed that the way to cope with this war on two fronts was to defeat France first before Russia was ready. Once the French were defeated, the Germans could then turn east and fight Russia. Von Schlieffen estimated that it would take the Russians at least six weeks to prepare for war because of the vast size of the country and its poor transport system.

In 1905 von Schlieffen finished drawing up a plan to defeat France within six weeks. The right wing of the German forces would attack France through Belgium and the Netherlands, leaving a much smaller force to hold off a French attack on Germany in Alsace-Lorraine. The plan was changed in 1914 by General Moltke: he attacked only through Belgium and strengthened the force in Alsace-Lorraine at the expense of the right wing.

VOICE YOUR OPINION!

'Germany fuelled the tension; Austria-Hungary was the first to attack. But it was Tsar Nicholas of Russia who turned the crisis into a world war.'

Do you agree?

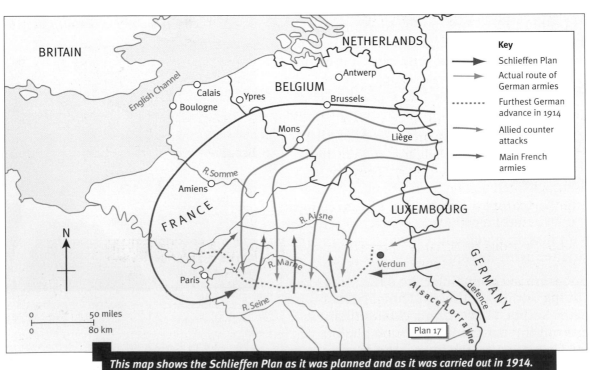

This map shows the Schlieffen Plan as it was planned and as it was carried out in 1914.

The Russian mobilisation in July 1914 threw the Germans into a panic. Their war plan depended on war with France and Russia breaking out at the same time and on defeating France before Russia was ready to fight. Now Russia was already preparing to fight, and every day that passed was a day less in which to defeat France. Chancellor Bethmann-Hollweg asked General Moltke, 'Is the Fatherland in danger?' Moltke's reply was 'Yes'.

On 1 August 1914, Germany supported its ally Austria-Hungary by declaring war on Russia and, two days later, on France.

The Schlieffen Plan was a critical factor in the outbreak of war because it was a plan of attack. Unlike Russia, Germany could not mobilise its forces merely as a threat of war or as part of a gradual preparation for war. When the German army mobilised, the fighting started. It is arguable that the Schlieffen Plan, more than any other individual factor, caused the war.

On 3 August 1914 the Germans launched the Schlieffen Plan and attacked France from the north through Belgium.

Britain enters the war

The British government was not keen on joining the war. At first the British foreign secretary, Sir Edward Grey, said Britain would remain **neutral** unless Germany attacked the north coast of France. Even after Germany declared war on Russia, the British cabinet stated on 2 August that they would go to war only if the neutrality of Belgium was violated.

On 4 August, the day after the Germans invaded Belgium, Britain declared war on Germany.

Why did Britain enter the war? In part because it had guaranteed the neutrality of Belgium in 1839. Once a treaty had been agreed, it had to be honoured. The invasion of Belgium by Germany broke international law. Furthermore, the coasts of Belgium and northern France were only a short distance away. They could easily be used to launch an attack on Britain. The British wanted to prevent these coastlines from falling into the hands of a potential enemy.

There were other reasons for Britain's entry into the war. The British wanted to prevent Germany from becoming too strong in Europe. They did not want the whole of Europe to fall under the control of a single power. Another important factor was public opinion. The vast majority of people in Britain supported Belgium and favoured war. The invasion of Belgium ensured that Britain was united in going to war.

SOURCE O

A photograph of British people signing up to join the army in 1914. This source shows how immensely popular the outbreak of war was in all the countries of Europe.

GradeStudio

To explain the importance of an event, you need to think about its results. For instance, if you were asked how important the Schlieffen Plan was in causing the First World War, you could offer three consequences:
1. Because it was a plan of attack, it turned ultimatums and mobilisations into actual fighting.
2. Because it attacked France, it brought France into the war even though it was Russia which was mobilising.
3. Because it went through Belgium, it brought Britain into the war.

VOICE YOUR OPINION!

'A peaceable, sensible mass of 500 million Europeans was hounded by a few dozen incapable leaders into a war which in no way was destined or inevitable.'
Do you agree?

This cartoon, entitled *A Chain of Friendship*, appeared in the *Brooklyn Eagle*, an American newspaper, in July 1914. The caption read: 'If Austria attacks Serbia, Russia will fall upon Austria, Germany upon Russia, and France and England upon Germany'.

The cartoon shows Austria, which is threatening Serbia, being threatened by Russia, which is being threatened by Germany, which is being threatened by Britain and France. In the event, things did not happen exactly as the cartoon predicted: Germany attacked France as well as Russia, and Britain entered the war to defend Belgium, not Russia.

This cartoon was published in August 1914 in the British humorous magazine *Punch*. The grumpy old man, sausages hanging from his pocket, represents Germany. He is waving a large club at a young boy, who represents Belgium. Though armed with only a small stick, the boy is determined to defend his right of way.

The cartoon sums up how the British felt about the invasion of Belgium – that a brave small nation was being unjustly attacked by a stronger, aggressive power.

Who was to blame for the war?

It is possible to formulate an argument which blames anyone and everyone for causing World War One.

- Serbia could be blamed for encouraging the assassination of Franz Ferdinand and for rejecting Austria-Hungary's ultimatum.
- Austria-Hungary could be blamed for manipulating the situation to gain an opportunity to invade Serbia.
- Russia could be blamed for an irresponsible mobilisation, which Russia must have known would provoke Germany.
- Germany can be blamed for wanting war – planning it as early, perhaps, as 1912 – and for not accepting Russia's assurances that the mobilisation was against Austria only. It can be argued that Germany's 'blank cheque' to Austria was a major factor in causing the war and that the Schlieffen Plan turned defensive mobilisations into an offensive conflict.
- Even Great Britain could be blamed – for the naval race and for becoming involved in a continental war on what was (as Belgian neutrality was in reality) a technicality.

Preparation - 'Describe'

- the Triple Alliance
- the Triple Entente
- Kaiser Wilhelm's foreign policy
- the Moroccan crises of 1905 and 1911
- the Bosnian crisis of 1908
- the military arms race
- the naval arms race
- Austria-Hungary's aims in the Balkans
- the Black Hand
- Serbia's aims in the Balkans
- the assassination in Sarajevo
- the events of 28 June to 4 August 1914
- the Schlieffen Plan

1. Looking back through this chapter, write a short paragraph describing IN GENERAL TERMS each item in the panel on the left.

2. Using this textbook, an encyclopaedia or the internet, ADD DETAIL by finding out two or more EXTRA FACTS about each item on the left. You could GO DEEPER by finding out more about a particular aspect. Or you could GO BROADER by putting each item in its wider context.

3. Choose ONE item and write a full 'Describe' essay of three paragraphs.

Preparation - 'Why?'

WHY...

- did Britain fear Germany?
- did Germany resent Britain?
- did Austria-Hungary fear Serbia?
- did Russia support Serbia?
- did Germany intervene in Morocco?
- did Austria-Hungary annex Bosnia?

- did Princip assassinate Franz Ferdinand?
- did Austria-Hungary declare war on Serbia?
- did Russia mobilise?
- did Germany declare war on Russia?
- did German troops invade Belgium?
- did Britain enter the war?

1. Working in a small group, think of TWO reasons for each situation in the list above.

Preparation - 'How?'

HOW did this...

- the system of alliances...
- the naval arms race...
- the Moroccan crises, 1906 and 1911...
- the Bosnian crisis of 1908...
- the assassination of Franz Ferdinand...
- alliances...
- the Schlieffen Plan...
- Austria-Hungary...
- Russia...
- Germany...

cause this?

- ★ greater international tension
- ★ hostility between Germany and Britain
- ★ tension between Germany and France
- ★ tension between Russia and Austria-Hungary
- ★ the First World War
- ★ the slide to war, 28 June to 4 August 1914
- ★ the outbreak of fighting in August
- ★ the First World War
- ★ the First World War
- ★ the First World War

1. Working as a whole class, think of TWO ways in which each factor on the left led to the outcome on the right.

 Source I suggests that Wilhelm II was responsible for the Moroccan crisis of 1905. Do you agree with the interpretation that Wilhelm II was the main cause of the crisis?

Explain your answer by referring to the purpose of the source, as well as using its content and your own knowledge.   (6 marks)

Full sample answer

Comments

Describe the cartoon's interpretation of events.

Source I shows Britain and France, backed by the British navy, stopping Wilhelm's schemes in Morocco. Wilhelm – dressed like the villain in a pantomime – accepts that he is beaten, but vows to try again. The cartoon blames Wilhelm, and makes out that he is wickedly trying to take more power.

> Begins by explaining what the cartoon shows and what its interpretation of events is.

Refer to the cartoon's provenance.

Looking at the provenance, I see that the cartoonist is Haselden, a patriotic British cartoonist. He drew the cartoon in 1905, so it is topical, but – being British – he would have been biased, and this makes his interpretation unreliable. A German cartoonist would have interpreted the incident in a very different way.

> TWO IDEAS about why the PROVENANCE might be important.

Show how the cartoon's interpretation of events is linked to its provenance.

Haselden makes Britain seem jolly and nice; a German cartoonist would have shown him as a greedy bully who already owned a fifth of the world.

Also, Haselden shows Wilhelm as a troublemaker; a German cartoonist might have shown him as a noble hero trying to get a place in the sun for Germany and the countries it traded with.

> TWO IDEAS explore the cartoon's interpretation of events, referring to its provenance.

Explain the event the cartoon is referring to.

When I look at the content of the source, I see that it is generally true. In a conference at Algeciras in 1906 Britain and Russia stood by France and it was agreed that Germany should have no say in Morocco.

> Provides facts about the cartoon's content.

Compare the cartoon's content in detail to the historical facts to examine whether the cartoon's interpretation of events is true or false.

Other facts support the cartoon's interpretation. Britain and France dancing together refers to the Entente Cordiale of 1904. Showing Wilhelm saying: 'a time will come' is a prophecy of the Agadir crisis of 1911.

However, some things about the cartoon are not true. It is not true that Wilhelm was the villain of the crisis – France was trying to take over Morocco, and Wilhelm tried to defend Morocco's independence. And it is not true that Britain's navy completely ruled the waves – in 1898, Wilhelm ordered Tirpitz to increase the German navy, so that it could challenge Britain's.

> Develops ideas FOR or AGAINST the interpretation. At this point, with detailed explanations of both the content and provenance of the source, the answer is of a very high standard.

Conclusion, assessing the cartoon's interpretation of events.

The cartoon is not a correct interpretation of the crisis – it is a British interpretation, produced to reassure the British public that the French alliance and the Royal Navy would protect Britain against Germany.

> Refers to the purpose of the source.

Which was the more important cause of Great Britain's entry into World War I:

- The naval race with Germany, 1906–1914
- The Schlieffen Plan?

You must refer to both causes when explaining your answer.   (10 marks)

Full sample answer

Comments

Describe the naval race.

In 1898, Wilhelm ordered Tirpitz to increase the German navy. After 1906 both sides began building Dreadnoughts. In 1907–14 Britain built 34, Germany 22. The race reached its peak in 1909, when Germans would not agree how many Dreadnoughts to build and public pressure in Britain demanded: 'we want eight and we won't wait'.

An opening statement. At least TWO extra facts.

Explain HOW the naval race caused tension and conflict.

The naval race helped bring Britain into the war. As an island with an empire, Britain needed a bigger navy, particularly since the British army was very small. The British believed the Germans were building up their navy to challenge British superiority and the empire. The naval race made the British resent and fear the Germans. This caused Britain to make a naval agreement with Japan (1902), and join the Entente Cordiale with France (1904).

TWO IDEAS have been introduced.

Assess how important the naval race was as a cause of Britain's entry into the war.

The naval race was not the main cause of Britain going to war in 1914, because by then Britain had won the race. The alliances with Japan and France came before the naval race, not because of it. Also, the height of the naval race came in 1909, long before the war, without causing a war.

Discusses the importance of the naval race by referring to facts.

Describe the Schlieffen Plan.

The Schlieffen Plan (1905) was Germany's answer to a 'war on two fronts'. It was to defeat France in the 6 weeks it would take Russia to mobilise. The right wing of the German forces would attack France through Belgium and Holland, leaving only a few troops to meet the French attack on Germany in Alsace and Lorraine.

An opening statement. At least TWO extra facts.

Explain HOW the Schlieffen Plan caused tension and conflict.

The Schlieffen Plan brought Britain into the war on 4 August because the neutrality of Belgium had been guaranteed by Britain in 1839. Also, Britain wanted to prevent the coastline opposite Britain from falling into the hands of a possible enemy. Belgium and the north coast of France could be used to launch an attack on Britain.

TWO IDEAS. At this point, with a full explanation of both possible causes of the major development, the answer is at a good level

Assess how important the Schlieffen Plan was as a cause of Britain's entry into the war.

But other reasons brought Britain into the war, which reduces the importance of the Schlieffen Plan. Britain also did not want the whole of Europe to fall under the control of one power. Also, public opinion in Britain overwhelmingly supported Belgium and going to war.

Discusses the importance of the Schlieffen Plan by referring to facts. Having assessed the importance of BOTH causes, this answer is now of a high standard.

Conclusion.

However, the Schlieffen Plan was more important. The naval race created underlying tensions, but still in 1914 the British government did not want war. Even after Germany declared war, the British stated on 2 August that they would only go to war if Germany went into Belgium, which was neutral. And the invasion of Belgium caused Britain to declare war.

This answer then makes a judgement. It explains how that judgement was reached and includes at least one fact.

1.2 Peacemaking 1918–1919 and the League of Nations

Overview

The costs of war

On 11 November 1918, at 11 a.m., an **armistice** (ceasefire) brought the First World War to an end. In France and Belgium alone, 300,000 houses, 6000 factories, 1600 kilometres of railway and 112 coal mines had been destroyed. In all, worldwide, eight million soldiers and nine million civilians had died, but the human cost of the war – in terms of ruined bodies and minds – was incalculable.

The terms of the November Armistice were harsh. They included:

- surrender by the German army of its equipment
- surrender by the German navy of all its submarines and most of its ships
- establishment of a neutral zone on the banks of the River Rhine
- '**reparations** for damage done'.

In January 1919 the countries of the world went to Paris to agree the terms of peace. This get-together was originally planned as a pre-conference meeting to sort out differences before the proper peace negotiations began. However, it turned into the Paris Peace Conference itself. As a result, this, unusually, was a peace negotiation in which the Germans took no part. Neither was the USSR allowed a say, as the Western allies did not trust communists.

The damage caused by the war.

HISTORIOGRAPHY

Immediately the Treaty of Versailles was signed, it was attacked as a failure. Most historians have presented it as a flawed treaty which in fact caused the Second World War.

However, recent historians – notably Margaret MacMillan, the great granddaughter of the wartime prime minister David Lloyd George – have re-interpreted the treaty. In their view, the treaty was not so bad; it was a genuine attempt to create a better world and was the best kind of peace that could be made in the circumstances.

TIMELINE

11 November 1918
Armistice

21 June 1919
German navy sinks its fleet

March 1920
US Senate refuses to sign the Treaty of Versailles

1918	1919	1920	1921	1926

January 1918
President Woodrow Wilson publishes the Fourteen Points

18 January 1919
Peace conference at Versailles

28 June 1919
Signing of Treaty of Versailles

16 January 1920
First meeting of the League of Nations

May 1921
Reparations are set at £6.6bn

Germar admitte the Lea of Natic

The Treaty of Versailles

By May the Treaty of Versailles – whose 200 pages contained 435 clauses – was finished. Germany was to lose large areas of territory, disband most of its armed forces, pay reparations and accept blame for the war.

The Germans, predictably, were outraged – not only by the terms of the treaty, but also by the fact that they had not been consulted. Nor were any of the Allies entirely happy with the treaty. In the end, the Treaty of Versailles pleased nobody. Delegates left the conference with the feeling that it was only a matter of time before there was another war.

The League of Nations

The League of Nations was set up in January 1920 under the terms of the Treaty of Versailles. The aims of the League were set out in a **covenant**, and the text of that covenant was included in all of the separate documents that together made up the Versailles Treaty.

Woodrow Wilson first came up with the idea of a League of Nations in his **Fourteen Points**, a list of peace aims. Wilson believed that a league would ensure that there was no repeat of the First World War. The aim of preventing another war was not in question; the only question was whether the League of Nations would be able to achieve it. Most ordinary people hoped that a League of Nations in which the USA took a leading role would be able to prevent another war. British and French politicians had their doubts, but they had no alternative to offer.

The Covenant of the League of Nations was a list of 26 articles, or laws, that all members agreed to follow. These articles encouraged countries to work together to ease international trade and improve working and living conditions for the world's people. The articles also encouraged nations to **disarm**. The most important was Article 10, which stated that members of the League would act together to ensure that any member threatened with war was protected by the other members. This agreement, known as 'collective security', was intended to keep the peace.

Germany, the country blamed most for the war, was refused membership. The **USSR** was also banned from joining, as the Allies did not approve of **communist** politics.

However, despite the League being Wilson's idea, he was unable to persuade the American Congress to approve the membership of the United States. As the United States had originally been viewed as one of the main economic and military supports for the League, this weakened the organisation from the start.

At first, in the 1920s, the League was quite successful but, during the economic **depression** of the 1930s, things began to go wrong. Japan, Italy and Germany began to look after their own interests by looking for 'living space'. They found this living space in other nations, which they then attacked and conquered.

The League was powerless to stop these acts of aggression. It did not have a permanent army, and member nations were unwilling to enforce economic **sanctions**. Sanctions hurt not only the country being punished – which could no longer buy certain goods – but also the countries enforcing them, because they could no longer sell certain goods to the country being punished. Therefore the League of Nations failed in its peacekeeping role, and in 1945 it was wound up and replaced by the United Nations.

29	1931–33	1932–34	1933	1935–36	1936	1937	1945

Germany and Japan leave the League

December 1935 Hoare-Laval Pact

Italy leaves the League

Wall Street Crash

Manchurian crisis

Disarmament Conference fails

Abyssinian Crisis

Germany occupies the Rhineland

End of the League

1.2a How did the Treaty of Versailles establish peace?

The Paris Peace Conference

In January 1919 the leaders of the USA, France and Britain – the 'Big Three' – met in Paris. They were under pressure to reach a peaceful settlement to Europe's huge problems.

Woodrow Wilson, president of the USA

The American president was an idealist: he believed that a perfect solution could be found. He had grand plans to make sure that war never broke out again. Wilson had made his views clear before the end of the war. In January 1918 he had published his Fourteen Points, a list of principles that he believed should guide peacemaking once the war had finished.

These were Wilson's core beliefs:

- To achieve world peace in the future, nations would have to co-operate.
- A nation had the right to **self-determination**. In other words, people of a single national group had the right to rule themselves. This idea was the guiding principle of Wilson's Fourteen Points. It made colonialism unacceptable.

Some of the Fourteen Points were easy to put into action. Others, such as self-determination, were good in theory but difficult to apply in practice. The peoples of Eastern Europe, for example, were scattered across wide areas. Some people were bound to end up being ruled by people who had a different language and culture.

Some of the Fourteen Points

1. No secret treaties
2. Free access to the seas
3. Free trade between countries
4. Disarmament
5. Colonies to have a say in their own future
8. France to regain Alsace-Lorraine
10. Self-determination for the peoples of eastern Europe
13. Poland to become an independent state
14. A League of Nations to be set up

SOURCE A

I consider it a distinguished privilege to be permitted to open the discussion in this conference on the League of Nations. We have assembled here for two purposes – to make the peace settlements, and also to secure the future peace of the world.

From a speech Woodrow Wilson made at the start of the Paris Peace Conference in January 1919.

Note Wilson's clear view of the conference's purpose – he called it 'a conference on the League of Nations.'

Wilson believed that Germany should be punished, but not too harshly. If the peace treaty was too harsh, Germans would be resentful and would want revenge.

Instead Wilson wanted all countries to join a League of Nations, which would resolve disputes peacefully. He believed that Germany should lose some territory but should not be made to pay the cost of war damage.

It might be argued that it was easy for Wilson to take this lenient attitude towards Germany. After all, the USA had not joined the war until April 1917, and American soldiers did not reach Europe until late 1917. Americans could take a more detached attitude than Europeans, who had suffered the full horrors of the long war.

Georges Clemenceau, prime minister of France

Georges Clemenceau was aged 77 when the peace talks began. He had become prime minister in November 1917, promising to win the war for France and to ensure that Germany could never inflict the same damage on France again. Clemenceau had three main aims:

- Alsace-Lorraine, taken by Germany in 1870, must now be restored to France.
- Germany must pay for the suffering that the French people had endured. Clemenceau was under great pressure from the French people to make Germany pay; the French argued that this payment should take the form of money and land.
- Germany must lose land on the border with France in order to make the French feel more secure from future attack.

With Clemenceau as their leader, the French people had a tough politician who would argue their case strongly.

David Lloyd George, prime minister of Britain

David Lloyd George was an experienced and wily politician. He understood that there would have to be many compromises in the peace talks, otherwise a settlement would never be reached.

- Lloyd George wanted Germany to be punished, but not too harshly – like Wilson, he did not want Germany to seek revenge in the future. This approach ran against the feelings of most British people. Lloyd George's government had won an election in December 1918 by promising to 'squeeze the German lemon until the pips squeak'.
- Lloyd George also wanted to protect British naval interests. Therefore he disliked Wilson's idea of free access for all countries to the seas. Lloyd George wanted to reduce the German navy and to extend the British empire. Yet at the same time he knew that Britain was primarily a trading nation. Therefore it was important that Germany was not crippled too much. He wanted the two countries to be able to start trading again.

The search for agreement

The 'Big Three' clashed dreadfully. Wilson, arrogant and irritable, would talk only of self-determination and a League of Nations. Clemenceau wanted revenge for the suffering and destruction inflicted by Germany during the war. In the middle was Lloyd George, who jokingly described his position as 'between Jesus Christ and Napoleon'.

By March, Wilson and Clemenceau were at each other's throats. It looked as though the peace process was going to fail. Lloyd George took control. First he persuaded Clemenceau to agree to a League of Nations. Then he forced Wilson to agree to a 'War Guilt' clause, which opened the way for Germany to be made to pay reparations.

The 'Big Three': from left to right, David Lloyd George (Britain), Georges Clemenceau (France), and Woodrow Wilson (USA).

SOURCE B

We must not let any sense of revenge, any spirit of greed, any grasping desire override the fundamental principles of righteousness.

From a speech given by Lloyd George to the British parliament on 12 November 1918, immediately after the Armistice.

SOURCE C

Germany is going to pay… I have no doubt that we will get everything out of her that you can squeeze out of a lemon and a bit more.

From a speech made by the parliamentary candidate Eric Geddes during the British election campaign of December 1918.

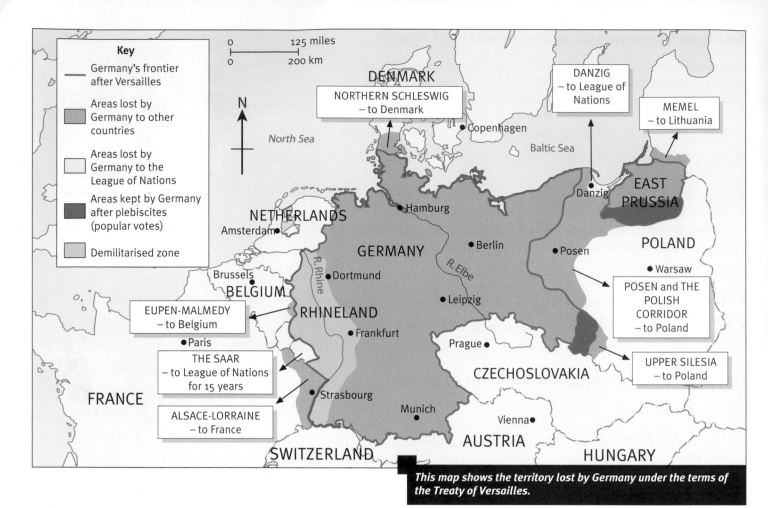

This map shows the territory lost by Germany under the terms of the Treaty of Versailles.

Key map labels:
- Germany's frontier after Versailles
- Areas lost by Germany to other countries
- Areas lost by Germany to the League of Nations
- Areas kept by Germany after plebiscites (popular votes)
- Demilitarised zone

- NORTHERN SCHLESWIG – to Denmark
- DANZIG – to League of Nations
- MEMEL – to Lithuania
- EUPEN-MALMEDY – to Belgium
- THE SAAR – to League of Nations for 15 years
- ALSACE-LORRAINE – to France
- POSEN and THE POLISH CORRIDOR – to Poland
- UPPER SILESIA – to Poland

The Treaty of Versailles, June 1919

The Treaty of Versailles was finally concluded by May. It was given to the Germans, who were forced to sign under threat of further war.

On 28 June 1919 the leading politicians from the victorious countries left Paris and made the 16-kilometre journey by train to Versailles. There, in the famous royal palace, they signed the Treaty of Versailles. Two representatives of the new German government were summoned. The Germans had been allowed no say in the discussions. In humiliating circumstances, they were given no choice but to sign, under threat of further war.

Territorial changes

The map above shows the main losses of land that Germany was forced to accept at Versailles.

- Alsace and Lorraine were returned to France.
- Eupen and Malmédy went to Belgium.
- Northern Schleswig went to Denmark.
- Memel was taken over by the League of Nations and transferred to Lithuania in 1923.

- West Prussia, Posen and part of Upper Silesia were given to Poland, a nation that had been erased from the map in 1795 and was now recreated. (East Prussia was now separated from the rest of Germany by Polish land.)

- The League of Nations was to control the Saar, in western Germany, for 15 years, but France controlled the coalfields.

- Danzig was made a free city under the control of the League of Nations. Poland had a corridor of land to the sea and could use the port of Danzig for trade.

- Germany lost all the land it had taken from Russia in the Treaty of Brest-Litovsk. This treaty had been agreed in March 1918, when Russia's new Revolutionary communist government decided to take Russia out of the war. (Estonia, Latvia and Lithuania became independent states.)

- Germany was forbidden to unite with Austria.

- Germany lost all its colonies. The League of Nations gave the colonies to Britain and France to rule until they were able to rule themselves.

In all, Germany lost 10 per cent of its land, all its overseas colonies, 16 per cent of its coalfields, half of its iron and steel industry and 12.5 per cent of its population.

Military restrictions

The Treaty of Versailles kept Germany's armed forces at a level far below where they had been before the war.

- The German army was limited to 100,000 soldiers.
- Conscription was banned; all soldiers had to be volunteers.
- Germany was not allowed tanks, submarines or military aircraft.
- Germany's navy could have only six battleships.
- The Rhineland, an area of western Germany near the French border, became a **demilitarised zone**. No German troops were allowed into this area, which included all the land west of the River Rhine and an area 48 kilometres wide on the river's east bank.
- The Allies were to keep an army of occupation on the west bank for fifteen years.

War guilt and reparations

The War Guilt Clause (clause 231 of the Treaty of Versailles) forced Germany to accept responsibility for the war:

231. The Allied governments affirm, and Germany accepts, the responsibility of Germany and her allies for causing all the loss and damage to which the Allied governments and their peoples have been subjected as a result of the war.

This clause provided the justification for Germany's punishment in the peace settlement. Germany was made to pay for the war. The payments were called reparations. The total sum was not fixed in the Treaty of Versailles but in 1921 was set at the huge figure of £6,600 million (£6.6 billion). The original intention was that Germany would pay a certain amount every year over a period of 42 years.

The League of Nations

The League of Nations was set up to maintain international peace. The League's covenant (binding agreement) was included at the beginning of the treaty. Therefore, the League's central role was to ensure that the details of the Versailles peace settlement were carried out. (For more information about the League of Nations, see pages 30–38.)

Strengths of the treaty

The Treaty of Versailles was initially signed by 45 countries. It was a worldwide agreement to end a World War. It reorganised the map of a world in which three major empires (the Russian, Austro-Hungarian and Turkish) had just collapsed. Most of the boundaries the treaty put in place still exist today. It was then (and is now) generally accepted as a genuine attempt to create a better world free from war.

SOURCE D

The time has come when the peoples of Europe will not want to live under masters, but to live under governments that they choose themselves. This is the fundamental principle of this great settlement.

From a speech given by President Woodrow Wilson at Pueblo, Colorado, on 25 September 1919. He made the speech during a campaign to win US support for the Treaty of Versailles.

GradeStudio

When considering the provenance of a source, it always makes sense to consider the intentions of the author. For instance, in Source D, the date is important because it is three months after the Treaty was signed, and Wilson was obviously trying to 'sell' the peace to a sceptical American audience.

VOICE YOUR OPINION!

Were reparations really set too high? The war had cost Britain £6.2 billion, and by 1919 the British national debt stood at £7 billion. Also, Britain owed almost £1 billion to the US. Britain needed reparations from Germany in order to pay this money back. Do you agree?

Weaknesses of the treaty

The Treaty of Versailles was deeply unpopular. The French general Ferdinand Foch – in front of Prime Minister Clemenceau – stood up at the Paris Peace Conference and attacked the Treaty. Foch asked the delegates to make the Rhineland an independent country, not just a demilitarised zone.

Japan and Italy were resentful. Both countries believed that the treaty did not reward them sufficiently for their contribution to the allied side in the war.

Many American delegates also hated the Treaty of Versailles and went home to try to persuade the US **Congress** (successfully, as it turned out) to reject it.

Many of the British delegates hated the treaty, too. The economist John Maynard Keynes believed that reparations were so high that they would damage world trade. Many ordinary British people came to believe that the treaty was too harsh (though this view was not universal – see Source E). Even Lloyd George predicted that it would cause, not prevent, another war (compare Source F).

Anger in Germany

The Germans were angry when they learned of the terms of the Treaty of Versailles. They did not even believe that they had lost the war. Having agreed to the armistice, they had expected negotiations to follow. Many Germans were outraged that Germany was not even represented at the Paris Peace Conference. Germany rejected the Treaty of Versailles as a 'Diktat' – a dictated peace.

Many Germans did not believe they had started the war and saw no reason why they should be blamed. Even if the Allies did blame Germany for the war, in 1914 Germany had not been a **democracy**. The person who might be held responsible, Kaiser Wilhelm II, had fled the country. Surely, the Germans thought, the Allies would want to support the new, democratic Germany (known as the Weimar Republic)?

Most German people did not want their government to sign the peace settlement. They felt that they had been 'stabbed in the back' by the so-called November Criminals – those who had agreed to end the fighting in November 1918. Many Germans would later come to accept Adolf Hitler's claim that a conspiracy of communists and Jews had betrayed Germany and brought about its humiliation in the war.

How Germans viewed the treaty

Many Germans believed that the Allies were attempting to destroy their country (see Source G). They believed that the combined effect of territorial losses and the Fourteen Points was especially unfair; the nations of Eastern Europe were given self-determination, while territorial losses condemned millions of Germans to life under the rule of a foreign government.

GIVING HIM ROPE?

German Criminal (*to Allied Police*). "HERE, I SAY, STOP! YOU'RE HURTING M[E] IF I ONLY WHINE ENOUGH I MAY BE ABLE TO WRIGGLE OUT OF THIS[.]"

This British cartoon was published in February 1919. It shows a German criminal being arrested by a French and a British policeman. The German shouts 'Here, I say, stop! You're hurting me!' Aside, he admits, 'If I only whine enough I may be able to wriggle out of this yet.'

The cartoon suggests that the rough treatment of Germany in the Treaty of Versailles was justified because Germany had done wrong. The Germans' complaints were just a trick to get the Allies to let them off.

VOICE YOUR OPINION!

Were the Germans correct to view the Treaty of Versaille as unfair and too harsh?

Germany's colonies were redistributed among Britain, France and other minor European powers. The Germans accused the two Great Powers of simply taking the opportunity to increase their own empires – even though the Fourteen Points opposed imperialism. Furthermore, it seemed that the requirement to disarm applied only to Germany and its allies.

The inclusion in the Treaty of Versailles of a War Guilt Clause – according to which Germany must accept the blame for starting the war – pained many Germans most of all. They felt humiliated by it.

However, German protests at the harshness of the treaty tended to ignore the equally harsh treatment of Austria-Hungary and Turkey. They also overlooked how harshly Germany had treated the Russians in 1918, when Germany had forced Russia to sign a peace treaty at Brest-Litovsk.

The Treaty of Versailles spread anger and resentment among Germans. When Adolf Hitler challenged the treaty's terms in the 1930s, he enjoyed widespread support. In Britain, France and the USA, persistent doubts about the treaty left many politicians without the stomach or the conviction to oppose Hitler.

This cartoon was published in the German newspaper *Kladderadatsch* in July 1919. A beautiful woman representing Germany lies defenceless on her bed, her weapons laid aside. Two vampire bats fly around outside, while a repulsive vampire with Clemenceau's features takes the lifeblood from her.

The cartoon is suggesting that France, with the help of Britain and the USA, was using the Treaty of Versailles first to disarm and then to destroy Germany.

SOURCE **F**

PEACE AND FUTURE CANNON FODDER

The Tiger : *"Curious! I seem to hear a child weeping!"*

This British cartoon was published in 1920. It shows, from left to right, David Lloyd George, Prime Minister Vittorio Emanuele Orlando of Italy, Georges Clemenceau (nicknamed 'the Tiger' because of his hatred of Germany) and Woodrow Wilson. They are looking at a child who has read the Versailles Treaty and thrown it on the floor. The child is crying because he will be in the 'class of 1940' and therefore would be called up to fight if a war were to break out in 1940.

The cartoon's implication is that the peace agreed at Versailles will only result in a war in 20 years' time.

SOURCE **H**

Today at Versailles a disgraceful treaty is being signed. Never forget it! There will be vengeance for the shame of 1919.

From the German newspaper *Deutsche Zeitung*, 28 June 1919

VOICE YOUR OPINION!

'The problem with the Treaty was that it had more of the Armistice than of the Fourteen Points.'
Do you agree?

1.2b Why did the League of Nations fail to keep peace?

The League of Nations

Membership

The League of Nations was set up in January 1920 as part of the Treaty of Versailles. It had been one of the key proposals of Woodrow Wilson, who believed the League would prevent war from breaking out again. British and French politicians may have doubted this, but they had no alternative to Wilson's idea. The League of Nations was established with a covenant, a set of 26 rules (or Articles) that encouraged all members to keep the peace, co-operate in trade and improve working and living conditions. Article 10 stated the members would act together to help any other threatened member, a policy known as 'collective security'.

Initially, 42 countries joined the League of Nations. However, the countries defeated in the First World War, notably Germany, were not allowed to join; nor was the Soviet Union, because its government was communist. This situation made the League appear to be a club for the benefit of the victorious countries in the First World War, notably Britain and France.

America and the League

Woodrow Wilson was confident that the USA would join the League of Nations. However, many Americans hated this idea. Here are some of the reasons why.

- Many Americans had been against US involvement in the war, and they certainly did not want the USA to get entangled in what many saw as Europe's petty squabbles after 1919.

- To remain entangled in Europe would cost Americans a lot of money and the lives of many young soldiers.

- In addition, the millions of German immigrants who lived in the USA opposed the League because Germany had not been allowed to join.

Woodrow Wilson campaigned hard to persuade Congress to support him. In spite of poor health (he had a stroke in 1919), Wilson toured the country by train and spoke in many cities and towns. However, in 1920 American politicians voted to reject the Treaty of Versailles and stay outside of the League of Nations. In the presidential election of November 1920, Americans voted for Warren Harding, who promised a 'return to normalcy'; in other words, he promised to keep the USA out of European political affairs with a policy of **isolationism**.

HISTORIOGRAPHY

After the Second World War, it was generally agreed that the League had been a failure. In 1961 the historian A.J.P. Taylor described it as a well-meaning gentlemen's club whose members were bewildered by Adolf Hitler's brutality. Taylor argued that the League's failure to resist Japan and Italy made war inevitable.

Recently, however, Susan Pedersen and other historians have argued that the League was a vigorous institution (it met 107 times in 20 years). According to this view, the League invented the diplomatic mechanisms needed to move the world on from the pre-1914 'leagues-of-empires' to the 'cooperating sovereign-states' of the modern world.

Strengths of the League

When the League of Nations was set up in 1919 and 1920, there was almost universal good will towards it from ordinary people and from most governments. People genuinely wanted to prevent a war like the one that had just ended from ever happening again, and most believed that this goal was achievable.

Most of the world's leading nations, including Britain, France, Italy and Japan had joined, and defeated countries were allowed to join later on. By the 1930s, the League had 59 members. Underpinning the League was the authority of the Treaty of Versailles, and every member had signed the League's binding covenant. By the 1920s, technological developments, such as international air travel and the telephone, suggested that it would be easier for countries to act together when conflict threatened.

Powers of the League

The Covenant of the League of Nations set out three ways in which the League could act to settle disputes:

- A hearing by an impartial, neutral country.
- A ruling by the International Court of Justice.
- An inquiry by the Council of the League of Nations.

If these methods did not resolve the dispute or if a country ignored the League's decision, then the League could take the following courses of action:

- Moral persuasion: the League could put pressure on the offending country by lining up world opinion against it.
- Economic sanctions: members of the League could refuse to trade with the offending country.
- Military force: the armed forces of member countries could be joined together and used against the offending country.

THE GAP IN THE BRIDGE.

This cartoon by Leonard Raven Hill, entitled *The Gap in the Bridge*, was published in December 1919 in the British magazine *Punch*. It reminds readers that Woodrow Wilson had promoted the League and had declared at the Paris Peace Conference that the League would be 'the keystone' of peace. Now, in December 1919 – three months before the Americans finally rejected the Treaty – the USA (represented by an Uncle Sam figure) appears unwilling to be part of the League.

The cartoonist is suggesting that the League without the USA, like a bridge without a keystone, will not be 'fit for purpose': it will be too weak to keep the peace.

GradeStudio

When considering the provenance of a source, it always makes sense to consider the intentions of the author. For instance, in Source J, the date is important because it is three months before the USA finally refused to join the League. Realising they were about to renege on their obligations, Raven Hill was trying to shame Americans into fulfilling them.

BE A HISTORIAN!

Use an internet search to find out something about these cases which came before the Permanent Court of International Justice:

- 1923 Jaworzina
- 1924 Saint-Naoum Monastery
- 1927 Danube
- 1929 Oder

THE ASSEMBLY

Every country in the League sent a representative to the Assembly. It could recommend action to the Council and could vote on various issues, including the budget and the admission of new members. It met once a year at the League's headquarters, in the Swiss city of Geneva. Decisions made by the Assembly had to be unanimous – that is, all members of the Assembly had to agree to them.

THE COUNCIL

The Council was a smaller group that met several times a year and during emergencies. The Council had permanent members (in 1920 these permanent members were Britain, France, Italy and Japan; a fifth place was reserved for the USA). The Council also had non-permanent members, who were elected by the Assembly for three-year periods.

Each of the Council's permanent members had a veto. As a result, a single 'no' vote could stop a decision from being passed. The Council had powers to act in various ways (see page 31) if it failed to persuade a country against a wrongful action.

THE SECRETARIAT

The Secretariat was much like an international civil service. It kept records of League meetings and prepared reports. Many of its staff were linguists. English and French were the main languages used. The Secretariat was very under-staffed.

THE PERMANENT COURT OF INTERNATIONAL JUSTICE

This institution, based at The Hague, in the Netherlands, was intended to help settle disputes peacefully. Its decisions were made by judges from the member countries. However, it had no way of enforcing its rulings.

THE AGENCIES

The League set up several bodies to deal with some of the world's major problems. These bodies included:

- Health Organisation
- International Labour Organisation
- Slavery Commission
- Commission for Refugees
- Permanent Mandates Commission (to deal with the former German colonies).

GradeStudio

To explain the importance of an issue, you need to think about its results. For instance, if you were asked how important the League's structure was in causing its eventual collapse you could offer three consequences:

1. Because decisions of the Assembly had to be unanimous, it was difficult to get agreement on a course of action.

2. Because Council members had a veto, they could stop the League taking any action.

3. Because the secretariat was small, any action by the League was often slow.

Weaknesses of the League

The League of Nations had a number of weaknesses. It relied heavily on good will and persuasion; it had very little real power and no permanent army. Although the League had many members, a number of important nations were missing. The USA never joined. Germany was allowed to join only in 1926 and left in 1933. Japan also left in 1933 and Italy in 1937. The Soviet Union did not join until 1934 and was expelled in 1939 after going to war with Finland. These absences greatly weakened the League of Nations.

Throughout the 1920s countries also continued to make treaties and alliances:

- 1921 – at the Washington Conference, the USA, Britain, France and Japan agreed to limit the size of their navies.
- 1925 – by the Locarno Treaty, France, Britain, Germany, Italy, Belgium, Poland and Czechoslovakia agreed to accept the borders set out by the Treaty of Versailles.

At the time, these agreements were regarded as steps towards peace but – because they were treaties between individual countries – they in fact undermined the League's principle of 'collective security'.

Then, in 1928–29, at the initiative of the US Secretary of State Frank B. Kellogg and the French foreign minister Aristotle Briand, sixty-one countries signed the Kellogg-Briand Pact, renouncing war as 'a way of solving international disputes'. Again at that time, it was regarded as the triumph of peace, but in fact it too undermined the League. It was an attempt to keep the peace by treaty, not by 'collective security'.

General disarmament was still a hope, not a reality. A Disarmament Conference (1932–34) tried without success to find a way forward. The French, for example, regarded disarmament as a threat to France's security, while the Germans could claim that if other nations failed to disarm, Germany had a right to rearm in order to protect itself. A great deal of wartime resentment and anger persisted. Countries were still suspicious of one another, and traditional rivalries remained in place.

Successes and Failures

It is all too easy to blame the League of Nations for its failure to prevent the Second World War. In fact, the League did solve some political disputes in the 1920s. Because they were solved peacefully, these disputes attracted little attention at the time. In 1921 Sweden and Finland clashed over the Åland Islands. In 1925, following an incident on the Greek border with Bulgaria, Greece reacted by invading its neighbour. In both cases the League of Nations restored order.

MORAL SUASION.

The Rabbit. "MY OFFENSIVE EQUIPMENT BEING PRACTICALLY *NIL*, IT REMAINS FOR ME TO FASCINATE HIM WITH THE POWER OF MY EYE."

This cartoon is titled *Moral Persuasion*. It appeared in the British humorous magazine *Punch* in 1936. In it, the League is represented as a rabbit, paralysed with fear in the face of a python, which represents 'International Strife'.

The cartoonist is suggesting that, with no power other than 'moral persuasion', the League is weak in the face of international aggression. Like a rabbit confronting a python, the League will be easily defeated in any attempt to prevent war.

Many of the League's agencies also enjoyed success in their work. The League attacked slave traders in Africa and Burma and closed down four big Swiss companies that were involved in the trade in narcotics (illegal drugs). It sent economics experts to help Austria and Hungary. The International Labour Organisation campaigned to persuade countries to adopt a 48-hour week. The Health Committee worked to reduce the impact of malaria and leprosy.

However, the very treaties that created the League of Nations also created the resentment that later destroyed it. Good will on the part of the League of Nations was not enough in itself to keep the peace. In the 1930s, the League proved powerless to act against the **dictatorships** of Japan, Germany and Italy.

The Manchurian Crisis 1931–32

Struggles in Japan

In October 1929 the New York Stock Exchange collapsed spectacularly. This event is known as the **Wall Street Crash**. The US economy went into depression, and world trade was badly affected. Countries put in place **tariffs** (taxes on imported goods) in an attempt to protect their own industries. Partly as a result of American tariffs on Japanese goods, Japanese industrial production fell by 30 per cent between 1929 and 1931. With less income from trade, Japan could not afford to import food.

The Japanese army

Japan was not a democracy. The country was ruled by an emperor who was believed to be divine. The Japanese army had a great deal of influence in Japan's government. The economic depression gave the leaders of Japan's army an opportunity to voice strong opinions about Japan's position in the world. Their views met with a sympathetic response among many Japanese people.

The army leaders were not happy with the way Japan was treated by other countries. They said that Japan had not gained as much as it had hoped in the Paris peace settlement. They claimed that Japan's government had allowed itself to be pushed around by western leaders. In the Washington Naval Agreements of 1922, for example, Japan had agreed to have only three ships to every five built by Britain and the USA. The army leaders believed that the only possible way of showing Japan's strength and solving its economic problems was territorial conquest.

Manchuria

Manchuria was a **province** of China and had **raw materials**, such as coal and iron ore, that Japan lacked. China, however, was weak. The last emperor (who was aged six at the time) had been overthrown in a revolution in 1911. China had collapsed into chaos as rival **warlords** divided the huge country between them and created numerous mini-kingdoms.

Japan had already taken advantage of Chinese weakness. The Japanese had an army stationed in southern Manchuria to protect the territory they had gained from Russia in 1905, and China had agreed that Manchuria should be a Japanese **sphere of interest**. Japan had numerous economic rights in the region, including the right to mine coal, fish, and use the ports and waterways. The Japanese also owned the South Manchurian Railway.

The Crisis

In September 1931, there was an explosion on the South Manchurian Railway, just outside the city of Mukden. The Japanese military leaders claimed that the explosion was an act of **sabotage** by the Chinese, who wanted to be rid of the Japanese. There was indeed a Chinese army in the area, but the Chinese claimed that all their soldiers were in their barracks at the time. Whatever the truth of the matter, the Japanese seized the opportunity to take full control of Manchuria and force the Chinese to withdraw from the area.

In February 1932 the Japanese set up a **puppet government** (that is, a government under the control of the Japanese). Manchuria was renamed Manchukuo, and the last Chinese Emperor, Pu Yi, was put in control of the province.

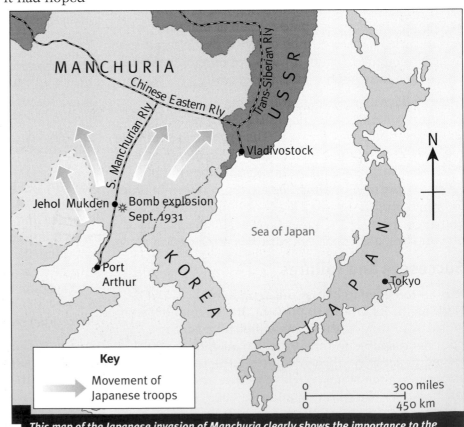

This map of the Japanese invasion of Manchuria clearly shows the importance to the region of the South Manchurian Railway.

The League of Nations responds

China appealed to the League of Nations about the Japanese takeover of Manchuria. Japan claimed it had done what it had done because the area was getting out of hand.

The League had to tread carefully.

- There was some truth in Japan's arguments, and Japan was a leading member of the League of Nations with a permanent seat on the Council.
- On the other hand, it appeared that the Japanese army had used military aggression to achieve its goals.

The League instructed Japan to withdraw its troops from Manchuria. Instead, the Japanese took firmer control of the area.

The League decided to set up a commission of inquiry under the British diplomat Victor Bulwer-Lytton. The commission was to travel to Manchuria, gather information and produce a report. The journey by sea took months, and the report was not published until October 1932 – a full year after the initial incident.

The Lytton Report came out firmly in favour of China. It declared that Japan had acted unlawfully and judged that Manchuria should be returned to China. All the League's member countries except Japan accepted the report. The Japanese response was straightforward. Japan ignored the report and in March 1933 left the League.

Japan invades China

The Japanese not only held onto Manchuria, they continued invading territory. In 1933 Japan invaded the province of Jehol, and in 1937 Japan invaded China itself.

The League did nothing. Imposing economic sanctions on Japan would have been useless, as Japan's main trading partner was the USA, which was not a member of the League. Britain in particular was concerned that further measures against Japan might harm British trade in Asia. Although people tried to make excuses for the League, nothing could really hide the truth. The League of Nations was powerless to prevent an aggressive dictator from invading another country.

GradeStudio

When considering the content of a cartoon, it is important that you interpret the cartoon correctly, so stick to the obvious. In Source L for instance, it is obvious that the cartoonist considered Japan to be trampling all over the League while Britain and France did nothing. You could then relate this to the fact that Japan ignored the League's instruction to leave Manchuria, and that the League did nothing.

THE DOORMAT.

This cartoon, drawn in 1933 by David Low, is called *The Doormat*. It shows a Japanese soldier trampling on the League of Nations while League officials bow down before him and the British foreign secretary, John Simon, powders the League's nose using a 'face-saving outfit'.

The cartoonist is suggesting that the League has weakly allowed the Japanese to break the covenant, ignore its orders and conquer Manchuria. The cartoon implies that the actions of the League (demands for troop withdrawal, the Lytton Commission and Report) are just attempts to 'save face' – to cover over its failure. The cartoon blames the British government in particular for not being tough enough.

In Source G, a figure representing Georges Clemenceau is shown trying to kill a beautiful woman representing Germany. Do you agree with the source's interpretation of the Treaty of Versailles – that the treaty was an attempt to destroy Germany?

Explain your answer by referring to the purpose of the source, as well as using its content and your own knowledge.　(6 marks)

Full sample answer

Comments

Describe the cartoon's interpretation of events.	Source G shows Clemenceau as a vampire sucking the life-blood out of Germany (in the form of a beautiful woman). He is helped by two more bats representing Britain and the USA. The meaning is that Germany has been forced to lay aside her weapons and allow the French in to take reparations and territory.	Begins by explaining what the cartoon shows and what its interpretation of events is.
Refer to the cartoon's provenance.	Looking at the provenance, I see that the cartoon appeared in July 1919 (a month after the Treaty of Versailles was signed) in the German newspaper <u>Kladderadatsch</u>. The cartoon is therefore contemporary, but – being German – would have been biased, and this makes its interpretation unreliable. British and French cartoonists interpreted the Treaty very differently.	TWO IDEAS about why the PROVENANCE might be important.
Show how the cartoon's interpretation of events is linked to its provenance.	The cartoon makes Germany seem beautiful and helpless, but a British cartoonist of the time showed Germany as a criminal. Similarly, the cartoonist shows the Allies as vampires, but the British cartoon showed them as policemen upholding justice.	TWO IDEAS explore the cartoon's interpretation of events, referring to its provenance.
Explain the event the cartoon is referring to.	When I look at the content of the source, I see that there is some truth in it. In the Treaty of Versailles Germany did have to pay huge reparations of £6.6 billion.	Provides facts about the cartoon's content.
Compare the cartoon's content in detail to the historical facts to examine whether the cartoon's interpretation of events is true or false.	Other facts support the cartoon's interpretation. In all, Germany lost 10 per cent of its land, all its colonies, 16 per cent of its coalfields, and half of its iron and steel industry. So there is some truth in the cartoon's view that the Treaty would ruin Germany. I also know that the Treaty limited Germany to an army of 100,000 and a navy of not more than 6 battleships, and no submarines or planes, so Germany had been forced to lay aside her weapons, as the cartoon shows. However, it is also true that Wilson and Lloyd George genuinely did not want to destroy Germany.	Develops ideas FOR or AGAINST the interpretation. At this point, with detailed explanations of both the content and provenance of the source, the answer is of a high standard.
Conclusion, assessing the cartoon's interpretation of events.	The cartoon is not a correct representation of the Treaty. It is a German exaggeration, produced as propaganda to spread the idea that the aim of the Treaty was not to bring peace, but to allow Clemenceau to get revenge on Germany.	Refers to the purpose of the source.

Which was the more important cause of the failure of the League of Nations:

• The decision by the USA not to join

• The Abyssinian crisis?

You must refer to both causes when explaining your answer.   (10 marks)

Full sample answer

Comments

Prompt	Answer	Comment
Describe the American decision.	In March 1920, the US Senate voted NOT to join the League of Nations. Wilson had campaigned hard for the League despite ill-health (leading to a stroke). But the USA did not want to get entangled in European affairs, and did not want to spend money and lose lives in Europe, and also the League was opposed by millions of German immigrants.	An opening statement. At least TWO extra facts.
Explain HOW the American decision caused tension and conflict.	This damaged the League in two ways. Firstly, it did not have access to the United States' wealth and power. Britain and France were damaged by the war and could not afford an army or sanctions, so the League could not do anything if it was ignored. Secondly, without the USA as a member (or the USSR or Germany), the League looked like a club run for the benefit of France and Britain. This meant countries did not pay it much attention.	TWO IDEAS are introduced here.
Assess how important the American decision was as a cause of the League's failure.	This was important in Manchuria – sanctions could have been applied against Japan if the USA had been a member. It was also important in Abyssinia, because sanctions could have been put on oil if the USA had been a member.	Discusses the importance of the American decision by referring to facts.
Describe the Abyssinian crisis.	In 1935, Italy invaded Abyssinia, after a border clash at Walwal. The Italians used tanks and poison gas, and Haile Selassie appealed to the League. The League, however, only banned the sale of arms and trade with Italy, it did not ban oil or coal, and the British did not close the Suez Canal. In December 1935, Hoare and Laval even planned to hand over the best bits of Abyssinia to Mussolini.	An opening statement. At least TWO extra facts.
Explain HOW the Abyssinian crisis caused tension and conflict.	This damaged the League in two ways. Firstly, the Hoare-Laval Pact made Britain and France seem to be traitors to the League. Secondly, as A.J.P. Taylor pointed out, Abyssinia showed the League's notion of collective security did not work. Violence and aggression were shown to pay. Small nations realised the League could not protect them.	TWO IDEAS. At this point, with a full explanation of both possible causes of the major development, the answer is of a good standard.
Assess how important the Abyssinian crisis was as a cause of the League's failure.	This was important because the Axis countries were encouraged, and soon afterwards Hitler remilitarised the Rhineland. Britain and France followed a policy of appeasement. As A.J.P. Taylor said, once people realised the League could not stop war, they came to think that war was inevitable.	Discusses the importance of the Abysinnian crisis by referring to facts. Having assessed the importance of BOTH causes, this answer is now of a high standard.
Conclusion.	Abyssinia was more important. The absence of the USA was a weakness, but it was there from the start, and in the 1920s the League was successful without the USA. But after Abyssinia, the League lost all authority, never to regain it, and war followed three years later.	The answer now makes a judgement. It explains how that judgement was reached and includes one fact.

1.3 Hitler's Foreign Policy and the Origins of the Second World War

Overview

The 1930s

The GCSE History syllabus artificially divides up the causes of the Second World War. In one category are the events relating to the failure of the League of Nations, especially Manchuria and Abyssinia. In another are the events relating to Hitler's path to war (first German re-armament, then remilitarisation of the Rhineland and the *Anschluss* (union) with Austria; later, the invasions of the Sudetenland, Czechoslovakia, and Poland). These events are divided from others that the syllabus does not cover, such as the Spanish Civil War, the economic depression, and the growth of Oswald Mosley's **fascist** blackshirt movement in Britain.

In reality, people living at the time did not see these events as divided up. For them, the world had turned wicked, and the fascist dictators were winning. The 1930s struck many people as a terrible but inevitable slide towards world war.

The Treaty of Versailles

Many historians believe that the Treaty of Versailles (see pages 24–29) helped cause the Second World War. Most Germans applauded Hitler's promise to destroy the treaty at every opportunity. Throughout Europe, many people felt that the treaty was too harsh, so as Hitler began to *challenge* the treaty's terms, he was able to *exploit* a lack of resolve among British and French politicians to resist what he was doing.

GradeStudio

To explain the importance of an issue, you need to think about its results. For instance, if you were asked how important the Treaty of Versailles was in causing the Second World War you could offer three consequences:

1. Because he so hated the Treaty, Hitler's first aggressions – the Saar, the Rhineland, Anschluss – were all designed to challenge it.

2. Because the Germans hated it so much, they supported Hitler's actions.

3. Because the Treaty was so harsh, it sapped British and French resolve to stand up to Hitler, and he got used to getting his own way.

TIMELINE

| 1919 | 1933 | 1934 | 1935 | 1936 | 1937 | 1938 |

Adolf Hitler becomes chancellor of Germany; Germany withdraws from Disarmament Conference

Hitler introduces conscription; Anglo-German Naval Agreement; Re-occupation of the Saar

May 1937
Neville Chamberlain becomes prime minister of Great Britain

Sept 1938
Sudetenlan crisis

28 June 1919
Signing of the Treaty of Versailles

Hitler signs non-aggression pact with Poland

Re-occupation of the Rhineland

March 1938
German *Anschluss* with Austria

This lack of resolve allowed Hitler to increase the territory under his control. After the Saar had voted to return to Germany from League of Nations control he marched troops into the demilitarised Rhineland. Then he bullied Austria, which was led by Chancellor Kurt von Schuschnigg, into an *Anschluss* (union) with Germany. Hitler was determined that no other country would decide what he could or could not do. In all three of these cases the League was either unable or unwilling to stop him, just as it had been when Mussolini had invaded Abyssinia.

Appeasement

By 1937 the League of Nations had clearly failed to curb German aggression. Neville Chamberlain, who became Britain's prime minister in May 1937, decided to negotiate directly with Hitler in an attempt to solve disputes and keep the peace. Chamberlain's policy has come to be called **appeasement**.

Appeasement was an unfortunate choice of word. The term comes from the animal world; it describes the cowering of a smaller dog, for example, in front of a bigger and more ferocious dog. In truth, Chamberlain did not cower before Hitler (as Schuschnigg had done). Chamberlain was quite capable of saying 'no' to Hitler. However, he truly believed that some of Hitler's claims were reasonable, and he thought that if he agreed to Hitler's reasonable demands, Hitler would be satisfied and war would be avoided.

Therefore, Chamberlain allowed Hitler to occupy Austria (March 1938), and he famously negotiated the Munich Agreement (September 1938), which gave Germany the Sudetenland (part of Czechoslovakia).

The policy of appeasement lasted only a short time. When Hitler occupied the rest of Czechoslovakia (March 1939), Chamberlain realised that Hitler could not be trusted. Appeasement was abandoned, and when Hitler invaded Poland in September 1939, Chamberlain declared war.

HISTORIOGRAPHY

Immediately after the Second World War, most historians agreed that Hitler caused the war deliberately. Alan Bullock, in his book *Hitler: A Study in Tyranny* (1952), claimed that it was Hitler's 'fundamental intention' to rule the world. Bullock argued that Hitler had declared his intention from the start; after coming to power, Hitler worked systematically to fulfill this intention. Historians who agree with Bullock's argument are called intentionalists.

In 1961, however, the historian A.J.P. Taylor, in his book *Origins of the Second World War*, gave a different interpretation. There was no grand plan, said Taylor – Hitler simply seized opportunities as they arose. The timidity of the British and French made it easier for him to take advantage of these opportunities. Historians who agree with Taylor's view are called functionalists.

| 15 September 1938 Berchtesgaden | 22 September 1938 Godesberg | 29 September 1938 Munich | **1939** | March 1939 Hitler occupies Czechoslovakia – appeasement ends | April 1939 Britain and France guarantee Poland | August 1939 Danzig Crisis Nazi-Soviet Pact | 1 Sept 1939 Hitler invades Poland | 3 Sept 1939 Britain declares war on Germany |

1.3a How did Hitler challenge and exploit the Treaty of Versailles to March 1938?

Hitler's Aims

In 1933 Adolf Hitler became chancellor of Germany. Back in 1924, while in prison (after an unsuccessful attempt to lead a revolution), Hitler had written a book called *Mein Kampf* (*My Struggle*). In it he had set out a list of aims for Germany's foreign policy. He wrote that he wanted:

1. to destroy the Treaty of Versailles, re-arm Germany and recover its lost lands
2. to bring all German-speaking people everywhere under German control
3. to expand eastwards in order to gain **Lebensraum** ('living space') for the German people
4. to destroy the communist USSR.

In the five years after 1933, Hitler's Germany re-armed, regained the Saar, marched into the Rhineland, and forced a union with Austria. Apparently, Hitler was doing exactly what he had promised to do a decade earlier.

SOURCE A

a. *What a use could be made of the Treaty of Versailles! Each one of the points of that treaty could be branded in the minds and hearts of the German people until sixty million men and women find their souls aflame with a feeling of anger and shame; they will answer with a common cry: 'We will have arms again.'*

b. *The reunion of Germany and Austria is our life task, to be carried out by every means possible at our disposal.*

c. *It will be the duty of German foreign policy to get large spaces to feed and house the growing population of Germany. Destiny points us towards Russia.*

d. *The menace of Russia hangs over Germany. All our strength is needed to rescue our nation from this international snake.*

Four extracts from Hitler's autobiography, *Mein Kampf*, published in 1924.

SOURCE B

"WELL – WHAT ARE YOU GOING TO DO ABOUT IT NOW?"

This cartoon by the British cartoonist David Low was published in October 1933. Low hated Hitler and accused him from the beginning of wanting war. Low also criticised British and French leaders for giving way to Hitler. For his part, Hitler hated Low's cartoons and once even asked the British foreign secretary to ban them.

The image shows Hitler, who already possesses weapons, challenging European leaders about their failed promises to disarm. All around is the evidence of Hitler's evasion and hypocrisy. The Europeans, by contrast, are scared, and the League of Nations is powerless.

A cartoon by the British cartoonist Sydney Strube, published in May 1933. It shows King Kong, wearing a German helmet and with the word "armaments" emblazoned on his chest, breaking the chains that bind him.

The cartoonist is suggesting that a re-armed Germany poses a great danger to the world. The name Professor Geneva, written on a placard, is a reference to the League of Nations, whose Disarmament Conference Hitler had wrecked by demanding an army equal to that of France. The League was supposed to keep Germany's armaments under control, but Germany was breaking free.

Hitler overturns the Treaty of Versailles

Re-armament

Nazi re-armament	1932	1939
Warships	30	95
Aircraft	36	8,250
Soldiers	100,000	950,000
Percentage of government spending on armaments	1	23

As soon as he came to power, Hitler started re-arming Germany. In 1933 he withdrew Germany from the World Disarmament Conference on the grounds that no other power was prepared to disarm. He claimed that Germany wanted peace and was prepared to disarm completely if its neighbours did the same.

Hitler also withdrew Germany from the League of Nations. However, in 1934 he signed a non-aggression pact with Poland. Under this agreement, each country promised not to attack the other for the next ten years.

At the same time, Hitler started building up the German army. In 1935 he introduced conscription. He justified this policy by pointing out that other countries were increasing their arms, and argued that Germany had to be strong enough to defend itself.

German conscription ran against the Treaty of Versailles, but no country was prepared to do anything to stop it. Britain even recognised Germany's right to re-arm by signing a naval agreement with Hitler in 1935. This agreement allowed the Germans to build a fleet on the condition that it was no larger than 35 per cent of the size of the British fleet. The British felt that if there was to be no general agreement on disarmament, then it was necessary to get a commitment from Germany in the one area that mattered most to Britain – the navy.

Many British people accepted German re-armament because they thought the Treaty of Versailles had been too harsh and because they wanted a strong Germany as a buffer against the communist USSR.

The Saar, 1935

The Treaty of Versailles had removed the industrial area around the Saar from Germany and placed it under the control of the League of Nations. A **plebiscite** (vote) among the Saarlanders was to be held after 15 years to decide whether the Saar should be returned to Germany.

As the voting date approached, the Nazis mounted a huge campaign to persuade Saarlanders to vote for reunification with Germany. Some communists and **socialists** tried to organise an opposition to the Nazis, but they were threatened and beaten up. An army of Nazi stormtroopers gathered on the border between the Saar and Germany, but this army disbanded when Britain and France threatened to send in troops.

In January 1935, 90 per cent of Saarlanders voted in favour of returning to Germany. The decision was very popular in Germany, and the Nazi Party celebrated a great victory. They presented the restoration of the Saar as the undoing of the first of the injustices of Versailles. This success encouraged Hitler to challenge more of the Versailles provisions.

The Rhineland, 1936

The Treaty of Versailles had made the Rhineland (the area of Germany which bordered France) a de-militarised zone. It was still part of Germany, but the Germans were not allowed to keep troops or weapons there. The German people regarded this ruling as particularly unjust and humiliating.

In a direct challenge to the Treaty of Versailles, on 7 March 1936 Hitler ordered 32,000 troops and armed police to march into the Rhineland. He feared that Britain and France would try to stop him, but they did nothing, and he had his way.

Hitler's action was popular with Germans. Rhinelanders went wild with delight, and Hitler felt encouraged to continue pursuing his policies.

Some historians believe that the remilitarisation of the Rhineland gave Britain and France their final opportunity to confront Hitler without going to war. Germany's armies were too weak to take on France in 1936, and German generals had orders to retreat if they were opposed. The French and British, though, were more worried about Mussolini's invasion of Abyssinia. Hitler had noticed the reluctance of the League to act against Mussolini. He correctly calculated that no action would be taken against Germany.

For its part, the British government believed that the Treaty of Versailles had been unfair. The British thought that by allowing Hitler to right the wrongs of Versailles, future peace with Germany would be secured.

The League of Nations condemned Hitler's action but did nothing more. Hitler offered to make a peace treaty that would last for 25 years. This offer was his way of calming those countries that wanted peace while at the same time getting his way. His combination of aggression and diplomacy succeeded.

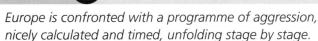

SOURCE D

Europe is confronted with a programme of aggression, nicely calculated and timed, unfolding stage by stage.

From a speech given by Winston Churchill in the House of Commons on 14 March 1938.

SOURCE E

The German bid for world domination found Europe weak and divided. At several points it could have been stopped without excessive effort or sacrifice, but was not: a failure of European statesmanship… of European morality.

The historian Louis Namier, writing in *Europe in Decay: A Study of Disintegration* in 1950.

Hitler's designs on Austria

A provision in the Treaty of Versailles forbade the joining together (*Anschluss*) of Austria and Germany. Yet the union of Germany and Austria was a key aim of Hitler, who wanted to unite all German-speaking people in one country. In 1934 Austrian Nazi Party activists murdered Engelbert Dolfuss, the chancellor of Austria. The Nazis then tried to take over the Austrian government, but they were prevented from doing so by Dolfuss's successor, Kurt von Schuschnigg, and by the opposition of the dictator of Italy, Benito Mussolini. Mussolini's threats forced the Nazis to back down, and Hitler promised to stay out of Austria's affairs.

When the Spanish Civil War broke out in 1936, Hitler and Mussolini both supported the Spanish fascist General Francisco Franco. Hitler used the war to give his new forces experience of fighting. In Spain, German aeroplanes practised dive-bombing, and the army practised tank formations. The Spanish Civil War brought Italy and Germany closer together, and in 1936 the two countries signed the Rome-Berlin Axis. This agreement was followed by the Anti-Comintern Pact of 1937, signed by Germany, Italy and Japan to prevent the spread of communism.

Hitler now felt strong enough to try to take over Austria.

Anschluss, March 1938

In January 1938 Chancellor Schuschnigg of Austria discovered that Austrian Nazis had been planning a revolution. Foolishly, he went to Germany to ask Hitler for help. Instead, Hitler berated Schuschnigg and insisted that he give positions in his government to Austrian Nazis, including the Nazi leader, Arthur Seyss-Inquart. Schuschnigg returned to Austria and tried to resist a Nazi takeover by arranging a plebiscite to ask the Austrian people whether they wanted union with Germany.

Fearing that the answer might be 'no', Hitler moved German troops to the Austrian border and threatened to invade. Austrian Nazis rioted in the streets, Schuschnigg resigned, and Seyss-Inquart invited the Germans into Austria to restore order. The Germans entered Austria and imprisoned more than 80,000 opponents of Hitler.

On 12 March 1938, Hitler entered Austria in triumph, and union with Germany was established on 14 March 1938. The plebiscite was then held; 99.75 per cent of Austrians voted 'yes'.

Hitler's skilful diplomacy had scored him another victory. Mussolini had not interfered because of the Rome-Berlin Axis, and there was no opposition from Britain and France, who were not prepared to go to war with Germany over Austria. Though the plebiscite result was influenced by pressure from the Nazis, many Austrians supported *Anschluss*. They wanted to be a part of the glory and success of Hitler's **Third Reich**.

SOURCE

GOOD HUNTING

This cartoon by Bernard Partridge was published in the British magazine *Punch* in February 1938. Hitler has poached a deer labelled 'Austrian integrity' (that is, independence). He is being allowed to carry off his catch by Mussolini, a gamekeeper, even though a sign indicates that the deer is 'strictly preserved'.

The cartoon presents Austria as a fragile deer whose life has been taken and Hitler as the killer of Austrian freedom. The cartoonist points out that Mussolini, who had stopped Hitler in 1934, did not do so in 1938, by which time he was Hitler's ally.

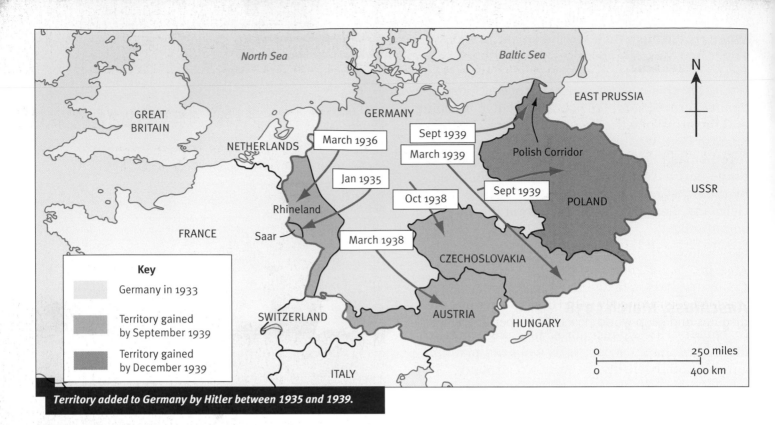

Territory added to Germany by Hitler between 1935 and 1939.

BE A HISTORIAN!

Use the internet and/or an encyclopaedia to find out about the 1937 Hossbach Memorandum.

Look back through the evidence presented in this chapter. What is your judgement of Hitler's foreign policy from 1933 to 1938? Was Hitler following a deliberate plan of aggression or just taking advantage of opportunities as they came along?

SOURCE G

INCREASING PRESSURE.

A cartoon by the British cartoonist David Low, published in February 1938. A Nazi soldier leans heavily on Austria, which is at the front of a line of countries. A British politician at the back of the line asks, 'Why would we take a stand… when it's all so far away?' The British man is too stupid to realise that it is only a matter of time before he, too, feels the pressure from Germany.

Low hated Hitler and thought that only a war would prevent the German leader from pursuing his goals. He also criticised British leaders for giving way to Hitler. The cartoon's message is that Nazi militarism is a danger to all the world and that Hitler ought to be resisted.

1.3b Why did Chamberlain's policy of appeasement fail to prevent the outbreak of war in 1939?

Down the Road to War

Chamberlain's new policy

After the failures of the League, Prime Minister Neville Chamberlain decided his only choice to prevent war was to negotiate directly with Hitler to solve any disputes and keep world peace. Chamberlain believed that Hitler had some reasonable demands. He also believed that if these demands were met, Hitler would be satisfied and war would therefore be avoided. This policy became known as appeasement.

It is sometimes stated that Britain 'appeased' Hitler before 1937 – for instance by signing a naval agreement with Germany in 1935, and allowing Hitler to remilitarise the Rhineland and annex Austria. But to say this is to misunderstand what 'appeasement' was.

Chamberlain's 'appeasement' was not simply 'giving way' to Hitler – in fact it was the opposite.

'Appeasement' of Hitler after 1937 involved negotiating with Germany – giving way to reasonable demands in return for concessions from Hitler. Just what those concessions ought to be was a subject of debate. Chamberlain's first Foreign Secretary, Anthony Eden, believed that the concessions ought to be tangible actions (such as disarmament). Chamberlain and Lord Halifax (who became Foreign Secretary after Eden's resignation in 1938) were prepared to accept promises and assurances.

In that respect, appeasement was a very cynical and selfish foreign policy. Chamberlain gave way on things that he felt did not matter to Britain (such as the Sudetenland) in return for assurances about things that he felt did matter to Britain.

Chamberlain understood that Hitler was expansionist, but by negotiating with him, he hoped to bring Germany gradually back into the international diplomatic community, where German foreign policy would once again be controlled by treaties and understandings. His failure was not that Hitler frightened and bullied him, but that Hitler failed to follow the promises he had made during his negotiations with Chamberlain.

On his return from signing the Munich Agreement, Chamberlain proclaimed "peace for our time!"

HISTORIOGRAPHY

In 1940, while most people were demonising Hitler for starting the war, three British journalists published the book *Guilty Men*. In it they blamed Chamberlain and the appeasers for the Second World War. The authors argued that the policy of appeasing Hitler had enabled him to become strong enough to start a war.

This view found support from Russian historians during the Cold War. The Russians argued that France and Britain, viewing Hitler as a useful weapon against communism, had allowed and even encouraged German aggression.

In the 1970s and 1980s, historians revised this view of Chamberlain. They instead portrayed him as a skilful negotiator who realised Britain was too weak to defend its empire against Germany in Europe and Japan in Asia at the same time.

More recent historians have, however, become critical of appeasement once more. After all, as a policy intended to stop war, it clearly failed.

Source U shows Hitler ignoring all the warnings and driving his Nazi tank to war. Do you agree with the source's interpretation of events – that Hitler was responsible for causing the Second World War?

Explain your answer by referring to the purpose of the source, as well as using its content and your own knowledge. (6 marks)

Full sample answer

Comments

Describe the cartoon's interpretation of events.

In Source U, the mailed fist stands for Hitler's determination for war, and the swastika wheels are his evil Nazi beliefs. The cartoonist is saying that Hitler, by attacking Poland, is forcing the world into war.

> Begins by explaining what the cartoon shows and what its interpretation of events is.

Refer to the cartoon's provenance.

Looking at the provenance, I see that the cartoon is contemporary (it appeared on 2 September 1939, the day after Hitler invaded Poland). However, it is British and so is biased against Hitler.

> TWO IDEAS about why the PROVENANCE might be important.

Show how the cartoon's interpretation of events is linked to its provenance.

The cartoon reflects the cartoonist's British standpoint, who had seen Chamberlain's appeasement, how he had given way to Hitler and tried everything to avoid war. It therefore criticises Hitler, claiming that he even ignored the appeals of the Pope and was determined to go to war.

> TWO IDEAS explore the cartoon's interpretation of events, referring to its provenance.

Explain the event the cartoon is referring to.

When I look at the content of the source, I see that there is truth in it. The Nazi emblem was a swastika, and Hitler did ignore the British warning in April 1939 that they would support Poland if Hitler invaded.

> Provides facts about the cartoon's content.

Compare the cartoon's content in detail to the historical facts to examine whether the cartoon's interpretation of events is true or false.

Other facts support the cartoon's interpretation. Hitler can be seen (e.g. by Bullock) as having intentionally sought war – re-arming, re-militarising the Rhineland, Anschluss, Munich, occupying Czechoslovakia and finally invading Poland.

However, A.J.P. Taylor denied that there was a 'grand plan' in 1961, and other historians have blamed many other things for the war, including the appeasers, the Depression of the 1930s, and the failure of the League of Nations. The cartoonist does not show Stalin, who had signed the Nazi-Soviet Pact with Hitler in August, and was invading Poland from the east.

> Develops ideas FOR or AGAINST the interpretation. At this point, with detailed explanations of both the content and provenance of the source, the answer is of a high standard.

Conclusion, assessing the cartoon's interpretation of events.

The cartoon is a biased view of why war broke out. It tells us what George Strube thought was the cause. It was not British government propaganda, but it was produced to convince the British people that Hitler was evil and that he was forcing Britain to fight a war against him.

> Refers to the purpose of the source.

Which was the more important cause of the Second World War:

- Chamberlain's policy of appeasement
- The Nazi-Soviet Pact?

You must refer to both causes when explaining your answer.   (10 marks)

Full sample answer

Comments

Describe appeasement.

Appeasement was the policy of negotiating with Hitler and giving way to him whenever his claims were 'reasonable'. Chamberlain followed this policy, partly to avoid war, and partly because Britain was too weak to fight Hitler in the west and Japan in the east. The high point of appeasement was the Munich Agreement of September 1938, when Chamberlain announced 'peace for our time'.

> An opening statement. At least TWO extra facts.

Explain HOW appeasement helped cause the war.

This helped cause the war in two ways. Firstly, it encouraged Hitler to demand more and more, because he thought Chamberlain would always back down. Secondly, because it allowed Hitler to re-arm, and re-occupy the Rhineland, and then take Austria and Czechoslovakia, it failed to stop him when he was weak. This meant that, when war came, it was against a massively powerful Germany which had invaded Poland.

> TWO IDEAS have been introduced here.

> Discusses the importance of appeasement by referring to facts.

Assess how important appeasement was as a cause of the war.

This was important because it created the underlying feeling that Hitler was unstoppable. Hitler invaded Poland in 1939 because he said that Chamberlain and Daladier were 'worms' who would not dare to stop him. Churchill said it would have been easier to stop Hitler in 1936.

> An opening statement. At least TWO extra facts.

Describe the Nazi-Soviet Pact.

On 23 August 1939, Hitler and Stalin signed a non-aggression pact. In secret clauses the USSR and Germany agreed to invade Poland and split the country between them. Britain had been negotiating an alliance with the USSR, but had taken so long that Stalin had become impatient.

> TWO IDEAS. At this point, with a full explanation of both possible causes of the major development, the answer is of a good standard.

Explain HOW the Nazi-Soviet Pact helped cause the war.

This helped cause the war because it freed Hitler to invade Poland. Firstly, Britain and France were too far away to help Poland. Secondly, the USSR – the only country which could have stopped Hitler – was now helping him to invade.

Assess how important the Nazi-Soviet Pact was as a cause of the war.

This was important because it allowed the critical event which caused the war. Knowing that the USSR would not stop him, Hitler invaded Poland on the 1st of September and Britain, honouring the promise it made to Poland in April 1939, declared war on the 3rd of September.

> Discusses the importance of the Nazi-Soviet Pact by referring to facts. Having assessed the importance of BOTH causes, this answer is of a high standard.

Conclusion.

Appeasement was more important. It was based on making little concession to Hitler, and Hitler was not satisfied with 'little concessions'. He kept on making bigger and bigger demands, and eventually he was going to do something (like invade Poland) that would force a military response from Britain. So appeasement was doomed from the start. Hitler was determined upon war, and his desire for Lebensraum meant that the Nazi-Soviet Pact did not last very long – in 1941 he invaded the USSR anyway.

> This answer now makes a judgement. It explains how that judgement was reached and includes at least one fact.

1.4 The Origins of the Cold War 1945–1955

Overview

From Allies to rivals

From 1939 to 1945, the Second World War was fought between the Axis countries (Nazi Germany, Japan and Italy) and the Allies (chiefly Britain, the USA and the USSR).

The Allies were bound together only by the need to defeat their common enemies: the Nazis and the Japanese. They were divided by **ideology**. In fact, the two sides – the USSR (also called the Soviet Union) on one side and the USA and Britain on the other – hated and feared each other. Even before the end of the war, the 'Big Three' had quarrelled at the conferences at Yalta and Potsdam.

The victory of the Allies in 1945 removed the threat of a world dominated by Nazi Germany. However, the Allies' victory created a world in which two 'superpowers', the USSR and the USA, vied for global domination. The conflict between them never quite broke out into open fighting – it never became a 'hot war'. Yet the two sides used every weapon short of actual warfare to attack each other. They fought what became known as the Cold War.

SOURCE A

The American attitude cooled once it became clear that Germany was defeated. It was as though the Americans were saying that the USSR was no longer needed.

Stalin's view of the cause of the Cold War, written in May 1945.

HISTORIOGRAPHY

Soviet historians always blamed American 'imperialism' for the Cold War. Documents discovered recently seem to prove that the USSR genuinely wanted peace.

At first, American historians blamed the Soviets for the Cold War. From the 1970s on, however, some American **revisionist** historians agreed with the Soviet historians that the USA was aggressive in expanding its power.

Most recently, 'post-revisionist' western historians have called the Cold War a 'clash of cultures' – a bitter conflict between two rival civilisations who were unable to trust each other.

VOICE YOUR OPINION!

Who – or what – was to blame for the Cold War?

TIMELINE

1945	1947			1948	1949			
Conferences at Yalta and Potsdam; bombing of Hiroshima	March 1947 Truman Doctrine	June 1947 Marshall Plan	October 1947 Cominform	Yugoslavia breaks with USSR	Comecon	June 1948–May 1949 Berlin blockade and air	Apr 1949 NATO	August USSR develop atom bo

Communism and capitalism

Although the USSR and USA were officially allies, their political systems were opposites of each other. The USSR was a one-party communist state. There were no free elections, and the state owned and controlled all the country's industry and agriculture. The Soviet ruler, Joseph Stalin, was a **totalitarian** dictator who put to death many of his own people and threw millions more into **labour camps**.

The USA and Britain were democratic and **capitalist**. Their governments came to power through free elections. Industry and agriculture were in private ownership and were run for profit.

Each side greatly feared the other. The Soviets believed that the West (principally the USA, but also Britain and other countries of western Europe) wanted to destroy communism. The West believed that the Soviets wanted to convert the world to communism. Soviet politicians were afraid that Germany would be allowed to rearm and become a threat to them once more. This fear prompted the Soviets to create a 'buffer zone' of friendly states between the USSR and Germany. Western politicians were afraid of a domino effect; they feared that once one country was allowed to fall to communism, others would soon follow.

The Cold War

Even before the war ended, the 'Big Three' met together – first at Yalta, then at Potsdam – to plan the shape of Europe after the war. There were open tensions between the Soviets on one hand and the British and the USA on the other. Critical was Soviet policy in eastern Europe, where communist governments were gradually coming to power with Stalin's help and under Stalin's control. In 1946 Churchill denounced this 'Iron Curtain' between the democratic West and Soviet-dominated East; Stalin regarded this as a declaration of war.

Even though, by possessing the atomic bomb, the USA possessed military superiority, President Truman decided he had to step in to 'contain' the spread of communism. After 1948 the USA handed out billions of dollars to help restore the economies of the countries of Western Europe. Stalin reacted by drawing the Soviet-controlled 'Iron Curtain' countries into a close bloc called 'Cominform'.

In 1947–48 economic tensions spilled over into the Berlin Blockade and Airlift, when Stalin tried to cut off West Berlin from the West and Britain and the USA reacted by supplying Berlin by air.

After Berlin

If the Berlin Crisis almost took the world to nuclear war, the Korean War could be argued to have taken it even closer. By this time the USSR had the atomic bomb and US policy had moved from 'containment' to 'roll back'.

However, in a strange way, the atomic bomb – soon to be followed by the hydrogen bomb – made the world safer, because neither side dared to risk a massive nuclear retaliation by the other. When Stalin died in 1953 and Nikita Khrushchev took over from him in Russia, Khrushchev came to power talking about 'peaceful co-existence' rather than military confrontation.

SOURCE **B**

The United States and the Soviet Union are engaged in a struggle for preponderant power [total dominance]... To seek less than preponderant power would be to opt for defeat. Preponderant power must be the object of US policy.

A statement made by Paul Nitze, President Truman's foreign affairs adviser, while planning US foreign policy in 1952.

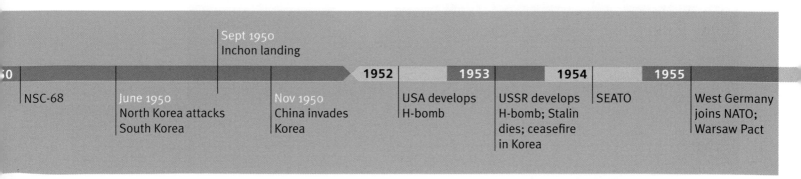

| | Sept 1950 Inchon landing | | 1952 | 1953 | 1954 | 1955 |
| NSC-68 | June 1950 North Korea attacks South Korea | Nov 1950 China invades Korea | USA develops H-bomb | USSR develops H-bomb; Stalin dies; ceasefire in Korea | SEATO | West Germany joins NATO; Warsaw Pact |

The Yalta Conference

In February 1945 the Allied leaders (Stalin, Prime Minister Winston Churchill and President Franklin D. Roosevelt) met at Yalta, a Soviet city on the Black Sea coast. There they agreed the principles of a peace settlement.

- Germany was to be divided into four zones. Britain, France, the USA and the USSR would each occupy a zone.
- Since Berlin, the German capital city, lay in the Soviet zone, it, too, was to be divided into four Allied sectors.
- Although Stalin was to have some influence over eastern Europe, the countries there would be allowed to choose their government in free elections.
- Germany should pay reparations.

Even before the war was over, however, there were tensions among the Allies. Relations between Stalin and Churchill were especially frosty.

The greatest source of conflict among the Allies was Poland. Soviet troops had already liberated much of Poland from German control and established a communist government there. Stalin insisted on the need for a 'friendly' government in Poland so that the USSR would have some protection from Germany. The Western Allies did not want a Soviet-dominated government in Poland. They persuaded Stalin to agree that Polish exiles who were opposed to communism should be included in the new government.

In the end, only a framework settlement was agreed at Yalta. The Allies had to agree that the details would be added at a later conference, due to be held at Potsdam, near Berlin.

The Potsdam Conference

In July 1945 the Allied leaders met again at Potsdam. By this time Germany had been defeated, and relations between West and East had cooled greatly. Roosevelt had died, and the new American president, Harry S. Truman, was determined to deal strictly with the Soviets.

Clement Attlee, the new British prime minister, was deeply suspicious of Stalin. In Poland Stalin had arrested the non-communists and refused to allow democratic elections to take place.

In an increasingly hostile atmosphere, the Allies sorted out the details of what they had agreed at Yalta. They set the boundaries of the four zones of Germany and agreed on how the zones would be governed. The USSR, which had suffered the worst damage in the war, was allowed to take reparations in the form of equipment and materials. These reparations were to be extracted mostly from its own zone; the Allied zones together would contribute an additional 10 per cent. Truman also agreed, bitterly, to recognise the Polish government.

In July 1945 the Allies met at Potsdam, near Berlin – but the strains were already beginning to show.

1.4a Why did the USA and USSR become rivals in the period 1945 to 1949?

The Effect of Hiroshima and Nagasaki

At 8:15 a.m. on 6 August 1945, an American B29 bomber named *Enola Gay*, piloted by Colonel Paul Tibbets, dropped an **atom bomb** onto the Japanese city of Hiroshima. A total of 78,000 people were killed outright. Three days after Hiroshima, the Americans dropped another atom bomb on the Japanese city of Nagasaki. This bomb killed a further 74,000 people. Japan surrendered, and it seemed that the Second World War was over.

The dropping of the atom bomb increased tension between the two superpowers. Stalin was angry that Truman had not told him at Potsdam that the USA had the atom bomb. For the Soviets, Hiroshima and Nagasaki marked not just a betrayal of trust, but a swing in the favour of the United States in the balance of global power.

The devastating destructiveness of the atom bomb and other **nuclear weapons** horrified many people in the West. There was a growth in what was at first called 'nuclear pacifism' but became known as the Campaign for Nuclear Disarmament (CND).

By 1949 the USSR had developed its own atom bomb. An armed conflict between two nuclear superpowers was unthinkable. It would be 'MAD' (that is, it would result in mutually assured destruction). Therefore, instead of engaging in a 'hot war', the USA and USSR had a series of tense confrontations which became known collectively as the Cold War.

The atom bomb probably prevented the conflict between the superpowers from turning into a 'hot war'. However, it created nearly half a century of terrifying and destructive Cold War.

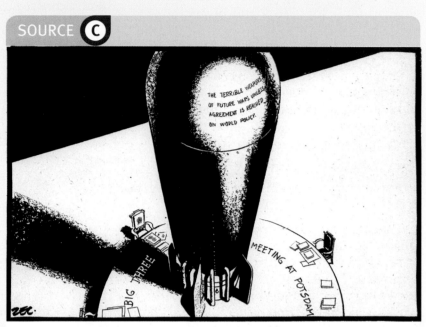

SOURCE **C**

In this cartoon, published in a British newspaper in 1945, the the atom bomb looms over the postwar peacemakers.

The cartoonist is suggesting that if the peacemakers fail to agree a 'just and workable peace', the world will face the terrifying prospect of a nuclear war.

SOURCE **D**

The madmen are planning the end of the world. What they call continued progress in atomic warfare means universal extermination, and what they call national security is organized suicide. There is only one duty for the moment: every other task is a dream or a mockery. Stop the atomic bomb.

From an article by the American journalist Lewis Mumford entitled 'Gentlemen, you are mad!' Published in the *Saturday Review* (2 March 1946).

The USSR and Eastern Europe: the Iron Curtain

During the latter stages of the war, the USSR's Red Army had liberated countries throughout eastern Europe from Nazi occupation. However, Nazi occupation was only replaced by Soviet occupation, since the Red army stayed in every country it 'liberated'. Communist governments loyal to – and protected by – Stalin's USSR took power in Albania, Bulgaria and Poland (1945) and Hungary and Romania (1947).

Stalinist politicians in these countries started by taking control of the police, army and radio stations. Then they arrested or murdered their opponents. Finally they held and won a rigged election. The communists often rose to power with the aid of Soviet military force. To the Americans, these takeovers proved that Stalin's plan was to spread communism throughout Europe.

The USSR's actions in eastern Europe alarmed the West. In March 1946 Churchill gave a speech to an American audience in Fulton, in the state of Missouri. In the speech Churchill described the division between West and East as an **Iron Curtain** that had descended between the two sides. The Iron Curtain was not a physical division, but a political and economic division. On one side of the curtain were the one-party communist states of the East, and on the other were the capitalist democracies of the West.

Churchill, who was speaking at Truman's invitation, wanted to convince Americans that they needed to maintain a military presence in Europe in order to prevent the spread of communism. Stalin claimed that Churchill's speech was a declaration of war.

BE A HISTORIAN!

Using an encyclopaedia or the internet, research how Stalinists took power in Hungary (1947) and in Czechoslovakia (1948).

SOURCE E

The Cold War set in. Churchill had given his famous speech in Fulton urging the imperialistic forces of the world to fight the Soviet Union. Our relations with England, France and the USA were ruined.

Nikita Khrushchev made this comment in 1971. Kruschev was president of the USSR from 1958 to 1964. In 1946 he had been a hard-line member of Stalin's government.

Khrushchev sees Churchill's Fulton speech as proof that the West wanted to spread its control and influence and to do battle with the USSR. In Kruschev's view, the Fulton speech started the Cold War.

SOURCE F

This British cartoon was published in a newspaper in March 1946. It shows Churchill looking under an 'Iron Curtain' which has split Europe in two. Behind the curtain is a world that is dark and frightening (ordinary people are running away from it) but industrially very powerful. 'Joe' is the Soviet leader Joseph Stalin.

The cartoon depicts Eastern Europe as Churchill saw it – out of bounds to western Europeans, it has been taken over by wicked but alarmingly powerful Stalinist dictatorships.

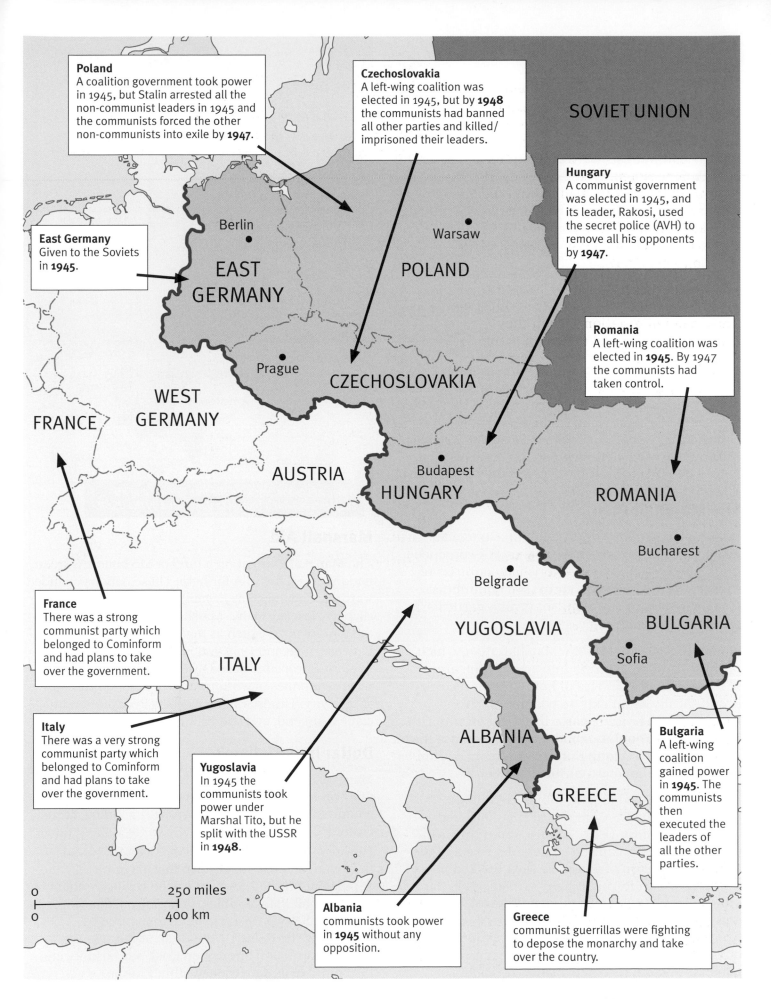

Poland
A coalition government took power in 1945, but Stalin arrested all the non-communist leaders in 1945 and the communists forced the other non-communists into exile by **1947**.

Czechoslovakia
A left-wing coalition was elected in 1945, but by **1948** the communists had banned all other parties and killed/imprisoned their leaders.

Hungary
A communist government was elected in 1945, and its leader, Rakosi, used the secret police (AVH) to remove all his opponents by **1947**.

East Germany
Given to the Soviets in **1945**.

Romania
A left-wing coalition was elected in **1945**. By 1947 the communists had taken control.

France
There was a strong communist party which belonged to Cominform and had plans to take over the government.

Italy
There was a very strong communist party which belonged to Cominform and had plans to take over the government.

Yugoslavia
In 1945 the communists took power under Marshal Tito, but he split with the USSR in **1948**.

Bulgaria
A left-wing coalition gained power in **1945**. The communists then executed the leaders of all the other parties.

Albania
communists took power in **1945** without any opposition.

Greece
communist guerrillas were fighting to depose the monarchy and take over the country.

SOVIET UNION

Berlin

Warsaw

EAST GERMANY

POLAND

WEST GERMANY

Prague

CZECHOSLOVAKIA

FRANCE

AUSTRIA

Budapest

HUNGARY

ROMANIA

Bucharest

Belgrade

YUGOSLAVIA

BULGARIA

ITALY

Sofia

ALBANIA

GREECE

0   250 miles
0   400 km

The Truman Doctrine and the Marshall Plan

The Truman Doctrine

Soviet power continued to spread in eastern Europe. In 1947 communists were threatening to take control in both Greece and Turkey. The situation became critical when the British announced that they were no longer able to offer the Greek government military support against communist rebels.

The USA had no wish to stand by while communism spread. In March 1947 President Truman declared in a speech that the USA would help any nation threatened by communism. This policy was known as the Truman Doctrine.

According to the Truman Doctrine, the countries of eastern Europe had been forced into communism by the Soviet Union. It was the USA's duty to protect other democratic countries under threat. The USA would take the lead in the containment of Soviet expansion. So the United States Congress announced that it was giving $400 million of aid to Greece and Turkey. This money helped the Greek government defeat the communists.

The Marshall Plan

In June 1947 the American general George Marshall visited Europe. He returned to the USA convinced that the war-torn and impoverished countries of western Europe were about to turn communist (the principles of communism can be particularly attractive to poor people).

Marshall came up with the Marshall Plan, which put the Truman Doctrine into action. The aim of the Marshall Plan was to help Europe recover economically as quickly as possible. A strong Europe would be better able to resist communism. The Marshall Plan also made economic sense for the Americans, as a strong Europe would once again be a valuable trading partner for the USA.

When it was asked to pour billions of dollars into Europe, the US Congress at first hesitated. Then, in February 1948, Stalinist communists in Czechoslovakia organised a general strike and the armed occupation of factories. Next the Stalinists seized power. A fortnight later Jan Masaryk, the only remaining non-communist minister, was found dead. He had 'fallen' from his bathroom window. Americans were alarmed by further evidence of the rapid spread of communism. Congress approved Marshall Aid on 31 March 1948.

A map of Europe, showing the Iron Curtain and the countries behind it that were dominated by the USSR.

Marshall Aid

The Marshall Plan set up a fund of $15 billion. Sixteen nations asked the USA for help. These nations included wartime allies, such as Britain, and former enemies, such as West Germany. Marshall Aid often arrived in the form of goods, such as machinery and fertilisers. Between 1948 and 1950, industrial production in western Europe increased by 25 percent. By 1952, most economies of western Europe were on the way to recovery. Unrest among workers in France and Italy came to an end, and communists lost influence.

Dollar imperialism?

Marshall's idea was that any European country could draw on Marshall Aid. The Marshall Plan offered aid wherever it was needed in Europe (including, at first, eastern Europe).

However, Stalin realised that Marshall Aid would make the countries of eastern Europe more dependent on the USA than on the USSR. Denouncing the Marshall Plan as 'dollar imperialism', he claimed that the USA was trying to build an empire by controlling the industry and trade of Europe. His fear and suspicion intensified Cold War hostility and further increased divisions within Europe.

Cominform and Comecon

In 1947 communist leaders from all over the world were summoned to a conference in Warsaw. At the conference, the Communist Information Bureau (Cominform) was created. This body was designed to spread communism and to protect communist states from US aggression.

In 1948 Stalin ordered Cominform to expel Tito, the communist leader of Yugoslavia, because Tito would not give in to Stalin's wishes. This action suggested to the West that Stalin wanted complete control of the communist world and would allow no opposition at all.

In 1949 the USSR introduced the Molotov Plan, which established the Council for Mutual Economic Assistance (Comecon). This body linked the USSR with Bulgaria, Czechoslovakia, Hungary, Poland, Romania and East Germany.

The USA saw Cominform and Comecon as serious threats. Relations between the superpowers deteriorated still further.

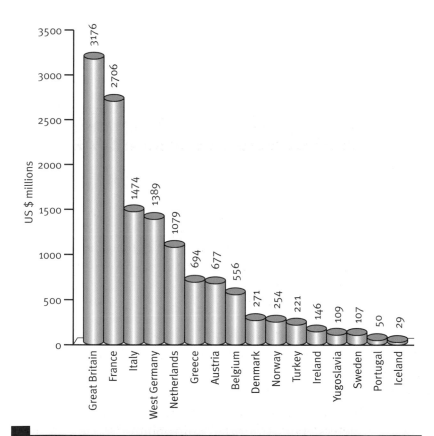

This diagram shows the levels of Marshall Aid received by the countries of western Europe.

This Russian cartoon of 1951 was drawn by Kukriniksky, a team of three Soviet cartoonists who worked for the Russian magazine *Krokodil*. The cartoon shows Marshall as a wicked ring-master who wants to harness the countries of Europe by tying them financially to the USA. The harness reads 'For Europe'. He is armed and in uniform and in his hand he holds a whip.

The meaning of the cartoon is that 'Marshall Aid' is merely US 'dollar imperialism'.

VOICE YOUR OPINION!

1. Was the Truman Doctrine 'the start of the Cold War'?
2. Who was most to blame for the deterioration of relations, 1945–46: the USA or the USSR?

GradeStudio

When considering the provenance of a source, it always makes sense to consider the situation of the author. For instance, in Source G, the team of Russian artists called Kukriniksy were working (in 1951) at the height of Stalin's dictatorship so they would not dare to do anything other than follow the official Soviet government line – that the Marshall Plan was American economic imperialism.

The Berlin Blockade and Airlift 1948–49

The post-war division of Germany

During the Second World War, Britain and the USA had sought to destroy Germany. After the war, however, they decided that the Soviet Union was a greater threat. A weak Germany might be taken over by the communists. A strong Germany, on the other hand, would act as a buffer against communism. Furthermore, the general economic situation in Europe would improve only with a strong German economy.

Stalin viewed the British and American attitude to Germany with suspicion. For the Soviets, the most important thing was to prevent a repeat of the Nazi invasion of 1941. Therefore Stalin weakened the Soviet zone of Germany by stripping it of all useful equipment and machinery. The Western countries, in contrast, strengthened their zones of Germany through industrialisation and reunification.

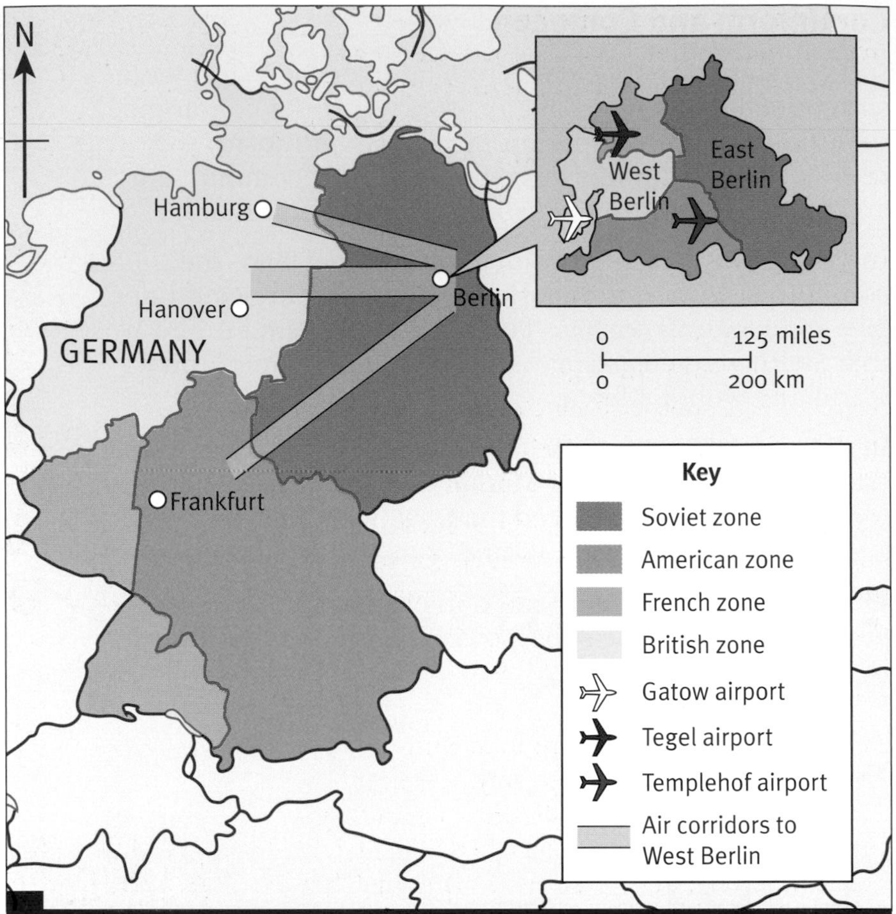

The occupied zones of Germany in 1945. Berlin, the capital of Germany, was divided into four zones of occupation, just like the rest of the country. As the city was in the Soviet zone, the West depended on the USSR to keep open the routes in and out of the city.

Map legend:

Key
- Soviet zone
- American zone
- French zone
- British zone
- Gatow airport
- Tegel airport
- Templehof airport
- Air corridors to West Berlin

Map labels: N, Hamburg, Hanover, GERMANY, Berlin, Frankfurt, West Berlin, East Berlin, 0 125 miles, 0 200 km

The Berlin crisis

A series of decisions made by the West triggered a major crisis in the Cold War.

By 1948 the western zones of Germany, including West Berlin, were beginning to recover thanks to Marshall Aid. The western Allies had stopped demanding reparations, and in 1947 Britain and the USA had joined their zones together (into 'Bizonia') to further aid recovery. A few months later the French zone joined them ('Trizonia').

Stalin saw these actions as betrayals. At Yalta and Potsdam the Allies had agreed that decisions about Germany would be taken jointly. Yet Stalin had not been consulted. He became increasingly suspicious of Western motives.

On 23 June the USA and Britain introduced a new currency, the Deutschmark, into Bizonia. This move was designed to strengthen the economy of western Germany. However, it caused an economic crisis in the eastern zone, where people rushed in their thousands to change their old Marks into new Deutschmarks. Stalin's response on 24 June 1948 was to close all roads, canals and railways that led from the West into West Berlin.

The Berlin Airlift

The Western powers claimed that Stalin was trying to force them to give up West Berlin by starving the city's two million inhabitants, who had enough food and fuel to last for only six weeks. The American commander in Germany, General Lucius Clay, suggested democracy in Europe was on the point of collapse:

> 'When Berlin falls, Western Germany will be next... Communism will run rampant.'

VOICE YOUR OPINION!

Who was to blame for the Berlin crisis of 1948–49?

President Truman seemed to have two options: surrender West Berlin or go to war. Surrendering West Berlin meant giving in to Stalin. On the other hand, an armed invasion of the Soviet zone of Germany might have dire consequences. Therefore, the British and Americans devised a less aggressive way of keeping the people of West Berlin from starving. They flew in supplies.

In 1945 the Soviets had granted each of the Allies an air corridor. These three corridors led from Allied zones in West Germany into West Berlin. To carry out their airlift, the Allies now made full use of these three air corridors.

The first flight was on 26 June. The airlift began slowly: on average, only 600 tonnes of fuel, food and other supplies were reaching West Berlin every day. If West Berliners were to survive Stalin's **blockade**, they needed over 4000 tonnes a day.

By September aircraft were landing in West Berlin every three minutes, day and night. By the spring of 1949, 8000 tonnes a day were being flown in. In response, the Soviets tried to put more pressure on West Berliners. They cut off electricity supplies to West Berlin and offered residents extra rations if they moved to East Berlin. Only 2 per cent of the population took advantage of this offer. West Berliners were clearly prepared to suffer hardship in order to remain part of the West.

Stalin realised that the Allies were determined to keep the airlift going. The only way he could stop it would be to shoot down the supply planes. Soviet planes did track the supply planes in case they moved out of the permitted air corridors. However, the USSR dared not shoot the planes down. This would have been an act of war – at a time when the USA had the atomic bomb and the USSR did not.

Stalin called off his blockade of Berlin in May 1949.

THE BIRD WATCHER

This British cartoon, entitled *The Bird Watcher*, was published in July 1948. Storks, representing the Allies' planes, fly supplies into the ruins of Berlin. Stalin could shoot them down, but he hesitates.

The cartoon praises the airlift, but warns that the crisis could easily escalate into conflict.

Results of the Berlin crisis

The Berlin Blockade was costly to the Allies in financial and human terms. 79 British and American pilots were killed in accidents. However, the Berlin Airlift ended the ill feeling between the USA and its former enemy, Germany. Furthermore, the West had now shown how determined it was to resist communism.

The Berlin crisis had dashed all hopes for a united Germany. In 1949 the three western zones, including West Berlin, came together as the Federal Republic of Germany. West Germany, as it was also known, had a freely elected government. The USSR responded by turning its zone into the German Democratic Republic (East Germany), which had a communist government.

1.4b How did the Cold War develop in the years 1949–1955?

NATO

The Berlin Blockade of 1949 greatly alarmed Ernest Bevin, the British foreign minister. Bevin feared that if it came to war, Western Europe was badly under-defended against the Soviets. Ten days after the start of the Berlin Airlift, Bevin opened talks with the Americans about a transatlantic defence treaty. These discussions led in 1949 to the formation of the North Atlantic Treaty Organisation (NATO).

The original NATO members were the USA, Canada, Britain, France, Belgium, the Netherlands, Iceland, Luxembourg, Italy, Norway, Denmark and Portugal. In 1952 Greece and Turkey became members, and in 1955 West Germany joined. All NATO members agreed to go to war if any one of them was attacked. After the Korean War broke out in 1950, NATO set up a unified command in Paris under US control.

NATO never assembled a force large enough to stop the Soviet army in the event of a war. However, the formation of NATO meant the permanent presence in Europe of a US army. The Americans had made a lasting commitment to defend Europe from communism – by force if necessary.

NATO members saw America's military presence in Europe as a deterrent against Soviet attack. Stalin saw it as an act of war. He speeded up plans for his own deterrent against the West: a Soviet nuclear weapon. In 1951 he even discussed with his Eastern European Allies the possibility of starting a war in Europe before the Americans got strong enough to resist the Russian army.

SOURCE K

A British cartoon by Illingworth, published 20 March 1949.

The cartoon is a Western response to Soviet anger about NATO. Illingworth shows a furious Stalin accusing the west of being 'warmongers'. However, the 'Atlantic Pact' is nothing more than a frail barbed-wire fence around the Allies, who huddle together for protection against the Soviet giant.

SOURCE J

The North Atlantic Treaty Organisation was a European initiative from the beginning: it was as explicit an invitation as has ever been extended from smaller powers to a great power to construct an empire and include them in it.

An extract from *We Now Know: Rethinking Cold War History* by John Lewis Gaddis (1997).

Gaddis, a post-revisionist historian, interprets the Cold War as a 'clash of cultures'.

War in Korea

The Japanese had occupied Korea from 1910 to 1945. After its defeat in the Second World War, however, Japan had to pull out of Korea. The country was divided in two along the 38th parallel (a line of latitude). Soviet forces occupied the north of the country, and American forces occupied the south. The division and occupation of Korea was supposed to be temporary.

In the north, a communist state was established under Kim Il Sung. In the south, elections were held. The result was an anti-communist, military government led by Syngman Rhee. Each side claimed to be the rightful government of all Korea. There were frequent clashes in the supposedly demilitarised zone along the border into 1950.

Background to war in Korea: the USA

Before 1950 the USA believed that Korea lay outside its 'sphere of interest'. However, in 1949 China became communist. The same year, the USSR developed the atomic bomb. US policy-makers now felt the need for a more aggressive approach to communism than 'containment'. In 1950 a policy document, coded NSC-68, made two key recommendations: a massive increase in armaments and a new policy to 'roll back' communism.

The Americans believed that if a state turned communist, neighbouring states would fall to communism one by one (like a row of dominoes knocking each other over). This belief is called the **domino theory**. The Americans began to worry that if South Korea fell to North Korean communism, then its neighbour, Japan, would soon follow.

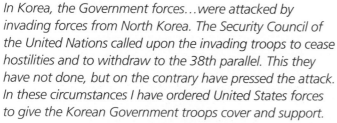
Background to war in Korea: the USSR

Before 1950 the USSR, too, believed that Korea lay outside its sphere of interest. However, in 1949 the USA formed NATO. The same year, the Americans began negotiating economic and military aid with Japan. It seemed to Stalin that the USA was becoming more aggressive.

Therefore, when Kim Il Sung visited Stalin and asked the Soviet leader's permission to attack South Korea, Stalin saw an opportunity to cause trouble for the Americans. He gave the North Koreans aid and military equipment (though he never involved the Soviet army directly in North Korea's military campaigns). In June 1950 North Korea invaded the South. The Korean War had begun.

What's in a name?

The different names given to the war by the different sides reflect their attitudes and beliefs. The North Koreans called the war 'The Fatherland Liberation War', while one Chinese newspaper called it 'The War to Resist US Aggression and Aid Korea'.

For their part however, the Americans claimed that all they were doing was supporting a United Nations action. They never declared war and sometimes call the war 'The Korean Conflict'.

The Soviet Union never become officially involved in the war. Soviet telegrams of the time, therefore, refer to 'military operations in Korea' or 'the war in Korea'.

HISTORIOGRAPHY

Although some people had reservations about US policy, most historians at the time approved of Truman's actions. They saw the Americans as defenders of democracy against a fanatical Soviet regime that was determined to take over the world.

From the 1960s, however, a number of revisionist historians began to criticise the Americans – especially Truman – and to blame the USA for the increasing tension in the Cold War. According to the revisionist view, the Korean War was a local conflict between the communists in North Korea and an unpleasant military dictator in the South. Yet the USA chose to make this civil war its battleground against communism.

Recently historians have been able to read Soviet government papers for the first time. These documents show that Stalin was much more aggressive than the revisionists thought. The papers prove that Stalin plotted with the North Koreans to start the Korean War and also tried to engineer a full-scale confrontation between China and the USA.

The Korean War

1. Initial North Korean success

The North Korean People's Army (NKPA) was successful at first. Most of South Korea fell. Only the Pusan Pocket in the south-east held out. In desperation, South Korea asked the United Nations for help. Normally the USSR would have vetoed any attempt to support South Korea. However, in 1950 the USSR was boycotting UN meetings in protest at the UN's refusal to admit communist China as a member. Therefore the UN Security Council declared North Korea to be the aggressor.

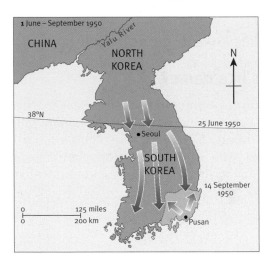

2. The NKPA is driven back

Sixteen nations, headed by the USA, immediately went to Korea. Later, 32 countries participated in the war. Their commander-in-chief was General Douglas MacArthur, an American hero of the Second World War. In September MacArthur organised a successful naval landing at Inchon that surprised the communists and forced them to retreat. North Korean resistance collapsed, and UN troops advanced into North Korea and towards China.

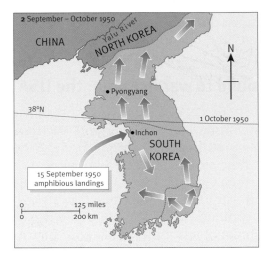

3. China intervenes

Communist China feared for its security and warned UN troops not to approach the Yalu River. MacArthur ignored this warning. He wished to invade China and was even prepared to use nuclear weapons. In November 1950 China sent 200,000 'volunteers' to help North Korea. UN forces were pushed back beyond the 38th parallel.

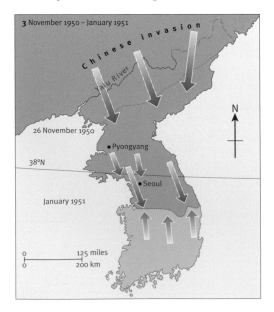

4. Stalemate

The Americans poured in more men and drove the Chinese back to the 38th parallel. Truman dismissed MacArthur in April 1951 and appointed General Matthew Ridgway as his replacement. The rest of the war was a **stalemate** in which neither side made gains and many lives were lost. Finally, both sides agreed a cease-fire in 1953.

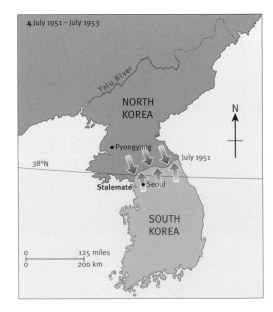

HISTORY DOESN'T REPEAT ITSELF

This British cartoon by David Low, published on 30 June 1950, portrays a heroic President Truman rushing with an armed United Nations to the aid of South Korea.

In the 1930s Low had been a harsh critic of appeasement.

He contrasts Truman's powerful reaction with the past failures of the League of Nations.

SOURCE **N**

Korea was the spearpoint of a drive made by the whole communist control group on the entire position of the West – it was also to unsettle Japan, Southeast Asia… and to affect the situation also in Europe. That is what the war in Korea is being fought about.

A statement made by Dean Acheson, the US secretary of state (foreign minister), in May 1951.

SOURCE **O**

I began to ask myself whether… we had contributed, and were continuing to contribute – by the overmilitarization of our policies and statements – to a belief in Moscow that it was war we were after.

A statement made by George Kennan, the US ambassador to the USSR, in 1952. Kennan hated the Soviets and held them responsible for the Cold War. However, he began to have doubts about US policy in Korea.

SOURCE **P**

President Truman, without hesitation, acted energetically, intelligently, with the sure instinct of bravery. He knew that no matter how remote the strategic value of Korea, the prestige of the US was now involved together with the future determination of the entire free world in resisting the pressures of communist Power.

From *A New History of the Cold War* by John Lukacs (1966). Lukacs was born in Hungary in 1942 but lives in the USA.

He is a respected historian and was a close friend of the American diplomat George Kennan. Strongly anti-communist, he blames Stalin for causing the Cold War. However, he believes that the USSR was a feeble power and would have collapsed if the USA had resisted it strongly.

The impact of the Korean War

During the Korean War the Cold War intensified. Hostilities spread beyond Europe and into new areas. The founding in 1954 of the South East Asian Treaty Organisation (SEATO) increased mistrust between the USA and the USSR. SEATO was an Asian version of NATO. Its goal was to contain communism in the Far East.

Korea was ruined by the war. One in ten Koreans died. However, the South had not fallen to communism. The country remained divided.

The Americans viewed the Korean War as a success. The advance of communism had been halted and the Truman Doctrine upheld. The USA now turned its attention to other areas in the Far East threatened by communism. Top of the list was Vietnam.

Korea was also a success for the United Nations, which had been formed in 1946 as a successor to the League of Nations. In Korea, the UN had shown that it was prepared to stand up to aggression. It seemed to be much stronger than the League of Nations.

The Korean war also revealed that China, no longer a weak nation, was prepared to stand up to the West.

BE A HISTORIAN!

1. Use an internet search engine, text book indexes or an encyclopaedia to find out about:
   - The domino theory
   - NSC-68
   - No Gun Ri
   - Human wave
   - General MacArthur in the Korean War
2. Looking again at pages 72–74, make the case that:
   a) the Americans
   b) the Soviets
   were to blame for the Korean War.

SOURCE Q

At the cost of the sacrifices of the Korean people a strengthening of the position at the 38th parallel has been won. North Korea and Northeast China have been defended.

The people of Korea and China, especially their armed forces, have received the possibility of being tempered and acquiring experience in the struggle against American imperialism.

In addition in the course of the struggle of the Korean and Chinese peoples, their might has been strengthened… This limits the mobility of the main forces of American imperialism and makes it suffer constant losses in the east… This will mean the delay of a new world war.

Telegram from Mao Zedung to Kim Il Sung, 15 July 1952, copied to Stalin on 18 July 1952.

SOURCE R

The victory in the last Fatherland Liberation War taught the truth of history that if wise leadership is provided by the party and leader and the army and the people display strong mental power, there is no formidable enemy in the world that they cannot defeat. Herein lies the great significance of the war.

From an article published in *Rodung Sinmum*, the official newspaper of the Central Committee of the Worker's Party of North Korea, 25 July 2008.

North Korea still claims it won the Korean War.

GradeStudio

To explain the importance of an event, you need to think about its results. For instance, if you were asked how important the Korean War was in worsening the Cold War, you could offer three consequences:
1. MacArthur saw it as an opportunity to move from 'containment' to 'roll back'.
2. The USA involved the whole of the United Nations in the war.
3. The USA considered using the atomic bomb on a number of occasions.

The Arms Race, 1949–55

After the formation of NATO, the Western Allies stepped up their spending on armaments. US military spending rose to 18 per cent of its Gross National Product (**GNP**), and British and French spending rose to 10 per cent of GNP.

Until 1949 only the USA had the atomic bomb (also called the A-bomb). Then in 1950 the Soviets announced that they, too, had developed an atom bomb (and had performed a trial detonation in August 1949). A nuclear arms race between the two superpowers began. In 1952 American scientists developed the hydrogen bomb, or H-bomb, which was 2500 times more powerful than the A-bomb. By 1953 Russian scientists, too, had developed an H-bomb.

By 1955 the Americans had about 2000 nuclear warheads. They also had the means to carry and fire them; the US airforce had 50 B-29 bombers in 1948 and more than a thousand five years later. Also in 1953, the American army in West Germany received its first nuclear weapons designed for use on the battlefield.

American politicians claimed that the USA had fewer nuclear weapons than the USSR. In fact the USSR had only about 50 atom bombs in 1953 and did not catch up with the USA until 1978. On the other hand, the USSR had a huge conventional army of soldiers, tanks, artillery, and so on. President Truman was fearful of the USSR's mighty conventional army. During the Korean War Truman ordered a massive increase in American spending on conventional weapons. He also increased spending on American NATO forces stationed in Western Europe.

The arms race increased the climate of fear between the two superpowers. In particular, each side was afraid that that the other might try to win a 'hot war' by launching a surprise **pre-emptive strike**.

"NOW, DON'T LET'S DO ANYTHING AS DANGEROUS AND RASH AS AGREEING ON SOMETHING."

A cartoon by Vicky (Victor Weisz), which appeared in the British newspaper the *Daily Mirror* in February 1955. Weisz feared that nuclear weapons would destroy humankind. He designed the famous logo for the Campaign for Nuclear Disarmament (CND).

In this cartoon, delegates at the United Nations Disarmament Talks warn each other not to do 'anything as dangerous and rash as agreeing on something!' Over their heads hangs a real danger: an atomic bomb that threatens to kill them all.

SOURCE **S**

And why has humanity survived the Cold War? The reasons that the Cold War never exploded into hot war was surely the invention of nuclear weapons. One is inclined to support the suggestions that the Nobel Peace Prize should have gone to the atomic bomb.

The highly respected American historian Arthur Schlesinger expressed this opinion in 1992 in his essay, *The End of the Cold War: Its Meanings and Implications.* Schlesinger twice won the Pulitzer Prize, a prestigious award for writers in various fields. Fiercely anti-communist, he blamed the Soviets for the Cold War.

BE A HISTORIAN!

Use an internet search engine, textbook indexes or an encyclopaedia to find out about:
- Joe One
- The Fulda Gap
- The DEW line
- Duck and Cover, 1951

Khrushchev and co-existence

Stalin was the dictator of the Soviet Union from the late 1920s to 1953. His regime was cruel and **repressive**. Anyone who opposed him was arrested, and his secret police were active everywhere.

When Stalin died in 1953, the Soviet people were relieved. The new leader of the Soviet Communist Party was Nikita Khrushchev, who immediately started to relax the Soviet state's grip on its citizens.

One of Khrushchev's first actions, in May 1955, was to sign the Austrian State Treaty. Austria, like Germany, had been occupied and divided among the Allies. The Austrian State Treaty ended this occupation and re-established Austria as an independent sovereign state. Khrushchev also pulled the Red Army out of the Soviet-occupied zone of Austria. He seemed to be a man who did not want to dominate the world.

In 1956 Khrushchev made a secret speech to the Communist Party. In it he denounced Stalin as a cruel **tyrant**. Stalin's statues came down, cities were renamed, the secret police became less active, Stalin's body was removed from the Kremlin, and more consumer goods were produced. This whole process, called 'destalinisation', proved to be very popular in the Soviet Union. Since the Soviet people seemed to be gaining more freedom, destalinisation was a popular policy in the West, too. The capitalist states particularly liked Khrushchev's change of attitude towards the West. Khrushchev wanted to replace the old policy of confrontation with a new policy of **Peaceful Co-existence**. The USSR would recognise the Western powers' right to exist. This change of approach led to a reduction in Cold War tensions. People called it a 'thaw' in relations.

This 'thaw' was an illusion, however. Destalinisation in the Soviet Union encouraged people living in the **satellite states** of Eastern Europe. They expected changes similar to those in the Soviet Union. They demanded concessions and tried to weaken Soviet influence in their countries.

However, they, like the West, had misunderstood Khrushchev's motives. Khrushchev could not grant widespread concessions in the satellite states because he feared the consequences: the end of communism in Eastern Europe and the destruction of the Soviet buffer against the West. Khrushchev was not prepared to compromise the security of the Soviet Union. So when revolts against Soviet control took place in East Germany in 1953 and Poland and Hungary in 1956, they were ruthlessly put down. Cold War relationships deteriorated once more, and the 'thaw' ended.

The Warsaw Pact

In 1955 West Germany was admitted to NATO. Ten days later, the Soviet Union joined with Poland, Czechoslovakia, Hungary, Romania, Bulgaria and Albania in a military alliance of 'friendship, cooperation and mutual assistance' called the Warsaw Pact. Soon after, the Soviet Union cancelled its wartime alliances with Britain and France and took East Germany into the Warsaw Pact.

After the Warsaw Pact was formed, it was impossible to deny that Germany – indeed, Europe – was absolutely divided between communist East and democratic West. It looked as though the Cold War was going to be a permanent fixture in international relations.

SOURCE U

Two final conclusions about the early Cold War years stand out: first, hostility on one side breeds hostility on the other… and second, adopting hard-line policies against the other superpower is at least as likely to trigger a hard-line response as it is to create moderate behaviour.

A comment written by the American historian Ralph B. Levering in 1982. Levering is a post-revisionist historian who believes that 'attitudes and policies on both sides' were to blame for the Cold War.

VOICE YOUR OPINION!

Argue with a friend about whether the Cold War got worse or better between 1949 and 1955. Support your argument with information from pages 70–76 and your own knowledge.

GradeStudio

Preparation - 'Describe'

- ideological differences between the USA and the USSR
- the conferences at Yalta and Potsdam
- the dropping of the atom bomb and its effects
- Soviet expansion in Eastern Europe
- the Truman Doctrine and its purpose
- the Marshall Plan and its effects
- Czechoslovakia, 1948
- the Berlin Blockade and Airlift, 1948–49
- NATO
- the arms race, 1945–55
- the Korean War
- the Warsaw Pact
- the 'thaw' and Peaceful Co-existence

1. Looking back through this chapter, write a short paragraph describing IN GENERAL TERMS each item in the panel on the left.

2. Using this textbook, an encyclopaedia or the internet, ADD DETAIL by finding out two or more EXTRA FACTS about each item on the left. You could GO DEEPER by finding out more about a particular aspect. Or you could GO BROADER by putting each item in its wider context.

3. Choose ONE item and write a full 'Describe' essay of three paragraphs.

Preparation - 'Why?'

WHY...

- did Britain and the USA fear the Soviets?
- did the Soviets hate and fear the West?
- did Truman declare his doctrine?
- did Marshall devise his plan?
- did Stalin set up the Berlin Blockade?

- did the Allies set up the Berlin Airlift?
- did the western democracies form NATO?
- did the USA support South Korea in 1950?
- did the USSR form the Warsaw Pact?

1. Working in a small group, think of TWO reasons for each situation in the list above.

Preparation - 'How?'

HOW did this...	cause this?
• ideological differences...	★ mistrust and fear between the USSR and the West
• Soviet expansion in Eastern Europe...	★ annoyance and alarm among the Western Allies
• Churchill's Fulton speech...	★ an increase in international tension
• the situation in Greece and Turkey...	★ the announcement of the Truman Doctrine
• Marshall Aid...	★ the 'containment' of communism
• the nuclear arms race...	★ increased tension in the Cold War

1. Working as a whole class, think of TWO ways in which each factor on the left led to the outcome on the right.

Source M shows President Truman and the United Nations rushing to the defence of Korea. Do you agree with this interpretation of American involvement in the Korean War?

Explain your answer by referring to the purpose of the source, as well as using its content and your own knowledge.   (6 marks)

Full sample answer

Comments

Describe the cartoon's interpretation of events.	Source M is a comment on the UN Security Council's decision to send an army (represented by the machine gun) to South Korea. At the time people such as the historian John Lukacs said that President Truman was being 'energetic... intelligent... brave' when he went to the defence of South Korea.	Begins by explaining what the cartoon shows and what its interpretation of events is.
Refer to the cartoon's provenance.	Looking at the provenance, I see that the cartoon is contemporary (it appeared in June 1950). However, being British, it is biased in favour of Truman; by contrast, Soviet propaganda denounced the Americans.	TWO IDEAS about why the PROVENANCE might be important.
Show how the cartoon's interpretation of events is linked to its provenance.	The cartoon praises Truman, who is portrayed as strong, energetic and determined. This reflects the cartoonist's British standpoint – David Low hated appeasement in the 1930s, and he is saying that the strong US/UN action is much better than the former, weak League of Nations. In the Korean War the British helped the Americans, and Low wanted to support this.	TWO IDEAS explore the cartoon's interpretation of events, referring to its provenance.
Explain the event the cartoon is referring to.	When I look at the content of the source, I see that there is truth in it. The UN Security Council did decide to send troops to Korea, and the presence of Truman in the cartoon reflects the fact that the USA provided most of the men, and UN forces were led by Douglas MacArthur.	Provides facts about the cartoon's content.
Compare the cartoon's content in detail to the historical facts to examine whether the cartoon's interpretation of events is true or false.	Other facts support the interpretation. Korea was a 'hot war' (as portrayed by the machine gun) – Truman even considered using nuclear weapons. Also, there was a rush in June 1950, because the North Koreans were defeating the South Koreans easily. However, US intervention was not just to defend. It was the result of a new American policy – NSC-68 – to 'roll back' communism. Truman has a look of determination in the cartoon, and he certainly was determined to stop the communists.	Develops ideas FOR or AGAINST the interpretation. At this point, with detailed explanations of both the content and provenance of the source, the answer is of a high standard
Conclusion, assessing the cartoon's interpretation of events.	The cartoon gives a biased view of the armed intervention in Korea by the UN and the Americans. It tells us Low's opinion of what happened. The cartoon was not government propaganda, but it was produced to reassure and convince the British people that the Americans were doing the right thing in going to war.	Refers to the purpose of the source.

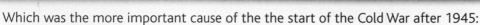

Which was the more important cause of the the start of the Cold War after 1945:

- Soviet expansion in eastern Europe
- The Marshall Plan of 1947?

You must refer to both causes when explaining your answer.   (10 marks)

Full sample answer

Comments

Describe Soviet expansion.

After 1945, Eastern Europe was taken over by governments supported by the Soviet Union. Communists took power in Albania, Bulgaria and Poland (1945), and Hungary and Romania (1947). First they took control of the police, army and radio stations. Then they systematically arrested or murdered their opponents.

> An opening statement. At least TWO extra facts.

Explain HOW Soviet expansion caused tension and conflict.

This caused tension because the Western Allies thought Communism was taking over the world. Also, they had democracies and hated the kind of communist dictatorships that were being set up in eastern Europe.

> TWO IDEAS are introduced here.

Assess how important Soviet expansion was as a cause of the Cold War.

This was a very important reason for the Cold War. The West was so worried that when it looked like Turkey and Greece might turn communist, President Truman announced his Doctrine to contain Communism.

> Discusses the importance of Soviet expansion by referring to facts.

Describe the Marshall Plan.

The war had left Western Europe very poor, and the aim of the Marshall Plan was to prevent Western Europe turning to communism. The plan was to help Europe recover economically as quickly as possible. The Marshall Plan set up $15 billion of aid, mostly in the form of products, such as machinery and fertilisers. Sixteen countries asked for aid, including allies like Britain and even former enemies such as West Germany.

> An opening statement. At least TWO extra facts.

> TWO IDEAS. At this point, with a full explanation of both possible causes of the major development, the answer is of a good standard.

Explain HOW the Marshall Plan caused tension and conflict.

This caused tension because Stalin thought America was trying to take over Europe with 'economic imperialism'. He thought America was trying to undermine the Soviet influence in Eastern Europe. The Marshall Plan was helping West Germany to grow stronger, and Stalin wanted to keep Germany weak so that the USSR could never be invaded again.

Assess how important the Marshall Plan was as a cause of the Cold War.

This was an important cause of the Cold War because Stalin was worried enough to order the communist countries not to accept Marshall Aid. Stalin responded by setting up Cominform (1947) and Comecon (1949) and he came up with a rival plan – the 'Molotov Plan'.

> Discusses the importance of the Marshall Plan by referring to facts. Having assessed the importance of BOTH causes, this answer is now of a high standard

Conclusion.

I think that the Soviet expansion was more important as a cause of the Cold War, because the Americans only came up with the Marshall Plan to stop the spread of communism. The US Congress only agreed the funding for Marshall Aid after Czechoslovakia turned communist in March 1948. So this shows that Soviet expansion was the main cause, and the Marshall Plan was just a response.

> The answer now makes a judgement. It explains how that judgement was reached and includes at least one fact.

1.5 Crises of the Cold War 1955–1970

Overview

Khrushchev and the West

When Nikita Khrushchev came to power in the USSR, he criticised Stalin and began a process of 'destalinisation'. The secret police became less active, there was less repression and more consumer goods were produced. He also talked openly about the importance of 'Peaceful Co-existence' in international relations. Western politicians hoped that there might be a 'thaw' in the Cold War.

There was no thaw. Khrushchev was certain that communism was a superior system of government to capitalism. By 'Peaceful Co-existence', he simply meant that each side ought to allow the other to compete equally on the world stage.

- Khrushchev made high-profile visits to foreign leaders and gave aid to poor Third World countries. In this way, he deliberately raised the political influence of the Soviet Union.
- He demanded the right to solve problems within the Soviet Union's 'sphere of interest'. His solutions included crushing the Hungarian Revolution and building the Berlin Wall.

HISTORIOGRAPHY

In the 1950s Khrushchev was regarded in the West either as a thug or a clown. In the 1960s he was hated as the man who had taken the world to the edge of nuclear annihilation.

After his fall from power in 1964, Khrushchev was viewed in the Soviet Union as an 'un-person' and was even denounced as a **renegade**.

After the fall of Soviet communism in 1991, Khrushchev's reputation rose. He was remembered as having led the USSR at a time when the USSR led the world. He was praised for his idea of Peaceful Co-existence.

The recent opening of Soviet archives has shed more light on Khrushchev's character and actions. Many modern biographers see him as a man whose over-optimism, risky schemes, aggression and downright ignorance led him time after time to misjudge situations and cause international crises.

TIMELINE

1955	1956	1957	1959	1960	1961
				May 1960 U-2 crisis; Paris Summit	April 1961 Bay of Pigs
Geneva Summit	Hungarian Revolution	Sputnik 1 (USSR); Atlas-A (USA)	Fidel Castro takes power in Cuba	Both powers develop Intercontinental Ballistic Missiles (ICBMs); Polaris (USA); Soviets put two dogs into orbit	Kennedy becomes US president; Yuri Gagarin orbits the Earth (USSR); Alan Shepard goes into space (USA)

- He challenged the West when he felt the Soviet Union was being threatened. Confrontations between Khrushchev and the West led to the U-2 crisis of 1960 and Khrushchev's demand at the 1961 Vienna **summit** that the Americans leave Berlin.
- He engaged in a space race with the USA in order to demonstrate the Soviet Union's technological superiority.
- He engaged with the West in a nuclear arms race, which ran out of control.
- Iron Curtain countries challenged the dominance of the USA in the Olympic Games.

One of the results of Khrushchev's actions was the election in 1961 of John F. Kennedy as president of the USA. Kennedy pledged to 'get tough' on the communists.

Therefore, although Khrushchev was not the malevolent tyrant Stalin had been, the Cold War was at its fiercest during his time in power.

End of the world?

People who lived in the 1960s remember feeling constantly afraid that life on Earth would be wiped out in a nuclear war. In the West, these were the years of peace campaigns with slogans like 'Ban the Bomb' and hippies who wanted to 'Make Love not War'. Yet the nuclear arms race accelerated and the Cold War showed no sign of ending.

The decade began with a number of confrontations between Kennedy and Khrushchev that culminated in the Cuban Missile Crisis (1962). Six years later, the decade seemed to be ending in despair. In 1968 the Soviet Army stomped into Czechoslovakia to put an end to the Prague Spring. While the Soviets were struggling to re-establish control behind the Iron Curtain, the endless atrocities and failures of the Vietnam War were plunging the USA into chaos.

Only in the final year of the decade did a glimmer of light appear at the end of the tunnel. In 1969 a human being stood on the moon and took a photograph that gave everyone a new perspective on the earth and its squabbles.

Space travel gave mankind a new perspective on the world.

BE A HISTORIAN!

1. Use the internet to find out FIVE significant facts about Khrushchev.
2. Invent a way of remembering how to spell his name.

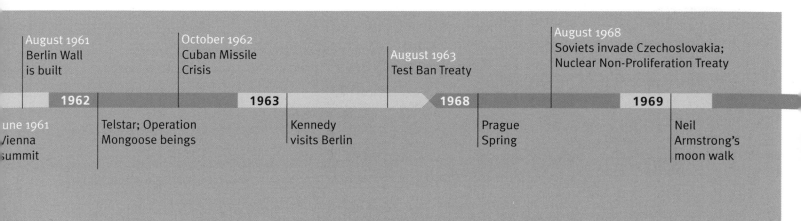

August 1961 Berlin Wall is built	October 1962 Cuban Missile Crisis		August 1963 Test Ban Treaty	August 1968 Soviets invade Czechoslovakia; Nuclear Non-Proliferation Treaty	
1962	**1963**		**1968**	**1969**	
June 1961 Vienna summit	Telstar; Operation Mongoose beings	Kennedy visits Berlin	Prague Spring	Neil Armstrong's moon walk	

1.5a How peaceful was Peaceful Co-existence?

The Geneva Summit

In 1955 world leaders met at the first summit held in ten years. They discussed world trade, the arms race and disarmament. President Dwight Eisenhower of the USA suggested an 'open skies' policy for aircraft. According to Eisenhower's proposal, each side would be free to monitor (from the air) the other's arms build-up. Neither would be able to stockpile weapons, and suspicion would be reduced. Although no decisions were made, the Geneva Summit marked the high point of the so-called 'thaw' in Cold War relations.

The arms race, 1955–63

The two superpowers competed to gain an advantage in the arms race:

- Until 1957 a nuclear bomb would have been carried to its target by a long-range aircraft and dropped. Then in October 1957 the USSR developed a rocket, the R-7, which could launch a satellite, Sputnik 1, into space. Two months later the Americans tested their own rocket, the Atlas-A. This rocket could be fitted with a nuclear warhead and launched at a target thousands of miles away.

- By 1960 both countries had Inter-Continental Ballistic Missiles (ICBMs). These land-based strategic missiles were stored in concrete silos in underground bases. From these bases they could be launched to strike targets up to 6400 kilometres away. Both sides tried to position ICBMs in friendly countries close to enemy borders. The Americans based missiles in Turkey, a country that bordered the USSR.

- The arms race moved on in 1960, when the Americans fired a new Polaris missile from a submarine. It was now possible to fire missiles with a range of over 1600 kilometres from under the sea. The Soviets soon developed their own nuclear submarines.

By 1960, both sides had enough nuclear weapons to destroy every living thing on Earth (this situation was called 'overkill').

SOURCE

" OF COURSE , DEAR , IT'S THE BOMB THAT'S CHANGED THE CLIMATE ... "

A British cartoon by Vicky (Victor Weisz), published in the *Daily Mirror* in 1955. The cartoonist likens the hot summer of 1955 to the warmth in international relations. On the left the British prime minister, Harold Macmillan, puts his arm round Khrushchev. British, American and Soviet politicians relax together, and a beach ball (drawn as a globe) rests peacefully on the sand.

The prospect of a nuclear war frightened Weisz. Macmillan's words to Khrushchev allude to popular fears that nuclear missile tests were changing the weather: 'Of course, dear, it's the bomb that's changed the climate'. These words have a clear double meaning.

The Hungarian Rising, 1956

People living in Hungary, a Soviet satellite state, took inspiration from the death of Stalin and the emergence of Khrushchev. Hungarians believed that destalinisation and the international thaw had created the right atmosphere in which to win reforms. After a revolt in Poland in June 1956, the Soviet Union had granted concessions to the Poles. The Polish concessions encouraged Hungarians to seek an end to the Soviet stranglehold on Hungary. They hoped to gain political freedom and economic improvements through increased contact with the West. Some hoped for the withdrawal of Soviet troops from Hungary.

Demonstrations and protests in Budapest, the capital of Hungary, led to the election of Imre Nagy as prime minister in October 1956. He had been prime minister from 1953 to 1955 and was known to be a moderniser. The Soviet Union, caught off guard by the riots, withdrew its army. Khrushchev hoped that this withdrawal would calm a difficult situation.

Nagy immediately announced a programme of reform. Government control of the press and radio was ended. Non-communists were allowed to participate in government, and Nagy promised free democratic elections. Finally, Nagy announced that Hungary would leave the Warsaw Pact.

This last move was completely unacceptable to Khrushchev. The Hungarian reforms had made communism 'look bad', but the threat to leave the Warsaw Pact was a different matter entirely: it threatened the Soviet Union's military safety. On 4 November 1956, the Red Army returned in strength and crushed the Hungarian uprising. In the fighting that followed, 4000 Hungarians were killed. Perhaps as many as 200,000 fled to the West.

Results of the rising

Nagy was arrested and later executed. Protesters were imprisoned, and 300 people were executed. A hard-line communist government under Janos Kadar abolished all Nagy's reforms.

The Hungarian episode was a military victory for Khrushchev. Hungary returned to being a pro-Soviet communist state. The United Nations passed a resolution in support of the Hungarians but did nothing more. The US was shown to be powerless to 'roll back' communism. People in the West complained that NATO stood for 'No Action: Talk Only'. Khrushchev joked that 'support by the United States... was like the support that the rope gives to a hanged man'.

However, in terms of propaganda, the Hungarian Rising was a defeat for Khrushchev. It made Soviet communism look brutal and cruel. In Britain, thousands of people resigned from the Communist Party.

On the whole, the West grew more frightened of the USSR, and the Cold War intensified.

SOURCE B

There is no stopping the wild onslaught of communism. Your turn will come, once we perish. Save our souls! We beg you to help us in the name of justice and freedom.

A plea broadcast to the West by Hungarian fighters on 4 November 1956.

SOURCE C

This was the painful point: Khrushchev had to be ruthless to hold his alliance together. He had hoped to make communism attractive enough that Stalinist methods would not be needed; but even the briefest experiment with destalinisation had set off separatist tendencies in Eastern Europe that ended in a bloodbath.

An extract from *We Now Know: Rethinking Cold War History*, by John Lewis Gaddis (1997). Gaddis, a post-revisionist historian, interprets the Cold War as a 'clash of cultures'. Writing after 1990, he had access to many Soviet as well as American records.

The U-2 crisis

The West had hoped that the rise to power of Khrushchev might lead to better relations with the Soviet Union. Events in Hungary in 1956, however, had shown that the Cold War was a long way from over. In 1960 the Cold War intensified.

The year had begun with great hope. The 'Big Four' – Eisenhower of the USA, Khrushchev of the USSR, Charles de Gaulle of France, and Macmillan of Britain – had arranged to meet at a summit to be held in Paris in May. Perhaps the time had come for East and West to patch up their differences and begin a new period of friendly relations. Yet before the leaders even arrived in Paris, those hopes had been dashed.

The 'spy in the sky'

By the 1950s the Americans had developed the U-2, a lightweight spy plane that could fly 75,000 feet above the Earth. Even if Soviet **radar** detected it, the plane would be too high to be intercepted by Soviet aircraft. Yet the U-2 carried hi-tech cameras which, even from that height, could take photographs of military sites in the Soviet Union.

On 1 May 1960, just a fortnight before the Paris summit, a U-2 piloted by Gary Powers took off from a US base in Pakistan. The flight went well, and Powers was able to take photographs deep inside the Soviet Union. Then came disaster. As Powers crossed the Ural Mountains, his plane was hit by a Soviet SAM-2 missile. It crashed near the Soviet town of Sverdlovsk. Powers ejected from the plane and parachuted to the ground, where he was captured by Soviet forces. The U-2 was recovered by Soviet scientists for study.

Instructions to Mr Powers and other pilots on similar missions is to feel free to tell the full truth about their mission. We think this is a firmly American way of behaviour – we can leave the bald-faced lying to the Soviets.

Printed in the *Washington Daily News* after Gary Powers' release from the Soviet Union. (In fact, it was the Americans who had been caught telling lies.)

SOURCE **D**

In this Soviet cartoon, called *The Art of Camouflage*, President Eisenhower is painting a dove, the symbol of peace, on a U-2 spy plane.

The cartoonist is accusing Eisenhower of pretending to want peace while really being a warmonger.

This map shows the intended route of Gary Powers' U2 spy plane over the USSR and indicates the point at which the plane was shot down.

Key
— U2 route
⊙ Where U2 was shot down
- - - Planned route

The American response

As soon as the Americans discovered that their plane had been shot down, they mounted an elaborate attempt to cover up what had happened. If they admitted to spying on the Soviet Union, the summit talks would be ruined. At first the Americans announced that a U-2 research plane studying weather conditions at high altitude had disappeared somewhere over Turkey.

What the Americans did not yet know was that Powers had ejected from the plane, been captured, and had admitted to spying. The Soviets had recovered the U-2, and Soviet scientists now had the remains of the plane together with thousands of photographs of Soviet territory.

On 7 May Khrushchev announced that he had both Powers and the U-2. The Americans had been caught spying and telling lies. There seemed to be no way of denying the truth of these charges.

The end of hopes for peace

Khrushchev offered to attend the summit as long as the Americans apologised. Eisenhower refused to apologise. He claimed that it was America's responsibility to protect itself from a possible surprise attack. Therefore, the U-2 flights were an important part of US defence strategy. Khrushchev was not satisfied with this answer and left the summit before talks had started. He then cancelled an invitation to Eisenhower to visit the Soviet Union. The Cold War had just got colder.

Postscript: Gary Powers

Powers was tried in Moscow on charges of spying. He was found guilty and sentenced to ten years imprisonment. After serving seventeen months of his sentence, he was sent back to the USA in return for the release of a top Soviet spy from a US prison.

A cartoon by Vicky (Victor Weisz), published in the *Daily Mirror* on 14 May 1955.

As the world leaders attending the Paris Summit (from left to right, de Gaulle, Eisenhower, Macmillan and Khrushchev) prepare to climb a mountain, the dove of peace is killed by a U-2 spy-plane. The mountain to be climbed is disarmament – a steep challenge.

GradeStudio

When considering the provenance of a source, it always makes sense to consider the date. Source F was drawn on 14 May, two days before Khrushchev walked out on the Paris Summit before it had actually convened. It is therefore contemporary and illustrates all the fear and worries of the time. It also turned out to be accurate; Khrushchev did walk out and the summit did collapse.

The Berlin Wall

Khrushchev had declared that his aim was Peaceful Co-existence with the West. Nevertheless, after 1958 he challenged the Western presence in Berlin on a number of occasions.

Berlin was a huge embarrassment to the USSR. American economic aid had helped transform the western part of the city into a showpiece of capitalism. While West Berliners were buying luxury goods and enjoying all the other benefits of economic recovery, East Berliners were working long hours and suffering food shortages. East Berliners rebelled in 1953, but this uprising was suppressed by the Soviet army.

Even more embarrassing for the Soviets was the defection of so many East Berliners to West Berlin. More than two million had fled by 1961. Some 2000 skilled workers were leaving for the West every day.

The border between East Germany and West Germany was protected with barbed wire, minefields and watch towers. Yet no such fortifications separated East Berlin from West Berlin. Therefore, it was easy for East Berliners to escape.

In June 1961, at the Vienna summit, Khrushchev again demanded that the West give up Berlin. President Kennedy refused. So Khrushchev decided to make it impossible for East Berliners to travel to and from West Berlin.

On 13 August 1961 the East Germans put up a barrier of barbed wire between East and West Berlin. They protected the new barrier with machine guns. President Kennedy protested, but he was unwilling to risk going to war over Berlin. Three days later work started on building a concrete wall 45 kilometres in length to replace the barbed wire. The gap in the frontier between East and West was now filled.

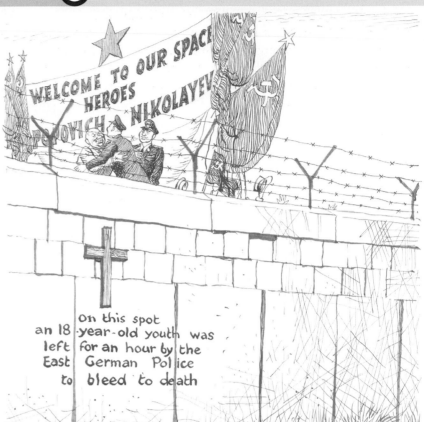

This British cartoon, drawn by Illingworth, was published in the *Daily Mail* newspaper in 1962. It shows Soviet leaders welcoming back successful cosmonauts and marvelling at the speed their spacecraft travelled. The cartoonist places this event on the Berlin Wall, above the spot where an 18-year-old East German was shot and left to bleed to death in August 1962. This man, a bricklayer named Peter Fechter, had recently been killed trying to escape over the wall.

For people in the West, the Berlin Wall symbolised Soviet oppression and the failure of communism. Many Western cartoons contrasted the USSR's claims of success with this symbol of its failure.

GradeStudio

It is not unusual for pupils to get muddled up between the Berlin Blockade and Airlift (1948–49), and the building of the Berlin Wall (1961). Make sure you remember the difference:

Blockade
- Stalin vs Truman
- Marshall Aid – Bizonia – New currency
- Roads, canals and railways closed.
- USA and Britain mounted an airlift
- Stalin called off the Blockade

Wall
- Khrushchev vs Kennedy
- Defection of skilled workers – Vienna Summit
- Barbed wire barrier + machine guns
- USA and Britain did nothing
- Soviet Union gradually strengthened the wall

The Soviets made it clear that anyone trying to cross the Berlin Wall would be shot. Even so, many were desperate enough to try. In the first year after the wall was built, 41 East Berliners were shot trying to cross. The wall separated family members and friends from one another. East Berliners also saw it as a clear sign of their inferiority to West Berliners. However, the wall greatly reduced the number of defectors from East to West Berlin.

Propaganda

Relations between the superpowers, already strained by the U-2 spying incident, got much worse. The Americans used the Berlin Wall for purposes of propaganda. If the communist system was so perfect, the Americans asked, why was it was necessary to turn it into a prison? 'Democracy may not be perfect but we never had to put up walls to keep our people in', said President Kennedy.

In 1963 Kennedy visited West Berlin. People turned out in large numbers to hear his famous speech. They applauded him warmly when he declared, *'Ich bin ein Berliner'* ('I am a Berliner'). He was demonstrating the USA's commitment to the people of West Berlin by promising that hc would never desert the city. The speech angered the communists, who saw Kennedy's visit as a deliberate attempt to cause trouble.

BE A HISTORIAN!

The Berlin Wall was a place of great tension and tragedy. To find out more enter (in inverted commas) 'Berlin Wall' into an Internet search engine, followed by these terms, and follow the links:

- construction
- 'Checkpoint Charlie'
- *Geisterbahnhöfe*
- 'Gunter Litwin'
- 'Conrad Schumann'
- 'Reinhold Huhn'
- 'Death Zone'
- 'Peter Fechter'
- Escapes
- '60 Westerstrasse'

SOURCE H

Officially the West was horrified… Behind the scenes many Western leaders were secretly relieved at the appearance of the Wall. For three years Berlin had threatened to be the flashpoint for an international confrontation, just as it had in 1948. Kennedy and other Western leaders privately agreed that a wall across Berlin was a far better outcome than a war.

The Wall ended Berlin's career as the crisis zone of world affairs.

An extract from Tony Judt's *History of Europe since 1945* (2005). Judt, a professor at New York University, is a moderately left-wing British historian.

SOURCE J

According to the West Berlin Senate we have walled ourselves in and are living in a concentration camp. But in that case why are the gentlemen so excited? Obviously, because in reality their spy centres, their seditious radio stations, their fascist solders' associations, their youth-poisoners, and their currency racketeers have been walled in. They are excited because we have erected the wall as an anti-fascist, protective wall against them.

An extract from an English-language pamphlet published in East Germany in 1962.

GradeStudio

During the Cold War, the Americans rated their intelligence information by reliability (A–D) and accuracy (1–4). Very rarely was their information A1 (impeccably reliable and irrefutably accurate); it was usually C3 (usually reliable and possibly accurate). You can use the same system. For example, Source J has some accuracy of content – the Americans did have spies and radio stations. But, since it is a piece of Soviet propaganda, it is hugely biased and unreliable, so perhaps we might grade it as a D3 source (or do you disagree?).

SOURCE K

The Berlin Wall is the defining achievement of socialism.

This statement was made by the right-wing American journalist George Will. A teacher of political philosophy at Harvard University, Will was a friend of Ronald Reagan, who was American president from 1981 to 1989.

The space race, 1957–62

The space race started in 1957, when the launch of the Soviet satellite Sputnik 1 upset US pride. The space race was an offshoot of the Cold War. Both the capitalist USA and the communist USSR claimed that their political system and way of life were superior. Winning the space race became a way to prove superiority.

At first, the Soviets led the space race.

1. In 1957 Sputnik 2 took the first dog into space, and in 1960 two Soviet space dogs (called Belka and Strelka) orbited the earth and were successfully returned.

2. In 1959 Luna 3 took pictures of the far side of the moon.

3. Finally, on 12 April 1961, Yuri Gagarin became the first person to orbit the earth. Soviet radio used this event as an opportunity to celebrate communist achievements and to attack western capitalism and the Christian religion.

By contrast, the US space agency, NASA (the National Aeronautics and Space Administration), at first experienced a number of embarrassing failures.

1. The first American satellite, Explorer 1, was not successfully launched until February 1958.

2. The Americans sent a chimpanzee named Ham into space in January 1961, and Alan Shepard flew 'Freedom 7' into space in May 1961. However, an American did not orbit the earth until 1962.

The Americans did, on the other hand, develop the first communications satellites. Telstar, the first satellite to transmit telephone and television signals, went on air in 1962.

In May 1961 President Kennedy, concerned about being left behind in the technological competition with the Soviet Union, launched the Apollo manned space flight programme. Kennedy set NASA scientists the challenge of putting a man on the moon before the end of the decade.

SOURCE L

The Sputniks prove that communism has won the competition between the communist and the capitalist countries. The economy, science, culture and the creative genius of people in all spheres of life develop better and faster under communism.

A comment by Khrushchev on the significance of the space race.

SOURCE M

LUNAR DARTS

This British cartoon by David Low, published in the *Guardian* newspaper in 1958, comments on the space race. American and Soviet scientists, watched by their generals, compete with each other in a darts match. Their target is the moon.

The cartoon captures the competitive nature of the space race and also the military significance of the rockets that the scientists are developing (they can be used to carry warheads as well as satellites).

1.5b How close to war was the world in the 1960s?

Throughout the 1960s, as competition between the USA and the USSR became more and more intense, many people lived in fear of the world ending in a nuclear war. Despite marches by groups such as the Campaign for Nuclear Disarmament, the nuclear arms race continued.

Cuba and the USSR

The location of Cuba – only 160 kilometres from the coast of Florida – gave it great strategic importance during the Cold War.

Before 1959 Cuba was a poor country controlled largely by American big business. It sold its main product, sugar cane, to the Americans. Cuba had been ruled by the dictator Fulgencio Batista since 1934, but Batista's cruel reign was ended in 1959 by **guerrillas** led by Fidel Castro.

Castro immediately started to **nationalise** all foreign-owned land, property and oil refineries. In January 1960 he made an alliance with the USSR, who promised to buy Cuba's sugar. The Americans did not like this arrangement, so in October 1960 they stopped all trade with Cuba. The USA now had an enemy on its doorstep.

The Bay of Pigs, 1961

John F. Kennedy became president of the USA in January 1961. In the early days of his presidency, he was persuaded by the Central Intelligence Agency (CIA) that Fidel Castro could be overthrown by supporters of the former Cuban ruler, Batista.

The rebels, backed by the Americans, landed at the Bay of Pigs, on Cuba's south coast, in April 1961. The attack was a total disaster. The rebels received no local Cuban support and were defeated in a few days. Kennedy was severely embarrassed. He realised that he had been wrongly advised.

The USSR arms Cuba

Castro, now certain that the USA was Cuba's enemy, looked to the USSR for even more support. In December 1961 he publicly declared himself a communist. This declaration convinced the Americans that Cuba had become a satellite state of the Soviet Union.

Meanwhile the Americans launched 'Operation Mongoose', a plan to replace Castro as ruler of Cuba by October 1962 at the latest. The Americans considered several options. One was sabotage – they aimed to disrupt the Cuban government and economy by attacking key installations, such as railway bridges, oil refineries or power plants. They also considered assassinating Castro. They even considered blowing up an American plane, blaming Cuba, and using the incident as an excuse to invade.

Cuba now had to depend on the Soviet Union for military protection. In June 1962 Castro began to receive huge shipments of Soviet arms such as aircraft, patrol boats and ground-to-air missiles.

In September, however, medium-range offensive nuclear missiles and bomber planes arrived in Cuba. The Americans knew about these weapons, but the Soviets insisted they were defensive. On 14 October 1962, U-2 spy planes photographed Soviet missiles in place on launch pads in Cuba. The photographs proved that the Soviets had lied. The missiles had a range of around 4000 kilometres. Therefore, most large American cities were within their range of attack. Nuclear destruction lay only a matter of minutes away. More ships carrying missiles were reported to be on the way from the USSR to Cuba.

HISTORIOGRAPHY

Historians disagree about the Cold War in the 1960s.

For some, the 1960s were the 'crisis years', a time when the world 'moved much closer to open conflict'.

For others, the 1960s saw the beginnings of **Détente** (the easing of tension), a time when the two sides 'learned to live with each other'.

Recently, historians have challenged both these interpretations, as well as the general view that the Cold War was a confrontation between one ideological group and another: East vs. West; Warsaw Pact vs. NATO; communism vs. capitalism. The real story, these historians argue, was much more complicated. In the USA different political and military pressure groups struggled for influence. America's allies were not always supportive – France, for instance, left NATO in 1966. Similarly, in the Soviet Union, different groups vied for power, and the Warsaw Pact countries quarrelled among themselves.

According to this view of the Cold War, neither side had a single fixed agenda. Instead leaders stumbled through events. Often they did not fully understand what was going on: they were just trying to 'come out on top'.

The Arms Race

The arms race during the 1960s was based on the principle of deterrence. According to this principle, a country had to have so many weapons that an enemy, however much it wanted to attack, would be deterred (put off) because it feared the terrible damage it would suffer.

The arms race was not only extremely costly for the countries involved, it also made the world a highly dangerous place. In March 1962, soon after the Cuban missile crisis, a Disarmament Conference opened in Geneva. It had some success. In August 1963 the Test Ban Treaty was signed in Moscow. This agreement banned the testing of nuclear weapons in the air or under water. On 17 October 1963, a UN resolution prohibited countries from placing nuclear weapons in space.

In the USA, the heads of the military continued to come up with terrifying proposals. Project Pluto was a supersonic missile powered by its own nuclear reactor. Project Dyna-Soar was a manned bomber spacecraft. Another proposal was for a manned orbiting military space-station. However, these projects were all shelved on account of their huge cost.

Meanwhile, the number of nuclear missiles increased rapidly. By 1970 the USA had 3900 warheads (with a total explosive force of 4300 **megatons**), and the USSR had 1800 warheads (3100 megatons).

In 1968, 187 countries signed the Nuclear Non-Proliferation Treaty. This agreement limited nuclear weapons to the five existing nuclear powers (the USA, the USSR, the UK, China and France).

The Space Race

The space race was an important feature of the Cold War. Not only did it give the superpowers a chance to 'beat the enemy', but space technologies could also be used in the arms race.

In the early 1960s, the Soviet Union had the lead in the space race. The USSR sent the first woman into space (Valentina Tereshkova in 1963), made the first flight without space suits (1964), and made the first spacewalk (1965).

In 1961 President Kennedy had set NASA the task of landing a man on the moon before the end of the decade. He made it clear that he saw this achievement as part of 'the battle that is now going

A human footprint on the moon.

on around the world between freedom and tyranny'. Kennedy's goal was 'mastery of space'.

During the later years of the decade, therefore, the superpowers were involved in a race to the moon. With far greater financial resources, the USA overtook the USSR. NASA completed the first manned orbit of the moon (1968) and landed the first man on the moon (Neil Armstrong on 21 July 1969). The moon landing was such a stupendous achievement that it is declared by some to be 'the defining moment of the 20th century'. On the other hand, there are still conspiracy theorists who claim that it never really happened.

There were other achievements of great importance during the 1960s space race. The Mariner probes, for example, which the Americans sent to Mars and Venus, completely changed astronomers' theories about these planets.

SOURCE T

One small step for man, one giant leap for mankind.

Neil Armstrong's comment as he placed his foot on the surface of the moon in 1969.

VOICE YOUR OPINION!

Do you agree that the moon landing was 'the defining moment of the 20th century'?

Preparation - 'Describe'

- Nikita Khrushchev's policies
- destalinisation
- Peaceful Co-existence
- Hungary, 1956
- John F. Kennedy's policies
- the nuclear arms race in the 1950s and 1960s
- the space race in the 1950s and 1960s
- the U-2 crisis, 1960
- the Berlin Wall, 1961
- the Bay of Pigs, 1961
- the Cuban missile crisis, 1962
- Czechoslovakia, 1968
- the Brezhnev Doctrine

1. Looking back through this chapter, write a short paragraph describing IN GENERAL TERMS each item in the panel on the left.

2. Using this textbook, an encyclopaedia or the internet, ADD DETAIL by finding out two or more EXTRA FACTS about each item on the left. You could GO DEEPER by finding out more about a particular aspect. Or you could GO BROADER by putting each item in its wider context.

3. Choose ONE item and write a full 'Describe' essay of three paragraphs.

Preparation - 'Why?'

WHY...

- did Hungary rebel against Soviet control?
- was there an arms race between the USA and USSR?
- was there a space race between the USA and USSR?
- did the Soviets build the Berlin Wall?
- did the USA and USSR clash over Cuba?
- was there a 'Prague Spring' in 1968?
- did Brechnev invade Czechoslovakia in 1968?

1. Working in a small group, think of TWO reasons for each situation in the list above.

Preparation - 'How?'

HOW did this...	cause this?
• the Hungarian Revolution...	• the Soviet invasion of 1956
• the U-2 crisis...	• Khrushchev's departure from the Paris summit
• the situation in Berlin in 1961...	• the building of the Berlin Wall
• Castro's revolution...	• the Cuban missile crisis
• the Cuban missile crisis...	• the 1963 Test Ban Treaty
• the Prague Spring...	• the invasion of Czechoslovakia by Warsaw Pact countries in 1968
• the Prague Spring...	• the Brezhnev Doctrine
• the Cold War...	• the space race
• the nuclear arms race...	• increased tension

1. Working as a whole class, think of TWO ways in which each factor on the left led to the outcome on the right.

GradeStudio

Source C suggests a reason why Khrushchev sent Soviet forces into Hungary in 1956. Do you agree with this interpretation of Soviet action in 1956?

Explain your answer by referring to the purpose of the source, as well as using its content and your own knowledge. **(6 marks)**

Full sample answer

Comments

Describe the source's interpretation of events.	Source C suggests that Hungary was Khrushchev's fault. It says that destalinisation 'set off separatist tendencies in Eastern Europe'. So destalinisation encouraged the Hungarians to leave the Warsaw Pact, and this led to the Soviet invasion of 1956.	Begins by explaining what the cartoon shows and what its interpretation of events is.
Refer to the source's provenance.	Looking at the provenance, I see that the source was written by John Gaddis in 1997. Gaddis is a secondary historian who has the advantage of hindsight, and also of being able to use a wide range of primary sources. Therefore his statement is probably true and fair.	TWO IDEAS about why the PROVENANCE might be important.
Show how the source's interpretation of events is linked to its provenance.	Gaddis is a 'post-revisionist' historian, which means that he is neither anti-Soviet nor anti-USA, but tries to be even-handed in his approach. It is also written after the Soviet archives opened up after 1990, so Gaddis had access to many new documents from the Soviet side, so it is likely to be well-sourced on both sides.	TWO IDEAS explore the cartoon's interpretation of events, referring to its provenance.
Explain the event the source is referring to.	When I look at the content of the source, I see truth in it. Khrushchev did try 'destalinisation'. And this did lead to trouble in Poland and Hungary, and to the Soviet invasion of 1956.	Provides facts about the cartoon's content.
Compare the source's content in detail to the historical facts to examine whether the source's interpretation of events is true or false.	Other facts support this interpretation. Khrushchev was ruthless. Despite his policy of 'Peaceful Co-existence' he still believed that he could do what he wanted behind the Iron Curtain. Secondly, it was Hungarian 'separatism' (Nagy's decision to leave the Warsaw Pact) that led Khrushchev to invade. However, recent documents from Soviet archives suggest that Hungary was not the 'bloodbath' source C describes. Instead of 30,000, less than 4000 died, so this is overstated.	Develops ideas FOR or AGAINST the interpretation. At this point, with detailed explanations of both the content and provenance of the source, the answer is of a high standard
Conclusion, assessing the source's interpretation of events.	The source is a very good interpretation of the invasion of Hungary. It tries to be an impartial description of what happened. It shows that the reason for the invasion was not the wickedness of Communism (as orthodox historians said) and it was not due to American meddling (as the revisionists said). Instead, the reason was the culture of Soviet Eastern Europe, which led Khrushchev to act ruthlessly when he thought the safety of the Soviet Union was at stake.	Refers to the purpose of the source.

Which was the more important cause of the growth tension in the Cold War after 1955:

- The Berlin Wall, 1961
- The Cuban missile crisis, 1962?

You must refer to both causes when explaining your answer. (10 marks)

Full sample answer

Comments

Describe the Berlin Wall.

In 1961, at the Vienna summit, Khrushchev demanded that the Americans leave West Berlin. When Kennedy refused, on 13 August 1961, the Soviets put up the Berlin Wall. At the time they said it was to stop American spies, 'youth poisoners' and racketeers; really it was to stop the 2000 skilled workers a day who were defecting to the West through Berlin. In its first year, 41 East Berliners (famously Peter Fechter) were shot trying to escape over the Wall.

An opening statement. At least TWO extra facts.

TWO IDEAS have been introduced here.

Explain HOW the Berlin Wall caused tension and conflict.

This caused tension because it proved to the Western Allies that Communism was a cruel and brutal system. They called the Wall 'the defining achievement of socialism'. In 1963 President Kennedy visited Berlin and declared: 'Ich bin ein Berliner', promising to defend Berlin against the Soviets. This made the Soviets angry.

Discusses the importance of the Berlin Wall by referring to facts.

Assess how important the Berlin Wall was as a cause of Cold War tension.

Actually, though, the Wall reduced tension. It stopped the drain of workers from the east, and both sides were just able to get on with life and ignore each other. As Kennedy said, a wall was better than a war over Berlin.

An opening statement. At least TWO extra facts.

Describe the Cuban missile crisis.

The Cuban missile crisis occurred in October 1962 when the Americans caught the Soviets building nuclear missile launch pads in Cuba. The crisis lasted 13 days, and came close to nuclear war twice – once when the Cubans shot down a U-2 plane, and once when the Americans stopped and boarded a Soviet ship.

TWO IDEAS. At this point, with a full explanation of both possible causes of the major development, the answer is of a good standard.

Explain HOW the Cuban missile crisis caused tension and conflict.

There was great tension when Kennedy mounted a blockade of Cuba and Soviet ships continued to sail towards Cuba. Many people expected the world to come to an end that day. There was another moment of great tension when Khrushchev sent a second letter demanding that the Americans close down their Turkish missile bases and Kennedy decided to ignore it.

Assess how important the Cuban missile crisis was as a cause of Cold War tension.

In the long term, the Cuban missile crisis also reduced tension. The leaders came so close to war that in 1963 they set up a 'hot line' to talk about problems, and also signed a Test Ban treaty to try to slow down the arms race.

Discusses the importance of the Cuban missile crisis by referring to facts. Having assessed the importance of BOTH causes, this answer is of a high standard.

Conclusion.

The Berlin Wall caused greater tension because it remained a symbol of Soviet oppression for the next 28 years, and because people died trying to cross it. Also, the Berlin Wall coming down in 1989 was the defining symbol of the collapse of Communism. By contrast, the Cuban missile crisis actually helped Détente.

The answer now makes a judgement. It explains how that judgement was reached and includes at least one fact.

1.6 The Failure of Détente and the Collapse of Communism, 1970–1991

Overview

Different views of Détente

In the 1970s the word '**Détente**' was used to describe a relaxing of tension between the USA and the USSR. People talked once again of a thaw in the Cold War.

Historians disagree about when Détente started. Soviet writers, including Brezhnev himself (see Source A), traced it back to 1953, and claimed that the Soviet Union had followed a consistent policy ever since.

Many Western historians suggest that Détente began with the scare Khrushchev and Kennedy gave themselves during the Cuban Missile Crisis of 1962.

However, it is difficult to argue that there was any real easing of tension during the late 1960s. During this period, which saw the Vietnam War and the invasion of Czechoslovakia, international relations seemed to be as bad as ever. Many historians, therefore, present Détente as a new idea of the 1970s, a decade that began with President Richard Nixon and his Nixon Doctrine (1969).

A period of success?

Under Détente a number of treaties were agreed between the two great powers. They were aimed at reducing the amount of nuclear weapons, agreeing Soviet and American spheres of influence and establishing protection of human rights in all countries.

SOURCE **A**

The Cold War has outlived itself and there is a need for a new, more sensible and realistic policy. Our calls for peaceful co-existence have begun to bring serious responses in many capitalist countries.

A comment made by the Soviet leader Leonid Brezhnev in 1975.

SOURCE **B**

The collapse of Soviet power was fast, unexpected and peaceful, and it swept across the region as a whole.

A comment made by the highly respected British historian Mark Mazower in 1998.

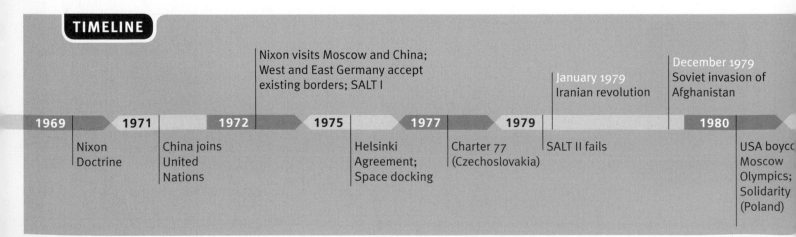

TIMELINE

1969	1971	1972	1975	1977	1979	1980
Nixon Doctrine	China joins United Nations		Helsinki Agreement; Space docking	Charter 77 (Czechoslovakia)	SALT II fails	USA boyc⟨ Moscow Olympics; Solidarity (Poland)

Nixon visits Moscow and China; West and East Germany accept existing borders; SALT I

January 1979 Iranian revolution

December 1979 Soviet invasion of Afghanistan

However, Détente was criticised by many as it did not prevent human rights abuses in the USSR. Both powers also remained suspicious of each other. President Jimmy Carter's inability to end a hostage crisis in Tehran in 1979 made many Americans worry that their country was weakening. The Soviet invasion of Afghanistan was also attacked by the American government as an aggressive action; this event effectively ended Détente. The new American President, Ronald Reagan, had been elected on a strong anti-communist stance and this started a new aggressive relationship between the two superpowers.

End of an era

In 1989 suddenly, amazingly, the Cold War ended. The arms race was over. Communist Eastern Europe collapsed. The Berlin Wall came down, and Germany was united. A McDonald's opened in Moscow, and the Soviets started drinking Coca-Cola.

When Mikhail Gorbachev came to power in the USSR in 1985, he proposed an end to the arms race and the Afghan War. Yet no one could have foreseen that within two years both the USA and the USSR would be dismantling all medium- and short-range nuclear weapons; that within four years the Soviet bloc in Eastern Europe would crumble with barely a shot fired in anger; and that within six years the Soviet Union would cease to exist.

East and West Berliners celebrate the fall of the Berlin Wall.

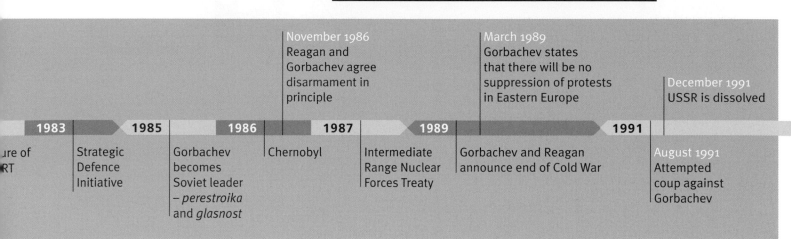

November 1986
Reagan and Gorbachev agree disarmament in principle

March 1989
Gorbachev states that there will be no suppression of protests in Eastern Europe

December 1991
USSR is dissolved

1983   1985   1986   1987   1989   1991

ure of RT

Strategic Defence Initiative

Gorbachev becomes Soviet leader – *perestroika* and *glasnost*

Chernobyl

Intermediate Range Nuclear Forces Treaty

Gorbachev and Reagan announce end of Cold War

August 1991
Attempted coup against Gorbachev

1.6a Why did Détente collapse in the 1970s and 1980s?

Détente

During the early 1970s the USA and the Soviet Union came to accept each other's areas of influence in the world, and both wanted to improve international relations.

Pressure for Détente in the USSR

- Brezhnev was keen to extend Khrushchev's policy of Peaceful Co-existence. Brezhnev also wanted to persuade the West to accept Soviet control of Eastern Europe.
- Soviet spending on arms amounted to 20 per cent of all government spending. By the mid-1970s, the USSR had caught up with the USA in the nuclear arms race. Therefore it made sense to cut back on military spending, particularly at a time when people in the communist bloc were fed up with low living standards.
- The Iron Curtain countries all had very poor industrial efficiency and needed to trade more with the West.
- The USSR had quarrelled with China and needed better relations with the USA.

Pressure for Détente in the USA

By the early 1970s the Americans had plenty to worry about at home. It was a bad time to be trying to fight an international Cold War in all corners of the globe.

- The USA was experiencing 'stagflation' – rising inflation coupled with economic stagnation. This situation, together with huge expenditure on the arms race and the war in Vietnam (see pages 236–249), was crippling the US economy.
- The American failure in the Vietnam War had seriously dented its confidence and produced a huge peace campaign. The campaign, which demanded an end to American military aggression abroad, was particularly popular among members of America's black Civil Rights Movemement.

This American cartoon, published in 1970, is critical of the US and Soviet leaders. Though they possess a huge stockpile of weapons, the two men refuse to reach an agreement at the SALT (arms reduction) talks. Yet the financial burden of military spending is killing taxpayers on both sides.

How successful was Détente in the 1970s?

The Beginnings of Détente

When Richard Nixon became US president in 1969, he appointed Henry Kissinger his secretary of state (foreign minister). Nixon and Kissinger were keen to establish better working relations with both the USSR and China.

President Nixon therefore announced what came be called the Nixon Doctrine. The United States would stick to its treaty obligations and would continue to hold a 'nuclear umbrella' over the free world. However, America expected its allies to take care of their own defence.

In the 1970s the leaders of the USA and the USSR began to meet each other. In 1972 Nixon went to Moscow. It was the first visit to the Soviet Union by a US president since 1945. Brezhnev made the return trip to Washington, DC, in 1974.

In 1972 East and West Germany signed agreements to recognise each other's borders. These border agreements removed an important source of tension between the superpowers. They also helped the USA and the Soviet Union to develop trade links. For example, the USA sold its surplus wheat cheaply to the Soviet Union.

At the same time, relations between the USA and China improved. In 1971 the USA agreed that China should be allowed to join the United Nations. Then the US table tennis team visited China. This 'ping pong diplomacy' opened the way for meetings between government officials from both sides. In 1972 Nixon himself visited China.

There was also co-operation in space. In July 1975 three US astronauts and two Soviet **cosmonauts** docked their Apollo and Soyuz spacecraft together while in orbit around the Earth. This pioneering event was a very visible sign of Détente.

SALT I (1972)

The Strategic Arms Limitation Talks (SALT) began in 1969 and produced the SALT I agreement in 1972. This agreement, which ran for five years, limited the number of inter-continental ballistic missiles (ICBMs) and anti-ballistic missiles (ABMs) both superpowers could hold. Each side was allowed to use spy satellites to check that the other was not breaking the agreed limits. Although it did not reduce existing stocks of weapons, the signing of SALT I in Moscow was seen as a huge achievement at the time.

Helsinki Agreement (1975)

In August 1975, 35 countries, including the USA and the USSR, signed the Helsinki Agreement in the Finnish capital:

- The West recognised the frontiers of Eastern Europe and acknowledged Soviet influence in that area; West Germany officially recognised East Germany.
- The Soviets agreed to buy US grain and to export oil to the West.
- All countries agreed to improve human rights, particularly freedom of speech, freedom of religion and freedom of movement.

As a consequence of the Helsinki Agreement, people in Eastern Europe formed groups to campaign for greater freedoms. These protest groups included Charter 77 in Czechoslovakia and the Helsinki Watch Group in Moscow and East Germany.

The Helsinki Agreement also had economic consequences for the Eastern bloc. The agreement opened the way for communist governments to borrow money from the West. By the 1980s, most were hugely in debt.

VOICE YOUR OPINION!

Make a judgement – how successful do you think Détente was in the 1970s?

Martin Walker (Source D) called the Helsinki Treaties a 'time-bomb in the heart of the Soviet Empire'. What did he mean?

SOURCE

The Helsinki Treaties of 1975 were the West's time-bomb planted in the heart of the Soviet Empire.

A comment by the journalist and broadcaster Martin Walker (1993).

Cummings

'DETENTE'

BRITISH LEFT

ANGOLA LEBANON

"Why not throw away your popgun, Mr. Wilson! This animal assures us it's vegetarian!"

A cartoon by the British cartoonist Cummings, published in the *Daily Express* in 1975.

The cartoonist attacks Détente by referring to a famous limerick about a woman who rode away on a tiger but came back as the smile on its face. The Soviet Union, the cartoon suggests, only wears the mask of a smiling Brezhnev. In truth it is a dangerous beast which is devouring countries (turning them communist). Riding this tiger are Kissinger and Harold Wilson, the British prime minister. The cartoonist is criticising these men and other Western politicians who are agreeing to arms cuts.

Criticisms of Détente

After the mid-1970s there were signs that Détente was falling apart.

- The West became frustrated because abuses of human rights continued in the Soviet Union.

- In the Eastern bloc, **dissidents** (those who disagreed with the government, even over issues as minor as pollution in a local marsh) were persecuted and suppressed. Members of Charter 77, for example, were dismissed from work, their children were expelled from school, and their driving licences and citizenship were cancelled. Many were **exiled** or imprisoned.

- When the USA tried to get human rights for Soviet Jews written into a trade agreement, Brezhnev cancelled the agreement.

- There were also suspicions about whether the USSR was keeping to the terms of SALT I. In fact, both the USSR and the USA were positioning more missiles against each other.

The SALT I agreement, which had been due to last for five years, ended in 1977. The new US President, Jimmy Carter, attempted to achieve further arms reductions through the SALT II talks. However, Carter annoyed Brezhnev by trying to link cuts in weapons with discussions on human rights. The talks went on and on until an agreement was finally reached in 1979. Before the agreement came into effect, however, something happened that shattered any hopes that Détente would continue. The Soviet Union invaded Afghanistan.

An anti-state, anti-socialist, and rabble-rousing, abusive piece of writing [written by] traitors and renegades.

A comment on Charter 77 that appeared in the official Czechoslovakian press in 1977.

Soviet involvement in Afghanistan

Although Afghanistan was a poor and mostly barren country, its location was important. It offered a land route between the oil-rich Middle East and the Soviet Union. Afghanistan had been under Soviet influence since 1947, although the USA also gave aid to the country.

Meanwhile, in January 1979, the shah (king) of neighbouring Iran was overthrown in a revolution by **fundamentalist** Muslims. The revolution was anti-American – in November 1979, 53 US hostages were seized at the American embassy in Tehran and held for over a year. However, the Soviets, too, had cause to worry about Muslim influence in the region.

Afghanistan had an unstable government. In 1979 Hafizullah Amin seized power and named himself president. Though a communist, Amin was not friendly with the Soviet Union. Furthermore, he was opposed by major Muslim groups in the country. The Soviet Union feared that these Muslim groups were planning to take control of Afghanistan and set up an Islamic state, as had happened in Iran. Large Muslim populations lived in areas of the Soviet Union bordering Afghanistan, and uprisings in Afghanistan might have knock-on effects on the Soviet Union.

SOURCE G

The invasion [of Afghanistan] was an attempt to put an end to the infighting and murders which had taken place among the leaders of the communist government in Kabul… it was a defensive move. It was far from obvious that the invasion showed that the USSR had gone back to being a predatory state.

An analysis by the respected historian Philip Thody in his book *Cold War* (1993).

SOURCE H

That secret operation drew the Soviets into the Afghan trap… The day that the Soviets officially crossed the border, I wrote to President Carter, "We now have the opportunity of giving to the Soviet Union its Vietnam War".

A comment made by Zbigniew Brzezinski during an interview in 1998. Brzezinski was President Carter's foreign policy adviser. He revealed that as early as July 1979, six months before the Soviet invasion, the Central Intelligence Agency (CIA) had been secretly training Muslim **Mujaheddin** fighters in Afghanistan to attack the communists. The goal was 'to induce a Soviet intervention'.

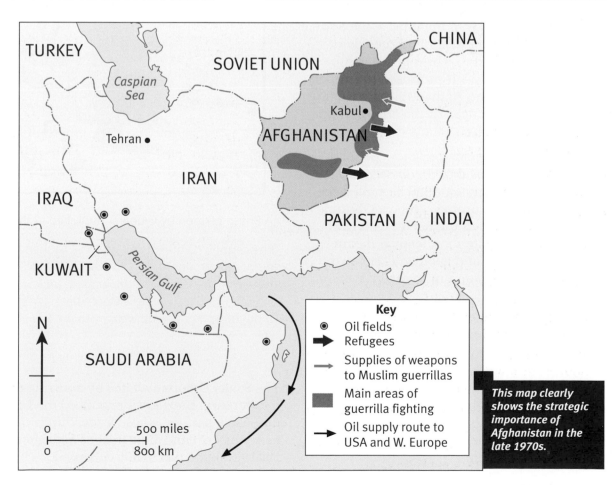

This map clearly shows the strategic importance of Afghanistan in the late 1970s.

The USSR invades

On 25 December 1979, Soviet troops invaded Afghanistan. The airport at Kabul was quickly captured, and in the next few days 350 Soviet aircraft carrying troops and equipment landed there. Within a week about 50,000 Soviet troops were in Afghanistan. The president's palace in Kabul was captured, and President Amin was killed. On New Year's Day 1980, a new government was set up in Kabul. It was led by Babrak Karmal, a former Afghan leader who had been specially flown back from exile in the Soviet Union to take over the government.

Reactions from around the world

President Brezhnev announced to the world that the airlift of Soviet troops and equipment was needed to restore order in Afghanistan. He claimed that Soviet troops had entered the country at the request of the Afghan government, which wanted protection. He also said that troops would be withdrawn from Afghanistan as soon as the situation stabilised.

However, the Americans reacted angrily (even though they later claimed that they tricked the Soviets into invading – see Source H). President Carter described the Soviet invasion as a threat to world peace. China also reacted angrily – it promised to support the Mujaheddin, the Afghan fighters waging **guerrilla warfare** against the Soviet troops in the name of Islam.

President Carter decided to show publicly America's disapproval of the invasion of Afghanistan. In January 1980 he pulled the USA out of the upcoming Moscow Olympic Games. He described the Soviet Union as an 'unsuitable site for a festival meant to celebrate peace and good will'. He also advised the US Senate not to **ratify** the SALT II treaty.

Carter sent a US Navy task force of 1,800 marines to the Arabian Sea to protect oil routes out of the Middle East. To inflict economic damage on the Soviets, he cut trade between the USA and the USSR. He stopped the export to the Soviet Union of 17 million tons of grain. He also stopped the sale of technological goods, such as computers and oil-drilling equipment.

SOURCE **J**

Russia's actions are a stepping-stone for a southward thrust towards Pakistan and the Indian sub-continent. There will be no peace in southern Asia with Soviet soldiers in Afghanistan.

From the *Peking People's Daily*, a Chinese newspaper, 1 January 1980.

GradeStudio

When considering the content of a cartoon, it is important that you interpret the cartoon correctly, so stick to the obvious. In Source K it is obvious that the cartoonist is suggesting that the Soviet invasion of Afghanistan has brought the end of Détente, and that the Cold War is coming again. You could relate this to American pulling out of the Olympics, refusing to ratify SALT II, and cutting trade with the USSR.

SOURCE **K**

A British cartoon by Gibbard, published in the *Guardian* in 1980.

The cartoon comments on how the Afghan War – seen in the distance – brought the Cold War back to life (in the form of a reawakened abominable snowman). Meanwhile Jimmy Carter looks on helplessly on as Détente flees. (At the time, Carter was thought by many to be weak with the Soviets.)

The Soviet Union retaliated by accusing the USA and China of interference. Brezhnev denounced the USA as 'an absolutely unreliable partner, whose leadership is capable – at any moment – of cancelling treaties and agreements' (January 1980). Détente had totally collapsed.

Reagan and Brezhnev and the renewed Cold War

Ronald Reagan became US president in January 1981, a time when criticism of Soviet involvement in Afghanistan was at its height. Reagan's tough anti-communist stance helped him win the election. He referred to the Soviet Union as 'that evil empire'. Reagan believed that Carter had been too soft on the Soviets. He said, 'America has lost faith in itself... we have to recapture our dreams, our pride.'

Development of new weapons

Reagan actively began a new Cold War with the Soviets. He increased the USA's defence spending from $178 billion in 1981 to $367 billion in 1986. New weapons, notably the **cruise missile**, were developed. NATO agreed that 464 American cruise missiles should be positioned in western Europe.

In 1981 Reagan announced that the USA had developed a new type of bomb. The **neutron bomb** could kill a great many people without destroying much property. The Americans were also developing the **MX missile**, which could be fired from different underground launch sites.

The Strategic Defense Initiative (SDI)

In 1983 US scientists began work on the Strategic Defense Initiative (SDI). This project was informally named 'Star Wars', after a popular sci-fi film. It was based on a system of satellites that would orbit the earth. The aim of Star Wars was to prevent Soviet nuclear missiles from reaching US targets by creating a huge laser shield in space.

Meetings between the USA and the USSR resumed in 1982 under the banner of START (Strategic Arms Reduction Talks). Reagan demanded huge cuts in Soviet nuclear capability. In response, the Soviets pulled out of the talks. Reagan's statements were so aggressive that by 1982, the Soviets were terrified that Reagan was secretly preparing the United States to fight a war he thought he could win.

SOURCE L

Washington has no brakes at all preventing it from crossing the mark before which any sober-minded person must stop.

A statement made by Yuri Andropov, the Soviet leader, in 1982.

SOURCE M

"*Now then, any time you want to start serious talks on arms limitation you let me know.*"

This British cartoon by Garland was published in the *Daily Telegraph* in 1981.

It criticises the increase in US aggression after 1981. Reagan pretends to the Soviets that he wants to start 'serious talks on arms limitations' while he himself is developing the neutron bomb and calling the Soviets 'warmongers, liars and cheats'.

Solidarity in Poland

The story of the Solidarity movement in Poland straddles the two topics in this chapter. In one way, the emergence of Solidarity can be seen as a factor in the collapse of Détente. It was a means by which Reagan, waging his 'New Cold War', aggressively attacked communism. In another way, however, Solidarity marked the beginning of the collapse of communism in Eastern Europe. Its emergence was the first hint that the communist system was beginning to unravel.

The formation of Solidarity

In 1980 protest movements emerged in Poland in response to high prices and food and fuel shortages. The shipyard workers in the key port of Gdansk went on strike. The strikers were led by an electrician, Lech Walesa. Walesa created Solidarity, the first free trade union in the whole Soviet system.

The unrest developed into nationwide strikes, and Solidarity soon had a membership of nine million. The Polish government was losing its grip, and many Poles feared a Soviet invasion (as had happened in Hungary in 1956 and Czechoslovakia in 1968). The invasion did not happen – partly because the Soviet Union had just invaded Afghanistan. Soviet troops were simply ordered to carry out 'training manoeuvres' near the Polish border.

In the end the communist Polish government, under a new military leader, General Jaruzelski, imposed martial law (rule by the army) in 1981. Ten thousand political opponents of the government, including Walesa, were arrested. Solidarity was declared an illegal organisation.

In 1982 the new leader of the Roman Catholic Church, Pope John Paul II – who was himself a Pole – met President Reagan. The two men discussed how they could destroy communism in Poland. Reagan poured money into Solidarity. The pope encouraged Poles, most of whom were devout Catholics, to speak out about their discontent. Catholic priests also worked as informants for the CIA.

Jaruzelski's attempts to destroy Solidarity failed. Walesa was put in prison, but imprisonment seemed to make him even more of a hero, and the Solidarity movement survived underground. In November 1982 Walesa was released from prison, and in 1983 he was awarded the Nobel Peace Prize.

SOURCE N

If you choose the example of what we have in our pockets and in our shops, then Communism has done little for us.

If you choose the example of what is in our souls instead, Communism has done very much for us. Our souls contain the exact opposite of what they wanted.

Lech Walesa

SOURCE O

If there was a central, key series of developments that began to unravel the entire system, it had to be events in Poland.

The American historian Daniel Chirot, analysing what happened in Eastern Europe in 1989.

BE A HISTORIAN!

Use an encyclopaedia or the internet to research the Solidarity movement, especially:

1. its formation and early growth
2. the Polish government's response
3. the 'Roundtable' talks.

GradeStudio

To explain the importance of an event, you need to think about its results. If you were asked how important Solidarity was in ending the Cold War, you could offer three consequences:

1. It was the first free trade union in the Soviet system.
2. It brought Pope John Paul II and President Reagan together to destroy communism.
3. The Soviet Union did not invade Poland and Solidarity survived to win the 1989 elections.

1.6b Why did communism collapse in Central and Eastern Europe?

Soviet failure in Afghanistan

After the first few months of 1980, Soviet troops controlled the towns in which they were based, but the Afghan rebels, the Mujaheddin, controlled the countryside. The Mujaheddin were not just fighting to get rid of Soviet troops. They were fighting to turn Afghanistan into a Muslim country. They were well equipped because both China and the USA gave them weapons.

The Soviets in Afghanistan found themselves in the same impossible position as the Americans in Vietnam (see pages 236–249). Though a superpower with all the advantages of modern technology, they were unable to win a guerrilla war. The Mujaheddin attacked Soviet supply routes and shot down Soviet helicopters. The Soviets suffered more and more casualties but succeeded only in propping up the unpopular communist government in Kabul. Although there were 125,000 Soviet troops in Afghanistan by the early 1980s, the Soviets found it impossible to defeat the Afghan rebels. In 1982 a massive attack against the Mujaheddin in the Panjahir Valley failed.

The Soviet Union also faced hostility from other Muslim nations, such as Pakistan. The Soviets became increasingly worried that some of the 30 million Muslims living within the Soviet Union might revolt in support of the Mujaheddin.

In 1985 the new Soviet leader, Mikhail Gorbachev, realised that the USSR could never win the war in Afghanistan. In 1987 he started talks with the USA, and he and President Reagan reached an agreement at Geneva in 1988. The last Soviet troops left Afghanistan in February 1989.

The Soviet war was disastrous for Afghanistan. Over 3 million Afghan refugees fled to Pakistan or Iran. About a million people died. After the departure of the Soviets, the fighting continued between rival Afghan groups. Afghans who remained in the country suffered from food shortages because the war had destroyed so much farmland.

SOURCE P

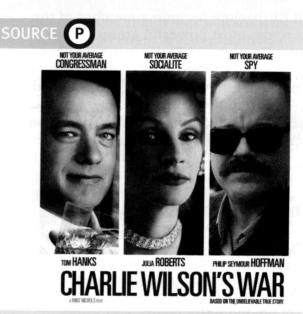

A poster for the American film *Charlie Wilson's War* (2007). Although factually quite accurate, the film attributes the Soviet defeat in Afghanistan to the work of one US senator, Charles Wilson, who succeeded in getting aid for the Mujaheddin, notably anti-aircraft weapons.

HISTORIOGRAPHY

Much of the historical debate about the collapse of communism focusses on the question, 'Did they fall or were they pushed... or did they throw themselves off?' Did communism collapse because of weaknesses within the system or because of external pressure applied by the Reagan administration? Or was it 'the Gorbachev factor'?

The Cold War caused great bitterness and cast a large shadow over the late twentieth century. However, historians still puzzle over the paradox of a 'war' whose contribution to international relations was 44 years of peace.

SOURCE Q

It was as if two horses were racing round a track and one broke its leg.

A comment on the collapse of the Soviet system in 1991, made by the left-wing American historian Bruce Cummings in 1992.

GradeStudio

Source Y shows a hammer and sickle defeated and in tears.

Do you agree with this interpretation of the state of communism in Europe in 1990?

Explain your answer by referring to the purpose of the source, as well as using its content and your own knowledge. (6 marks)

Comments

Describe the cartoon's interpretation of events.

Source Y is a comment on the collapse of communism in Eastern Europe in 1989. The hammer and sickle are the symbols of communism. They sit hunched with the body-language of defeat and are in tears. The message of the cartoon is that communism has lost.

> Begins by explaining what the cartoon shows and what its interpretation of events is.

Refer to the cartoon's provenance.

Looking at the provenance, I see that the cartoon is contemporary (it appeared in 1990), so it has been drawn by someone who was experiencing the events at the time. However, as Krauze was Polish, it may have been biased against the Soviet Union.

> TWO IDEAS about why the PROVENANCE might be important.

Show how the cartoon's interpretation of events is linked to its provenance.

The cartoon reflects the cartoonist's Polish and British standpoint. Krauze hated communism and produced a number of cartoons attacking the Polish communist government, so he (like his British public) is probably taking delight in the fall of communism, rather than impartially reporting it. Also Krauze's cartoons often criticised oppressors, so it is possible that he is over-stating communism's defeat in this cartoon. The purpose of a cartoon is to exaggerate.

> TWO IDEAS explore the cartoon's interpretation of events, referring to its provenance.

Explain the event the cartoon is referring to.

When I look at the content of the source, however, I see that there is truth in it. Communist-controlled Eastern Europe did collapse in the revolutions of 1989, and communism was defeated by 1990.

> Provides facts about the cartoon's content.

Compare the cartoon's content in detail to the historical facts to examine whether the cartoon's interpretation of events is true or false.

Other facts support this interpretation. Lithuania, Latvia and Estonia left the USSR in 1990, and also in 1990 there were riots and demonstrations against communism in Moscow. Communism had been completely defeated. As Arthur Schlesinger said, democracy and the market had 'won' the Cold War. The only question is whether the tears are accurate in the cartoon – the people of Eastern Europe were delighted to overthrow their governments. Perhaps the tears were from their former rulers and Communist Party officials.

> Develops ideas FOR or AGAINST the interpretation. At this point, with detailed explanations of both the content and provenance of the source, the answer is of a high standard.

Conclusion, assessing the cartoon's interpretation of events.

The cartoon is not an impartial representation of events. It tells us what Krauze thought communist leaders would be feeling about the collapse of communism. It was not government propaganda, but it was produced to amuse the British newspaper readers who were delighted that they had 'won' the Cold War.

> Refers to the purpose of the source.

Grade Studio

Which was the more important cause of the collapse of Soviet power in Eastern Europe, 1989–1991:

- The 'Gorbachev factor'   • President Reagan's 'New Cold War'?

You must refer to both causes when explaining your answer.   (10 marks)

Comments

Describe the Gorbachev factor.

Gorbachev tried to reform communism. He introduced glasnost (openness = personal freedoms) and perestroika (restructuring = economic reforms). He also began disarmament talks with Reagan which culminated in the INF Treaty in 1987; in 1989 he and George Bush announced the end of the Cold War.

> An opening statement. At least TWO extra facts..

Explain HOW the Gorbachev factor caused the collapse of Soviet power.

Gorbachev caused the collapse of communism firstly, because glasnost got out of hand in every communist state in Eastern Europe, especially after Gorbachev said in March 1989 that he would not suppress protest by force. This led to the 1989 revolutions. Secondly, it made communist hard-liners think he was weak, which led to the failed coup of August 1991, and then the collapse of communism in the USSR.

> TWO IDEAS have been introduced here.

> Discusses the importance of the Gorbachev factor by referring to facts.

Assess how important the Gorbachev factor was as a cause of the Soviet collapse.

Gorbachev was the figurehead of reform, an international celebrity, a Nobel Prize winner. He was the one who started the process. Most historians accept that the 'Gorbachev factor' was an element in the fall of communism.

> An opening statement. At least TWO extra facts.

Describe Reagan's actions.

Reagan came to power determined to 'recapture our pride' by starting a New Cold War. He poured billions into defence, including the SDI 'Star Wars' project and the neutron bomb. He kept up rhetoric against the Soviets, calling them 'the evil empire'. In 1983, the Soviet leadership were convinced he intended to start a nuclear war against them.

> TWO IDEAS. At this point, with a full explanation of both possible causes of the major development, the answer is now of a good standard.

Explain HOW Reagan's actions caused the collapse of Soviet power.

This led to the Soviet defeat firstly, by winning the arms race; the Soviet government, spending 25% of its GNP on defence, could not keep up – which was why Gorbachev had to seek disarmament. Secondly, the support Reagan (plotting with the Pope) gave Solidarity in Poland started the collapse of communism in that country – and one historian calls events in Poland 'the key series of developments that began to unravel the entire system'.

> Discusses the importance of Reagan's actions by referring to facts. Having assessed the importance of BOTH causes, this answer is now of a high standard.

Assess how important Reagan's actions were as a cause of the Soviet collapse.

If Reagan had never applied pressure, but had continued with Détente like Jimmy Carter, the Soviet system might not have collapsed, but might have struggled on. Reagan panicked the Soviets into collapse.

Conclusion.

In the end, the real cause of the collapse of communism was probably neither Gorbachev nor Reagan, but the popular hatred of communism that had been growing in Eastern Europe since Helsinki in 1975. If this is true, then Gorbachev is probably more important than Reagan, since it was glasnost which let people express this hatred. Glasnost then ran out of control and destroyed communism.

> This answer now makes a judgement. It explains how that judgement was reached and includes at least one fact.

20th Century Depth Studies – Section A

How should I study the main events of the 20th century?

Unit 2A in the AQA History Specification B GCSE lists three topics from the 20th century:

1. From Tsardom to Communism: Russia, 1914–1924
2. Weimar Germany, 1919–1929
3. The Roaring 20s: USA, 1919–1929

Your teacher will be asking you to undertake a Depth Study of one topic from this list. This unit provides a wonderful opportunity to study one country in depth through some of the most exciting times in its history. During the years in question, all three countries went through a period of rapid development and great turmoil.

There are three questions in section A of Paper 2 – one for each topic. You must answer one of the questions. Your answer is worth 20 marks. Each question has three parts:

1. An 'Inference' question (4 marks)

This part of the question tests a sourcework skill: understanding a source. You have to show that you understand not just what the source says on the surface, but what its underlying point is. If you know what was going on at the time the source refers to, this question should be easy.

To help you deal with 'Inference' questions, a box on every page in this unit asks 'What Was Going On?'. The Grade Studio gives you lots of topics to discuss with your classmates.

2. An 'Explain how' question (6 marks)

This part of the question tests your understanding of development through time. You have to show that you understand how an event grew out of the events before it and affected events afterwards.

The examiners want to make sure that you understand the PROCESS of change through time – the HOW of history. What were the causes of an event? What were the results? How did the event change things?

The chapters in this unit have been specially written to help you understand the 'whys' and the 'hows' of history. Therefore the first thing you should do is read through the chapter to get an overview of how events developed. To help you revise, there is a list of 'Explain how' questions in the Grade Studio.

3. A 'Usefulness' question (10 marks)

This is the most important part of the question, and it is worth the most marks. It tests a sourcework skill: evaluating a source's usefulness (utility).

There is a knack to answering this kind of question. You have to look at the source's provenance and content and then use this information to come up with ideas about how useful the source is going to be.

Once you have learned how to approach a 'Usefulness' question, it is just a matter of practice, practice, practice. A visual and/or a written source has been included on every page of this unit, so that you can get used to discussing the usefulness of sources.

How do I approach an 'Inference' question?

For this part of the question, you will simply be asked:

What does Source X suggest about [something]?

Your answer is worth 4 marks. It is the easiest part of the Paper 2 question, and you should be looking to spend no more than 5 minutes on it.

Here is the really simple bit: you can start your answer well just by looking for facts *in the source itself*. Here is a specimen question from the AQA exam board. It is simply a factual statement taken from a textbook:

Source A

The Bolshevik Revolution of October/November 1917

Although later communist propaganda said differently, the Bolshevik revolution was quite a small-scale affair. Although Lenin was in charge, Trotsky did most of the planning. There was little fighting, much less than there had been in March. Success was achieved by a small group of dedicated revolutionaries.

What does Source A suggest about the reasons for Bolshevik success in seizing power in October/November 1917?

There are plenty of ideas in the source, and you can start to build your answer simply by copying the correct ones. You need to make sure that you are copying the bits that are relevant to the question you have been asked. So in this case, what 'reasons for Bolshevik success', are provided in the source?

- Trotsky did most of the planning.
- There was little fighting, much less than there had been in March.
- Success was achieved by a small group of dedicated revolutionaries.

However, to improve your answer for this part of the question, it is vitally important that you also draw a couple of INFERENCES.

Drawing an inference means 'reading between the lines' to find out what is what is going on 'beneath the surface'. For example, if a teacher picks on a particular student, your inference might be that he dislikes that student. Or your inference might be that the teacher is very finicky. You are looking for the general truth that underlies the specific surface facts.

So let's look again at the specimen question above. Reread the source and try to infer what it is saying about the Bolshevik success. You could earn a point by writing something along these lines:

Source A is suggesting that the revolution was not a spontaneous uprising of the people, as the March Revolution had been. Instead, it was a planned seizure of power by a small group of extremists.

Every page in this unit of the book includes a list of 'underlying issues' to give you ideas of some inferences you might draw from the surface facts.

Who and Why

To draw inferences from a source, ask yourself what the author is trying to get you to think.

Have a look at the provenance of the source and think about what the author would probably want you to come away believing.

BE A HISTORIAN!

Using the ideas on this page and any extra ideas you might have, write out in your own words an exam-style answer to the specimen question.

Make a list of things that adults say to you that have an underlying meaning beneath the surface words. What do you infer from phrases like 'I don't know what's got into you!'?

How do I write an 'Explain how' essay?

The second part of the question is worth 6 marks. Spend about 10 minutes on it.

Confusingly, this part of the question may take a number of forms:

1. It may simply ask you to explain why something happened. Here's an example:

In August 1914 Russia became involved in the First World War. Explain why Nicholas II became increasingly unpopular as Tsar during this war.

Like so many exam questions, this one starts off by giving you a factual statement to prompt your memory and make it clear what topic you're going to be asked about. The actual question, as always, is in the second sentence.

2. Or it may ask you to explain the consequences of an event:

Explain the consequences of Prohibition for the USA in the 1920s.

3. Or finally, it may ask you to explain a process:

Explain how Stresemann helped the German economy to recover in the years 1923–29.

When dealing with an 'Explain How' question like the examples above, it is always a good idea to pause and think: 'OK – so what is it really asking?'. Then try to rephrase the question in your own words: 'Why did the war make people hate the Tsar?'; 'What were the results of prohibition?'; 'What did Stresemann do to help the German economy?'.

Remember, when you write a 'how' essay, you need to give REASONS and EXPLANATIONS.

An answer that simply detailed what Nicholas or Stresemann did or what Prohibition was is of a low quality as this question is not looking specifically for factual information.

For a WHY question give REASONS.
For a HOW question give WAYS.
For a CONSEQUENCES question give RESULTS.

To get a high mark on this part of the question, you need to think of AT LEAST TWO reasons, ways, or results. Devote one paragraph to each. A really good way to start each paragraph is:

'The first reason [or way or result] was...'
'The second reason [or way or result] was...'

All these different kinds of questions revolve around the 'how' of history. How did one thing lead to another?

CAUSES ━ HOW ➡ CONSEQUENCES

This part of the question is asking you to explain how one thing led to another. The better your explanation, the more marks you will get.

Let's take the first of the three example questions: 'Explain why Nicholas II became increasingly unpopular as Tsar during this war'. An answer that just mentions two or three unpopular decisions – one might be that Nicholas left Rasputin and the Tsarina in charge when he went to the Front – will score only a couple of marks (grade E).

To do well on this question, you would then need to EXPLAIN HOW each of these decisions made Nicholas unpopular. So you would need to explain that Rasputin and the Tsarina governed very badly. People who had loved the Tsar came to hate Rasputin and the Tsarina. They also grew to resent the Tsar for leaving the pair in charge, and so the Tsar became unpopular.

The knack here is to 'explain right through' to the situation given in the question. The situation here is the Tsar's unpopularity (the question is 'why did the Tsar become unpopular'), so you explain right through by ending your paragraph with: '... and so the Tsar became unpopular'.

The BEST answers will include a fact or a couple of facts as part of this explanation.

How do I approach a 'Usefulness' question?

The third part of the Paper 2 question asks you to evaluate the usefulness of a source. It is worth 10 marks. When dealing with this part of the exam, you should be looking at the source and asking yourself, 'How might this information be useful to a historian?' Do not forget that this part of the Paper 2 question is worth as much as the other two parts put together. You should be looking to spend about 15 minutes on it. As for ALL questions about sources, to answer this question you must address TWO issues:

1. The provenance

The first issue is the source's provenance. Where does the source come from? Who wrote it, drew it or said it? Is that person a reliable witness whose opinions might be useful?

- In a basic answer, you would need to identify basic facts about the source, such as when it was written and who wrote it. You would then need to explain how these basic facts might affect the source's usefulness for historians. For example, if a source was written (or said or drawn) around the time of the events it describes, it is a useful guide to what people thought at the time. If it was written by someone who strongly supported a particular point of view, it is probably biased.

- In a more advanced answer, you would need to look at the MOTIVE and PURPOSE of the writer. You would then need to EXPLAIN HOW these factors might make the source both MORE useful and LESS useful. For example, if the writer's purpose was to suggest a new policy, the source might show us clearly how government leaders were thinking. If the writer's motive was to deny responsibility for an unpopular action, the source might be deceptive and untruthful.

2. The content

The second issue is the source's content. What is its message? How might the information it holds be useful to historians?

- In a basic answer, you will need to write about the source in general terms: the source tells us certain facts/shows us what the author thought/provides reliable factual evidence, and so on.

- In a more advanced answer, you will need to give SPECIFIC INSTANCES of HOW the information might be useful to different historians. The source might, for example,
  - provide facts which illustrate [some underlying issue you know about]
  - provide facts which cast doubt on [some underlying issue you know about]
  - show historians how [here, use your inference skills to draw some inferences]
  - supply facts for historians who want to study [a particular topic]
  - supply facts for economic or political or social historians or other specialists
  - tell historians [some specific thing] about the author
  - show historians [some specific thing] about one political or social grouping.

GradeStudio

Thinking about sources

Whenever you answer a question about a historical source, before you start writing, take a little time to **SWIPE** the source. Ask yourself:

1. What does the source say on the **S**urface?
2. **W**ho wrote the source (and how might that have affected what it says)?
3. What is the source's underlying truth – what can you **I**nfer from reading between the lines?
4. What is the source's **P**urpose – what was it trying to achieve?
5. When was it written – what **E**vents were happening at the time, and how might they have affected what the source says?

BE A HISTORIAN!

- Practise thinking about the usefulness of sources by asking your teacher to bring in a selection of random cuttings, photos and objects from his or her house. Discuss as a class which of these items gives the most useful insight into what your teacher is really like – and why.

- As a whole class, make a list of all the different kinds of sources you can think of. Then think of specific ways in which each kind of source might be useful to different historians.

2.1 From Tsardom to Communism: Russia, 1914–1924

2.1a Why did the rule of the Tsar collapse in February/March 1917?

The nature of Russian society

The Russian empire was huge. It extended 4,000 miles from east to west and had a population of 150 million. A census (survey of the population) in 1926 found people from 172 different ethnic or national groups living within the empire's borders. Most of these people hated being part of the Russian Empire and called it 'the prison of nations'.

The Russian Empire was old-fashioned and backward. In 1914 it still had not adopted the **Gregorian Calendar**, which had first been introduced in 1582 and was widely in use by 1700. As a result, Russia was out of sync with most of the rest of the world by 13 days.

Across most of Russia's vast expanse, there was no modern transport system. Most roads were primitive mud tracks. The country's 68,400 kilometres of railway track – including the famous Trans-Siberian railway, completed in 1904 – did not even begin to meet Russia's needs. Britain, a hundred times smaller, had over 32,000 kilometres of track.

There was a huge gulf between Russia's wealthy nobles and landowners and the poor. Four-fifths of the population were peasant farmers. The Russian economy was technologically backwards and based

SOURCE A

A metal-worker's home in Petrograd before the revolution.

mainly on **subsistence farming** (people ate what they grew). **Famine** regularly swept the countryside.

After 1900 there were signs of **industrialisation**. The early years of industrialisation were very problematic. Large numbers of peasants migrated from the countryside into Russia's new towns. There, they found poverty, overcrowding, pollution and appalling working conditions in the factories.

TIMELINE

1861	1903	1904–5	1905	1906	1914	1916
Abolition of serfdom	Social Democrats split into Bolsheviks and Mensheviks.	Russia defeated in war with Japan	Bloody Sunday and the 1905 revolution	Fundamental Laws	First World War breaks out	Rasputin assassinated

The government of Nicholas II

Nicholas II was the tsar (emperor) of Russia. He was an **autocrat** (that is, he alone ruled and made laws; there was no parliament). Nicholas's rule was enforced at a local level by councils called *zemstvos* that were run by local noblemen. Nicholas could also call on the army and the *Okhrana* (secret police).

Although Nicholas was a tyrant, his was a very weak tyranny. Personally, he was out of touch, foolish and indecisive.

The 1905 Revolution

The years after 1900 were a period of failure and crisis. A series of bad harvests reduced the peasants to starvation. In 1904 Plehve, the minister of the interior, who was in charge of the secret police, was assassinated. In 1904–05 Russia fought and lost a war with Japan.

Unrest in Russia came to a head on 22 January 1905, when 200,000 people marched in St Petersburg, the capital. The march was peaceful and was led by a priest named Father Gapon. The marchers, who sang hymns and carried pictures of Nicholas II, were simply asking the tsar to improve their working conditions. Yet tsarist troops attacked the marchers, and perhaps as many as 1,000 people were killed. The day became known as 'Bloody Sunday'.

Events in St Petersburg sparked the 1905 Revolution. Millions of workers joined a strike that had been organised by workers' councils called **soviets**. Sailors on the battleship *Potemkin* mutinied.

The strikes forced Nicholas to issue the 'October Manifesto', in which he promised reforms. These reforms including the establishment of a parliament, to be called the **Duma**.

Yet the reforms were short-lived. In 1906 Nicholas issued the 'Fundamental Laws': he was 'the supreme autocratic ruler' and the Duma could not make laws. Nicholas dismissed the Duma if it questioned him.

Some government figures, such as Prime Minister Pyotr Stolypin, had hoped to combine repression with reforms (Stolypin dissolved the Duma twice, but also proposed bills to reform local government and improve economic conditions of the peasants). However, Stolypin was assassinated in 1911, and his successors as prime minister fully supported the tsar in his re-establishment of autocratic rule.

In 1914 the Russian Empire covered one-sixth of the world's land area.

WHAT WAS GOING ON?

- Russia was too big and backward to be governed efficiently.
- The tsar's government was inefficient and old-fashioned and had huge underlying weaknesses.
- The people were impoverished, repressed and **oppressed**, and resentment of the government was growing.
- The tsar finally had to hold onto power by force – by using the army and the *Okhrana* (secret police).

April 1917
Lenin's April Theses

August 1917
Kornilov uprising

1918–1921
Russian Civil War

1917 | **1918** | **1921** | **1923**

March 1917
March Revolution; Tsar Nicholas abdicates; Provisional Government

July 1917
July Days

November 1917
November Revolution

March 1918
Treaty of Brest-Litovsk

July 1918
Royal Family executed

Famine; Kronstadt Rebellion; New Economic Policy

Creaton of USSR

Opposition groups

Russians opposed the tsar for a variety of different reasons (and not simply because he was an autocrat):

- Some opposition came from middle-class **liberals** who wanted a British-style parliamentary system of government. In 1905 liberals formed a party called the Constitutional Democratic Party (also known as the Cadets).

- Other opponents of the tsar were more violent. The Social Revolutionaries wanted the tsar overthrown in a peasant revolution.

- The **Marxists** (sometimes called the Social Democrats) based their aims on the ideas of Karl Marx, the political philosopher who invented communism. The Marxists wanted a revolution of the workers. In 1903 the party split into two groups:
    - The **Bolsheviks** ('majority'), led by Vladimir Ilich Lenin, believed that only a committed group of conspirators could start the revolution.
    - The **Mensheviks** ('minority') believed that a revolution could be sparked by a spontaneous uprising of the masses.

Traditional loyalties

Not everyone opposed the tsar, though. He found support among various groups:

- The nobles realised that if the monarchy was thrown out, they would be too. A group of nobles called the 'Rights' or the 'Black Hundreds' wanted to return to full, unrestricted autocratic monarchy.

- The 'Octobrists', named after the October Manifesto, supported Nicholas because they were satisfied with the Duma and the limited reforms Nicholas had granted in 1905.

- Leaders in the Russian Orthodox Church supported the tsar because they realised that revolutionaries who wanted to depose the tsar also wanted to destroy the church. Priests, who were very influential in Russian society (especially among the peasantry), taught that it was a sin against God to oppose the tsar.

- Among the peasantry — a class of people who were mostly illiterate and poorly educated — it was widely believed that the tsar was God's representative on earth. Many peasants worshipped him as their 'little father'.

In 1913 the opposition parties were weak and divided (and Lenin was in exile in Switzerland). The rule of the tsar looked safe and secure. The 300th anniversary of the Romanov family's rule was marked with heartfelt celebrations.

SOURCE **B**

Sire – We, working men and inhabitants of St Petersburg, our wives and our children and our helpless old parents, come to You, Sire, to seek for truth, justice and protection. We are near to death… We ask but little: to reduce the working day to eight hours, to provide a minimum wage of a rouble a day… Do not refuse to help Your people.

The petition issued to Tsar Nicholas II by Russian workers on Bloody Sunday (1905).

SOURCE **C**

The Revolution of 1905 was provoked by an attack by Nicholas II's troops on a peaceful march. This drawing of the events of Bloody Sunday is a French picture from 1905.

WHAT WAS GOING ON?

- The opposition to the tsar was violent but divided and weak. A tradition of loyalty to the tsar still held fast among large sections of Russian society.
- Some opposition was based on ideology. The aim of this kind of opposition was not reform but the overthrow of the government.
- The supporters of the tsar – principally the nobles and the church – were the forces of the past; his opponents – middle class liberals and working class communists – were the forces of the future.

The impact of the First World War

In 1914 Russia went to war alongside Britain and France against Germany and Austria-Hungary. The war was greeted with enthusiasm and patriotism. The city of St Petersburg was renamed Petrograd because its original name sounded too German. Crowds cheered the tsar. Strikes were called off. The Duma swore to support the tsar.

However, the Russian army was poorly equipped. Soldiers lacked basic supplies, such as boots, medical supplies and food. Nearly a third of Russian soldiers did not even have rifles. Unarmed men were ordered to charge at the enemy and capture a gun. Unsurprisingly, they were machine-gunned down by the thousand.

Although millions of men were called up, they were badly trained and prepared. By 1917 discipline had broken down, and soldiers were deserting or refusing to obey orders. Officers, who were drawn from the nobility, had won promotion on the basis of birth rather than military ability. As a result, the army's leadership was incompetent. For example, military leaders used radio to co-ordinate troop movements – but they did not use code. Therefore, the Germans simply listened in on the Russian plans and were ready for a Russian attack when it came. The Russians suffered heavy defeats at Tannenburg and the Masurian Lakes, and the Germans invaded Russia.

WHAT WAS GOING ON?

- The First World War highlighted the underlying weaknesses of the tsar's government and Russia itself.
- The war created resentment of the government among Russians.

SOURCE D

A photograph of Russian prisoners of war in 1915.

GradeStudio

When studying the usefulness of a source, it sometimes makes sense to think about what it does NOT show/tell us. Source E, shows the almost religious veneration the Russians had for the Tsar – but it does not show the slaughter and despair of the soldiers on the front (compare with Source D).

SOURCE E

Tsar Nicholas II blesses his troops.

The collapse of the tsar's government

Effects of the war

The war reduced Russia to chaos.

- Millions of peasants were conscripted into the army, so there were not enough people left behind to farm the land.
- Food did not reach the towns because railways were being used to transport troops and supplies.
- Millions of refugees flooded into the towns to escape from the advancing German armies.
- As shortages of manpower and fuel forced factories to close down, unemployment rose.
- Food and fuel prices rose, and people died of starvation and cold.
- Reports from the front brought news of defeat in battle and the death of loved ones.

In 1915 the tsar took personal command of the army. The military situation did not improve, and now the tsar himself was blamed for the military defeats.

Rasputin

The tsar placed the day-to-day running of Russia in the hands of Alexandra, the tsarina (empress). This was a mistake. Alexandra was incapable of governing Russia. Moreover, she was of German birth, and many suspected her (wrongly) of being a spy.

Alexandra would not work with the Duma. Instead she turned to Rasputin, a faith healer who appeared to be able to heal Nicholas's son, Alexis, from the effects of **haemophilia** (a blood disorder). Rasputin had a great deal of power over the tsarina. Deeply religious, she was convinced Rasputin had been sent by God.

Unable to cope with running the government by herself, Alexandra soon became completely dependent on Rasputin's advice. She even wrote letters to Nicholas in which she passed on Rasputin's suggestions about how to run the war.

Rasputin used his influence over the tsarina to promote bad ministers and interfere with the war. Because of Rasputin's drinking and womanising, Russian people began to despise their government. Opposition pamphlets openly suggested that Rasputin was sleeping with the tsarina. He was assassinated in 1916, but his death came too late to save the reputation of the royal family.

Meanwhile, because the tsar was out of Petrograd, he was powerless to reduce the terrible effects of the war on the Russian people. His popularity continued to fall.

SOURCE F

The main and worst enemy of our country is not at the front, but here, in our midst. There is no salvation for our country until we force the removal of those who ruin and insult it.

A speech made in the Duma by Alexandr Kerensky, who was attacking Rasputin (1916).

SOURCE G

A Russian cartoon of Rasputin with the tsar and tsarina.

WHAT WAS GOING ON?

- Rasputin's unpopularity rubbed off on the royal family – especially the tsarina, who became a laughing stock.
- The fact that Rasputin could do the damage he did proves how incompetent and inadequate the tsar's rule was.

A queue outside a bread shop in 1917.

On 12 March Mikhail Rodzianko, the president of the Duma, telegraphed the tsar to tell him how serious the situation had become. Rodzianko wrote: 'Something has to be done immediately. Tomorrow is too late. The last hour has struck. The future of the country and the royal family is being decided.' The tsar read the message and then made this comment:

Again, that fat-bellied Rodzianko has written me a load of nonsense, which I won't even bother to answer.

The March Revolution

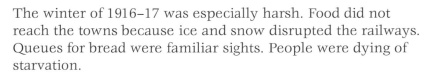

There was growing anger at the tsar's government.

The winter of 1916–17 was especially harsh. Food did not reach the towns because ice and snow disrupted the railways. Queues for bread were familiar sights. People were dying of starvation.

On 4 March 1917 workers demanding higher wages went on strike at the Putilov armaments factory in Petrograd. Within three days 40,000 workers were on strike, and the factory had closed down. As the strike spread, there were clashes between workers and the army. Some of the strikers were killed. On 8 March, thousands of women came out onto the streets to demand bread.

Law and order was breaking down in Russia. On 10 March the tsar ordered the army to put an end to the rioting. The Duma advised the tsar to return to Petrograd, but he chose to ignore the warning and instead ordered the Duma to stop meeting.

The turning point of the Revolution came on 12 March; soldiers in Petrograd refused to fire on demonstrators and joined them instead. The Duma met and agreed to set up a Provisional (temporary) Government.

At the same time, leaders of the soldiers and the strikers met and set up the Petrograd Soviet, a council of 2,500 deputies who were determined to have a say in the government of the city.

Nicholas now realised how serious the situation had become. He tried to return to Petrograd, but his train was stopped outside the city. On 15 March he was forced to **abdicate**. Within a week he and his family were arrested and taken to a prison camp in Siberia.

WHAT WAS GOING ON?

- Resentment of the government had been brewing for a long time. The hardships caused by the war and the harsh winter deepened this resentment. The strike at the Putilov factory was all that was required to trigger the March Revolution.
- The March Revolution was a spontaneous outbreak of popular anger against the tsar.
- Because of his personal inadequacies, the tsar was unable to respond in a way that would calm the situation.

GradeStudio

'Inference' is a really hard skill to learn, but all it really means is: 'what is the underlying message?' Source G shows Rasputin, holding the tsar and tsarina. From the cartoon you can easily infer that the cartoonist thought that Rasputin was evil, that the tsar and tsarina were a bit simple in the head and that Rasputin was controlling them both like puppets.

2.1b Why were the Bolsheviks able to seize power in October/November 1917?

Problems facing the Provisional Government

The Duma planned to hold elections for a constituent assembly that would put in place a new parliamentary government. Until those elections, the Provisional Government set up by the Duma would rule Russia.

The most important minister in the Provisional Government was Alexandr Kerensky, a member of the Duma and one of the leaders of the March Revolution (see Source F on page 124).

At first the Provisional Government was popular. It awarded Russians basic rights, such as freedom of speech and the right to strike.

Soldiers and workers continued to set up numerous soviets (workers' councils). These soviets sent representatives to the Petrograd Soviet, which had played a central role in the revolution.

The soviets effectively controlled day-to-day life in Petrograd. The Provisional Government gave orders, but the soviets carried them out only if they wanted to. Historians sometimes call this period the time of 'Dual Government'.

Problems soon emerged in the Provisional Government. It was made up of members of various political parties – including Social Revolutionaries, Cadets, Liberals and Mensheviks. These parties had different views on how Russia should be governed. The disagreements among them made it hard to make decisions. By contrast, the Petrograd Soviet was united and had a clear idea of what it wanted to achieve.

Two issues made the Provisional Government unpopular:

- The first was land. The government avoided making a decision on the ownership of land by peasants. It wanted to leave the decision to the Constituent Assembly when it was elected. This delay angered the peasants, many of whom refused to wait and seized the land for themselves.

- An even more important issue was the war. The government decided to go on fighting. It feared that any peace settlement with Germany would involve harsh conditions being imposed on Russia. The decision to fight on was unpopular with the army and the Russian people. Soldiers demoralised by defeat were deserting. People at home were suffering food and fuel shortages.

SOURCE K

Putilov factory workers meet in 1920 to elect a representative to the Petrograd Soviet.

SOURCE L

- *The orders of the Petrograd Soviet shall be carried out only when they do not go against the orders and decisions of the soviets.*

- *All weapons must be under the control of the soviets. They must not be handed over to officers.*

- *All ranks and titles in the army are abolished.*

From Order No.1 of the Petrograd Soviet (March 1917).

WHAT WAS GOING ON?

- The Provisional Government failed to take control fully; the true rulers were the soviets.

- The Provisional Government tried to carry on governing almost as the tsar had governed. This failure to break with the past made the Provisonal Government unpopular. People were ready to accept an alternative government.

The growth of the Bolsheviks

The Revolution in March caught Lenin, the exiled Bolshevik leader, by surprise. Returning to Russia as quickly as possible, he arrived in Petrograd on 16 April. He had travelled through Germany in a sealed train carriage provided by the German government (the Germans hoped that Lenin might cause a revolution and take Russia out of the war).

Lenin announced that the Bolsheviks would not co-operate with the Provisional Government but would work for its overthrow. He also declared that Russia should withdraw from the war and that land should be distributed to the peasants. These announcements were called the 'April Theses'. They were summarised in the slogans 'Peace, Bread and Land' and 'All Power to the Soviets'.

The April Theses were popular not only among the people but also among the Bolsheviks. Lenin gave his party leadership and a clear direction.

July Days and the Kornilov Uprising

The Bolshevik Party was disciplined and well-organised. It ran a successful propaganda newspaper called *Pravda* ('Truth'). By August 1917, the Party had 2 million members and a private army (called the Red Guards). Two events helped the Bolsheviks grow even more powerful:

- In July a Russian attack on the Germans ended in a massive Russian defeat. News of this defeat reached Petrograd. On 16 and 17 July, soldiers, sailors and workers demonstrated against the government. The Red Guards joined in the rioting that followed. Troops loyal to the government put down the rising. Lenin fled to Finland, but the Bolshevik Party was not banned.

- In August the commander of the Russian army, General Lavr Kornilov, tried to seize power and bring back the tsar. Kornilov was defeated when his troops were persuaded not to fire on fellow Russians. Yet the Bolsheviks won popularity because they were ready to fight Kornilov – with arms supplied to their Red Guards by the government. After the confrontation with Kornilov, the Red Guards held onto the weapons.

Support for the Bolsheviks grew throughout the summer. In September they took control of the Petrograd Soviet.

SOURCE M

This painting was produced by a Bolshevik artist. It shows Lenin returning in triumph to Petrograd in April 1917.

In reality, Lenin returned quietly and in secret.

SOURCE N

The Bolshevik party was waging a determined struggle to win over the masses. The struggle was headed by Lenin, who frequently addressed mass rallies and meetings. Lenin's speeches, noted for their profound content and brilliant delivery, inspired the workers and soldiers. Bolshevik membership began to grow rapidly.

Written by a Soviet historian in 1981, at the height of the Cold War, when President Reagan was accusing the Soviet Union of being 'an evil empire'.

WHAT WAS GOING ON?

- The Bolsheviks' growth was due partly to Lenin's successes but mainly to the Provisional Government's failures.
- The Bolsheviks were opposed by the Mensheviks in the Soviet as well as the Provisional Government.

The Bolshevik plan

Lenin had spent many years preparing the Bolsheviks for revolution. He had criticised Russia's involvement in the First World War from the start. He saw it as a capitalist war. Lenin soon became aware of the discontent among soldiers and civilians.

By 1917 Lenin had a small group of dedicated revolutionaries ready and able to seize power. Leon Trotsky, a leading Menshevik, did not join the Bolsheviks until the summer of 1917. However, he quickly became a close colleague of Lenin. Although Lenin was in charge, Trotsky was given the task of planning the seizure of power.

In October Lenin returned secretly from Finland to attend a meeting of the Central Committee of the Bolshevik Party. The Committee voted 10-2 in favour of carrying out a second revolution. The Bolsheviks' plan was to launch their strike at the same time as the All-Russian Congress of Soviets was meeting in Petrograd.

The Bolshevik Red Guards were to seize the important buildings and bridges in Petrograd. They had already won over some of the government troops in the city. The *Aurora*, a ship with a Bolshevik crew that was moored in the River Neva, would fire its guns. This sound was to be the signal for the Red Guards to capture their targets.

Trotsky was a Marxist who was exiled in 1900 for opposing the tsar. He took part in the 1905 revolution, but was exiled again. In 1917 he returned and joined Lenin's Bolsheviks. In this photograph he addresses workers and soldiers after the Revolution in October and November 1917.

SOURCE O

The Red Guards poured out of the adjacent streets in an irresistible rush across the square in front of the Winter Palace. The last bastion of the counter-revolution fell. This marked the victory of the armed uprising of the working people in Petrograd, which began a new era in human history.

The Soviet historian D.Y. Kukushkin, writing in 1981.

SOURCE P

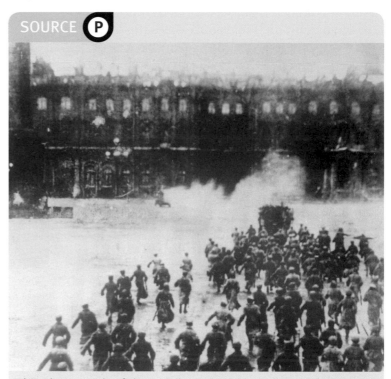

This photograph of the attack on the Winter Palace was staged for the camera in 1920 by the Red Army.

Trotsky was chairman of the Military Revolutionary Committee. From his office in Room 10 of the Smolni Institute, he issued arms to the Red Guards and drew up the plans for the seizure of the key sites in Petrograd.

Kerensky knew of the Bolshevik plan. He did not, however, have enough loyal troops to protect his government.

WHAT WAS GOING ON?

- The November Revolution was a **coup d'état** by a small group of Revolutionaries.
- The November Revolution was led by Lenin but masterminded by Trotsky.
- Later Bolshevik propaganda tried to make out that the revolution had been a heroic and popular uprising of the masses.

The Bolshevik Revolution

Later Bolshevik propaganda portrayed the events of November 1917 as a 'popular revolution' brought about by mass support from the **proletariat** (the working classes) for communist ideas.

In fact, the revolution was quite a small-scale affair. There was little fighting during the November uprising, much less than there had been in March.

The Bolshevik Revolution succeeded because it was a well-organised coup, because it had the support of the navy, and because the Provisional Government was so unpopular that it simply collapsed as soon as it was challenged.

1. On the night of 6 November the Red Guards set up road blocks and blockaded the bridges into Petrograd. They were helped by large numbers of sailors from the nearby Kronstadt naval base.

2. By the morning of the 7th, the Red Guards had taken control of the railway stations, the telephone exchange, the telegraph agency, the state bank and the electricity supply. The *Aurora* prepared to bombard the Winter Palace, the headquarters of the Provisional Government.

3. Kerensky went to the front line in search of loyal troops who would save his government. He failed and went into hiding.

4. The same night (7/8 November), the Red Guards took the Winter Palace.

5. The All-Russian Congress of Soviets was meeting while these events took place. The Mensheviks and most of the Social Revolutionaries walked out of the meeting in protest at the Bolshevik Revolution. This walkout left the Bolsheviks in control.

6. The ministers of the Provisional Government – except Kerensky, who fled abroad – were arrested in the Winter Palace.

7. The following day, Lenin set up a new government called the Council of the People's Commissars. He announced that he had taken power in the name of all the soviets of Russia.

A few days later, on 15 November, the Bolsheviks seized Moscow. They now had control of Russia's two largest cities – but little else.

SOURCE Q

The Provisional Government had dwindled to a meeting of ministers in the Winter Palace. A few Red Guards climbed in through the servants' entrance and arrested them.

The British historian A.J.P. Taylor, writing in *Revolutions and Revolutionaries* (1980), describes events in Petrograd.

GradeStudio

When you are assessing the usefulness of the provenance of a source, you need to look at the AUTHORITY of the author. Source Q was written by a famous and respected British historian, A.J.P. Taylor. This makes it VERY useful, because he was a brilliant historian who had reflected academically on the events of the times. But you might also want to point out that since he was British and living at the height of the Cold War, he may have been a little emotionally hostile to the subject to be wholly objective – did he subconsciously want to demean and diminish the Bolshevik achievement of 1917?

SOURCE R

The Winter Palace in Petrograd, the headquarters of the Provisional Government, sustained little damage during the Bolshevik Revolution.

WHAT WAS GOING ON?

- The Bolshevik Revolution in Petrograd met with almost no opposition. The Provisional Government simply collapsed.
- The Bolshevik Revolution in Petrograd was well-organised and slick.

2.1c How successful was Lenin in creating a new society in Russia?

The Bolsheviks take power

On 8 November the Bolsheviks set up their new government. Most of the ministers were Bolsheviks. Lenin himself was chairman of the Council of Commissars – in effect, he was the leader of the government. Trotsky was commissar for foreign affairs. Joseph Stalin was commissar for nationalities (that is, he was in charge of all the non-Russians living in Russia).

As soon as he came to power, Lenin announced an immediate end to Russia's involvement in the First World War. Peace talks with the Germans began in December. On 3 March 1918, Germany and Russia signed the Treaty of Brest-Litovsk. Russia gave away 750,000 square kilometres of land, three-quarters of its coal and iron mines, 37 per cent of its best farmland, and 26 per cent of its population (60 million people). Lenin also issued a land **decree**. It gave him the power to seize land owned by the tsar, the church and rich landlords and hand it over to peasants.

The Constituent Assembly

Before the Provisional Government fell from power, Kerensky had promised elections for a permanent parliament, to be called the Constituent Assembly.

Lenin allowed the election to go ahead. However, most voters were peasants who supported the Social Revolutionary Party. It won 370 of the 700 seats available, and Lenin's Communist Party won only 175 seats. Lenin therefore shut down the Constituent Assembly after only one day and instead began ruling by decree. He described this phase of the revolution as the 'Dictatorship of the Proletariat'. It was a transitional stage – it would last only until communism could be properly established among the people.

In December 1917 Lenin set up the Cheka, a secret police force. When opponents of Lenin tried to assassinate the Russian leader in 1918, he launched the 'Red Terror'. During this backlash, as many as 50,000 opponents of communism were arrested, tortured and executed.

SOURCE S

This Bolshevik poster reads: 'Beat up the noblemen – and don't forget the lords'.

SOURCE T

The Council of People's Commissars resolves to abolish all the existing judicial institutions such as district courts…

In order to fight the counter-revolutionary forces and to protect the revolution against them, and also to try cases of marauding and pillage, and the sabotage and other misdeeds of merchants, industrialists, officials and other persons, worker-peasant revolutionary tribunals shall be set up consisting of a chairman and six assessors elected by the city Soviet of Workers, Soldiers and Peasants.

A decree issued by Lenin on 5 December 1917.

WHAT WAS GOING ON?

- Lenin kept his two key promises: peace and land.
- From the start, Bolshevik rule was a dictatorship backed up with terror.
- The terms of the Treaty of Brest-Litovsk were exceptionally harsh for Russia.

The Russian civil war

Opponents of the Bolsheviks were known as the 'Whites'. This group included:

- landowners who had lost land during the Bolshevik Revolution
- religious groups who opposed the Bolsheviks' seizure of church property
- royalists who wanted to bring back the tsar

The White armies were led by officers loyal to the old regime, including Nikolay Yudenich, Anton Denikin, Aleksandr Kolchak and Jozef Pilsudski.

Lenin had opponents abroad as well as at home. His threat of a global revolution alarmed Britain, France, the USA and Japan. These countries were also annoyed by Lenin's peace with Germany and his refusal to pay the tsar's debts. They wanted Russia back in the war.

These countries supplied weapons and troops to the Whites. A British force landed at Murmansk, in the north. British and French troops landed in the south. A joint British-Japanese force landed in the far east. Finally the Czechoslovak Legion, a unit that had fought with the Allies during the First World War in order to win Czechoslovakian independence from Austria-Hungary, took control of the Trans-Siberian Railway.

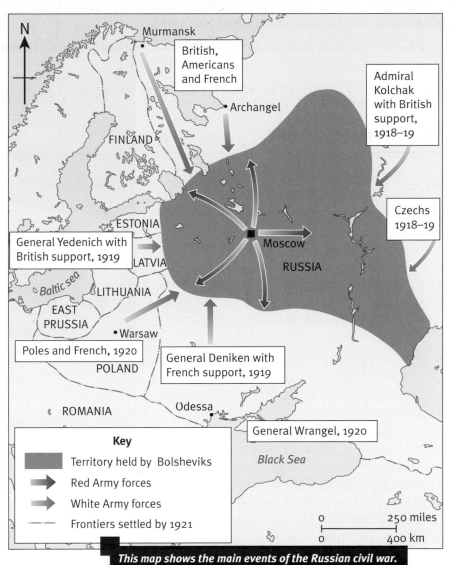

This map shows the main events of the Russian civil war.

Key
Territory held by Bolsheviks
Red Army forces
White Army forces
Frontiers settled by 1921

The Events of the Civil War

1. In the north-west, an army led by General Yudenich was helped by the British. By 1920 this army had advanced to within a few kilometres of Petrograd. Then Trotsky went to the front and inspired the Bolshevik forces to drive their enemies back.

2. In the south-west, General Denikin advanced on Moscow. He was stopped in 1919, and in March 1920 his force was destroyed. A small number of soldiers survived. This band, led by General Wrangel, was finally defeated in the Crimea in November 1920.

3. In the east, Admiral Kolchak used brutal tactics. He filled 'death trains' with Red Army prisoners. These trains would be driven up and down the trans-Siberian railway, its passengers poorly fed and never allowed off the trains. Many died from this treatment. Executions and mass shootings were also common. Kolchak's army was defeated in 1919. Its leaders were arrested and shot.

4. General Pilsudski led a Polish army that hoped to gain some advantage from the Russian civil war. Pilsudski invaded Russia in spring 1920. The Red Army responded brutally and drove him back. The Poles and Russians finally signed the Treaty of Riga in March 1921.

WHAT WAS GOING ON?

- At the start, lots of people wanted to get rid of the Bolsheviks, who had to fight for their lives.
- The Bolsheviks were literally surrounded by enemies.

Reasons for the Bolsheviks' success

- The Whites had several weaknesses:
  - Their armies were thousands of miles apart. The different commanders concentrated on winning their own victories instead of working together. As a result, the Whites' attacks were never co-ordinated.
  - Some White leaders were brutal. General Denikin, for example, was accused of slaughtering 100,000 Jews in the Ukraine. This 'White Terror' drove many Russians to support the Reds.
- Meanwhile, the Bolsheviks controlled the towns and the railways, so they could rush supplies and troops to any part of their front line under threat.
- The Bolsheviks had a cause – communism. Trotsky succeeded in motivating people to fight for this cause.
- Trotsky's leadership of the Red Army was vital. By using harsh discipline, he turned it into a formidable fighting force. When the Red Army did not have enough officers, Trotsky conscripted tsarist officers. He made sure they stayed loyal by threatening to kill their families.
- The Bolsheviks were ruthless. Cheka units ran an ongoing campaign of 'Red Terror', and the tsar and his family were executed.

War Communism

Lenin's greatest challenge in the war was feeding and supplying the Red Army. Russia had to produce more weapons and food. To achieve this goal, Lenin extended state control over the economy. He called this policy 'War Communism'.

- The state took control of the factories and appointed managers to run them.
- People had to work long hours in the factories.
- Trade unions were banned, and strikers were shot.
- Food was **rationed**, and ration cards were issued only to those in work.
- The Cheka seized all surplus grain from the peasants. Peasants who hid food were punished.

Many peasants preferred to grow less grain than give it away for free to feed people in the towns. Grain production fell even more as a result, and drought and severe famine hit the country in 1921.

A Bolshevik propaganda poster shows Britain, France and the USA as evil capitalists trying to destroy Russia using Denikin, Kolchak and Yudenich as their fighting dogs.

Bolshevik propaganda portrayed the Whites as the tools of foreign powers and the Reds as defenders of Russia.

GradeStudio

When you are assessing the usefulness of the CONTENT of a source, you need to look at both surface, and inferred facts. Source U is useful because you can see from the picture that the three main White generals' names were Denikin, Kolchak and Yudenich. But you can also infer from the cartoon that the artist thought that the three generals were really fighting for the USA. This is a very useful insight into the attitudes of the Bolsheviks at the time, and it helps to explain why the Soviets hated the Americans so much during the Cold War.

WHAT WAS GOING ON?

- The White Army was top-heavy (it had too many officers). It was also disunited and dispersed. The Reds had too few officers, but the army was united and motivated by the communist dream.
- Both sides used Terror as a weapon.

Results of the civil war

At the end of the civil war in 1921, the Bolshevik Revolution had survived, and the Reds controlled most of the tsar's former empire.

An important consequence of the civil war was the death of the tsar and his family. After Nicholas II's abdication in March 1917, members of the royal family were arrested and imprisoned. First they were taken to Siberia and then to the town of Ekaterinburg in the Ural Mountains. In July 1918, as the White Army advanced to free them, the royals were executed by their communist guards. Officially the local Soviet had responsibility for the decision. In reality it was taken by Lenin.

The civil war had disastrous effects on a population already devastated by the First World War. Atrocities were commonplace on both sides. Prisoners were often tortured and killed. In total, 21 million Russians died between 1914 and 1921. The fighting ruined both agriculture and industry. Land was only 50 per cent cultivated. Steel production was down to 5 per cent of its pre-war output. Poor hygiene and rat infestations led to disease, and there was a shortage of doctors and hospitals.

There was a famine in 1921. At times food shortages in the towns were so bad that a person's bread ration fell to 30 grams per day. Industrial production fell as workers left the cities for the countryside in the hope of finding more food. Those who stayed behind salvaged what they could by using the black market. It is estimated that the famine killed about five million people.

Some historians believe that the atrocities Russia suffered during the civil war desensitised the Bolshevik leaders — that is, it took away their ability to feel bad about human suffering. This desensitisation, they argue, explains why the Bolshevik leaders were able to accept the mass-slaughters that occurred during Stalin's Great Terror (1930s).

The Reds never forgave the Western governments who had helped the Whites to try to destroy them. In March 1919, the Communist International (Comintern) was set up to help communist parties in other countries to work for an international communist revolution.

SOURCE X

Of all the tyrannies in history, the Bolshevik tyranny is the worst, the most destructive, the most degrading.

The atrocities committed under Lenin and Trotsky are far more hideous and more numerous than anything for which the Kaiser was responsible.

Winston Churchill, then Britain's secretary of state for war, giving his reasons for opposing Bolshevism in 1919, when British forces were fighting in Russia to help the Whites destroy the Bolshevik government by force.

A communist society

The Bolsheviks did not just want power. They wanted the power to create a new, different kind of society – one run according to communist values.

On one hand, this society relied on 'the Dictatorship of the Proletariat', the brutal suppression of any opposition by the Cheka, and absolute state control of the newspapers.

The state took control of the factories. Religion was banned; many churches were destroyed, and many priests were killed.

Yet at the same time, the Bolsheviks truly believed that they were creating a better world for the workers.

In the countryside, Lenin confiscated land from the nobles and gave it to peasants. In the towns, a Labour Law gave workers an eight-hour day, unemployment benefits and pensions.

The Bolsheviks believed that if Russia was to become an advanced communist state, people would have to be educated. There was a huge campaign in the countryside to teach everyone to read. Science was encouraged, and 'useless' subjects, such as Latin and history, were banned.

There was also a relaxation of social rules. The Bolsheviks allowed free love, divorce and abortion.

WHAT WAS GOING ON?

- The civil war caused great suffering in Russia.
- The Bolsheviks tried to set up a society based on communist ideas and beliefs.

The New Economic Policy

War Communism made the government unpopular. There was violence in the countryside and strikes in the towns. In March 1921, the sailors at the Kronstadt naval base revolted. The sailors had been Lenin's strongest supporters, and their revolt made Lenin realise how unpopular War Communism was.

Lenin therefore introduced a 'New Economic Policy' (NEP), which had been Trotsky's idea. The government relaxed its control over the economy and returned smaller factories to private ownership. Grain was no longer seized from the peasants. Instead, they had to give some to the government but could sell any surplus at a profit.

Lenin called the NEP 'a breathing space'. Production of industrial goods and grain increased.

	Output (in millions of tonnes)		
	1913	1921	1928
Coal	29.0	9.0	35.0
Iron and Steel	8.5	0.3	7.3
Grain	80.0	37.6	73.3

However, there was some opposition to the NEP from within the Party. Some peasants (the Kulaks) and some traders and businessmen in towns (called 'Nepmen') made huge profits.

The fact that such profits could be made caused great resentment. 'Old' Bolsheviks thought that gearing trade and business towards profit was against communist principles. To many, the NEP was a return to old ways and a betrayal of communism. Many resigned from the party.

The creation of the USSR

The Red Army captured new regions during the civil war. They set up communist governments and declared these regions 'socialist republics'. In 1923 all of these socialist republics were brought together into the Union of Soviet Socialist Republics (USSR). In theory this huge new state was a democracy. In practice the Communist Party was the only party. Therefore, the USSR was run by a dictatorship of the Communist Party.

By the time Lenin died in January 1924, he had made sure that the Communist Party had full control of the country. He achieved this goal partly by introducing popular policies, but mainly through force and terror.

The cover of a Russian book on the New Economic Policy (1924).

WHAT WAS GOING ON?

- The Kronstadt Rebellion scared Lenin into relaxing War Communism. Many Bolsheviks disapproved of this move.
- The civil war set the pattern for the way Russia was governed and its foreign policy.

SOURCE **W**

Parties which were sent into the countryside to obtain grain by force might be driven away by the peasants with pitch-forks. Savage peasants would slit open a belly, pack it with grain, and leave him by the road-side as a lesson to all.

A communist describes unrest in the countryside caused by government attempts to requisition grain during the period of War Communism.

Preparation – 'Inference'

- Russia still had not introduced the Gregorian Calendar by 1914.
- Tsar Nicholas ruled with the help of the *Okhrana* and the army.
- The influential Orthodox Church taught that it was a sin against God to oppose the tsar.
- The three-hundredth anniversary of the Romanov family's rule was marked by genuine celebrations.
- In 1914 the city of St Petersburg was renamed Petrograd.
- On 8 March 1917, thousands of women came out onto the streets to demand bread.
- On 12 March 1917, soldiers in Petrograd refused to fire on demonstrators and joined them instead.
- Lenin returned to Russia in a sealed carriage provided by the German government.
- Later Bolshevik propaganda portrayed the October/November Revolution as a 'popular revolution'.
- General Denikin killed 100,000 Jews in the Ukraine.
- Trotsky conscripted tsarist officers and kept them loyal by threatening to kill their families.
- The tsar and his family were executed.
- During the civil war, the Bolsheviks controlled the towns and the railways.
- In March 1921 the sailors at the Kronstadt naval base revolted.
- Lenin called the NEP 'a breathing space'.
- Some peasants (the Kulaks) and some businessmen (called 'Nepmen') made huge profits.
- The Communist Party was the only party in the USSR.

What can you INFER from these facts?

Working in pairs, draw TWO inferences from each of these facts. What general issues or events of the time does each fact hint at?

Preparation – 'Explain how'

- Why was Russia so difficult to rule?
- Why did anger and resentment build up in Russia before 1914?
- Why did some groups oppose the tsar in the years before 1914?
- Why did some groups support the tsar in the years before 1914?
- Why was the Russian army so often defeated by the Germans during the First World War?
- Why was the tsar increasingly unpopular as the war went on?
- What consequences had the war had for the people of Petrograd by 1917?
- Why did Rasputin gain so much influence in Russia during the war?
- How did Rasputin cause so much damage to the tsar's reputation during the war?
- Why did rioting break out in Petrograd in March 1917?
- How did the rioting in March 1917 lead to a revolution and the abdication of the tsar?
- Why was the Provisional Government unpopular in the period between the revolutions?
- How did the Bolsheviks become popular in the period between the revolutions?
- Why did the Bolshevik Revolution succeed?
- Why did a civil war break out in Russia in 1918?
- Why did the 'Reds' win the civil war, 1918–21?
- What were the consequences of the civil war for Russia?
- How did the Bolshevik takeover affect the everyday lives of people in Russia?
- Why did Lenin introduce the New Economic Policy?

Using this textbook or the internet, answer each question above by finding THREE REASONS ('Why?'), WAYS ('How?'), or RESULTS ('What consequences?'). Then EXPLAIN HOW all three led to or arose from the situation given in the question.

Why did the 'Reds' win the Civil War, 1918–1921?   (6 marks)

Full sample answer

Comments

Explain one reason.

The first main reason why the Reds won the Civil war was that the Whites had several weaknesses (even though the Whites had large armies and the support of Britain, France and America). The White armies were thousands of miles apart, attacking from the north-west (General Yudenich), the south-west (General Denikin) and the east (Admiral Kolchak). Also, the different commanders were jealous of each other. Therefore the White leaders were disunited, and their attacks were never co-ordinated. The Bolsheviks, who controlled the towns and the railways, were able to rush supplies and troops to any part of their front under threat, and they could defeat the Whites' attacks one by one.

No introduction – it wastes time. Goes straight to the first reason.

States the first reason. Supports this idea with facts. EXPLAINS HOW this was a reason for the Reds' victory.

Explain a second reason.

A second main reason why the Reds won the Civil war was Trotsky's brilliant leadership of the Red Army. By harsh discipline, he turned the army into a fighting force. When the Red Army did not have enough officers, Trotsky conscripted Tsarist officers and kept them loyal by threatening to kill their families. And when General Yudenich (helped by the British) advanced to within a few kilometres of Petrograd in 1920, Trotsky went to the front and inspired the Bolshevik forces to drive the Whites back. Trotsky's skills as an organiser and motivator together with his ruthlessness lay behind the Bolshevik success. He turned them into a disciplined, war-winning Army which was able to defeat the Whites.

States the second reason. Supports this idea with facts. EXPLAINS HOW this was a reason for the Reds' victory. This section can get you to full marks, depending on the depth of your explanation.

Summary of other reasons.

There were other reasons for the Red Army's success. Some White leaders were cruel and brutal – General Denikin killed 100,000 Jews in the Ukraine, and Admiral Kolchak filled 'death trains' with Red Army prisoners. This 'White Terror' led many Russians to support the Reds. Finally, the Bolsheviks were also fighting for the communist cause, and were motivated by their beliefs. They were fighting to the death for the survival of the only communist state in the world. They had plotted and rebelled their whole lives, so they were prepared to undergo any suffering, or commit any atrocity, to win the war. This was why the Bolsheviks were so ruthless – Cheka units ran a 'Red Terror' which used fear to keep people fighting for the Reds. By contrast, the Whites had no 'big idea' to fight for after the tsar was executed.

Briefly summarises all the other reasons you know. Supports these ideas with facts and brief explanations. To further improve your answer, you might want to explain a third reason in depth.

Source B

Sire – We, working men and inhabitants of St Petersburg, our wives and our children and our helpless old parents, come to You, Sire, to seek for truth, justice and protection. We are near to death... We ask but little: to reduce the working day to eight hours, to provide a minimum wage of a rouble a day... Do not refuse to help Your people.

Full sample answer

How useful is Source B for studying the growing anger in Russia before the First World War?
Use Source B and your own knowledge to explain your answer. (10 marks)

Comments

Briefly describe the source and its content.

Source B is from a Russian trade union leaflet of 1898, and it shows how the workers were complaining about poor working conditions and blaming the bosses.

This gets you started.

Compare the source's content in detail to the historical facts to assess whether the source is useful.

When I look at the content of the source, I see that it would be useful for a historian collecting evidence of the poor working conditions in Russian factories before the war. I know that at this time in Russia there were all the problems of the early years of an industrial revolution. Large numbers of peasants were migrating from the countryside, and there was poverty, overcrowding, pollution, and appalling conditions in the factories. I know of photographs of the time showing factory workers living in appalling conditions – and Source B reinforces those facts.

The source is also useful because it is an outcry against the bosses. It would be useful to a historian researching the causes of the Russian Revolution because it shows the growing anger of the workers and helps to explain the causes of the March Revolution, which began with a strike of 40,000 workers at the Putilov factory.

Use the CONTENT of the source and your own knowledge to come up with TWO IDEAS about the source's USEFULNESS.

Examine the source's provenance to find further ways it might be useful.

Looking at the provenance, I see that it is from 1898, which is quite a long time before the War. It proves that there was growing anger towards the bosses before the 1905 Revolution, but I know that in the years after 1905 Stolypin was able to re-establish autocratic rule. So it might be more useful to a historian studying how Russians felt in 1905 than a historian studying how people felt in 1914.

Secondly, being a trade union leaflet, it would have been on the side of the workers and against the bosses. In one way, this is useful because it shows how angry people working at the Putilov armaments factory felt. However, it is not a useful indication of the views of all Russian people – I know that the peasants had a deep traditional loyalty to the Tsar.

Use the PROVENANCE of the source and your own knowledge to come up with TWO MORE IDEAS about the source's usefulness.

Conclusion summarises the usefulness of the source.

This source is quite useful to a historian because it is evidence of poor factory conditions. However, a historian would have to remember that it is biased – it may not represent the feelings of all workers.

However, it was written as an appeal against the bosses' cruelty, and was probably designed to attract other workers to join the Union, so it is a very useful indication of the feelings and intentions of Russian Trade Unionists in 1898.

Notice how the conclusion explicitly refers to the PURPOSE of the source.

German attitudes to the treaty

Germans were outraged by the unfairness of the Treaty of Versailles and especially by the fact that Germany had not been included in negotiations. Instead, Germany had been presented with the Treaty as a 'Diktat' (a dictated peace). As a result, Germans felt deeply resentful towards foreign nations and were eager for revenge. As he was rising to power, Hitler found it easy to tap into German resentment. He channeled it into support for his racism and his aggressive foreign policy. Hitler openly promised that he would tear up the Versailles Treaty.

The Germans were furious that the Treaty of Versailles blamed Germany for causing the war. They felt that the blame lay with Russia. Over the next few years, they published all their foreign policy documents in order to prove that they had not caused the war on purpose. They managed to convince some historians, including the American Sydney Bradshaw Fay.

Reparations ruined the German economy. In 1923 the country experienced economic meltdown, causing anger, riots and rebellion. Later, the USA stepped in and propped up the German economy with huge loans. Many Germans greatly resented the American domination of their country's economy. Again, Hitler was able to exploit this resentment as he rose to power.

When Germans sought the armistice in 1918, they did so in the belief that a peace treaty would be based on the principles set down in President Woodrow Wilson's Fourteen Points. In the end, the treaty was much harsher. A clause that particularly annoyed the Germans reduced the German army to only 100,000 soldiers. The Fourteen Points had called for mutual disarmament. Yet the Treaty of Versailles disarmed only the defeated nations. Germans complained that this lopsided disarmament left their country weaker than even small neighbouring nations, such as Poland and Czechoslovakia. This unfair treatment not only gave Hitler genuine grounds for complaint, it gave him the excuse to re-arm Germany in the 1930s and gear up for war.

Loss of territory was another ground for complaint. Wilson's Fourteen Points called for self-determination – the principle that people of one national group should be allowed to rule themselves. Yet the Treaty of Versailles left millions of Germans living under the rule of foreigners in Czechoslovakia, Danzig (in the Polish Corridor), Lithuania and Poland. It also forbade Germany to unite with German-speaking Austria. Many Germans were eager to take up Hitler's call for the creation of a 'Greater Germany'.

SOURCE C

The disgraceful Treaty is being signed today. Don't forget it! We will never stop until we win back what we deserve.

From the German newspaper *Deutsche Zeitung*, 28 June 1919.

SOURCE D

In our high school in Stuttgart, after 1918, a noticeable rightist trend prevailed. We believed that it was the stab in the back alone that had prevented a German victory; we had one Pan-German history teacher who defended this worst form of the legend. We were convinced that one could only be patriotic on the rightist side… We took up nationalistic slogans, while the Republic of which we were trying to make fun was trying to pull the wagon out of the mud.

The German historian Fritz Ernst (writing in *The Germans and Their Modern History*, 1966), remembering his schooldays.

GradeStudio

When you are assessing the usefulness of the provenance of a source, you need to look at the AUTHORITY of the author. Source D was written by a German historian who had lived through the events. This makes it REALLY useful, because he was an eye-witness who had then reflected academically on the events of the times. But you might also want to point out that, being German, he may have been a little too emotionally close to the subject to be wholly objective.

WHAT WAS GOING ON?

- The Germans' hatred of the Treaty of Versailles was a continual problem for the Weimar government – which was blamed for signing the treaty.

Challenges to the Weimar Republic

The new government found itself attacked by groups from both the extreme left and the extreme right.

The German Communist Party was large. It had close links with the Bolsheviks, who in 1917 had led a successful communist revolution in Russia. The communists wanted to take control of Germany's factories and farms and bring in a Russian-style system of government based on soviets (workers' councils).

In January 1919, even before the Weimar Government was officially constituted, the Spartacists (named after Spartacus, a Roman slave who rebelled) led a communist uprising. Most of the army had been disbanded, but groups of ex-soldiers formed themselves into volunteer private armies called Freikorps (free companies). With the help of the regular army, the Freikorps brutally put down the Spartacists. Thousands of Spartacists were captured and shot. The leaders of the revolt, Rosa Luxemburg and Karl Liebknecht, were killed.

The Freikorps and the army put down further communist revolts in Berlin in March 1919. When Bavaria declared itself an independent Soviet Republic in April 1919, the army and the Freikorps **besieged** Munich and massacred the communists.

Extreme right-wing agitators also wanted to destroy the Weimar government and bring back the old autocratic monarchy of the Kaiser. They then wanted to rebuild the army and re-establish the power and pride of the German nation.

In March 1920 the Freikorps rebelled. The **Putsch** (rebellion) was led by a right-wing nationalist called Wolfgang Kapp. The rebels took over Berlin and tried to bring back the Kaiser. The army refused to attack the rebels. However, the Kapp Putsch came to an end when the workers of Berlin called a general strike and brought the city to a standstill.

The right-wing groups were supported not only by many ex-soldiers and ex-officers, but also by the police and the judges. As a result, they could literally get away with murder. In August 1921 Matthias Erzberger, a politician who had agreed the armistice (and was therefore a 'November criminal'), was shot. In 1922, the foreign minister Walther Rathenau was assassinated because he had made a treaty with Russia.

SOURCE E

The Spartacus League is now fighting for total power. The government, which wants the people to decide their own future freely (by voting in the election), is to be overthrown by force. The people are not allowed to speak. You have seen the results. Where Spartacus rules, all personal freedom and security is abolished.... The government is taking all measures necessary to destroy this rule of terror.

From a document published by Friedrich Ebert's government in January 1919.

SOURCE F

A German photograph taken during the Kapp Putsch.

The photo's original caption reads, 'Loyal German government troops in Berlin distributing anti-communist pamphlets, March, 1920'. This caption is almost certainly wrong. The photo probably shows members of the Freikorps distributing pamphlets supporting the Putsch.

WHAT WAS GOING ON?

- The Weimar government found itself attacked from both Left and Right.
- The Weimar government survived by using the Freikorps (right-wing) to put down the communists, and by using the trade unions (left-wing) to defeat the Kapp Putsch.

2.2b How far did the Weimar Republic recover under Stresemann?

Weimar's 'golden age'

The crisis in the Weimar Republic reached its peak in November 1923. Then Germany enjoyed a six-year period of prosperity that is sometimes called the 'golden age of the Weimar Republic'.

Gustav Stresemann was the leader of the German People's Party (DVP). He organised Germany's moderate political parties into a stable coalition called the 'Great Coalition'. During a short spell as chancellor in 1923, Stresemann replaced the worthless Mark with a new currency, the Rentenmark. He ordered the striking workers in the Ruhr back to work and agreed that Germany should start paying reparations again.

These moves made Stresemann unpopular, and he was forced to give up the post of chancellor in November 1923. However, he had created a basis for economic and political stability, and the Weimar Republic had a chance to establish itself.

Economic recovery

The introduction of the Rentenmark stabilised the German currency and ended hyperinflation. The government then took other measures to prevent a financial collapse in the future. In 1924 Germany agreed the Dawes Plan. It was named after Charles Gates Dawes, the US politician who negotiated it. Under the terms of the plan, the USA lent Germany 800 million gold marks. The Germans used this money to build new factories in a bid to kickstart the country's economy. The Dawes Plan also spread the load of the reparations payments. Germany's payments would start at £50 million per year and would rise to £125 million over the next few years. After that time, payments would be linked to the prosperity of the German economy.

The Dawes Plan restored confidence in the German economy, and investment poured in from abroad. German industry produced more goods, exports rose, unemployment fell and most Germans were better off.

In 1929 the Young Plan, which was arranged by a US businessman named Owen D. Young, reduced the total amount of reparations and extended the deadline for payments by a further 59 years.

SOURCE **K**

The Siemens power plant in Nuremburg, 1926.

SOURCE **L**

Divided on political matters, the Germans want to become a united nation of gum chewers. No other item enjoyed such a rapid increase of turnover during the stabilisation crisis. Chewing gum is the cheapest way to Americanise oneself, and the Germans of today harbor an intense yearning for the USA.

Ernst Lorsy, *The Hour of Chewing Gum* (1926).

WHAT WAS GOING ON?

- Right-wing and nationalist Germans did not thank the people – Ebert and Stresemann, for example – who got Germany out of its crises. They hated them for collaborating with Germany's foreign enemies.
- The Dawes Plan triggered a period of economic prosperity.

International relations

From 1923 to 1929, Stresemann was Germany's foreign secretary. During this period, Germany once again gained acceptance among the European powers.

When Stresemann started paying reparations, the French and Belgians took their troops out of the Ruhr. They had withdrawn by 1925.

Other countries began to treat Germany as an equal:

- In 1925 the Germans and the French signed the Locarno Pact. They agreed never to try to change the border between their two countries.
- In 1926 Germany was allowed to join the League of Nations.
- In 1928 Germany signed the Kellogg–Briand Pact with over 60 other countries. These countries promised never to go to war against one another.

Germany was now more stable than it had been at any time since 1919. Support for extremist parties, such as the communists and the National Socialists, fell away. Support for the moderate Social Democrats, on the other hand, grew.

Germany still had problems, however. Its economy was very dependent on US loans. After 1927 industrial growth started to slow down, and there was a depression in the farming sector.

Cultural flowering

The late 1920s also saw a cultural boom in Germany. People had more money to spend. Berlin became the pleasure capital of Europe.

- Going to clubs and cafés became an important part of Berlin life.
- Numerous cabaret artists and singers – the most famous was Marlene Dietrich – came to work in Berlin.

There was little censorship, so writers and artists could try out new ideas.

- Artists such as George Grosz and Otto Dix created work that criticised German society.
- Erich Remarque wrote the anti-war novel *All Quiet on the Western Front* (1929). The following year it was made into a successful film.
- These were also the years of the famous Bauhaus school of architects.
- People were much freer in their attitudes towards sex and more relaxed about homosexuality and abortion.

Some critics saw the new Weimar culture as **decadent**. They said it did not represent traditional German virtues and was causing a decline in moral standards.

GradeStudio

Some sources are more useful than others; Source N for instance simply shows us a group of women in a café. To assess its utility, we need to know how representative this picture was of women in general – and in fact such women were more the exception than the norm (which is why the photographer thought them unusual enough to warrant a picture).

SOURCE N

German women in a Berlin café, 1927.

WHAT WAS GOING ON?

- The Weimar Republic only SEEMED safe during the Stresemann years. The underlying problems of economic weakness and political opposition to the government remained.
- The brilliant but decadent Weimar culture created more right-wing hostility to the government.

2.2c How far did the Nazi Party develop its ideas and organisation up to 1929?

Adolf Hitler

Adolf Hitler was born in Austria in 1889. His father, a customs officer, died when he was fourteen. His mother died when he was eighteen. Hitler had little education and no job. He drifted to Vienna, the capital of Austria, to become an art student. Yet the Academy of Art would not enrol him. He was forced to live in poverty in hostels for the homeless and take whatever work he could find. He developed an interest in politics and supported nationalist parties. He also developed a dislike for foreigners and a particular hatred of Jewish people.

In 1913 Hitler left Austria to avoid military service. He went to live in Munich. When war broke out he volunteered to join the German army. He was on active service throughout the war and was wounded twice. He was promoted to corporal and won the Iron Cross, First Class – the highest award for a German soldier. In 1918 he was hospitalised in a British gas attack.

It was in hospital that Hitler learned that Germany had surrendered and signed the armistice. He was bitter and angry. Like many other Germans, he could not accept that Germany had been defeated fairly. He looked for other people to accuse. Drawing on his prejudices and political beliefs, he blamed a conspiracy of communists and Jews. He also blamed the Weimar politicians, who had, he said, given the German army a 'stab in the back'.

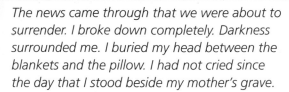

SOURCE O

The news came through that we were about to surrender. I broke down completely. Darkness surrounded me. I buried my head between the blankets and the pillow. I had not cried since the day that I stood beside my mother's grave.

Hitler describes his reaction to the German surrender in 1918 in his autobiography *Mein Kampf* (1924).

WHAT WAS GOING ON?

- Hitler's only skill was talking politics, yet he found himself in the right party at the right time.
- Hitler based his politics on blaming the November criminals/the Jews/the communists for Germany's defeat in the First World War.

The beginnings of the Nazi Party

After the war Hitler returned to Munich. He remained in the army, which used him to spy on political parties to find out if they were a threat to the new government. One of the parties he spied on was the newly formed German Workers Party.

The German Workers Party was a small group led by a railwayman named Anton Drexler. It was nationalist, socialist and anti-Semitic (that is, anti-Jewish). Hitler found he agreed with the party's ideas and decided to join (he became its seventh member). Before long, he was the leader of the party. He began to reorganise it to increase its popularity.

The Nazi Party

One of Hitler's first moves was to change the party's name to the National Socialist German Workers Party (NSDAP). It was commonly called the Nazi Party.

In 1921 Hitler set up a private army, the *Sturmabteilung* ('stormtroopers'). This army is usually called the SA. Its members, young men and some former soldiers, were known as the Brownshirts because of their uniforms. Their official role was to protect Nazi meetings. In practice they went much further – they attacked political opponents and broke up their meetings.

Hitler also devised a symbol for his new party – the swastika. The Party published its own newspaper, *Der Stürmer*, to put forward its ideas.

The Nazi Party was based in Munich, the capital of the German state of Bavaria. Hitler was well known there. In its early years, the party was financed by rich people who hoped Hitler would prevent the communists from growing strong. He began to make a name for himself by giving powerful, angry speeches.

Even though the Nazi Party was relatively small elsewhere in Germany, Hitler was confident that Nazi ideas would appeal to all German people.

SOURCE **P**

This Nazi election poster (c. 1933) is entitled 'We are building'. It contrasts 'our building blocks' – work, freedom and bread – with the 'plans of the others' – which include welfare cuts, corruption, terror, haste and lies.

Nazi beliefs

In 1920 the Nazis set out their 'National Socialist' beliefs in their 'Twenty-Five Point Programme'.

Some Nazi policies appealed to nationalists and racists. Such policies included unifying all Germans into one country, abolishing the Treaty of Versailles, gaining more land and colonies to feed Germany's population, and expelling **immigrants**. Other policies appealed to socialists because they involved sharing the nation's wealth. These policies included **nationalising** industry, profit-sharing (sharing the profits of major businesses in Germany amongst the population), improving pensions, and giving tenant farmers (farmers who rented their farmland from other landowners) the right to own their land.

Finally, the Nazis demanded 'a strong central government with unrestricted authority'. This idea appealed to Germans who longed to return to the days of the Kaiser.

The Nazi Party was 'all things to all men'. Its policies were popular and influential in the chaotic and rebellious early years of the Weimar Republic, 1919–23.

GradeStudio

When you are assessing the usefulness of the CONTENT of a source, you need to look at both surface, and inferred facts. In Source Q you may want to point out that the artist is caricaturing the Jewish man's clothes, beard and love of money. But you could also point out the inference that Jews are in league with the communists, and that they want to control Germany (symbolised by the whip). Most of all, you can infer the massive anti-semitic hatred which the artist clearly had towards the Jews. These are very useful insights into how Germans of the time may have been feeling.

WHAT WAS GOING ON?

- In its early days, the Nazi Party used violent tactics and a message of hatred.
- The Nazi programme promised everything to everybody; it was a blend of nationalist and socialist ideas.

SOURCE Q

GROSSE POLITISCHE SCHAU IM BIBLIOTHEKSBAU DES DEUTSCHEN MUSEUMS ZU MÜNCHEN · AB 8. NOVEMBER 1937 · TÄGLICH GEÖFFNET VON 10-21 UHR

This poster of 1937 features a **caricature** of a Jew. It suggests that the Jews want to help the communists take over Germany.

SOURCE R

We are Nationalists because we, as Germans, love Germany. And because we love Germany, we demand the protection of its national spirit and we battle against its destroyers.

We are Socialists because we see in Socialism the only chance for maintaining our racial existence… because for us the social question is a matter of necessity and social justice…

We are enemies of the Jews because we are fighters for the freedom of the German people. The Jew is the cause and the beneficiary of our misery. He is the real cause of our loss of the Great War. He has corrupted our race, fouled our morals, undermined our customs and broken our power.

Josef Goebbels, *Why Are We Enemies of the Jews* (1930). Goebbels was in charge of the Nazi Party's propaganda.

The Munich Putsch

During the economic crisis of 1923, Hitler became convinced that conditions gave him a good chance of a successful Putsch (rebellion). Thanks to the French invasion and hyperinflation, public anger was at its height. Hitler had the support of the First World War veteran General Ludendorff. He also expected to be supported by the German army and the right-wing Bavarian government, which was led by Gustav von Kahr.

When Kahr began to show signs of wavering, Hitler decided to force his hand. On 8 November 1923, Kahr was speaking at a meeting at a beer hall in Munich. Hitler burst in with 600 stormtroopers and forced Kahr at gunpoint to support the Putsch. That night the stormtroopers seized key positions in Munich.

However, Kahr, who had been freed after agreeing to support the Putsch, had alerted the army and the police. The following day, when the Nazis tried to march triumphantly into the city centre, their route was blocked by armed police and soldiers. Shots were fired, and sixteen Nazis and three policemen were killed. Hitler and Ludendorff were arrested.

Mein Kampf

The Putsch had failed, but Hitler turned what could have been a disaster into a propaganda opportunity. At his trial, the judge allowed him to deliver a number of nationalistic speeches and let him off with a light sentence.

While in prison, Hitler wrote a book about his life and ideas. Called *Mein Kampf* (*My Struggle*), Hitler's book became the 'bible' of the Nazi movement. In it Hitler wrote down many of the ideas that he later put into practice. After he became chancellor of Germany in 1933, *Mein Kampf* became a school textbook and was the most-borrowed book in German libraries. A copy was given to every newly married couple as a wedding gift from the state.

The following ideas appeared in *Mein Kampf*:

- Territorial expansion: Germany must conquer more Lebensraum ('living space') for its people.
- Racism: the superiority of the pure German Aryan 'master race' over other races.
- National Socialism: aggressive national pride, centralised government, and state control of the economy.

Hitler's failure in Munich convinced him that he would not gain power by a revolution. He decided instead to try to win power through the ballot box.

Police about to attack the Nazis in Munich, 9 November 1923.

I am not a criminal. There is no such thing as high treason against the traitors of 1918. History will judge us as Germans who wanted only the good of their people and fatherland.

From a speech Hitler gave at his trial in 1924.

WHAT WAS GOING ON?

- The Munich Putsch failed because Hitler overestimated the support of the army and the public.
- Hitler wrote *Mein Kampf* while in prison to spread the idea of National Socialism.

The Wilderness Years

The years from 1924 to 1929 were a difficult period for the Nazi Party. After the Munich Putsch, the party was banned by the government.

On Hitler's release from prison in December 1924, the ban was lifted. The Nazi Party re-formed. However, it struggled to attract the support of German voters. These were the Stresemann years, a time when the economy was doing well. The extremist policies of the Nazi Party were not attractive in such stable conditions. The Nazi Party therefore did badly in elections. In May 1924 it won 32 seats in the Reichstag. By December it had only 14 seats, and by 1928 only 12 seats.

Yet the Nazi Party did not fade away during these years. Hitler increased his control of the party. In 1925 he set up a personal bodyguard called the *Schutzstaffel* (the SS). Josef Goebbels was put in charge of party propaganda. The Nazis set up organisations such as the **Hitler Youth** and the Nazi Teachers' League and staged public meetings and rallies throughout Germany.

As a result, although the elections were going badly, membership of the Nazi Party increased slowly but steadily. In 1925 it had 27,000 members. In 1928 it had more than 100,000.

Even so, the Nazis were a long way from becoming a major national political party. Something was needed to push the Nazi Party forward. That 'something' came in 1929, when a severe economic depression hit Germany.

SOURCE **U**

Adolf Hitler at a Nazi Party rally in 1928.

WHAT WAS GOING ON?

- The Munich Putsch convinced Hitler to use the ballot box.
- Hitler used the years 1923–29 to build and organise the Nazi Party.
- The Nazi Party did badly in elections during the years 1923–29; the economy was booming, and nobody wanted to know about National Socialism.

SOURCE **V**

Hitler had extraordinary political abilities. He possessed tremendous energy and will power and a remarkable gift for public speaking which enabled him to put forward his ideas with great emotional force. Large numbers of Germans began to look towards him as some sort of Messiah figure.

The British historian Norman Lowe, writing in 1988, in a school GCSE history revision book.

Preparation – 'Inference'

- The Freikorps put down the Spartacists with great brutality.
- Right-wing politicians believed the army had been 'stabbed in the back' by the 'November criminals'.
- The army refused to attack the Kapp Putsch.
- The Kapp Putsch was stopped when the workers of Berlin went on strike.
- During the Kapp Putsch, right-wing groups were supported by the police and the judges.
- In 1921 French, British and Belgian troops invaded the Ruhr to force Germany to agree to reparations.
- The German government ordered the people of the Ruhr to carry out passive resistance.
- A loaf of bread cost 4 marks in 1921 but 200,000 million marks in November 1923.

- In 1924 Germany agreed the Dawes Plan.
- The republic under Stresemann was more stable than at any time since 1919.
- Attitudes towards homosexuality and abortion relaxed in Weimar society.
- The SA consisted of young men and some former soldiers.
- On 9 November 1923, the Nazis tried to march triumphantly into Munich's city centre.
- While in prison, Hitler wrote a book about his life and ideas called *Mein Kampf*.
- In May 1924 the Nazi Party won 32 seats in the Reichstag. By 1928 it had only 12 seats.
- Hitler set up the *Schutzstaffel* (SS) as his personal bodyguard in 1925.

What can you INFER from these facts?

Working in pairs, draw TWO inferences from each of these facts. What general issues or events of the time does each fact hint at?

Preparation – 'Explain how'

- Why is the Weimar Republic described as 'a brave attempt to set up a democratic government'?
- Why is the Weimar Republic sometimes described as 'doomed from the start'?
- What were the consequences of the Treaty of Versailles for Germany?
- Why did Germans hate the Treaty of Versailles?
- Why was the Weimar Republic in danger of collapsing, 1919–23?
- How and why did left-wing extremists challenge the Weimar Republic, and why did they fail?
- How and why did right-wing extremists challenge the Weimar Republic, and why did they fail?
- Why did the French invade the Ruhr in 1923?
- Why was there crisis, hyperinflation and violent unrest in 1923?
- What consequences did hyperinflation have for many Germans?

- Why is 1923–29 sometimes called 'the golden age of the Weimar Republic'?
- Why was 1923–29 a time of political stability for Germany?
- How did Stresemann help the German economy recover after 1923?
- Why did Germany's international importance grow after 1923?
- Why did Hitler hate communists, Jews and the 'November criminals'?
- How did the Nazi Party grow, 1919–23?
- Why did Hitler call his new party the 'National Socialists'?
- Why did Hitler attempt the Munich Putsch in 1923? Why did it fail?
- Why did the Nazis have little success in elections, 1923–29?
- How did Nazi Party membership grow, 1923–29?

Using this textbook or the internet, answer each question above by finding THREE REASONS ('Why?'), WAYS ('How?'), or RESULTS ('What consequences?'). Then EXPLAIN HOW all three led to or arose from the situation given in the question.

How did the Nazis try to appeal to the German people, 1919–23?   (6 marks)

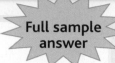

Full sample answer

Comments

Explain one way.

The first way the Nazi Party tried to appeal to the German people in the years 1919–23 was by the use of violence. In 1921 Hitler set up a private army, the Sturmabteilung (SA – the 'Stormtroopers'), also known as the Brownshirts because of their uniforms. The SA consisted of young men and some former soldiers – these were the men Hitler used in the failed Munich Putsch of 1923. Their official role was to protect Nazi meetings. In practice they went much further and attacked opponents and broke up their meetings. This helped the Party grow because people were frightened and unable to oppose it.

No introduction – it wastes time. Goes straight to the first way.

States the first way. Supports this idea with facts. EXPLAINS HOW this was a way the Nazis appealed to the Germans.

Explain a second way.

The second way the Nazis tried to appeal to the German people was by developing policies which were 'all things to all men'. The Nazis set out their 'National Socialist' beliefs in 1920 in their 'Twenty-Five Point Programme'. This included 'nationalist' policies, such as the union of all Germans into one country, the abolition of the Treaty of Versailles, land and colonies to feed Germany's population, and the expulsion of immigrants. It also included 'socialist' ideas (such as nationalisation of industry, profit-sharing, the improvement of pensions and a scheme to give tenant farmers the right to own their land). Finally, they wanted 'a strong central government with unrestricted authority'. Ideas like this were popular and influential in the chaotic and rebellious early days of the Weimar Republic, 1919–23. They appealed to the nationalists because they wanted to make Germany strong. They appealed to the socialists because they proposed sharing the nation's wealth. The demand for a strong government appealed to Germans who longed to return to the days of the Kaiser.

States the second way. Supports this idea with facts. EXPLAINS HOW this was a way the Nazis appealed to the Germans.

Summary of other ways.

There were many other ways that the Nazi Party tried to appeal to the German people. One of the first things Hitler did was to change its name to the National Socialist German Workers Party (NSDAP) – the Nazi Party. Hitler also devised a symbol for the new party – the swastika. In the early years of the Party, Hitler was financed by rich people who hoped he would prevent the communists growing strong. The Party published its own newspaper, Der Stürmer, to put forward its ideas, and also Hitler began to make a name for himself by making powerful, angry speeches. All these things brought Hitler and the Nazis to the public's attention, and helped the Nazi Party to grow in numbers.

Briefly summarises all the other ways you know. Supports these ideas with facts and brief explanations. To further improve your answer, you might want to explain a third way in depth.

How useful is Source H for studying conditions in Weimar Germany during the hyperinflation of 1923?

Use Source H and your own knowledge to explain your answer. (8 marks)

Comments

Briefly describe the source and its content.

Source H is a photograph from 1923, and it seems to be a family photograph showing children playing with building blocks made from banknotes, because they had become worthless.

> This gets you started.

Compare the source's content in detail to the historical facts to assess whether the source is useful.

When I look at the content of the source, I see that it would be useful for a historian collecting evidence of how money became worthless during the hyperinflation. I know that at this time prices were rising to incredible figures (a loaf of bread rose from 4 marks to 200 thousand million marks by November 1923) and that workers had to collect their wages in wheelbarrows. Source H reinforces this impression of the time.

> Use the CONTENT of the source and your own knowledge to come up with TWO IDEAS about the source's USEFULNESS.

It is also useful to a historian researching the condition of Germans during the hyperinflation. I know that during the hyperinflation people with fixed incomes or savings (e.g. like pensioners) suffered badly, but people on wages were able to renegotiate their wages each morning, and people who had borrowed money actually did well. The children are playing and do not look as though they are starving – in fact, they look quite well-fed, clean, well-dressed and prosperous. This photo seems to show that not everyone starved in 1923.

Examine the source's provenance to find further ways it might be useful.

Looking at the provenance, I see that it is from 1923 and is therefore contemporary. So the photograph is useful evidence of what people looked like at that time. It has not been posed or 'set up' after the event. I know of similar photographs and sources from the time showing the worthlessness of money. One woman wrote how a vicar came to Berlin to buy some baby shoes with his month's wages, but when he arrived, he only had enough for a cup of coffee.

> Use the PROVENANCE of the source and your own knowledge to come up with TWO MORE IDEAS about the source's usefulness.

Secondly, if this is a normal family photograph, in one way it might be useful because it is just showing how one family responded to the hyperinflation. However, a historian might question its usefulness because you have to ask how 'normal' this family is – they seem very comfortably off, and I know that hyperinflation caused great suffering and hardship for many people, especially pensioners. I know that cartoons of the time showed German people naked, thin and starving.

Conclusion summarises the usefulness of the source.

This source is useful to a historian because it shows how paper money during the hyperinflation quickly became absolutely worthless.

> Notice how the conclusion explicitly refers to the PURPOSE of the source.

I think that it is particularly useful because it seems to be a family photograph. Although it shows that people of the time were amazed and fascinated by the worthlessness of their money, it does not seem to be a political propaganda photograph, and appears to be simply a genuine record of what happened in this family.

2.3 The Roaring 20s: USA, 1919–1929

2.3a How and why did the USA achieve prosperity in the 1920s?

The USA after the war

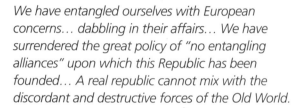

The USA did not enter the First World War until April 1917. Only 100,000 Americans died in the war. Each death was a huge personal tragedy for an American family that lost a son, but the total number was small compared to the losses sustained by European nations. In some ways, the USA had even done well out of the war – European countries had paid the USA to provide food, raw materials and weapons.

President Woodrow Wilson had taken the USA into the war, and his Fourteen Points had been the basis for the peace settlement. After the war, Wilson saw it as the USA's duty to help preserve world peace. To that end, he proposed a League of Nations (see pages 22–23).

WHAT WAS GOING ON?

- After the war, isolationists won political arguments in the USA.
- Isolationism had connections with racism, tariffs, the Red Scare, and immigration controls.

SOURCE A

We have entangled ourselves with European concerns… dabbling in their affairs… We have surrendered the great policy of "no entangling alliances" upon which this Republic has been founded… A real republic cannot mix with the discordant and destructive forces of the Old World.

From a speech by the Republican senator William Edgar Borah, an isolationist (1919).

GradeStudio

'Inference' is a really hard skill to learn, but all it really means is: 'what is the underlying message?' In Source A Senator Borah is giving some reasons for rejecting the Treaty of Versailles. But as you read the words 'discordant and destructive', it is easy to infer that he despised Europeans as old-fashioned and wicked. Similarly, the word 'dabbled' reveals that he regarded Woodrow Wilson's ideas as superficial and dangerous.

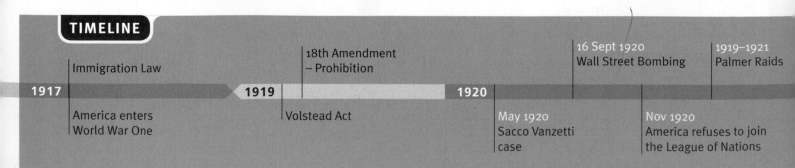

TIMELINE

1917		1919		1920		

Immigration Law

18th Amendment – Prohibition

16 Sept 1920 Wall Street Bombing

1919–1921 Palmer Raids

America enters World War One

Volstead Act

May 1920 Sacco Vanzetti case

Nov 1920 America refuses to join the League of Nations

The mood of isolation

To many Americans, the war seemed a remote conflict. It had been fought thousands of miles away over issues that did not concern their country. They did not want more American soldiers killed trying to keep peace around the world. They were worried that the USA, as the strongest and richest country in the world, would end up paying the cost of keeping world peace.

President Wilson wanted the USA to sign the Treaty of Versailles and join the League of Nations. However, his party, the Democrats, did not control Congress (the American parliament). Their opponents, the Republicans, who were led by Henry Cabot Lodge, rejected the Treaty of Versailles and with it the USA's entry into the League.

The Republican candidate in the 1920 presidential election was Warren Harding. His campaign slogan was 'America First'. He talked about a return to 'normalcy' (a word he invented). What he meant was a return to how things had been before the war.

The Americans voted in Harding as their new president. By rejecting the Democrats, the people were also rejecting the Treaty of Versailles and the League of Nations.

Isolationism grew even stronger in the USA during the 1930s. Certain American historians decided that Germany had not started the First World War and that 'German atrocities' had been cooked up by British propaganda. In the 1930s, through several Neutrality Acts, the USA formally refused to get involved in European wars and refused to sell weapons to either side in a European conflict. As a result, until the invasion of Czechoslovakia in 1939 forced the USA to revise its policy, American firms were not allowed to sell arms to Great Britain when it faced Germany.

Effects of isolationism

Isolationism kept the USA out of European affairs. Internationally, it weakened the League of Nations. Isolationist policies have therefore been held responsible for allowing the rise of Hitler.

Within the USA, isolationism – fuelled by racist ideas of white supremacy – helped to create a 'Red Scare' (see page 162). The desire to keep America exclusively for 'WASPS' (white Anglo-Saxon Protestants) also led directly to attempts to control immigration (see page 162).

Economically, isolationism led to a tariff policy to try to keep foreign goods out of the US economy (see page 158). Tariffs eventually helped to cause the **Great Depression** of the 1930s.

GradeStudio

When you are assessing the usefulness of the CONTENT of a source, you need to look at both surface, and inferred facts. Source B tells us simply a list of things that Warren Harding said America needed. But he was saying these things because he thought that Americans wanted to hear them and that this would make them vote for him. You can sense the desire of the American people to leave behind the killing and the upheaval of the First World War, and to get back to peace and 'business as normal'. So the Source gives us a very useful insight into how Americans of the time were feeling.

1921	1922	1924	1927	1929	1933
				Oct 1929 Wall Street Crash	
May 1921 Emergency Tariff					
May 1921 Emergency Quota Act	Sept 1922 Fordney-McCumber Tariff Act	National Origins Act	The Jazz Singer – the first 'talkie'	Feb 1929 Valentine's Day Massacre	Dec 1933 Prohibition repealed

The Boom of the 20s

In the 1920s the USA went through a period of economic prosperity – a boom. During this time it became the richest country in the world. Between 1920 and 1929, the number of motor cars on American roads, for example, increased from 9 million to 26 million. In the same period, the number of telephones increased from 13 million to 20 million.

Economic growth created a 'cycle of prosperity'. An increase in the production of consumer goods created more jobs. As a result, people had more money to spend on consumer goods. This increase in wealth encouraged an increase in production – and so on.

Throughout the 1920s there was a feeling of confidence among the American people. Many Americans invested in companies by buying shares. The result was a boom in the American stock market, which was based on Wall Street in New York.

The Growth in Industry

The motor car industry was among the first to use **assembly lines** to produce goods in large quantities. The pioneer of this method of production was Henry Ford. Ford's big idea was to make a motor car for the ordinary man and his family.

Ford's car was called the Model T. The first Model T was produced in 1911. By the 1920s a Model T was being produced every ten seconds. The high volume of production allowed Ford to reduce his prices. In 1911 a Model T had cost $850; by 1920 it could be bought for $295. One Model T was identical to another. They were all the same colour (black), and all engines were the same size. This uniformity did not bother Americans. The 'Tin Lizzie', as it was known, became the most popular car in the USA.

The car industry expanded during the 1920s. It also helped other industries to grow – steel, rubber, glass, leather and oil were all in greater demand because of the car industry. The construction industry built roads for all the new traffic.

Other industries also grew during the 20s. Other consumer goods made using mass-production methods included radios, telephones, refrigerators, vacuum cleaners, washing machines and ovens. These new 'gadgets' were very attractive to Americans. Sales rocketed.

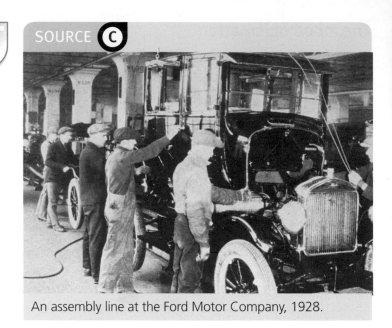

SOURCE C

An assembly line at the Ford Motor Company, 1928.

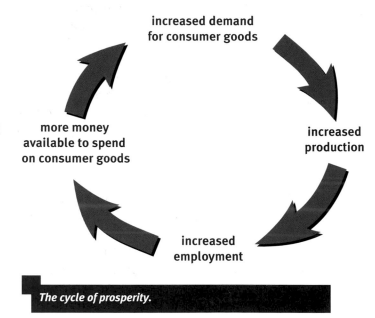

increased demand
for consumer goods

increased
production

increased
employment

more money
available to spend
on consumer goods

The cycle of prosperity.

WHAT WAS GOING ON?

- The 1920s saw the start of 'consumerism' in the USA.
- The 1920s saw a 'cycle of prosperity'; growth in one industry stimulated growth in another.
- The basis of the 1920s boom was consumer goods, such as electrical items and cars.
- The basis of the 1920s boom was mass-production.

Causes of the boom

There were many causes of the economic boom during the 1920s:

1. The USA was rich in raw materials – especially land, people and oil.
2. American industry grew during the First World War; the USA sold food and weapons to Europe with no competition from European countries.
3. American industry developed new production techniques.
   - The mass production of goods allowed **economies of scale**. As a result, the cost per unit of producing goods came down.
   - By placing workers on an assembly line and giving each worker one specific task, factories could produce goods much more quickly and much more cheaply.
   - **Time and motion** studies (which looked for ways of making each worker's task as quick as possible) improved efficiency even further.
4. People could buy consumer goods more easily thanks to new credit facilities, especially **hire purchase** (which allowed a buyer to pay for something in installments over a period of time).
5. Advertisements in magazines and newspapers, on the radio, in cinemas and on billboards, all tried to convince Americans that they should 'keep up with the Joneses'.
6. Mail order extended the market for consumer goods beyond towns and cities.
7. Government policy also fuelled the boom. The Republican governments of the 1920s encouraged the growth of business by a policy of non-interference in the ecomomy. This approach is called **laissez-faire** – 'leave things alone'. The governments of the 1920s did not place any controls on industry or on financial institutions. They also lowered taxes on people's incomes and on company profits. As a result, people had more money to spend on consumer goods, and companies had more money to invest in new factories and buildings.
   The government also protected American industry by placing tariffs on foreign goods coming into the USA. This approach, called **protectionism**, made a foreign product more expensive than the same American product.
8. Thousands of ordinary people bought **stocks and shares** in US businesses. The American Stock Exchange enjoyed a sustained bull market (a rise in all prices). Between 1921 and 1929, share prices rose 500 per cent. As far as the market was concerned, it seemed as though the only way was up.

SOURCE D

In 1928 Herbert Hoover declared, 'We in America are nearer to the financial triumph over poverty then ever before in the history of our land.' Hoover was to be the next President of the USA and he was convinced, as were many others, that American economic progress was unstoppable.

The British historian Tony Howarth, writing in *Twentieth Century History: The World Since 1900* in 1979.

SOURCE E

This advertisement for a washing machine appeared in the 1920s.

WHAT WAS GOING ON?

- The boom of the 1920s was fuelled by increases in supply and increases in demand. Improvements in production boosted the supply of goods, and improvements in people's ability to buy goods increased demand. In other words, there were 'push' factors and 'pull' factors.
- The government helped through laissez-faire economic policies and protectionist tariffs.

Tariffs

Before the First World War, most Americans believed in low tariffs. Low tariffs encourage world trade, and Americans wanted to trade with the rest of the world.

After the war, however, more and more Americans came to demand higher tariffs.

1. This development was due partly to isolationist attitudes and to the general feeling that the USA did not need the rest of the world.

   Primarily, however, tariffs stop imports, and Americans thought that putting high tariffs in place would help American businesses.

2. American business had boomed during the war – possibly because the countries involved in the war had not been able to sell goods to the USA. American business leaders wanted this boom to continue.

3. American wages were high. American business leaders feared that European firms that could pay low wages would undercut them as they would be able to produce goods at a lower cost and, therefore, sell them cheaper. Joseph Fordney claimed that tariffs would protect American jobs; by requiring American citizens to buy more American goods, they would guarantee American jobs.

4. Overproduction was causing a depression in farming, and American farmers wanted to keep foreign grain out to keep grain prices up.

As soon as he became president, Warren Harding passed an Emergency Tariff (May 1921) to increase duties on food imports. In 1922 Congress passed the Fordney-McCumber Tariff. This tariff had two main elements:

- The scientific tariff, which placed higher tariffs on goods coming from countries with low wages.
- The American Selling Price, which adjusted the tariff in such a way that the selling price of imported goods was always higher than the selling price of US goods.

SOURCE F

The Senate Finance Committee meets in July 1929 to formulate a new, even tougher tariff bill. The chairman of the committee was Reed Smoot.

Effects of US tariff policy

The Fordney-McCumber Act established the highest tariffs in history. The average import duty was 40 per cent, and duty on some imported items was as high as 400 per cent.

At first, tariffs helped American industry. By pushing up the price of imports, high tariffs protected American industry and agriculture from foreign competition. Farms and factories prospered, and the US economy continued to grow.

As time went on, however, tariffs began to have a damaging effect on the US economy:

- By keeping prices high, tariffs made life more difficult for poor people.
- Protected from foreign competition, American firms became inefficient. Wage rises made it more expensive to produce goods.
- Other countries began to respond to high American tariffs by imposing high tariffs of their own. American business, especially the agriculture sector, relied on exports, and high tariffs abroad were disastrous.
- Economic prosperity comes from trade. By blocking trade, high tariffs worldwide damaged the global economy and eventually helped cause the Great Depression of the 1930s.

WHAT WAS GOING ON?

- The aim of tariffs was to help American industry and farming by shutting out foreign competition.
- Tariffs were a form of economic isolationism.

The entertainment industry

In the 1920s young Americans wanted fun. They had money in their pockets, and the entertainment industry gave them great ways to spend it.

Jazz was a new kind of music. It developed from early African–American musical forms. Jazz was played in night clubs such as New York's Cotton Club by black musicians. Two of the most famous were Duke Ellington and Louis Armstrong.

Another popular form of music at this time was blues, which was played by black guitarists such as W.C. Handy. People could buy gramophone recordings of their favourite singers and play these records at home on a **phonograph**. Another way of listening to musc at home was to turn on the radio. The number of homes with radios rose from 60,000 in 1920 to 10 million in 1929. Local and national commercial stations were set up. These stations made money by advertising. As people bought the consumer goods they heard about on the radio, American business boomed.

Above all, going to the movies became a national habit during the 1920s. By 1929 more than 110 million Americans were going to the movies each week, and nearly every town had its own cinema. People went to the movies because they could afford to pay a few pennies for a ticket. Ironically, most movies allowed audiences to escape into a fantasy world far different from the impoverished, disease-ridden, harsh real world most Americans lived in.

The first movies were silent films in black and white. Words were shown on the screen, and cinemas employed piano players to provide background music. In 1927, however, people flocked to see Al Jolson in *The Jazz Singer*, which was the first talkie (move with a soundtrack). By the mid-1930s, films were also being produced in colour, and Walt Disney had made the cartoon characters Mickey Mouse and Donald Duck into household names.

Most of the films were made in Hollywood, a district of Los Angeles, in the Pacific state of California. Hollywood became the film capital of the world. The leading movie companies, notably United Artists, MGM and Paramount, produced more than 500 new films every year. They created international film stars, such as Charlie Chaplin, Gloria Swanson and Mary Pickford. When the movie heart-throb Rudolph Valentino died in 1926, thousands of fans attended his funeral.

This is the great picture upon which the famous comedian has worked a whole year.

6 reels of Joy.

Charles Chaplin IN "THE KID"

Written and directed by Charles Chaplin

A First National Attraction

A poster for *The Kid* (1921), starring Charlie Chaplin.

WHAT WAS GOING ON?

- The entertainment industry assumed that people had surplus cash in their pockets.
- The entertainment industry was based on technological innovation (the phonograph, the radio, talkies and so on.)

Fads and flappers

After the traumatic events of the First World War, many young people rejected convention. They just wanted to have fun. They rebelled against the social rules of their parents and were purposefully controversial and decadent.

The 1920s became known as 'the Roaring 20s' largely because of the pace of social life. Young people turned away from old-fashioned dances such as the waltz. New, wilder dances, such as the Charleston, the sexually suggestive tango, and the bunny hug became very popular.

Young Americans went to the cinema. They watched basketball, baseball and American football. Jazz became a craze. It appealed to young Americans partly because the music itself was wild and dramatic. Another part of its appeal was its origin: as a product of black American culture, jazz was something controversial and daring.

Many young women became 'flappers'. A flapper's hair was short and bobbed. She tried to look flat-chested and wore a skirt that rose to the knee. She used lipstick and rouge, smoked cigarettes and drove a 'Tin Lizzy'. Some flappers were openly lesbian. Meanwhile, young men wore pinstriped suits, trilby hats and **spats** on their shoes.

The older generation disliked what was happening in American society. The Anti Flirt Association was set up to try to control the excesses of the young. It distributed badges and organised speeches.

The 20s was a time of crazes and fads, a time when youngsters joined in never-ending dance marathons or sat on top of a flagpole for weeks just to break a record. Popular heroes emerged. One was Charles Lindbergh, who in 1927 became the first man to fly solo across the Atlantic. Other famous personalities included sportsmen, such as the boxer Jack Dempsey and the baseball player Babe Ruth.

SOURCE H

The parties were bigger, the pace was faster, the shows were broader, the buildings were higher, the morals were looser and the liquor was cheaper.

The American author F. Scott Fitzgerald, commenting on the Jazz Age in 1931.

SOURCE J

An 'it girl' dancing the Charleston.

GradeStudio

When studying the usefulness of a source, it sometimes makes sense to think about what it does NOT show/tell us. Source J, for instance, shows us a flapper dancing the Charleston – but it does not tell us that many Americans disapproved hugely of the new fads and fashions.

WHAT WAS GOING ON?

- Women won greater personal freedom in the 1920s and enjoyed shocking their strait-laced and disapproving elders.
- The Roaring 20s was a time of rebellion, experimentation, loss of inhibition and the pursuit of pleasure.
- Youngsters adopted black American jazz and wild new dances because they seemed more exciting than traditional forms.

2.3b How far was the USA a divided society in the 1920s?

Rich and poor

Although the 1920s were a 'boom' time for some, many Americans still lived in poverty. The richest 5 per cent of the population earned 33 per cent of the wealth. And in 1929, a survey found that 60 per cent of Americans lived 'below the poverty line' – that is, they earned less than $2,000 a year. Some sections of the population had a particularly hard time:

1. Farmers struggled during the 1920s – and almost half of all American people were involved in farming. Tractors, combine harvesters and other new machines helped farmers to produce more food. However, farmers ended up producing a **surplus** of food. As a result, food prices dropped. Many small farmers found themselves with a lower income and had difficulty keeping up their mortgage repayments. Some were evicted, others were forced to sell their land. Farm labourers also found themselves out of work and drifted to towns or to California, where there was the promise of work on fruit farms.

2. Black Americans had a similar experience. Almost one million black farm workers lost their jobs in the 1920s. Many moved from their homes in the south to the cities of the north. In the cities, black migrants from the south and also new immigrants to the country were usually able to find work, but only for very low pay.

3. Workers in older industries also did not share in the prosperity of the 20s. The coal industry, for example, suffered as new forms of power – oil, gas and electricity – became more widely used. The overmining of coal led to wage cuts or, worse, job losses and mine closures. Other older industries, such as cotton farming and textiles, suffered in a similar way.

SOURCE K

Half of all US citizens lived in rural areas. Not for them the new fridge and the vacuum cleaner: even if they could afford it, very few rural areas had electricity. Rural Americans felt isolated; 6 million left the land for the cities. Many of these were black farm labourers and small farmers from the southern USA.

From a GCSE revision guide written by the British historian Christopher Culpin.

SOURCE L

An American cartoon from the 1920s. A farmer looks wistfully at the millions of dollars being made by industry, while he struggles in poverty.

WHAT WAS GOING ON?

- The boom was centred on the production of modern, high-tech goods; farmers, black people and workers in the old industries did not prosper.
- Money was unfairly shared out in American society – 5 per cent earned 33 per cent of the wealth, and 60 per cent were below the poverty line.

Isolationism

Immigration

More than 40 million people moved to the USA between 1850 and 1914. By the end of the First World War, American society was a mixture of a hundred different nationalities. Although life during the Roaring 20s was filled with pleasure and excitement for many, there was also a dark side of intolerance and racism.

The political leaning towards isolation, together with some people's desire to keep America for the 'WASPS' (white Anglo-Saxon Protestants), also led directly to attempts to restrict immigration. Those who were against immigration wanted to in particular keep out people from Asia and Eastern Europe. Americans feared that new immigrants would take their jobs or, worse still, that they might try to spread communist ideas.

The Immigration Law (1917) required all would-be immigrants to prove that they could read English. The Emergency Quota Act (1921) limited the number of immigrants to 357,000 per year. The number of people coming to the USA from any one country could not exceed 3 per cent of the number from that country already living in the USA in 1910. This rule kept out people from Eastern European countries because there were fewer of them already living in the USA. The National Origins Act (1924) reduced the quota to 2 per cent of the population and set the date back to 1890. In 1929 the number of immigrants each year was reduced to 150,000, and immigration from Asia was blocked altogether.

The 'Red Scare'

Another effect of isolationism was distrust and intolerance of immigrants. Immigrants were restricted to the lowest-paid jobs. Areas of the cities became immigrant **ghettos**. In these ghettos, housing was poor, and violence and crime were high. Immigrants were often despised because they were poor.

Especially after the Russian Revolution (1917), Americans greatly feared communism. They felt that their free lifestyle and the capitalist economy that funded it were under serious threat.

In the early 1920s this fear became widespread. The idea that immigrants were communists was called the 'Red Scare.' The fear intensified after a number of bombs were planted by Italian communists and **anarchists**.

On 16 September 1920, a bomb on a horse-drawn wagon was detonated outside the Stock Exchange on Wall Street. The bomb was on a timer. It consisted of 45 kilograms of dynamite surrounded by hundreds of small metal slugs, which sprayed into the lunchtime crowd; 38 people died, and some 400 were injured. The American newspapers called the bomb 'an act of war' and blamed Italian anarchists (the bombers were never captured).

In response to this and the other bombs, the US attorney-general, Alexander Palmer, ordered the arrest of 10,000 people suspected of holding left-wing political views. The arrests were made during the so-called 'Palmer Raids'. Any of those rounded up who were discovered to be immigrants were deported without trial.

Sacco and Vanzetti

The most famous case of injustice against immigrants involved two Italians, Nicola Sacco and Bartolomeo Vanzetti.

Sacco and Vanzetti were openly anarchist. In 1920 they were charged with the murder of two guards in an armed robbery. 61 witnesses identified the Italians as the killers. However, these witnesses could not agree on the details of the crime, and the defence produced 107 witnesses who swore to seeing the two men somewhere else at the time of the robbery. Largely because most of the defence witnesses were Italian immigrants, the jury found both men guilty of murder. They were executed in 1927.

The Klu Klux Klan

The Ku Klux Klan, a militant organisation of white supremacists, launched what it saw as a moral crusade to save the USA. In doing so, it stirred up racial and religious hatred. The Klan would accept as true Americans only those people who were WASPs – that is, people who had originally come from northern Europe and whose families had lived in the USA for several generations. All other people were condemned as not being true Americans: Jews, Catholics, immigrants from southern Europe (such as Italians), from Eastern Europe (such as Russians), from Asia, and especially black people.

Membership of the Ku Klux Klan grew from fewer than 5000 members in 1920 to five million members in 1925. Klan members were often poor whites who felt that their jobs were threatened by people who were willing to work for lower wages – blacks and immigrants. However, the Klan also had rich and influential members, including state politicians. The Klan was strongest in the southern states, where there was a large black population and a history of slavery.

Klan members:

- held ceremonies in which they dressed in long white robes
- spoke to each other in secret codes known as 'Klonversations'
- used torture and violence against people who were not 'true Americans'
- most often attacked black people; blacks were beaten, raped or lynched (hanged without trial), and their homes were set on fire and their property destroyed.

Klansmen who committed violence were often protected by police or judges who were themselves members of the Klan. In addition, white juries were reluctant to find people guilty of Klan activities. However, the Klan's appalling crimes were widely reported, and after 1925, Klan membership fell.

SOURCE O

A photograph of the aftermath of the Wall Street bomb of 16 September 1920.

SOURCE P

'Native, white, Protestant supremacy!' The Klan is intolerant of the people who are trying to destroy our traditional Americanism… aliens who are constantly trying to change our civilisation into something that will suit them better.

From a speech by Wesley Evans, 'imperial wizard' (leader) of the Ku Klux Klan', dated 1923.

SOURCE Q

A store designed only for Black Americans to use in the 1920s. It is rundown and on the left is a sign stating 'Colored only'.

WHAT WAS GOING ON?

- In the 1920s parts of American society were extremely racist, and this racism found an outlet in the violent atrocities commited by the Ku Klux Klan.
- There was serious discrimination against black Americans during the 1920s.

Prohibition

'The era of **Prohibition**' was the time when the making, selling or transporting of alcoholic drink became illegal in the USA.

Prohibition marked the final success in a long campaign by groups such as the Women's Christian Temperance Union (founded in 1874) and the Anti-Saloon League (1895) to have alcohol banned. These groups claimed that alcohol brought poverty, broke up marriages, caused crime and insanity, and disrupted industry. By 1917, 18 American states had already banned alcohol, and in 1919 the ban became national. The 18th **Amendment** made Prohibition part of the US Constitution. A separate law, called the Volstead Act (1919), defined an alcoholic drink as any drink that was more than 0.5 per cent alcohol.

Effects of Prohibition

The alcohol ban was not popular. Most people saw nothing wrong with having a drink and found ways to get round the law. Many produced their own home-made alcoholic drink. Called 'moonshine', it was usually of poor quality and often caused illness and even death.

Town dwellers often looked to others to provide the alcohol they wanted. An illegal industry started up. Secret bars called **speakeasies** were set up behind locked doors in cellars and back rooms. By 1930 there were nearly a quarter of a million speakeasies in the USA – and more than 30,000 in New York alone. The speakeasies sold alcohol smuggled from abroad by **bootleggers**. They brought in rum from the West Indies and whisky from Canada.

WHAT WAS GOING ON?

- In 1919 the moral right-wing persuaded legislators to ban alcohol.
- Prohibition was driven by religious conservatives but also by sociologists who saw the damage drink did to families.
- Prohibition simply drove drinking 'underground' into the speakeasies.

SOURCE S

Daddy's in There---

And Our Shoes and Stockings and Clothes and Food Are in There, Too, and They'll Never Come Out.
—*Chicago American*

WANTED--A FATHER; A LITTLE BOY'S PLEA
JULIA H. JOHNSON

A shy little boy stood peering
 Through the door of a bright saloon;
He looked as if food and clothing
 Would be thought a most welcome boon.

And one of the men, in passing,
 As if tossing a dog a bone,—
Asked, "What do you want this evening?"
 In a rude and unkindly tone.

"I am wanting"—the boy's lips trembled—
 "I am wanting my father, sir."
And he gazed at the little tables
 Where the careless onlookers were.

It was there that he saw his father,
 But the man only shook his head,
And the boy, with his thin cheek burning,
 Ran away with a look of dread.

Oh, the fathers—the fathers wanted!
 How the heart-break, and bitter need,
With the longings, deep and piteous,
 For the wandering children plead.

May the children's call arouse them,
 May the fathers arise and go
With the young souls waiting for them,
 For the little ones need them so!

SERIES G NO. 23

The American Issue Publishing Co
Westerville Ohio

This cartoon, entitled *'Daddy's in There'*, appeared on a poster published by the Anti-Saloon League in 1910.

GradeStudio

When you are assessing the usefulness of the provenance of a source, you need to look at the AUTHORITY of the author. Source S was published by the Anti-Saloon League. This makes it REALLY useful, because it is an example of the actual arguments used by pro-Prohibition campaigners to get alcohol banned. But you might also want to point out that it is also therefore biased, and represents the views only of one lobby group; as it turned out, it did NOT represent the opinion of the majority of the American people.

Organised crime

The vast profits to be made from the illegal alcohol trade attracted gangsters. One of the most famous gangsters was the Italian immigrant Al Capone, who operated in Chicago. Capone's gang of 700 men, armed with with sawn-off shotguns and machine-guns, was like a private army. Rivals were 'rubbed out' (killed), and many of the city's leading police officers, judges and politicians were in his pay. Capone became a celebrity – he mixed with businessmen, politicians and movie stars.

The gangsters ran speakeasies and **protection rackets**. They were involved in prostitution and drug trafficking. They also bought their way into legal business activities and trade unions. Gangland murders increased as rival gangs fought to take over one another's 'territory'. In Chicago 227 gangsters were murdered in four years without anyone being convicted. In one day in 1929, in the St Valentine's Day massacre, Al Capone's men machine-gunned seven members of the gang run by Capone's rival 'Bugs' Moran.

The failure of Prohibition

The Prohibition Bureau employed only 4000 agents for the whole of the USA. Some agents, notably Eliot Ness, achieved some success. Most, however, were ineffective in the face of organised crime. Nearly one in ten agents was sacked for taking bribes.

Despite the strength of the temperance groups, most Americans did not agree with Prohibition. This lack of popular support was the most important reason for the failure of Prohibition. Americans were prepared to break the law in order to consume alcohol.

Prohibition ended in December 1933 when President Franklin D. Roosevelt repealed the 18th Amendment. The crime associated with Prohibition was gradually brought under control. The only crime the FBI could hang on Al Capone was tax evasion, for which he began a prison sentence in 1932.

SOURCE V

In 1930, Al Capone made the front page of *Time*, America's leading magazine.

WHAT WAS GOING ON?

- Crime thrived under Prohibition; criminal activity became unstoppable and corrupted American society.
- Prohibition failed because many people were prepared to break the law to have a drink.

2.3c Why did the US Stock Exchange collapse in 1929?

The US Economy

During the 1920s the American economy appeared to be strong, but it had some serious weaknesses.

1. Overproduction – once Americans had bought their cars, radios and other consumer goods, the demand for these items fell. Factories were forced to produce fewer goods. Therefore they had to cut back on their workforces. Therefore, fewer people could afford to buy consumer goods.

2. Unequal distribution of wealth – even during the boom years, more than half of Americans lived 'below the poverty line'. So although the American economy was generating lots of money, the money was not going into the pockets of the people who needed it most.

3. Tariff policy – tariffs protected US industry at home. However, when American businessmen tried to sell their grain and goods abroad, they found that foreign governments had imposed similarly high tariffs on American goods. Therefore US businessmen had great difficulty in selling their goods abroad.

4. Financial speculation – during the 1920s more and more Americans were buying shares in American companies. It was possible to buy shares 'on the margin' by paying 10 per cent of the cost in cash and borrowing the remaining 90 per cent from the banks. Wall Street was enjoying a 'bull market', and share prices kept rising. Investors fully expected to be able to sell their shares for a profit and settle their debts. This form of gambling on the stock market is called 'speculation'.

During 1928 share prices did not rise by as much as they had done in previous years. Some more experienced investors began to sell their shares before values fell. When other investors noticed these sales, they began to sell too. Suddenly, the bubble burst, and the 'bull' market quickly became a 'bear' market (one in which prices fall).

The Wall Street Crash, 1929

Prices began to fall dramatically as investors tried to sell their shares.

1. On Thursday 24 October – later known as Black Thursday – nearly 13 million shares were sold. Nobody wanted to buy, and prices dived.
2. A group of bankers spent nearly $250,000,000 buying shares. They hoped to encourage investors to buy rather than sell shares. The tactic seemed to work, and share prices stopped falling.
3. However, on Monday 28 October there was renewed panic, and over 9 million shares were sold at falling prices.
4. Finally, on Tuesday 29 October, panic-stricken investors sold over 16 million shares for whatever price they could get. As a result, prices tumbled. Shareholders lost a total of $8 billion on that day alone.

Prices of some US shares in 1929:

Company	3 Sept	13 Nov
Anaconda Copper	$132	$70
General Electric	$396	$168
US Steel	$261	$150
Woolworths	$100	$52

Effects of the Wall Street Crash

Although Tuesday was the worst single day on the stock market, share prices continued to fall for the next few weeks. Finally they 'bottomed out' (stopped falling) in mid-November. By then, though, the damage was done. Confidence in the American economy was destroyed. Many Americans had lost all their money in the Wall Street Crash. Instead of a 'cycle of prosperity', the USA now became trapped in a 'cycle of depression'.

Banks suffered particularly in the crash. Many had invested their customers' money in shares. People lost confidence, and there was a 'run' on the banks (that is, people rushed to withdraw their savings). The banks began to run out of money. In 1929 alone nearly 700 banks collapsed.

In an attempt to recover some of their money, banks began to call in loans from the companies and the ordinary people who had borrowed money from them. However, the banks were asking people to repay money they did not have. More companies closed, and some people had to sell their homes and possessions. Companies that managed to stay open had to dismiss some of their workforce. During the worst period of the Great Depression (1929–33), more than 100,000 businesses shut down.

SOURCE **Y**

A newspaper headline from 30 October 1929.

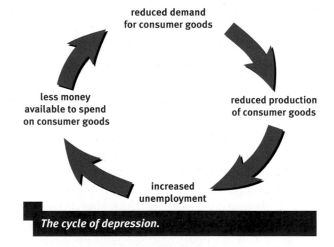

The cycle of depression.

WHAT WAS GOING ON?

- The boom was based on confidence; as soon as that confidence was dented, the economy collapsed.
- The Wall Street Crash began on the stock market; when it spread to the banks and then industry, it caused the Great Depression.

GradeStudio

Preparation – 'Inference'

- In the 1920 election, Warren Harding talked about a return to 'normalcy'.
- Between 1920 and 1929, the number of motor cars on the roads increased from 9 million to 26 million.
- The Republican governments did not place any controls on industry or financial institutions.
- In 1922 Congress introduced the Fordney-McCumber tariff.
- By 1929 more than 110 million Americans were going to the cinema every week.
- When Rudolph Valentino died in 1926, thousands of fans attended his funeral.
- In 1929, 60 per cent of Americans lived 'below the poverty line'.
- During the 1920s, some farmers were evicted; others were forced to sell their land.

- In 1921 the Emergency Quota Act limited the number of immigrants to 357,000 a year.
- The jury found Sacco and Vanzetti guilty of murder, and they were executed in 1927.
- Juries made up of white people were reluctant to convict people for Ku Klux Klan activities.
- During the 1920s, new wilder dances, such as the Charleston, became very popular.
- The Anti Flirt Association was set up to try to control the excesses of the young.
- By 1930 there were nearly a quarter of a million speakeasies in the USA.
- Al Capone became a celebrity – he mixed with businessmen, politicians and movie stars.
- Ordinary people bought shares 'on the margin'.
- On Tuesday 29 October, shareholders lost a total of $8 billion.

What can you INFER from these facts?

Working in pairs, draw TWO inferences from each of these facts. What general issues or events of the time does each fact hint at?

Preparation – 'Explain how'

- Why did a mood of isolationism grow in the USA after 1918?
- Why did the USA refuse to join the League of Nations in 1920?
- What were the effects of isolationism in the USA during the 1920s?
- Why did American industry experience a boom in the 1920s?
- Why was Henry Ford so successful?
- Why did the US government impose high tariffs on imports in the 1920s?
- What were the consequences of the Fordney-McCumber tariff?
- Why did the entertainment industry prosper in the 1920s?
- Why were the 1920s called 'the roaring twenties'?
- Why did jazz appeal to young people in the 1920s?

- How were the 1920s a bad time for some farmers, black people and workers in old industries?
- Why did the US government impose strict immigration controls in the 1920s?
- Why was there a 'Red Scare' in the 1920s?
- Why were black Americans so often attacked in the 1920s?
- Why was the Ku Klux Klan able to attack black Americans so often in the 1920s?
- Why did the US government impose Prohibition in 1919?
- Why did Prohibition fail?
- What were the effects of Prohibition in the 1920s?
- Why did organised crime flourish in the 1920s?
- In what ways was the US economy weak in the 1920s?
- Why did Wall Street 'crash' in 1929, and what were the consequences?

Using this textbook or the internet, answer each question above by finding THREE REASONS ('Why?'), WAYS ('How?'), or RESULTS ('What consequences?'). Then EXPLAIN HOW all three led to or arose from the situation given in the question.

What were the consequences of isolationism for America, 1919–1929?   (6 marks)

Full sample answer

Comments

Explain one result.

Firstly, isolationism kept the USA out of European affairs. President Wilson wanted the USA to sign the Treaty of Versailles and join the League of Nations, but the Republicans, led by Henry Cabot Lodge, rejected the Treaty of Versailles and the USA's entry into the League. In the 1920 election, the Republican Warren Harding campaigned with a slogan of 'America First', and talked about a return to 'normalcy'. The Americans voted in Harding as their new President – by rejecting the Democrats, they were also rejecting the Treaty of Versailles and the League of Nations. Isolationist Americans did not want to spend American money and lose American lives to help what they called 'the discordant and destructive forces of the Old World'.

No introduction – it wastes time. Goes straight to the first result.

States the first result. Supports this idea with facts. EXPLAINS HOW this situation was a result of isolationism.

Explain a second result.

Secondly, isolationism also led directly to a number of attempts to control immigration, especially from Asia and Eastern Europe. In 1917, an Immigration Law required all immigrants to prove they could read English. In 1921 the Emergency Quota Act limited the number of immigrants to 3 per cent of the number from that country already living in the US in 1910; this stopped people from eastern European countries because there were fewer of them living in the US. In 1924, the National Origins Act reduced the quota to 2 per cent of the population in 1890. In 1929, the number of immigrants each year was reduced to 150,000, and immigration from Asia was stopped altogether. Isolationism had this result because isolationists wanted to keep America for the 'WASPS' (white Anglo-Saxon Protestants). Americans also feared that new immigrants would take their jobs – or, worse still, that they might be communists.

States the second result. Supports this idea with facts. EXPLAINS HOW this situation was a result of isolationism.

Summary of other results.

Isolationism also had other consequences. Economically, it led to a tariff policy to try to keep foreign goods out of the US economy (the Fordney-McCumber Act established the highest tariffs in history, with an average duty of 40%, and duties on some items up to 400%). Also, isolationism helped to create a 'Red Scare' – after a number of bombs were planted by Italian communists and anarchists, thousands of people were arrested in the 'Palmer Raids', and any that were found to be immigrants were deported.

Briefly summarises all the other results you know. Supports these ideas with facts and brief explanations. To improve your answer, you might want to explain a third result in depth.

How useful is Source S for studying the reasons why Prohibition was introduced in the USA in 1919?

Use Source S and your own knowledge to explain your answer.   (8 marks)

Comments

Briefly describe the source and its content.

Source S is a poster published by the Anti-Saloon League in 1910. It portrays a drinker's children as poor abandoned waifs. They lack not only clothes and food but also their father's love.

This gets you started.

When I look at the content of the source, I see that it would be useful for a historian collecting evidence of what Americans thought about alcohol in the years before Prohibition. I know that at this time many Americans were complaining about the damage that alcohol did to homes and families, and that many states had therefore introduced prohibition by 1917.

Compare the source's content in detail to the historical facts to assess whether the source is useful.

It is also useful to a historian researching Prohibitionist propaganda. This cartoon really 'pulls the heart strings' by showing two little children longing to see their father. I know of other Prohibitionist sources from this time which similarly claimed that alcohol 'inflicts disease and untimely death upon hundreds and thousands of citizens, and leads to their children being born handicapped'. This poster gives further evidence that prohibition campaigners tried to appeal to people's emotions.

Use the CONTENT of the source and your own knowledge to come up with TWO IDEAS about the source's USEFULNESS.

Examine the source's provenance to find further ways it might be useful.

Looking at the provenance, I see that it is from 1910. Since it is more or less contemporary, the poster gives a useful indication of how people at that time felt. It is from the time leading up to Prohibition, so it is particularly relevant in explaining why people voted as they did in 1919.

Secondly, as this is a prohibition poster, in one way it may be useful because it shows how the Anti-Saloon League presented its case. However, a historian might question its usefulness because of course it is very one-sided; it only shows what Prohibitionists felt about alcohol. This is particularly important because, in fact, I know that most Americans did not agree with Prohibition, and from 1919 to 1933 they made moonshine and went to speakeasies to get alcohol.

Use the PROVENANCE of the source and your own knowledge to come up with TWO MORE IDEAS about the source's usefulness.

Conclusion summarises the usefulness of the source.

This source is of some use to a historian because it could be used as evidence of attitudes towards alcohol in pre-Prohibition America. But a historian would have to remember that it is biased – it does not represent the feelings of all Americans.

However, it was written as a direct appeal to the public, and was designed to attract other Americans to support Prohibition, so it is a very useful indication of the feelings and intentions of the Prohibitionists in the years leading up to the 18th Amendment in 1919.

Notice how the conclusion explicitly refers to the PURPOSE of the source.

20th Century Depth Studies – Section B

Unit 2B in the AQA History Specification B GCSE lists seven different 20th century topics:

1. Stalin's Dictatorship: USSR, 1924–1941
2. Hitler's Germany, 1929–1939
3. Depression and the New Deal: The USA, 1929–1941
4. Race Relations in the USA, 1955–1968
5. The USA and Vietnam: Failure Abroad and at Home, 1964–1975
6. Britain: The Challenge in Northern Ireland, 1960–1986
7. The Middle East, 1956–1979

Your teacher will be asking you to undertake a Depth Study of two topics from this list.

This unit provides a wonderful opportunity to study in depth two fascinating topics in the history of the twentieth century – from the horrors of Hitler to the marvels of Martin Luther King.

There are seven questions in section B of Paper Two – one for each topic. You must answer two of the questions. Each answer is worth 20 marks. Each question has two parts:

1. A 'Describe' question (8 marks)

Each unit identifies a number of important developments. The first part of a Paper 2B question asks you simply to describe one of these developments. You will be asked to write about something quite 'big' in scope (bigger, for example, than the single event you are asked to describe in a Paper 1 question). The 'Grade Studio' section at the end of each chapter lists the kinds of developments you will be asked to describe. However, do not be alarmed by the big scope of the developments. This part of the question is simply asking you to 'tell the story' – you are not required to give any kind of in-depth 'explanation'.

You MUST learn about these developments. The 'Describe' part of the question is worth 8 marks, or 40 per cent of the whole question.

2. An 'Analysis and explanation' question (12 marks)

For the second part of a Paper 2B question, you have to 'debate' an issue. The question puts forward a provocative statement and then asks you whether you agree or disagree with the statement. This is *real* history. You have to show that you are able to debate the ins and outs of a historical issue.

It is vital that you fully understand the historical topics you are studying. Therefore the first thing you should do is read through each chapter you are studying from beginning to end in one go. If you do, you'll get an overview of how events developed through time. As you read, you will notice that useful 'Summary' boxes list the main points you need to make when debating some of the important issues.

On the other hand, you will find very few sources in this unit. There are no sourcework questions to prepare for on this section of the paper.

The key to improving your answer in an 'Analysis and explanation' question is to argue (or explain) your case well. The basis of your explanation will be the 'whys' and 'hows' of the issue. Two sections in the Grade Studio give you practice in considering some of these 'whys' and 'hows'.

Now let's examine in more detail how to approach each kind of question.

2.4 Stalin's Dictatorship: USSR, 1924–1941

2.4a To what extent had Stalin become a personal dictator in communist Russia by the end of the 1920s?

Background

In November 1917, the Bolsheviks seized power in Russia after a brief military takeover. The Bolsheviks' **vozhd** (leader) was Lenin.

The Bolsheviks believed that true Communist Revolution could only be achieved by the industrial working class (the proletariat), but 85 per cent of the people of Russia were at this time rural peasants. Lenin's idea was that the Bolsheviks would have to rule FOR the people, until the people were industrialised and educated in communism.

So Lenin ruled by decree as dictator of Russia. His two right-hand men – the only two people allowed to see him without an appointment – were Leon Trotsky and Joseph Stalin.

Trotsky and Stalin

Trotsky and Stalin disliked each other. Stalin complained about Trotsky's conduct of the civil war; Trotsky complained about Stalin's excesses in Georgia (Stalin had executed a number of White Russian officers).

Trotsky and Stalin particularly disagreed about which direction the revolution ought to take after 1917. Trotsky advocated 'permanent revolution'; there were communists all over Europe, he argued, and they ought to be encouraged to rebel and set up communist governments too. Stalin's opinion was known as 'socialism in one country'; he argued that the revolution would be best protected by making Russia strong.

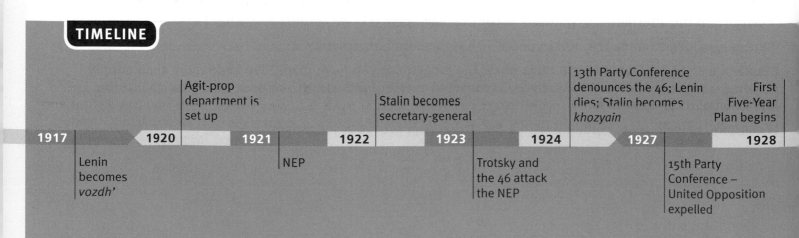

TIMELINE

1917	1920	1921	1922	1923	1924	1927	1928

Agit-prop department is set up (1920–1921)

Stalin becomes secretary-general (1922)

13th Party Conference denounces the 46; Lenin dies; Stalin becomes *khozyain* (1924)

First Five-Year Plan begins (1928)

Lenin becomes *vozdh'* (1917)

NEP (1921)

Trotsky and the 46 attack the NEP (1923)

15th Party Conference – United Opposition expelled (1927)

Lenin's *Testament*

By March 1923, after three strokes, Lenin was bed-ridden and so weak that his doctors ordered him to stay calm. With Lenin ill and dying, power passed to the **Politburo** (the group of **Commissars** who ran the government's day-to-day business):

- Trotsky
- Stalin
- Kamenev (chairman of the Moscow Soviet)
- Zinoviev (president of the Petrograd Soviet)
- Tomsky (leader of the Trade Unions)
- Rykov (chairman of the Council of National Economy)
- Bukharin (President of the Communist International).

The Politburo decided that – to reduce the pressure on Lenin – Stalin should be the only person allowed to see him. Rather than helping Stalin's career, this almost ended it. Lenin came to hate this man who would not allow him to run the government, and when Stalin had a disagreement with Lenin's wife, Lenin wrote a *Political Testament* saying that Stalin was too rude, would abuse his power, and should be removed from his post.

The initial concern of the Politburo, however, was not Stalin, but Trotsky. Kamenev and Zinoviev especially did NOT want Trotsky to take power. So they formed an alliance (called the *troika*) with Stalin.

Stalin is sometimes presented as an unremarkable and dull man, but this is far from the truth. He was a brilliant politician and organiser. He had been editor of *Pravda* (the Bolshevik newspaper).

In 1917 he was made Commissar for Nationalities. He believed that his job was to destroy the different nationalities (he was particularly brutal in Georgia). In 1922 Lenin made Stalin also secretary-general – a role for which he was mocked as 'Comrade Card-index'. Stalin was well-liked; he was cheerful and friendly.

Leon Trotsky was the man who organised the Bolshevik Revolution and who ran the Red Army; it was Trotsky who organised the 'Red Terror' against the opponents of the Revolution during the civil wars. In 1917 he was made Commissar for Foreign Affairs. Trotsky was a brilliant man, but he was unpopular – he had become a member of the Bolshevik Party only in 1917, and he was arrogant and aloof.

Joseph Stalin

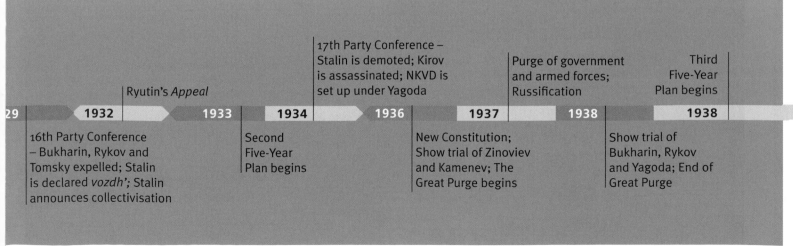

29	**1932**	Ryutin's *Appeal*	**1933**	**1934**	**1936**	**1937**	**1938**	**1938**

17th Party Conference – Stalin is demoted; Kirov is assassinated; NKVD is set up under Yagoda

Purge of government and armed forces; Russification

Third Five-Year Plan begins

16th Party Conference – Bukharin, Rykov and Tomsky expelled; Stalin is declared *vozdh'*; Stalin announces collectivisation

Second Five-Year Plan begins

New Constitution; Show trial of Zinoviev and Kamenev; The Great Purge begins

Show trial of Bukharin, Rykov and Yagoda; End of Great Purge

Getting rid of rivals

1. Trotsky

Trotsky was the first person to try to stop Stalin's rise to power. In May 1924, he forced the Politburo to consider Lenin's *Testament*. It was a tense discussion, which could have seen Stalin dismissed, but Stalin was saved by Zinoviev and Kamenev.

Instead, the conflict ended Trotsky's political power. In 1925, he was forced to resign as Commissar for War. He was expelled from the Politburo in 1926, and in 1928 the OGPU took him to a prison camp in Siberia. He was exiled in 1929 and assassinated on Stalin's orders by a Soviet agent in 1940.

2. Zinoviev and Kamenev

Having got rid of Trotsky, Stalin next plotted to get rid of Zinoviev and Kamenev (who had supported him against Trotsky). He removed their supporters from key positions in the Moscow and Leningrad Parties and replaced them with his own supporters.

For the next three years, 1925–1928, there was furious argument. Zinoviev and Kamenev attacked the New Economic Policy and accused Stalin of trying to become sole ruler. Joining them, Trotsky accused him of being the 'gravedigger of the revolution'. The alliance of these three became known as the 'United Opposition'.

However, Stalin was supported by Bukharin, Rykov and Tomsky. He denounced Zinoviev and Kamenev as 'factionalists', and when Trotsky tried to bring up Lenin's *Testament* again, Stalin retorted: 'Yes I am rough, comrades, in regard to those who are roughly and disloyally ruining and splitting the Party'. At the 15th Party Conference in 1927, Trotsky, Zinoviev, Kamenev and more than 1500 of their supporters were expelled from the Party.

After 1928, nobody in Russia used the word 'opposition' again. Nobody dared to admit that they opposed Stalin, and Stalin refused to admit that there was any opposition to his ideas.

3. Bukharin, Rykov and Tomsky

In 1928 Stalin moved against Bukharin, Rykov and Tomsky – the three 'rightists' who had supported him against Zinoviev and Kamenev.

Stalin announced a forced requisition of grain from the peasants and declared that the peasant farms would be **collectivised** (see page 184). Bukharin, Rykov and Tomsky realised, correctly, that this was a move to replace the NEP with the 'modernisation-by-force' of War Communism. However, when they tried to stop it, the 'rightists' found themselves denounced as 'factionalists' and 'deviationists'. At the 16th Party Conference in November 1929, they publicly admitted their guilt and were demoted.

The politburo of the Soviet Union at the end of 1930 (after the Removal of Rykov). By this time, none of the original members of the Politburo survived. Stalin is in the middle, Kirov on the far right.

2.4b How did Stalin reinforce his dictatorship in the 1930s?

Becoming sole ruler

By 1929 Stalin had got rid of his chief rivals in the Politburo. Nobody disagreed with him in public. And on his 50th birthday, in December 1929, he was celebrated as Lenin's successor, the new *vozhd'*.

Yet it is arguable that he was not yet sole ruler of the Soviet Union. Other people, including Kirov, the Leningrad Party leader, were powerful and popular. And there were still people in the Soviet Union who opposed Stalin's policies.

In 1932, Ryutin, an old friend of Bukharin, published *An Appeal to All Bolsheviks*. It called for a return to the New Economic Policy, an end to forced collectivisation and 'the elimination of Stalin'.

Stalin, interpreting this as a call for his assassination, wanted the death penalty, but was stopped by members of the Politburo, notably Kirov. In the end, Ryutin was merely expelled.

At the 17th Party Congress in 1934, more discontent with Stalin surfaced. Some delegates asked Kirov to take over as general secretary. When he refused, the Congress abolished the position of general secretary altogether – effectively reducing Stalin to the same level as the other three secretaries. In the ballot, Kirov gained 300 more votes than Stalin.

The Kirov affair

In December 1934 Kirov was shot. Many people suspected Stalin, but there is little proof. Instead, Stalin set up the **NKVD** (a strong secret police, which included the old OGPU) and appointed the ruthless Genrikh Yagoda as its head. When Yagoda's agents investigated Kirov's death, they claimed to have found evidence of a 'Moscow Centre' led by Zinoviev and Kamenev. In January 1935, Zinoviev, Kamenev and thousands of ordinary Leningrad Party members were arrested and imprisoned.

The Great Purge (sometimes called the Great Terror) had begun.

Engineering workers in Leningrad pass a resolution supporting the trial and execution of Zinoviev, Kamenev, and 14 others for crimes including the murder of Kirov.

SUMMARY

Was Stalin all-powerful by 1929?

YES

1. Had removed all his rivals – Trotsky, then Zinoviev and Kamenev, then Bukharin, Rykov and Tomsky
2. General secretary – appointed the *nomeklatura*
3. Had established himself as the 'heir of Lenin' – very popular with the 'Lenin levy'
4. Could use the OGPU and agitprop
5. Was declared the *vozhd'* in 1929

NO

1. Other leaders were popular (especially Kirov)
2. Opposition within Party – e.g. Ryutin's *Appeal to All Bolsheviks*
3. Trotsky, Zinoviev, Kamenev, Bukharin, Rykov and Tomsky were dismissed but were still alive
4. In 1934 Congress abolished the post of general secretary and demoted Stalin
5. Other people still thought for themselves; Stalin was not yet 'worshipped', as he later came to be
6. Russia was weak agriculturally and industrially

The growth of industry

Russian industry changed and expanded enormously because of the Plans. Old industrial areas were re-developed and expanded, and new ones were created to the east, in the Urals and Siberia, well away from areas most likely to be attacked by enemies, such as Germany.

New towns were built, such as Magnitogorsk in the Urals and Komsomulsk in Siberia. In eight years Magnitogorsk was transformed from a tiny village to a massive industrial city producing steel.

Other achievements included the construction of a hydro-electric dam on the River Dnieper, which by itself produced more electricity than was produced in the whole of Tsarist Russia.

Enthusiastic bands of young 'pioneers' went out to build the new industrial cities with Soviet zeal. The government celebrated the achievements of successful factories and workers – the most famous was the miner Stakhanov, who in 1935 mined 102 tonnes of coal in five hours (40 times his quota). Workers were urged to become '**Stakhanovites**', and those who did so received medals.

A more practical (though un-communist) encouragement was to give scientists, engineers and skilled workers higher wages. The authorities also used terror; workers who were absent would be sacked, and 'idlers' and 'wreckers' could find themselves arrested or shot.

Results of the Five-Year Plans

In all the key industries – coal, iron and steel, oil, electricity – the USSR grew to be a major industrial power strong enough to resist the Nazis when they invaded in 1941:

	1928	1937
Coal (million tonnes)	35	128
Steel (million tonnes)	4	18
Oil (million tonnes)	12	29
Electricity (000 million kwh)	5	36

At the same time, there was a growth in Soviet science and technology.

The words on this Soviet poster read: 'We strike down lazy workers'.

The human cost of this achievement, however, was high.

Much of the workforce consisted of forced labour from the gulags or peasants driven off the land by collectivisation. Working conditions were harsh and dangerous, and literally millions of workers died as a result of accidents, starvation or cold. In the towns and cities, which were unable to cope with the mass influx of new workers from the countryside, slums and poor sanitation flourished.

The Five-Year Plans supplied production goods, but not consumer goods. There wasn't enough food, and rationing was common. Working conditions were poor, and hours of work were long. Wages fell. Improvements made by the government – including schools, housing blocks and social insurance schemes – could not meet the level of demand (especially as the *apparatchiki* made sure that they got all the best new housing). Crime and alcoholism increased.

Politically, the Five-Year Plans marked the triumph of Stalin's policy of 'socialism in one country' over the Old Bolshevik idea of 'permanent revolution'. They turned the Soviet Union into a strong state capable of resisting Hitler. At the same time, Stalin used them to destroy the Kulaks, to reduce the numbers of peasants and to increase the proletariat. However, as Trotsky wrote before he was murdered, the Five-Year Plans increased Stalin's control over the USSR, and reduced the proletariat almost to the level of slaves of the state – they gave their labour and their lives, but received little in return.

The propaganda poster below– which looks forward to 'a prosperous and cultural life' – shows Russian women giving their labour to the Revolution. Women in Stalin's Russia were educated and given more opportunities than ever before. Some became doctors and scientists. They played an important part in Russian industrial expansion. Ordinary working women were still expected to look after the household, however.

SUMMARY

Were the Five-Year Plans a success?

YES
1. Increased production – coal/steel/oil/electricity
2. New industrial areas in the Urals and Siberia
3. New towns such as Magnitogorsk
4. Dnieper Dam
5. Enthusiasm – 'pioneers'/Stakhanovites
6. Growth in science and technology

AGAINST
1. Use of terror
2. Forced labour
3. Poor conditions in the new towns
4. Poor working conditions
5. NOT consumer goods – people didn't benefit

A propaganda poster showing the role of women in Stalin's Russia.

Preparation - 'Describe'

- the story of how Stalin destroyed his rivals and came to power
- how Stalin took sole power in the 1930s
- the Terror/the Purges and their effects
- the government of the USSR in the 1920s
- the government of the USSR in the 1930s
- collectivisation
- the Five-Year Plans
- the cult of Stalin and Soviet culture
- the Kulaks and their fate

Using this textbook, an encyclopaedia or the internet, make sure you know enough to write at least TWO detailed descriptions of each item in the list above.

Preparation - names and specialist terms

- Trotsky
- Kamenev
- Zinoviev
- Tomsky
- Rykov
- Bukharin
- Ryutin
- Kirov
- Yagoda
- Yezhov
- Vyshinskii
- Tukchachevskii
- Stakhanov
- proletariat
- 'socialism in one country'
- 'permanent revolution'
- Politburo and the Troika
- Lenin levy
- *Khozyain* and *vozdh*
- the *nomenklatura* and the *apparatchiki*
- the OGPU and NKVD
- agitprop, agit-trains and *agitki*
- *kolkhozi* and Kulaks
- Gosplan and pioneers
- the Yezhovshchina
- the gulag
- Russification

Using this textbook, an encyclopaedia or the internet, make sure you know about each of the above so that you can include them in your exam answers.

Preparation - 'Why?'

WHY...

- was Stalin able to become a dictator?
- did Stalin encourage collectivisation?
- did Stalin want rapid industrialisation?
- did Stalin start the Purges in the 1930s?
- did Stalin eliminate the Kulaks?

Working in a small group, think of TWO reasons for each situation in the list above.

Preparation - 'How?'

HOW did this...	cause this?
• being Party Secretary...	• Stalin's rise to *khozyain*
• Zinoviev and Kamenev...	• Stalin's defeat of Trotsky
• Bukharin, Rykov and Tomsky...	• Stalin's rise to *vozdh'*
• The Ezhovshchina...	• Stalin's rise to sole ruler
• control of culture...	• Stalin's rise to sole ruler
• collectivisation...	• a decline in agricultural production
• the Five-Year Plans...	• industrial growth
• the Five-Year Plans...	• untold suffering
• Terror...	• a 'smiling mask'

Working as a whole class, think of TWO ways in which each factor on the left led to the outcome on the right.

'Stalin had defeated his rivals for power by 1928 mainly because he had been able to use his position as general secretary'. Do you agree? Explain your answer. (12 marks)

Full sample answer

Comments

Defends the null hypothesis.

There is an argument that being general secretary did help Stalin to defeat his rivals for power in a number of ways.

Firstly, as general secretary, Stalin could organise meetings to suit himself – for example, he misinformed Trotsky about the date of Lenin's funeral, so Trotsky missed the funeral (which made him unpopular).

Secondly, as general secretary, he could disadvantage opponents during Party Conferences because he prepared the agendas. He appointed the top 5000 Party officials (the nomenklatura) – and they appointed the 20,000 apparatchiki. He was able to put supporters in important positions. And at the Party Conferences, the delegates (70 per cent of whom were party officials) knew who to vote for! Stalin's opponents were heckled and hissed – but Stalin received cheers and applause.

All this suggests that being general secretary was very important in helping Stalin defeat his rivals.

However, there were many other reasons why Stalin was able to defeat his rivals for power in the 1920s.

Argues that the null hypothesis is not true.

Firstly, Stalin was brilliant at politics. First he used Kamenev and Zinoviev to help him survive when Trotsky tried to use Lenin's Testament to get him dismissed. Then he used Tomsky, Rykov and Bukharin to help him survive the attack of the 'United Opposition' on the NEP in 1925 to 1928. But then, in 1929, he turned on the 'rightists' for supporting the NEP! His opponents united to oppose him, and he could 'pick them off' one at a time.

Secondly, Stalin used dirty tricks. He took advantage of the Russian people's hero-worship of Lenin by writing a short book summarising Lenin's ideas, then organised a mass recruitment campaign (the 'Lenin levy') to flood the Bolshevik Party with his supporters. He also used the OGPU to arrest and imprison his opponents.

All this suggests that factors other than being general secretary were important in Stalin's defea of his rivals.

Reaches a conclusion.

Nevertheless, Stalin's control of the Party as general secretary was probably the main reason he came to power. If he had not been general secretary, he would not have been able to play his politics or do his dirty tricks on his opponents. His policies may have earned him some support, but Stalin switched his support for the NEP on and off, so that cannot have been the main factor. In the end, it was his popularity at the Party Conferences which defeated his rivals – and that came from his position as secretary.

> At least TWO reasons why the null hypothesis IS true. EXPLAIN HOW the null hypothesis is true. Include FACTS.

> Begin the second section with a connective of comparison. At least TWO reasons why the the null hypothesis IS NOT true. EXPLAIN HOW the null hypothesis is not true. Include FACTS.

> Begin the third section with a connective of comparison. EXPLAIN HOW you reached your judgement. Include FACTS.

2.5 Hitler's Germany, 1929–1939

2.5a How and why was Hitler able to become chancellor in January 1933?

Background

In 1924, the Dawes Plan had rescued Germany from the financial crisis of 1923, had spread the load of reparations payments and had poured 800 million gold marks in loans into the Germany economy. For a while, the Weimar Republic had flourished economically and culturally (see pages 144–145).

In October 1929, however, Gustav Stresemann, the most able minister in the government, died. Shortly after, the American financial market, based on Wall Street in New York, crashed. The effects of the collapse were felt across the world. Germany was hit particularly badly because of the scale of its loans from America – American bankers and businessmen demanded repayment and, of course, were not in a position to lend any more money.

The result was a disaster for Germany. Trade ground to a halt and businesses closed down. Germany slumped into a depression.

Most unemployed workers in Germany (apart from those employed directly by the Nazis as

Hitler at a rally in Dortmund

Stormtroopers) voted for the communists, who showed a steady rise in seats in the Reichstag (the German parliament).

The growth in votes for the Nazis, however, was much greater. Support came from lower middle-class professionals and businessmen, who suffered less from the Depression but were worried by the growth of communism.

TIMELINE

1929	1931	1932			1933		
Wall Street Crash	Bruning becomes Chancellor	6 million unemployed	June 1932 Bruning resigns – von Papen's government	December 1932 Von Schleicher fails to form a government	January 1933 Hindenburg asks Hitler to form a government	March 1933 Election, followed by the Enabling Act; Dachau concentration camp opened	

April 1932 Presidential elections; Hitler stands against Hindenburg

July 1932 Elections; Nazis become the largest party in the Reichstag

February 1933 Reichstag Fire

July 1933 Law against Parties; Concorda with the Pope

The Weimar government and the Depression

The Depression hit Germany badly. Unemployment rose to six million by 1932. Millions became homeless and set up camps on the outskirts of towns. They became dependent on charity food and soup kitchens.

The government was taken by surprise at the speed and extent of the Depression. It also had no idea how to deal with it. Taxes were falling because people were being thrown out of work. So the only way to increase government expenditure to help the poor would be to print more money – and after 1923 this was an unthinkable idea.

In fact, when he came to power in 1931, the new German chancellor – Heinrich Bruning of the Catholic Centre Party – introduced a series of measures which in fact made things worse. He raised taxes to reduce the shortfall in government revenue, but this caused further problems for the businesses and companies being taxed. He reduced unemployment benefit and also the wages of public officials, but as a result they bought less, demand fell and the Depression got worse.

These policies also caused the collapse of the government, as political parties withdrew from the coalition in protest. It proved impossible to put together another coalition that could form a government. In such a political emergency, the constitution allowed the president to take control of the government. So the 84-year-old German President Hindenburg – who wanted to reduce the power of the Reichstag – started ruling under Article 48 by emergency decree.

The Depression brought out all the weaknesses of the Weimar Republic, which seemed to be incapable of doing anything to end it.

The Nazis and the Depression

Bitterness about the past – the old anger about Versailles and reparations – resurfaced. The German people began to listen to extremist parties who promised to do something – such as the communists and the extreme right-wing nationalist parties.

In particular, support for the Nazi Party grew. The Nazis promised jobs for the unemployed in state-financed public works programmes, help for employers to increase their profits and help for farmers and shop-keepers. They promised that Germany would be great again.

The Nazis were also well organised and disciplined – which appealed to middle class people in a time of chaos. Joseph Goebbels, who was in charge of propaganda, ran a 'Hitler over Germany' campaign, which involved flying Hitler from one mass rally to the next. This was reinforced by a poster campaign, strong in emotional appeal, which portrayed Hitler as a strong leader who would 'save' Germany.

The Nazis were supported financially by wealthy industrialists – such as Fritz von Thyssen, the German steel businessman, Alfred Krupp, the owner of the Krupp steel and armaments firm, and Henry Ford, the American car manufacturer – who saw the Nazis as a way to prevent the growth of communism.

The SA (the thugs Hitler hired to 'protect' the Nazi party) also played a role. By 1933 there were half a million Nazi 'Stormtroopers'. With their motto, 'All opposition must be stamped into the ground', they beat up opponents, especially the communists, mainly in street-fights called *Zusammenstöße* ('clashes')… and then Hitler complained about the violence on the streets and promised that the Nazis would bring proper law and order.

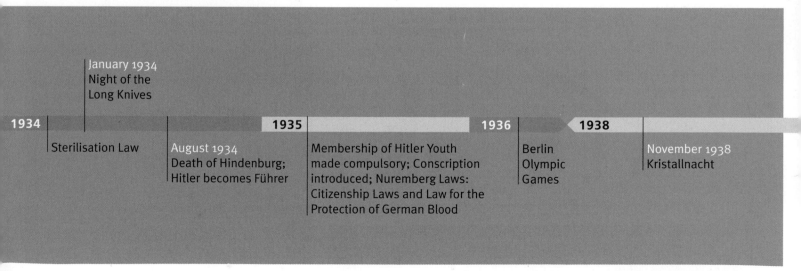

1934 | 1935 | 1936 | 1938

January 1934
Night of the Long Knives

Sterilisation Law

August 1934
Death of Hindenburg;
Hitler becomes Führer

Membership of Hitler Youth made compulsory; Conscription introduced; Nuremberg Laws: Citizenship Laws and Law for the Protection of German Blood

Berlin Olympic Games

November 1938
Kristallnacht

Nazi election gains, 1930–32

Nazi election campaigning was effective. By contrast, the Social Democrats and other moderate parties seemed to have little to offer. In 1930 the Nazis won 107 seats, and in July 1932 this increased to 230 seats. Although this fell to 196 in the November election, the Nazis remained the largest single party in the Reichstag.

In the presidential elections of April 1932 Hitler stood against Hindenburg for the presidency of Germany. Hindenburg won with 19 million votes against Hitler's 13 million. In contrast to their tactics during the Munich Putsch, the Nazis were using the democratic process in an attempt to win power.

Hitler becomes chancellor

In June 1932, Hindenburg forced Bruning to resign. But he refused to make Hitler chancellor despite his electoral success – he disliked the Nazi Party and its leader. Instead, he used his emergency powers to appoint the leader of the smaller Centre Party, Franz von Papen, as chancellor.

However, von Papen's government collapsed when one of Hindenburg's advisers, von Schleicher, told him that the army opposed von Papen and might take action unless he was replaced.

In December 1932, therefore, Hindenburg asked von Schleicher to become chancellor. But von Schleicher failed to get enough support in the Reichstag and resigned after only eight weeks.

Hindenburg and von Papen realised that they needed the support of a major party in the Reichstag – so they decided to risk a coalition with the Nazis. At first they offered Hitler the post of vice-chancellor. Hitler refused.

Finally, on 30 January 1933, Hindenburg asked Hitler to become chancellor. He made von Papen vice chancellor and put von Papen's supporters into the government. In this way Hindenburg and von Papen thought they would be able to control Hitler.

However, they had underestimated Hitler.

The text on this Nazi election poster of 1932 reads: 'Women! Millions of men out of work! Millions of children without a future! Save our German families. Vote for Adolf Hitler.'

SUMMARY

How was Hitler able to become chancellor?

1. Long-standing anger at the Treaty of Versailles
2. Weaknesses of the Weimar government – coalition government collapses; Hindenburg rules by Article 48
3. The Depression created unemployment and despair
4. Nazi organisation and propaganda – 'Hitler over Germany' campaign
5. Support of rich industrialists who feared Communism
6. The SA beat up opponents
7. Nazi promises led to electoral success, which made the Nazis the biggest party in the Reichstag
8. Hindenburg and von Papen OFFERED Hitler the chancellorship, thinking they could control him

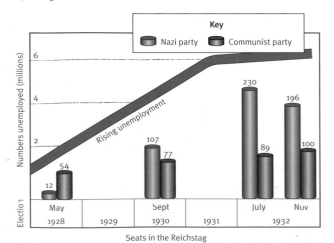

This graph shows growing support for the Nazis, and growing unemployment in Germany, 1928–33.

2.5b How did Hitler change Germany from a democracy to a Nazi dictatorship, 1933–1934?

Establishing a dictatorship

The Reichstag Fire

Having become chancellor, Hitler set about seizing total power.

On 27 February 1933, the Reichstag building was set on fire. Inside the building a Dutch communist, Marinus van der Lubbe, was found with matches in his pocket. He confessed and was later executed. The crime was so convenient for the Nazis that anti-Nazi groups have claimed ever since that the real culprit was the SA. It is alleged (though far from proven) that Van der Lubbe – who was of limited intelligence – was 'set up'.

Whoever caused the Reichstag fire, Hitler benefited. He claimed that the fire was proof of a communist plot and persuaded President Hindenburg to sign an emergency decree, the Law for the Protection of People and the State. It ended all the freedoms guaranteed in the Constitution and gave the police total control.

The police and the SA arrested communist leaders. communist meetings were broken up, and communist newspapers were closed down. Other political opponents of the Nazis also suffered.

Nazi stormtroopers arresting suspected communists in 1933.

The 1933 election

At the same time, the Nazi propaganda machine encouraged the German people to vote for the Nazis. There were mass rallies, torchlight parades and radio broadcasts.

The election results of March 1933, not unexpectedly, brought victory for the Nazis. More people (44 per cent of voters) voted for them than ever before, and the Party won more seats (288) than ever before. With the support of the Nationalist Party (52 seats), this gave the Nazis a slender majority of the 647 deputies in the Reichstag.

The Enabling Law

Hitler now moved for complete power. On 23 March he introduced an **Enabling Law** which would allow him to make laws without consulting the Reichstag and without the approval of the president.

Because this would change the Constitution of the Republic, it had to be approved by two-thirds of the Reichstag (not just a simple majority).

Great pressure was now put on the other parties. Hitler banned the 81 communist members from taking their seats using the emergency powers under the Law for the Protection of the People and the State. The next largest party in the Reichstag was the Social Democrats. Its members were threatened by the SA. Other deputies gave in to Nazi pressure or failed to turn up. The Enabling Law was passed by 444 votes to 94.

The Enabling Law destroyed the Weimar Constitution. After March 1933, the Reichstag did not meet very often, and then only to hear a speech from Hitler. In November 1933 new 'elections' were held for the Reichstag. The Nazis were the only party allowed to stand.

The removal of opposition

With the powers given to him by the Enabling Law, Hitler now moved against the Nazis' opponents. The communists had already been destroyed. In June 1933 the Social Democrat Party was banned. Other political parties soon followed – in July the Law against the Formation of New Parties ruled that the Nazi Party was the only party allowed in Germany. Germany was now a one-party state.

Trade unions, which tended to be anti-Nazi, were also abolished and their offices destroyed. The leaders of political parties and trade unions were arrested and imprisoned. Many were to die in labour camps.

Hitler put Nazis into important positions in the state and the government. Soon all the ministers were Nazis. Nazi officials were also put in charge of local government. Many judges and civil servants were Nazis or sympathised with the Nazis; those who did not were removed from office. In this way Hitler took complete control of Germany's political, administrative and legal systems.

The Night of the Long Knives

Now that Hitler was in control of Germany, he did not need the SA, which was now a threat to his control.

- It was an undisciplined body, with many of its members no more than thugs. Many – including their leader, Ernst Roehm – were homosexual, which conflicted with the new image of 'respectability' Hitler wanted to create.

- In addition, Roehm's views were more socialist than those of Hitler; he wanted the state to take over the major industries. Hitler had won the support of the leading industrialists and, at this stage, did not want to lose that support.

- Above all, Roehm wanted the SA to control the German army. This alarmed Hitler because it would make Roehm more powerful than he was. Throughout 1933 Hitler had been trying to win the support of the army leaders for the Nazi take-over. Now he had to decide – Roehm and the SA, or the army. He chose the army.

On 30 June 1934 – 'the Night of the Long Knives' – Hitler claimed that the SA was plotting to seize power and ordered the SS to arrest its leaders. Over the next few days, hundreds of SA leaders were shot, including Roehm. At the same time, Hitler also took the opportunity to remove other opponents; for example, von Schleicher, the former Chancellor, was murdered. In July Hitler explained his actions to the Reichstag. It accepted his claim that he had 'saved the nation'.

SUMMARY

How was Hitler able to create a Nazi dictatorship in Germany?

1. The Reichstag Fire gave Hitler the opportunity to pass the Law for the Protection of the State.
2. The General Election of March 1933 gave Hitler a majority in the Reichstag.
3. The Enabling Act of 23 March 1933 gave Hitler the power to make his own laws.
4. The Law against the Formation of New Parties (July 1933) made Germany a one-party state.
5. He also banned the trade unions and filled civil service and the courts with Nazis.
6. The Night of the Long Knives (30 June 1934) destroyed the power of Roehm and the SA.
7. When Hindenburg died, Hitler proclaimed himself Führer; the army swore loyalty to him.

GradeStudio

Describe how Hitler established a dictatorship after 1933.

1933 Became Chancellor	❑
Feb 1933 Reichstag Fire (arrested the communists)	❑
March 1933 Election (Enabling Law)	❑
June–July 1933 Other parties/ trade unions banned	❑
SS/Gestapo concentration camps	❑
1934 Night of Long Knives (i.e. Nazi opponents)	❑
August 1934 Hindenburg died, Hitler Führer	❑

The Death of Hindenburg

Now President Hindenburg was the only person with more authority than Hitler. On 2 August 1934, he died at the age of 87. Hitler immediately declared himself president as well as chancellor and took the new title of 'Führer and Reich Chancellor'. On the same day the German army swore an oath of personal loyalty to Hitler. The army, the only force with the power to oppose and remove Hitler, had promised to support him.

The one-party state

The SS (*Schutz-Staffel*) started as a small private bodyguard for Hitler. By 1934 it was a 50,000-strong terror organisation, led by Heinrich Himmler and totally devoted to Hitler. It could search houses, confiscate property and send people to concentration camps without a trial. The camps were run by a branch of the SS called the Death Head Units.

The Gestapo (the state secret police) had authority to spy on people, read their mail and tap their telephones. Gestapo agents pretending to be rebels would visit people suspected of being disloyal to the government, trying to trick them into incriminating themselves and their friends.

Some historians have suggested that Hitler was a 'weak dictator' – that he only *looked* all-powerful; in reality the Nazi government was chaotic. When war broke out, opposition groups such as the 'Edelweiss Pirates' and a student organisation called the 'White Rose' movement sprang up. Before 1939, though, there was very little open opposition or even underground resistance, and what did exist was soon destroyed. The SS and the Gestapo terrified most Germans.

The concentration camps

After 1933 the Nazis established **concentration camps**, initially to detain political prisoners. Six large concentration camps were built: Dachau, Sachsenhausen, Buchenwald, Flossenbürg, Mauthausen and Ravensbrück. At first, the camps

Political prisoners with red triangles at Sachsenhausen concentration camp, 1938.

Dachau concentration camp, near Munich, in 1930.

were austere rather than brutal, but by 1939 they had become places where prisoners were tortured and murdered.

After 1939, under the pressure of war, prisoners were used as slave labour to help the war effort. As one prisoner later wrote, 'death took place daily'. During the war, some of these camps became extermination camps.

The police were controlled by the SS, and all judges were re-appointed after taking an oath of loyalty to Hitler. The courts were, therefore, used for political as well as criminal cases.

Propaganda

Joseph Goebbels was Minister for Propaganda and National Enlightenment. He used all the resources of the state to carry out his task.

- Newspapers printed only stories that were favourable to the Nazis; newspaper editors were even told what the headlines should be. (Newspapers that did not support the Nazis were closed down – over 1,500 were closed by 1934.)

- The Nazis also used radio to send the Nazi message to mass audiences. Goebbels took control of all the local radio stations. Cheap radio sets called 'People's Receivers' were produced so that every German household could afford one. They were made so that foreign stations could not be picked up; the only view of the world people received was the Nazi one. Loudspeaker pillars were set up in public places so that people could hear the radio wherever they were.

- The Nazis also used cinema in their propaganda campaign. The German film industry made over a hundred films a year, all closely censored to reflect Nazi principles. Special films carrying the Nazi message were made for the young. A typical programme at the cinema would also include newsreels and documentaries with a Nazi slant.

The Nazis also used the 1936 Olympic Games in Berlin as a massive propaganda event to demonstrate the superiority of the Aryan race. When the black American athlete Jesse Owens won four gold medals, however, some of the Nazi celebrations were dampened.

After 1933 Nazi rallies became even more spectacular. The most famous was the Nuremberg rally held every year for a week in August. There were army parades, gymnastic displays, bands and choirs, firework displays, fly-pasts by the airforce… and set-piece speeches by Hitler. 'Love for the Führer' reached fever pitch in the mid-1930s, and Hitler was mobbed by screaming girls much like a modern pop-star.

Suspicion and distrust

The Nazis encouraged a climate where nobody ever criticised the government or Hitler. Each block of flats had a 'staircase ruler' who reported grumblers to the police. Children were encouraged to report their parents to their teacher if they said anything against the state. People were taken into mental hospital for re-education merely for saying that business was bad.

German people learned to 'speak through a flower' – always saying nice, positive things whatever their private thoughts were.

Hitler at the Nuremberg rally in 1936

The Church

Hitler tried to get the churches to encourage their congregations to support the Nazis. At first Hitler tried to reach agreement with the churches – in 1933 a Concordat was signed with the Catholics by which the Church promised to keep out of politics and, in turn, the Nazis would not interfere with the Church.

A harder line was taken against Protestant churches. They were brought together in one Reich Church – a Nazi-dominated Church. Ministers who opposed this, such as Martin Niemoller and Paul Schneider, were arrested and put in concentration camps.

Education

Hitler wanted to create a 'Thousand-Year Reich'. He therefore began a programme of **indoctrination** of young people. This could be done by controlling the education system.

Teachers had to belong to the German Teachers' League, a Nazi organisation, and were forced to teach Nazi principles. Any teachers who refused were dismissed.

The teaching of school subjects was controlled in order to indoctrinate Nazi beliefs.

- In history, children were taught that the Weimar Republic had betrayed Germany.

- Biology was used to explain Nazi ideas on race – that Germans were the 'master' Aryan race and that others were inferior. Nazi schoolteachers would bring Jewish childen to the front of the class to point out (and mock) their 'racial features'.

- Maths questions asked pupils to calculate the fuel needed to drop a bomb on the Jews of Warsaw, or to work out how much it cost to feed mentally ill patients in Germany's hospitals.

- Physical education was stressed and given extra time in the timetable. The Nazis considered it more important to have fit and healthy young people than to learn 'dead facts' in the classroom and academic standards were relaxed in favour of physical fitness.

Able boys aged from 12 to 18 might be sent to one of the ten special *Reichsführer* schools. The best pupils from here were then sent for three further years to the *Ordensburgen*, which were in effect elite military training academies, after which they were expected to become leaders in the SS or the army.

Hitler wanted German men to be 'violent, masterful, fearless and cruel...indifferent to pain, without weakness and tenderness'.

By contrast, German girls were taught how to book, clean and sew, so that they might grow up to be good mothers. They were also taught eugenics (the science of selective breeding), so that they might be able to look out for the perfect genetic husband.

PERIODS	Monday	Tuesday	Wednesday	Thursday	Friday	Saturday
1. 8:00–8:45	German	German	German	German	German	German
2. 8:50–9:35	Geography	History	Singing	Geography	History	Singing
3. 9:40–10:25	Race Study	Race Study	Race Study	Race Study	Party Beliefs	Party Beliefs
4. 10:25–11:00	Break – with sports and special announcements					
5. 11:00–12:05	Domestic Science with Mathematics – Every day					
6. 12:10–12:55	The science of breeding (Eugenics) – Health Biology					
	2:00–6:00 Sport each day					

A 1935 timetable for a girls' school in Nazi Germany. A girl's education was a preparation for the role of wife and mother.

Hitler Youth

Another way Hitler appealed to young people was through a movement called the Hitler Youth (*Hitler Jugend or HJ*), which was organised and run by members of the SS. Its aim was to indoctrinate young people into accepting Nazi ideas, to train them for future service in the armed forces, and to ensure that they were loyal and obedient to Hitler. After 1933 other youth organisations were forced to shut down, and by 1935 it was compulsory to join the HJ. By 1939 eight million young Germans belonged to the movement.

A parallel movement for girls – the League of German Maidens (*Bund Deutscher Mädel* or BDM) – prepared them to be good mothers and child-bearers.

Young people enjoyed the HJ. They wore smart uniforms and paraded through their towns. They took part in a range of leisure activities, such as sport, gymnastics, walking and weekend camps.

Older members were trained to use rifles. Every young person had a 'performance book' in which the marks gained in these activities were recorded. Those with the best marks were sent to special schools – the Adolf Hitler Schools – where they were trained to be the future leaders of Germany.

GradeStudio

Describe how Hitler imposed Nazi ideals on German people.

1933 Concordat with Catholic Church ❏

Propaganda (newspapers/radio/films/rallies) ❏

Control of education/Hitler Youth ❏

Economic success (SdA, KdF) ❏

Terror (SS/Gestapo/concentration camps) ❏

Members of the Hitler Youth on parade outside a town hall.

2.5c To what extent did Germans benefit from Nazi rule in the 1930s?

Economic policy

When Hitler came to power in 1933, Germany was still in economic depression. Five million Germans were out of work. Hitler was now expected to make good his promise to end the Depression.

Hjalmar Schacht was minister of the economy, 1934–37. His 'New Plan' for Germany aimed to reduce unemployment, build up the armaments industry and make Germany self-sufficient.

A National Labour Service was set up for young men aged 18 to 25. They did jobs such as digging ditches and planting forests. They wore uniforms and lived in camps and were given pocket money rather than wages. These schemes were then extended to ambitious public works programmes – building new *Autobahns* (motorways), hospitals, schools, sports stadiums and other public buildings. These schemes created thousands of jobs.

The greatest fall in unemployment was brought about by re-armament. In 1935 Hitler ignored the Treaty of Versailles and introduced compulsory military service (conscription); the army alone increased by over one million men between 1935 and 1938. An armaments industry grew up to make the weapons and equipment needed to support this rearmament – this also employed thousands of men.

Other Nazi policies reduced unemployment. Women were forced out of work to look after their homes and families. Jews were dismissed from their jobs. The increasing numbers of people being sent to concentration camps made available the jobs they had vacated.

Unemployment in Germany fell. By 1939 there was no unemployment – the Nazis were even declaring that there was a shortage of labour.

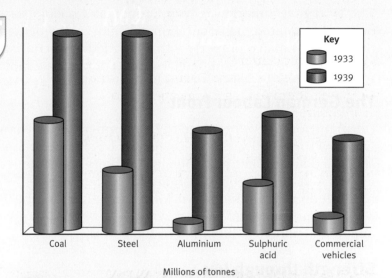

German industrial growth under the Nazis.

However, Nazi public spending created inflation and 'over-heated' the economy – some historians suggest that Hitler HAD to go to war in 1939 to stop the economy going into crisis.

Self-sufficiency

Hitler wanted Germany to be **self-sufficient** – to be able to produce all its own food and raw materials. This policy was called '**autarky**'. In 1936 a Four-Year Plan was drawn up to make Germany self-sufficient. More raw materials, such as coal, oil and iron were produced, and synthetic (artificial) raw materials, such as rubber, fuel and textiles, were developed.

Despite massive state investment in industry, however, in 1939 more than a third of Germany's raw materials were still being imported from other countries. Instead, the Nazis decided to take over countries with the raw materials and food it needed – the policy of finding Lebensraum (living space). Nazi economic policy and foreign policy began to overlap.

Nazi social policy

The Nazis restored Germany's honour and pride. There was more optimism and self-confidence. However, the price was heavy. The German people lived in a police state where their whole lives were controlled by the Nazis – their education, their religion, their work, even their leisure time. It is difficult to judge exactly what the German people thought about Nazi rule. On balance, it would seem that most Germans were happy to accept Nazi rule in the 1930s.

The Nazi government was very 'proper' and middle class in its outlook. It treated the population as children and demanded that people behave properly – this is called '**paternalism**', because the government behaves like a demanding father.

The German Labour Front

German workers were forced to be members of the German Labour Front (DAF), run by Dr Robert Ley. Trade unions were abolished and strikes made illegal. Workers could not leave a job without permission or bargain for higher wages. There was no limit on the number of working hours. Instead, the 'Beauty of Work' movement (*Schönheit der Arbeit*, or SdA) was set up to encourage people to be proud of their work.

Strength through Joy

The Nazis also tried to control people's leisure time. A branch of the German Labour Front, called 'Strength through Joy' (*Kraft durch Freude*, or KdF), organised people's leisure activities so that free time was not 'wasted'. Cheap holidays were arranged, including foreign travel and Mediterranean cruises – these 'rewards' were an incentive to work hard. The KdF was also involved in the plan to manufacture a car cheap enough for workers to buy. This was the Volkswagen ('people's car'). Workers could pay for it on a hire purchase scheme into which they paid weekly sums in advance. Actually, very few German workers managed to buy a Volkswagen and the whole scheme was a failure.

The government's social welfare programmes (such as KdF) were advanced for their time. The Hitler Youth and the BDM were set up to provide children with 'wholesome' pursuits. Heavy drinking was discouraged – drunkards were humiliated by having their heads shaved, and alcoholics were sent to concentration camps.

The Nazis took care of people's health – the Nazi government was the first in the world to realise that smoking caused cancer and the first to introduce regular screening of women for breast cancer.

The government also introduced a Reich Nature Protection Act (1935) to protect the environment and encourage tree-planting. One of its first laws was an act to prevent cruelty to animals.

SUMMARY

Were Nazi economic policies successful?

YES

1. Unemployment ended
2. *Autobahns* – road transport system
3. Motivated workforce (SdA/KdF)
4. New inventions (e.g. synthetic oil, rubber, cloth)

NO

1. Full employment achieved by rearmament and persecution of Jews/women
2. Repression of trade unions/control by RAD
3. Self-sufficiency not achieved
4. Public works spending brought the economy to the brink of collapse in 1939

Built as part of the SdA programme, Prora holiday camp, on the Baltic Sea, had 10,000 identical rooms. It was a place where German workers would go for 'true relaxation' – by which Hitler meant a diet of sun, sport and Nazi propaganda.

Culture

All German culture was controlled by the Nazis. Goebbels formed the Reich Chamber of Culture. Musicians, actors, writers and artists had to be members of the Chamber before they could work or perform. Membership depended on supporting the Nazis. Many could not accept this requirement and left Germany.

Music had to be German. German composers, such as Wagner, Beethoven and Mozart (an Austrian) were in favour. German folk songs and marching music were also encouraged. Nazi architecture was neoclassical (based on Roman architecture). German art was encouraged to be realistic and heroic, and to celebrate the family and the values of 'decency'; modern art was dismissed as 'degenerate'. Unlike in Weimar Germany, homosexuality was condemned; homosexuals were sent to concentration camps.

Books written by Jews or by authors opposed to the Nazis were banned. In 1933 students were encouraged to burn huge piles of banned books looted from libraries. The work of Jewish composers was banned – as was jazz, because it was black American music. The theatre and the cinema were censored in the same way.

Women

In the new Nazi order, women were limited to the 'three Cs' – Church, Cooker, Children.

The Nazis were worried about the declining birth rate in Germany, so they encouraged marriage through the Law for the Encouragement of Marriage (1933). This granted newly married couples a loan of 1000 marks. To encourage married couples to have children they allowed them to keep 250 marks for each child they had.

Mothercraft classes were introduced. Homes for unmarried mothers were set up to allow unmarried women to become pregnant, often by a 'racially pure' member of the SS. These measures worked. The birth rate rose throughout the 1930s.

A woman was also encouraged to stay at home to look after her husband and children, and many female teachers, civil servants and doctors were dismissed from their jobs. Women were given advice on what to cook and were even advised on how to appear: no make-up and hair arranged in a bun or plaits. Slimming was discouraged because it was not good for childbearing.

This Nazi poster celebrates the ideal Nazi family. The text reads, 'The Nazi Party protects the people's community. Race-comrades – for help and assistance, turn to the Regional Organisation'.

SUMMARY

Did the German people benefit from Nazi Rule?

YES
1. Full employment
2. *Autobahns* and public buildings
3. KdF activities/Volkswagen
4. HJ and BDM for young people
5. Law and order
6. Pride and hope

NO
1. Loss of personal and political freedom
2. Fear of SS and Gestapo
3. Propaganda and indoctrination
4. Control of workers, culture
5. Women reduced to 'the three Cs'
6. Persecution of Jews, gypsies, disabled and others

The Jews

The Nazis believed that Jews were an inferior race. In their view the inter-marriage of Jews and Germans over the years had weakened the German people. The Jews were also resented for their influence in Germany. Although they formed less than 1 per cent of the German population, Jews were prominent in the professions as lawyers, bankers and doctors. Once in power, the Nazis made life difficult for the Jews.

- In 1933 a boycott of all Jewish shops and businesses was ordered.

- After 1934 Jewish shops had to be marked with a yellow star to identify them.

- Jews were also dismissed from important jobs in the civil service, education and the media. In parks and public transport, they had to sit apart from other Germans.

- In 1935 Hitler passed the Nuremberg Laws. A Citizenship Law stated that Jews were no longer German citizens; as a result, they could not be employed in any public position and were not protected by the law.

- At the same time, the Law for the Protection of German Blood and Honour banned marriages and sexual relations between Jews and non-Jews.

In November 1938 a Jew shot dead a Nazi official in Paris. Hitler ordered the SS to begin a campaign of terror against the Jews which became known as *Kristallnacht* (the Night of Broken Glass). Jewish shops, synagogues and homes were destroyed. Thousands of Jews were arrested, and nearly a hundred were killed. This was followed by a collective fine on the Jews of one billion marks. Jews were publicly humiliated by being forced to clean the streets or mend the roads.

Kristallnacht was followed by the mass arrest of Jews at the beginning of March 1939; within weeks, 30,000 Jews had been sent to concentration camps.

Nazi stormtroopers oversee the arrest and internment of German Jews after Kristallnacht.

Genocide

The Second World War brought the Nazi treatment of the Jews to its terrible conclusion. Hitler – who blamed the Jews for starting the war – began implementing his 'Final Solution'.

At first, SS units called *Einsatzgruppen* tried shooting the Jews; but the process was slow and distressing for the troops. Eventually, the Nazis decided to build 'extermination camps' such as those at Auschwitz, Treblinka and Sobibor with their aim of the total extermination of the Jewish people.

Genocide is the attempt to destroy a whole race of people, and the Nazi state was organised as efficiently as possible to exterminate the Jews. The Ministry of the Interior supplied birth records so that Jews could be identified. The Finance Ministry confiscated their property. Transport offices organised trains to take them to the camps.

Arriving at the camp, their possessions were collected and sorted, to be used for the war effort. Healthy prisoners were sent for forced labour until they fell too sick to work. Nazi doctors such as Dr Josef Mengele used some Jews for medical experiments. The old, the sick, pregnant women and children were told they were to be deloused and were sent straight to the gas chambers.

Six million Jews died in the Nazi Holocaust.

Other groups

Not only the Jews were persecuted by the Nazis. Anyone who did not fit into the ideal of an Aryan 'master race' was persecuted.

Gypsies did not look like Aryans, and because they were homeless and tended not to have permanent jobs, they were not 'socially useful'.

Black people were seen as another 'inferior race' and were a target of persecution, even though there were relatively few of them in Germany.

Others who suffered because they were not 'socially useful' included tramps and beggars, alcoholics, homosexuals, the mentally and physically disabled and political prisoners (see page 195). Many of them were sent to concentration camps.

Other measures were also taken. In 1934 the Nazis passed a Sterilisation Law. This allowed the sterilisation of people with certain illnesses, especially mental illness. The law was extended to other groups. From 1939 until 1941 – when the Catholic Bishop, Clemens von Galen, denounced the practice and had it stopped – the Nazis had a euthanasia programme for what they called 'life unworthy of life' (such as babies born 'mentally retarded' or 'deformed').

Hungarian Jews arrive at Auschwitz concentration camp in spring 1945. In the background are the chimneys of the crematoria, in which the bodies of the murdered prisoners were burnt.

GradeStudio

Preparation – 'Describe'

- how the Depression affected Germany
- how the Nazis built their support, 1929–32
- how Hitler became chancellor, 1929–33
- how Hitler established a dictatorship, 1933–34
- the aims and methods of Nazi economic policy

- the Nazi state established in Germany after 1933
- the Nazi regime of 'terror'
- the Nazi idea of 'culture'
- how some Germans benefited from Nazi rule
- how the Nazis persecuted the Jews

Using this textbook, an encyclopaedia or the internet, make sure you know enough to write at least TWO detailed descriptions of each item in the list above.

Preparation – names and specialist terms

- SA
- Article 48
- SS
- Gestapo
- DAF
- SdA
- KdF
- 3 C's

- Enabling Law
- Aryan Race
- *Hitler Jugend*
- BDM
- Auschwitz
- Concordat
- autarky
- Führer

- Social Democrats
- Death Head Units
- Edelweiss Pirates
- White Rose
- *Lebensraum*
- genocide
- *Kristallnacht*
- Bruning

- von Papen
- von Schleicher
- van der Lubbe
- Ernst Roehm
- Josef Mengele
- Clemens von Galen
- Niemoller

Using this textbook, an encyclopaedia or the internet, make sure you know about each of the above so that you can include them in your exam answers.

Preparation – 'Why?'

WHY...

- did Hindenburg ask Hitler to become Chancellor?
- did Nazi electoral success improve after 1930?

- did Hitler destroy the SA?
- did the Nazis persecute the Jews?

Working in a small group, think of TWO reasons for each situation in the list above.

Preparation – 'How?'

HOW did this...	cause this?
Great Depression...	Hitler's rise to chancellor
Fear of communism...	Hitler's rise to chancellor
Reichstag fire...	Hitler's rise to dictator
The Enabling Act...	the death of the Weimar Republic
Nazi propaganda...	Hitler's rise to dictator
Nazi Youth policies...	Hitler's rise to dictator
Nazi terror...	Hitler's rise to dictator
Nazi social policy...	the quality of life in Germany
Nazi propaganda...	Hitler's rise to dictator
the Second World War...	the Holocaust

Working as a whole class, think of TWO ways in which each factor on the left led to the outcome on the right.

'The Nazis' use of threats and violence was the main reason why Hitler became chancellor of Germany in January 1933.' Do you agree? Explain your answer. (12 marks)

Full sample answer

Comments

Defend the null hypothesis.

There is an argument that the use of threats and violence was the main reason Hitler became Chancellor. There were half a million Nazi 'stormtroopers' by 1933 and, with their motto: 'All opposition must be stamped into the ground', they beat up opponents in street-fights called Zusammenstöße ('clashes'). This helped Hitler come to power, because it terrified the Nazis' opponents and prevented them from campaigning.

Secondly, it helped Hitler because – when there was violence on the streets because of his Stormtroopers – Hitler then complained about the violence and promised that the Nazis would bring proper law and order! This then increased his vote amongst the middle class, who were worried that the communists might take over control of the government.

> At least TWO reasons why the null hypothesis IS true. EXPLAIN HOW the null hypothesis is true. Include FACTS.

Argue that the null hypothesis is not true.

However, there were many other more important reasons why Hitler became Chancellor in 1933. There was long-standing anger in Germany at the Treaty of Versailles, and Hitler made himself popular when he promised to destroy it. The Depression also helped Hitler because it created unemployment and despair, which led people to turn to extremist solutions such as those offered by Hitler and the Nazis – the Nazi vote rose in step with the rise in unemployment.

Also important was Nazi organisation and propaganda, and Josef Goebbels' brilliant 'Hitler over Germany' election campaigns – if the Nazis had not won so many seats, Hindenburg would not have offered Hitler the position of Chancellor in 1933.

> Begin the second section with a connective of comparison. At least TWO reasons why the the null hypothesis IS NOT true. EXPLAIN HOW the null hypothesis is not true. Include FACTS.

The Nazis could not have done any of this without the financial support of rich industrialists who feared Communism.

Hitler also benefitted directly from the weaknesses of the Weimar government. In 1932, the coalition governments of Bruning, von Papen and von Schleicher all collapsed, leaving Hindenburg ruling by Article 48. And it was this chaos which led Hindenburg and von Papen to offer Hitler the Chancellorship in January 1933, thinking they could control him.

Reach a conclusion.

Therefore, it seems that the use of threats and violence was not the main reason why Hitler became Chancellor; it seems that the SA was only one small reason among many for his success. The strongest argument for this is that Hitler did not take power by violence in 1933 – he did not even win it in an election – but was given power by Hindenburg and von Papen.

> Begin the third section with a connective of comparison. EXPLAIN HOW you reached your judgement. Include FACTS.

2.6 Depression and the New Deal: The USA, 1929–1941

2.5a How serious was the Depression for the American people?

Background

In October 1929 – as you will know if you have studied the USA, 1919–1929 (see pages 154–170) – the price of shares on the US stock market collapsed dramatically. This event was the Wall Street Crash.

The Wall Street Crash need not have caused a depression – barely half a million **speculators** were affected – but it did.

One important factor was timing: the crash happened when there were key weaknesses in the American economy, especially in the 'old industries' (see pages 166–167).

Another factor was the indebtedness of the American economy. Many people had bought shares 'at the margin' – with borrowed money – so when share prices fell, these people simply went bankrupt. Speculators were not just foolhardy

individuals but also major businesses, which reacted by laying off staff and trying to cut costs. So the crash translated into unemployment. In fact, the American boom of the 1920s had been largely based on borrowed money – for example, the buying of goods on hire purchase. When firms began to sack workers, those workers lost their wages and began to default on their repayments.

Therefore it was the banks that were hardest hit by the Wall Street Crash. They had lent money that people were now unable to pay back. Bank after bank went bankrupt. Naturally, the banks reacted by calling in loans, especially loans to foreign countries.

However, world trade had come to depend on American money (from 1924 to 1928, America had lent 6 billion dollars abroad). When this money dried up, world trade plummeted. Global imports fell from $125 billion in 1929 to $35 billion in 1933. What had been an American depression became a global depression.

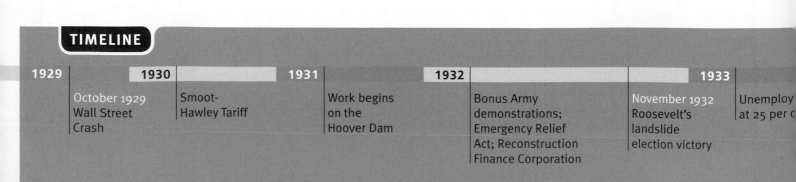

TIMELINE

1929	1930	1931	1932	1933
October 1929 Wall Street Crash	Smoot-Hawley Tariff	Work begins on the Hoover Dam	Bonus Army demonstrations; Emergency Relief Act; Reconstruction Finance Corporation	November 1932 Roosevelt's landslide election victory	Unemploy[ment] at 25 per c[ent]

Import and export

Two factors worsened the slump in world trade.

The first was a 'tariff war'. As their economies collapsed into depression, many countries put high tariffs on imports to protect their home industries. This had the effect of 'freezing out' American firms from their usual export markets and further damaged the American economy.

The second complicating factor was that many countries came off the **gold standard**. The gold standard linked the exchange rate of a country's currency to the amount of gold in that country. This system often kept exchange rates with US dollars unrealistically high (for instance, in 1931, one British pound was worth $4.86). With their economies in crisis, countries now abandoned the gold standard and let their currency fall to its 'natural' value (thus the pound fell to $3.50). This helped non-American economies by making imported goods from the USA more expensive. On the other hand, it damaged American industry, because it made American exports more expensive.

Collapse of business and industry

Many American industries – especially American agriculture – depended on their export trade. When foreign countries stopped importing American goods, it had a disastrous effect on the US economy.

The raw figures show the extent and depth of the Great Depression in the United States.

- US exports fell from $10 billion to $3 billion, 1929–32.
- More than 100,000 businesses shut down; industrial production fell 40 per cent, and one-third of farmers lost their farms.

- Sales in American shops fell 50 per cent.
- Wages fell 60 per cent.
- 10,000 American banks went bankrupt between 1929 and 1933; the worst failure was the Bank of America, in 1931 ruined 400,000 depositors.
- Unemployment soared, from 1.6 million (2.3 per cent of the workforce) in 1929 to 12.1 million (23.6 per cent) in 1932.

SUMMARY

Was the Wall Street Crash the main cause of the Depression in the USA?

YES

1. Loss of confidence
2. 600,000 individuals ruined = reduced spending
3. Companies ruined = workers laid off
4. Banks ruined = run on the banks = banks call in loans = world trade ruined
5. Kick-started a 'cycle of depression'

OTHER CAUSES

1. Underlying weaknesses of American economy – 'old industries'/dependence on borrowing (especially credit schemes, such as hire purchase, buying 'on the margin')
2. Tariff war caused a drop in American exports
3. America stayed on the gold standard, so the exchange rate damaged American exports
4. The 'cycle of depression'

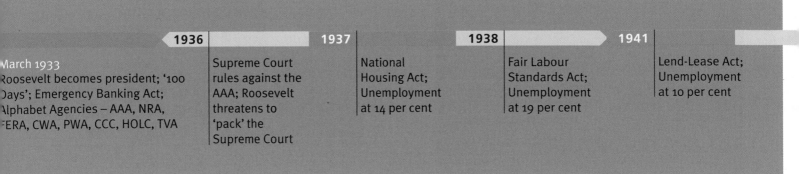

	1936	1937	1938	1941
March 1933 Roosevelt becomes president; '100 Days'; Emergency Banking Act; Alphabet Agencies – AAA, NRA, FERA, CWA, PWA, CCC, HOLC, TVA	Supreme Court rules against the AAA; Roosevelt threatens to 'pack' the Supreme Court	National Housing Act; Unemployment at 14 per cent	Fair Labour Standards Act; Unemployment at 19 per cent	Lend-Lease Act; Unemployment at 10 per cent

Human effects of the Depression

It is important to realise that not everybody suffered during the Depression. Some industries (for example electronics, aviation and the film industry) continued to prosper, and people who had a job and an income actually *benefited* from the lower prices.

Nevertheless, the statistics of the Depression underlie many real-life human tragedies, stories of people thrown into poverty and despair.

Unemployment

By 1933 unemployment reached 25 per cent. In the industrial cities of the north, the rate was even higher as factories and businesses cut down on production or shut down completely. In Chicago, for example, nearly half the labour force was unemployed in 1933. Black people were especially hard hit – in Charleston in 1931, 70 per cent of black people of working age were unemployed. In Memphis the figure was 75 per cent.

Hundreds of thousands of Americans took to the roads and travelled as **hobos** from place to place, trying to find work wherever they could.

An unemployed worker during the Depression.

SUMMARY

How serious were the effects of the Great Depression on Americans, 1929–32?

SERIOUS

1. Fall in exports, production, sales, wages
2. Banks bankrupted = run on banks/ banking crisis
3. Farmers bankrupted = drift to California
4. Unemployment – esp. in the north and among Black communities = hobos and beggars
5. Homelessness = Hoovervilles
6. Charity = soup kitchens and breadlines
7. Bonus Army, riots and demonstrations

NOT SO SERIOUS

8. Not everybody suffered – 'new industries' prospered, and people with steady wages benefited from falling prices

Unemployment in the USA, 1929–33

Unemployed (millions)

Year	Unemployed (millions)	Unemployed as a percentage of the labour force
1929	1.6	2.3%
1930	4.3	8.7%
1931	8.0	15.9%
1932	12.1	23.6%
1933	14.0	24.9%

Homelessness

The Depression made many Americans homeless. When people became unemployed, there were no dole payments to help them. They had to sell their possessions to pay back loans or credit taken out during the good years. If they had mortgage payments they could not meet, their homes were re-possessed. If they fell behind with their rent, they were evicted. In 1932 alone a quarter of a million Americans lost their homes.

The homeless ended up on the streets, sleeping on park benches or in bus shelters. Some deliberately got themselves arrested so that they could spend the night in jail. Many moved to waste ground, where they built shelters from whatever they could find – corrugated iron, scrap metal, old wood. They called these collections of shelters **Hoovervilles** as an insult to the President, Herbert Hoover.

The Bonus Army

At the end of the First World War, the government had promised soldiers that in 1945 they would get a 'bonus' (pension). By 1932, however, many of the war veterans hit by the Depression were asking the government to pay the bonuses up front. In 1932 up to 20,000 veterans went to Washington to protest to the government. They set up a Hooverville opposite the White House.

Although Congress voted against paying the bonuses, the Bonus Army stayed in Washington. Hoover first used the police to contain the veterans. Then he called in the army. Troops, using tanks and tear gas, cleared the Bonus Army out of the camp and set fire to the tents and shelters. Two veterans were killed, and nearly a thousand others were injured. The Bonus Army had been defeated, but President Hoover became even more unpopular.

The Bonus Army shanty town is attacked by the US army, 1932.

Help from charities

The homeless needed help. It did not come from the state – unlike Britain, the USA did not have a social security system which would pay unemployment benefit to the jobless. Some towns and cities set up their own public relief programmes which provided temporary homes, food, clothes and even jobs for the unemployed. Private charities run by bodies like the Salvation Army were also set up. In some cases, wealthy individuals gave help (even the gangster Al Capone provided food in Chicago).

These charities set up soup kitchens, bread kitchens or cheap food centres to feed the hungry. Breadlines, long lines of men and women queuing for free bread and soup, became a common sight in most American towns.

America was in deep depression. Many people ended up begging – one of the most popular songs of the time sums up the mood: 'Buddy, Can You Spare A Dime?'

Farmers

Because of unemployment in the towns, farmers sold less of their produce. Prices of farm produce fell so much that it was not profitable even to harvest crops – wheat was left to rot in the fields and farmers went bankrupt.

Around 1930 another problem hit some farmers – the **dust bowl**. In the states of the South and Midwest, such as Oklahoma and Kansas, farmers had moved from cattle farming to growing crops during the First World War. Crop growing continued in the 1920s, but the land was being over-farmed, and the soil was damaged. Then in the years after 1930 there was drought. Strong winds and low rainfall turned the top soil to dust. The land became like a desert. Thousands of farmers were ruined. They were left with no choice but to abandon their farms and look for work elsewhere. Many drifted to California to work on the fruit farms there.

Limits to the depression

It would be wrong, however, to imagine that 1930s America was comprised only of starving people and closed factories.

The Empire State Building was opened in 1931, the Hoover Dam in 1936 and the Golden Gate Bridge in 1937. 'New industries' – particularly electrical goods – continued to develop. 1938 saw the first sales of 'nylons', non-stick pans and fibreglass. The first television channels were established in 1939. Air travel grew – in 1928, American airlines carried 48,000 passengers; in 1938, they carried more than 1.1 million.

The 1930s also saw the continued development of mass entertainment. Millions of people went to the movies or to lavish stage musicals. Bingo boomed and so did sales of beer – in the newly introduced cans.

Describe how serious the Depression of the 1930s was in America.

October 1929: Wall Street Crash	☐
Bank bankruptcies	☐
Collapse of trade and industry (fall in exports/business bankruptcies/unemployment/fall in wages)	☐
Homelessness/Hoovervilles and Bonus Army	☐
Agriculture (Dust Bowl and drift to California)	☐

SUMMARY

Do you agree that Hoover failed to act against the Depression?

YES

1. Hoover believed in rugged individualism and laissez-faire economics
2. Smoot-Hawley Tariff ruined America's exports
3. Attacked the Bonus Army
4. Just hoped America would 'turn the corner'
5. Blamed by Americans: 'In Hoover we trusted...'

plus Hoovervilles, Hoover blankets, Hoover leather

NO

1. Cut taxes
2. $4 billion for building projects (e.g. Hoover Dam)
3. Emergency Relief Act ($300 million to unemployed)
4. Reconstruction Finance Corp ($1.5 billion loans to businesses)

Hoover and the Depression

The Republican government of Herbert Hoover believed in 'rugged individualism' – that is, people should sort out their own problems.

It is sometimes said, therefore, that Hoover's government did not try to improve the situation, but this claim is not true. In 1930 taxes were cut to increase people's spending power. The government pumped over $4,000 million into the construction industry in a bid to create new jobs; for example, in 1931 work began on the Hoover Dam on the Colorado River. In 1932 an Emergency Relief Act gave $300 million to the states to help the unemployed. Also in 1932 the Reconstruction Finance Corporation provided loans of $1,500 million to businesses. However, these actions were not enough to halt the Depression.

Then, in June 1930, the Hoover government passed the Smoot-Hawley Tariff Act, which raised American tariffs to their highest level ever. It was an attempt to protect American industry, but all it did was trigger a wave of retaliatory tariff increases which destroyed US trade and deepened the Depression.

The 1932 presidential election

Americans blamed Hoover for the Depression. With bitterness, they said: 'In Hoover we trusted, now we are busted.' They talked of 'Hoover leather' (cardboard soles for shoes) and 'Hoover blankets' (newspapers that people slept in). Resentment turned to violence, and marches and demonstrations by unemployed people often turned into riots.

In the 1932 presidential election campaign, Hoover offered only the hope that the USA would soon 'turn the corner' back towards prosperity. By contrast, the Democrat candidate, Franklin D. Roosevelt, offered 'a New Deal for the American people'. Roosevelt promised action to provide jobs and relief for the poor and unemployed, to help industry and agriculture and to resolve the banking crisis.

The American people wanted a positive approach to the Depression, and they voted for Roosevelt. Roosevelt won in 42 of the 48 states – the biggest victory ever in an American presidential election.

A cartoon, dated 3 March 1933, showing President Roosevelt throwing out the policies of the Hoover government, which are shown as rubbish.

2.5b How did Roosevelt deal with the Great Depression?

The New Deal

During the period between the election victory of November 1932 and taking office in March 1933 – the 'lame duck months' when the new administration is not yet in place – Roosevelt worked out the New Deal in greater detail. He adopted the theories of the British economist J.M. Keynes: that the way to end the Depression was to put money in people's pockets. This would increase spending, which would stimulate industry and thereby kick-start a new 'cycle of prosperity'.

The 'Hundred Days'

The New Deal required massive state involvement in the economy and the setting up of government-controlled agencies. Roosevelt was given the authority to do this when Congress granted him 'emergency powers' – the sort of powers he would have had if the USA had been at war.

Roosevelt acted quickly during his first hundred days in office and set up a number of agencies which became known as the 'Alphabet Agencies' because people found it easier to remember them by their initials than by their full names.

Roosevelt also realised the need to explain to the American people what he was doing. They needed to have trust and confidence in his measures and in the recovery of the economy. As he said when he was sworn in as President: 'The only thing we have to fear is fear itself.'

He used the radio to reach a large audience of millions of Americans and to talk directly to them. In his 'fireside chats', in which he sat in a chair by a fire in his office, he explained in simple terms why the USA had fallen into depression and what he proposed to do to end it. The broadcasts were hugely successful – especially the first one, which dealt with the banking crisis.

Ending the banking crisis

During the Depression, people lost confidence in the banks. Many banks had been forced to close when savers withdrew their money and businesses were unable to repay back bank loans.

In March 1933 Roosevelt introduced an Emergency Banking Act. All banks were closed for four days. During that time government officials inspected the accounts of every bank. Only those banks that were properly managed were allowed to re-open – and these were supported by government loans.

When the banks re-opened after the four-day 'holiday', savers kept their accounts open and customers who had withdrawn their money even started to put it back into their accounts. The banking crisis was over.

In June 1933, the Government passed the Glass-Steagall Act, which stopped banks speculating with their customers' money by insisting that 'savings' banks could not also be 'investment' banks. In addition, the Act forbade banks to own other finance companies and gave the US Federal Reserve the right to set interest rates. These rules improved the honesty and stability of the US banking system.

Roosevelt gives one of his 'fireside chats' on the radio in 1935.

Agriculture

In May 1933 Roosevelt set up the Agricultural Adjustment Administration (AAA) to help farmers increase their income. It was controversial because it paid farmers to produce less food, either by ploughing less land or by reducing their livestock. This meant that food prices went up and farmers' income increased. Government subsidies made up for any loss of profit. Government money was also used to help farmers who were having difficulty meeting their mortgage payments. As a result of these measures, farmers' incomes doubled in the period up to 1939. However, the AAA failed to help farm workers. Many were evicted as there was less work for them to do.

Industry

Roosevelt tried to help both sides of industry – employers and workers – through the National Recovery Administration (NRA).

- Employers and businessmen were invited to follow codes fixing fair prices for the goods being sold.
- They also agreed to fair conditions of work – setting the minimum wages to be paid to workers, laying down maximum hours of work and forbidding child labour and cheap 'sweated' labour.
- Businesses that signed the NRA code could advertise using the Blue Eagle emblem with the motto 'We Do Our Part' – Americans were encouraged to buy goods with the Blue Eagle on them.

The scheme was a success. By the end of 1933 two million employers, employing 22 million workers, had agreed to the codes.

Unemployment

A number of agencies were set up to deal with unemployment.

As a start, the Federal Emergency Relief Administration (FERA) was created in 1933 to give quick relief to the hungry and homeless. $500 million was spent on providing soup kitchens and clothing and setting up employment schemes.

The Civil Works Administration (CWA) aimed to provide as many jobs as possible in the short term. During the winter of 1933–34 more than four million jobs were created on projects such as building and improving roads, schools, airports and other public installations. People were paid to sweep up leaves in local parks – even to frighten pigeons away from public buildings. Once the winter of 1933–34 was over, the CWA ended – and so did the four million jobs it created.

In the meantime, the Public Works Administration (PWA), set up in 1933, aimed to organise large-scale work schemes that would be of lasting value to Americans: these included building schools, hospitals, airports, dams, bridges and battleships. The PWA also directed improvements in sewage and drainage systems. Such schemes created jobs, but generally they were for skilled workers rather than for the millions who lacked a skill or trade.

To help meet this need, the Works Progress Administration (WPA) was set up in 1935. In some ways it was similar to the PWA – it organised smaller-scale schemes building roads, schools and other public buildings. It also gave work to writers, artists, actors and photographers – for example, unemployed writers were paid to write a series of guide books on American states and cities, and 12,000 actors were paid to tour the country and perform plays. The WPA became the country's biggest employer. It gave work to two million Americans each year.

The young

Some of the agencies set up in the New Deal had more than one aim. For example, the Civilian Conservation Corps (CCC) not only provided work but also helped agriculture and the environment. This agency gave work to single, unemployed young men between the ages of 18 and 25 for a limited period – usually six months. They lived in camps in the countryside, planted trees to stop soil erosion, cleared land, created forests and made reservoirs. In return they received food, clothing and shelter, and pocket money of one dollar a day. By 1938 over two million young people had served in the CCC. It was criticised by some Americans as amounting to cheap labour, but it was not compulsory, and through it, many young men learned skills which later allowed them to get a job.

SUMMARY

How did Roosevelt try to end the Depression?
1. Bank Holiday (financial security)
2. AAA (farming)
3. NRA (industry)
4. CWA, PWA, WPA (reduce unemployment)
5. HOLC (address homelessness)
6. FERA (alleviate poverty)
7. TVA

Other measures of the New Deal

The New Deal introduced a number of measures which tried to help the American people in other ways. The Home Owners Loan Corporation (HOLC) helped people who were having difficulty meeting their mortgage repayments. Through the Corporation, the government lent money to people at low interest rates to prevent them from losing their homes.

The Tennessee Valley Authority

The setting up of the TVA is one example of a permanent change for the better under the New Deal.

Roosevelt called the Tennessee Valley 'the nation's number one economic problem'. The Tennessee river flooded in spring, washing away good soil, and almost dried up in summer, causing dust-bowl conditions. Because it ran through seven different American states, it was also difficult to get common agreement on what actions to take to solve the problems. As a result the people of the Tennessee Valley lived in poverty.

So Roosevelt set up the Tennessee Valley Authority (TVA) to improve the whole area. Forests were planted to stop soil erosion. Twenty-one dams were built to control the river and prevent flooding. Power stations were built at the dams to provide cheap electricity for homes and industry. The dams also created lakes which were used for water transport, and also provided sporting and leisure facilities.

Cheap power and good transport attracted industries to the Tennessee Valley. As a result the Tennessee Valley recovered and became a prosperous area. Thousands of jobs were created, the land became fertile and the quality of life of the people who lived there was greatly improved.

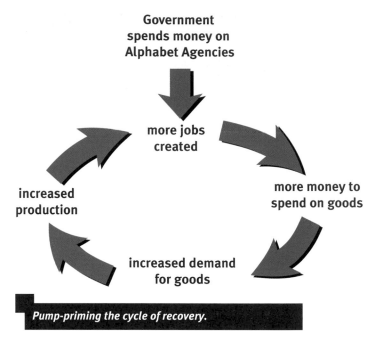

Government spends money on Alphabet Agencies → more jobs created → more money to spend on goods → increased demand for goods → increased production → (back to more jobs created)

Pump-priming the cycle of recovery.

The Norris Dam, Knoxville, Tennessee, in about 1935. Norris Dam is 80 metres high and 567 metres wide. The lake it created has a flood-storage capacity of 14.5 billion cubic metres. The town of Norris, a planned 'garden city' built to house workers on the dam, was a model community. It contained some of the first all-electric homes in America.

2.5c How far was the New Deal successful in ending the Depression in the USA?

Opposition to the New Deal

Some people opposed the New Deal – especially Republican politicians, who claimed that it involved spending lots of money but did not end the Depression. They felt Roosevelt was behaving like a *dictator*, forcing Americans to do what he wanted.

Many American businessmen also did not like government interference in their affairs. They especially resented the NRA and Roosevelt's support for trade unions and his attempts to increase wages. Roosevelt was accused of 'deserting his class'.

The Supreme Court

The New Deal also met opposition in the Supreme Court.

Under the terms of the US Constitution, the Supreme Court can declare illegal any measure passed by the president and Congress which it decides is unconstitutional.

Roosevelt was unfortunate in that a majority of the judges on the Supreme Court were Republicans. They felt that the New Deal ran against the Constitution because the federal government (the government of the whole country) had taken powers which belonged to the separate states. As a result, the Supreme Court ruled against the Alphabet Agencies in eleven cases. For example:

- In 1935 the NRA had to be withdrawn when the Supreme Court ruled that the government did not have the right to impose rules of fair competition.

- In 1936 the AAA was also declared unconstitutional when the Supreme Court ruled that it was 'oppressive coercion' to pay a subsidy only if farmers reduced production.

Roosevelt was furious with the Supreme Court. After his 1936 election victory he threatened to add six judges to the Supreme Court to create a Democrat majority. This attempt to 'pack' the Court made Roosevelt unpopular throughout America, even among Democrats. He backed down – but so too did the Supreme Court. After this no more of Roosevelt's measures were rejected by the Court.

This 1933 cartoon comments on Roosevelt's claim that he was 'priming the pump' of the American economy. To prime a pump is to get it started with a flow of water. Here, the priming water Roosevelt is pouring down the pump is really taxpayers' money, which he is wasting.

More opponents

There were also some Americans who felt that Roosevelt was not doing enough.

Huey Long, Senator for Louisiana, set up the 'Share Our Wealth' movement. He wanted to confiscate all fortunes over $3 million and share out the money so that every American family would have between $4000 and $5000. He also wanted free education for all Americans, a national minimum wage and old age pensions. His ideas were popular, especially in Louisiana. However, they did attract opposition for being too extreme. When Long was assassinated in 1935, support for his movement collapsed.

Another opponent was Francis Townsend, an American doctor who campaigned for an old-age pension of $200 a month.

The Second New Deal

Roosevelt's reaction to the opposition was what some historians call 'the Second New Deal'.

In the first years of the New Deal, Roosevelt had introduced measures to ease the Depression. This programme was continued. To replace the banned NRA, he passed the National Labour Relations Act (1935 – sometimes called the Wagner Act), which protected workers' right to join a trade union. He also set up the National Labour Relations Board (NLRB) to prevent employers from victimising workers.

Also, anticipating the Supreme Court's decision against the AAA, the Soil Conservation Act (1935) allowed the government to continue subsidising farmers.

In the second phase of the New Deal, however, Roosevelt also introduced measures to change the underlying structures of society.

The Social Security Act (1935) provided America's first system of social welfare – it set up a national system of old-age pensions and a national system of unemployment insurance. It also provided help for children in need and people with physical disabilities.

By 1936 Roosevelt's first term of office as president was coming to an end. He sought re-election for a second term and based his campaign on the promise not only to continue with the New Deal, but to make it more radical and far-reaching. Only two states out of the 48 voted against Roosevelt. He had received a clear vote of confidence for his policies from the American people.

The National Housing Act (1937) reduced excessive rents and made loans available so that people could buy their own houses. And the Fair Labour Standards Act (1938) fixed the hours and conditions of work and set a minimum wage.

GradeStudio

Describe how Roosevelt tried to end the Depression.

'Emergency powers'/'New Deal'/the 'Hundred Days' ☐

Bank holiday ☐

Fireside Chats ☐

Alphabet Agencies (AAA, NRA, FERA, CWA, PWA, WPA, CCC, HOLC, TVA) ☐

'Second New Deal' after 1935 – Soil Conservation/Social Security/ National Housing Acts ☐

SUMMARY

Which Americans were in favour of the New Deal?

IN FAVOUR

1. All the people helped by the FERA
2. Everybody given jobs by the CWA, PWA or WPA, or loans by the HOLC
3. Trade unionists and everyone protected by the NRA/National Labour Relations Act/Fair Labour Standards Act
4. Residents of the Tennessee Valley
5. People with money in banks
6. People helped by the Social Security Act
7. Tenants protected by the National Housing Act

NEUTRAL

1. Black Americans, who did not benefit as much but still supported Roosevelt
2. Farmers, one-third of whom lost their farms

NOT IN FAVOUR

1. Republicans who claimed it was wasted money
2. Businessmen who did not like interference
3. Rich people who felt 'deserted'
4. Supreme Court – especially when Roosevelt threatened to 'pack' it with six Democrats
5. Huey Long and Francis Townsend

Was the New Deal a success?

The New Deal achieved much and helped millions of Americans who had suffered in the years of Depression, but there were areas where it was less successful.

Black people generally benefited less from the New Deal than white people – in 1935 about a third of black people were dependent on relief payments. Many farmers and especially farm labourers also continued to have a low standard of living. Those who lived in the areas affected by the dust bowl were even worse off.

It is also true that the New Deal had other weaknesses. Roosevelt was cautious financially, and he allowed the Federal Reserve to set high interest rates, which prevented economic recovery. Also, because he kept America on the gold standard, the exchange rate continued to make world trade difficult for American firms.

In the first phase, from 1933 to 1936, there was limited recovery as the government spent millions of dollars creating jobs and reviving American industry. Unemployment fell from 14 million to 9 million between 1933 and 1936.

But when in 1937 Roosevelt tried to reduce spending on the New Deal, demand decreased, production began to fall again and businesses started to collapse again. By 1938 unemployment was back to 11 million. Roosevelt pumped more money into the economy, and unemployment fell in 1939 – but only to 9.5 million. It seemed as if the New Deal had achieved all it could.

The Second World War

What *did* help the American economy to recover was the Second World War. Although the USA did not enter the war until December 1941, the war's impact was felt from 1939.

At first, America was able to sell weapons to Britain. As the war continued, Britain found it harder to pay for armaments. So in March 1941, Roosevelt passed the Lend-Lease Act. Under this agreement, Britain handed over its overseas military bases to the USA. In return, America supplied Britain and the USSR with war materials as necessary, to be paid for after the war. In all, America supplied armaments worth $50 billion to its allies. The manufacture of these armaments stimulated American industry.

Finally, when the USA entered the war in 1941, its full resources – manpower, industry and agriculture – were dedicated to the fight against Japan and Germany. The US government spent billions of dollars buying military equipment and supplies, and to produce those goods, American industry employed many more people... who then went out and spent their wages on food and consumer goods. In this way, the war lifted the US economy out of depression.

Although the New Deal was not an unqualified success economically, socially it was a great success. Poor people idolised Roosevelt as the man who had saved them from starvation or from their employer. Roosevelt and the New Deal brought great changes to America. The federal government became much more involved in people's lives, and Americans came to accept that the federal government ought to protect the weaker sections of society – the unemployed, the homeless, the old and the poor. Roosevelt had helped to redefine the role of government in America.

SUMMARY

Did the New Deal help the American Economy to recover?

YES
1. Restored confidence (fireside chats)
2. Ended banking crisis
3. The Alphabet Agencies combated unemployment and homelessness, created jobs, supported business and farming
4. TVA
5. Social benefits of the Second New Deal

NO
1. Limited help to black people and farmers
2. Unemployment was reduced, but stayed high
3. The attempt to reduce funding in 1937 failed
4. America stayed on the gold standard, which continued to damage exports
5. Interest rates stayed high, which held back industry
6. Needed Second World War and Lend-Lease to get the economy going again

Preparation - 'Describe'

- the effects of the Wall Street Crash
- what Hoover's government did to try to end the Depression
- the economic effects of the Depression
- the effects of the Depression on the American people

- how Roosevelt solved the banking crisis
- how the New Deal helped industry
- how the New Deal helped agriculture
- the TVA
- the 'Second New Deal'
- Roosevelt's conflict with the Supreme Court

Using this textbook, an encyclopaedia or the internet, make sure you know enough to write at least TWO detailed descriptions of each item in the list above.

Preparation - names and specialist terms

- AAA
- NRA
- FERA
- CWA
- PWA
- WPA
- CCC
- HOLC
- TVA

- speculators
- shares
- stock market
- Wall Street
- tariff war
- hobos
- breadlines
- dust bowl
- gold standard

- Hoovervilles
- Bonus Army
- Rugged individualism
- Smoot-Hawley Tariff
- lame duck months
- emergency powers
- Alphabet Agencies
- fireside chats
- Blue Eagle

- Huey Long
- Francis Townsend
- National Labour Relations Act
- Soil Conservation Act
- Social Security Act
- National Housing Act
- Fair Labour Standards Act
- Lend-Lease Act
- 'oppresive coercion'

Using this textbook, an encyclopaedia or the internet, make sure you know about each of the above so that you can include them in your exam answers.

Preparation - 'Why?'

WHY...

- did the Wall Street Crash develop into the Great Depression?
- did Hoover become so unpopular?

- was Roosevelt so loved by the American people?
- did the Second World War get the US economy going again?

Working in a small group, think of TWO reasons for each situation in the list above.

Preparation - 'How?'

HOW did this...	cause this?
- the Wall Street Crash...	- the Depression
- the Smoot-Hawley Tariff...	- the Depression
- the gold standard...	- the Depression
- the Depression...	- human misery
- the Depression ...	- Roosevelt's landslide election victory
- the New Deal...	- a fall in unemployment
- the TVA...	- increased prosperity in the Tennessee Valley area
- the New Deal...	- opposition to Roosevelt

Working as a whole class, think of TWO ways in which each factor on the left led to the outcome on the right.

The New Deal led to the economic recovery of the USA in the 1930s.' Do you agree? Explain your answer.   (12 marks)

Comments

There is an argument that the New Deal did lead to economic recovery.

Defend the null hypothesis.

Firstly, Roosevelt's 'bank holiday' (the Emergency Banking, Act March 1933) restored confidence in the banking system. Also, Roosevelt's 'fireside chats' helped restore confidence. No more banks failed after 1933.

> At least TWO reasons why the null hypothesis IS true. EXPLAIN HOW the null hypothesis is true. Include FACTS.

Secondly, the New Deal helped to create jobs. The CWA created 4 million jobs during the winter of 1933–34, the PWA created jobs for skilled workers, and the WPA employed another 2 million. The CCC gave work to 2 million young people. The AAA helped farmers, and the NRA helped American industry. These 'Alphabet Agencies' combated unemployment and homelessness, created jobs and supported business and farming. They pumped money into the American economy to keep it going.

Argue that the null hypothesis is not true.

However, many historians argue that the New Deal did not do anything permanent to help the US economy.

> Begin the second section with a connective of comparison. At least TWO reasons why the the null hypothesis IS NOT true. EXPLAIN HOW the null hypothesis is not true. Include FACTS.

Firstly, it did not do anything specifically to help farm labourers or black people, two groups that suffered greatly during the Depression.

Secondly, at 9 million, unemployment was still high. When in 1937 Roosevelt tried to reduce spending, demand decreased, production began to fall again and businesses started to collapse again. By 1938, unemployment was back to 11 million. Roosevelt increased spending again and unemployment fell in 1939 – but only to 9.5 million. It seemed as if the New Deal had failed to end unemployment.

Reach a conclusion.

Therefore, it seems that – although it arguably saved the American economy from total meltdown – the New Deal did not bring economic recovery. Only when it was supplying Britain (to be paid for after the war under the Lend-Lease Act of March 1941) and later the USSR with $50 billion worth of armaments, did American industry begin to recover. This was later helped by the billions of dollars the government spent buying military supplies, after the USA entered the war in 1941. To produce these, American industry employed more people who then went out and spent their wages on food and consumer goods. In this way, it was the Second World War, not the New Deal, which lifted the US economy out of Depression.

> Begin the third section with a connective of comparison. EXPLAIN HOW you reached your judgement. Include FACTS.

2.7 Race Relations in the USA, 1955–1968

2.7a To what extent did racial inequality exist in the USA in the 1950s and 1960s?

Background

Attitudes towards black people in the United States were formed during the era of slavery. Slavery was not just a question of white people having legal ownership of black people. It created certain attitudes towards African Americans – that they were stupid, lazy, and untrustworthy. It also established a social situation in which white people were the HAVES and black people the HAVE NOTS.

Although the legal status of black Americans has changed, the effort to improve their economic status and to change underlying racial attitudes has been a long and difficult struggle (and it is a struggle that continues). The story of race relations in the USA is the story of this struggle.

Before the Second World War

In 1865 the United States gave slaves freedom but not equality. In the southern states, the Ku Klux

Klan terrorised and lynched black Americans. At the same time, local laws called 'Jim Crow Laws' discriminated against black Americans ('Jim Crow' was a slang term for a black person). Local authorities insisted that black people pass certain tests before they were allowed to enrol as voters. Literacy tests, for example, kept many blacks off the register because a lack of educational opportunities had prevented them from learning to read and write. In the same way most black people were legally prevented from voting or sitting on juries.

The idea of **segregation** grew up in many states. Black Americans went to separate schools and separate restaurants. They sat on separate seats at the back of buses. Things were worst in the South, but there was racism in the north too, and there were race riots in some cities, notably in Chicago in 1919.

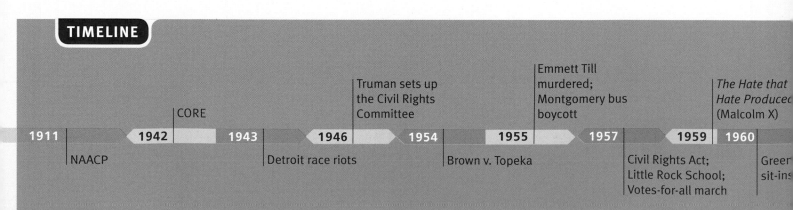

TIMELINE

1911	1942	CORE 1943	1946	Truman sets up the Civil Rights Committee 1954	1955	Emmett Till murdered; Montgomery bus boycott 1957	1959	*The Hate that Hate Produced* (Malcolm X) 1960
NAACP			Detroit race riots		Brown v. Topeka		Civil Rights Act; Little Rock School; Votes-for-all march	Green sit-ins

The 1920s and 1930s saw 'scientific racism' and bogus theories about 'race types' and 'inferior races'. On the other hand, the 1930s also saw the 'Harlem Renaissance' – the development of black awareness and culture. Jazz music and 'black' dances, like the Charleston, became internationally popular (see page 160). People talked of 'the New Negroes', who were starting 'to realize the great possibilities within themselves'.

The National Association for the Advancement of Colored People (NAACP) had been set up in 1911. By 1945 it had 450,000 members. During the 1930s it conducted a campaign against lynchings. One black NAACP lawyer, Charles Houston, trained an elite team of black lawyers who challenged segregation laws in the courts. These lawyers won a number of rights for blacks, particularly the right to postgraduate education and the right to sit on juries.

The impact of the Second World War

During the Second World War, black activism grew. A black Christian socialist called James Farmer founded the Congress of Racial Equality (CORE) which organised sit-ins at segregated restaurants and insisted its members sit in white seats on interstate buses.

But there was also increased racism during the war. In 1941, the Fair Employment Practices law had abolished discrimination against black workers in defence industries, which employed two million blacks by the end of the war. But many white workers resented what they saw as black people taking their jobs and moving into their neighbourhoods. They called strikes, picketed black housing projects and

attacked black workers. In 1943 there were race riots across America, notably in Detroit.

Tension increased further after the war. More than a million black people had served in the US Army and fought against Nazi racism and oppression. Now they felt that they had earned equality – as one ex-corporal said: 'I went into the Army a nigger; I'm coming out a man'.

But black Americans were not equal. They had the lowest paid jobs and the lowest standards of education. The principle behind the Jim Crow Laws – 'separate but equal' – was still underpinned in law by the Supreme Court. Most returning black soldiers found themselves unemployed and called 'boy'. In the southern states of the USA, black soldiers who questioned their place in society were beaten and even murdered.

GradeStudio

Describe how Black Americans achieved Civil Rights, 1955–65.

1946 Truman (Civil Rights Committee) ❑

1954 Brown vs. Topeka (vs. segregated schools) ❑

1955–56 Montgomery Bus Boycott ❑

1957 Little Rock ❑

1960s Restaurant sit-ins/Freedom Rides (buses) ❑

Freedom Marches (Birmingham/Washington/Selma) ❑

Civil Rights Act (1964)/Voting Rights Act (1965) ❑

61	1962	1963	1964	1965	1966	1967	1968	
Freedom Rides; Albany campaign; First Freedom March		Birmingham campaign; University of Alabama desegregated; Washington Freedom March – 'I have a dream' speech		Voting Rights Act; Selma March; Watts Riots; Malcolm X assassinated		*Where Do We Go From Here?*		
	Law to reduce housing discrimination		Civil Rights Act; CORE freedom houses		Carmichael elected president of SNCC; McKissick elected president of CORE; Huey Newton forms the Black Panther Party; Meredith March		Mexico Olympics – Black Power salute; Martin Luther King assassinated; Fair Housing Act	

Civil rights in the 1950s

President Harry S. Truman (1945–53) held racist views in private and had once joined the KKK, but now he spoke out for civil rights, particularly for returning black soldiers. He gave black workers equality in the armed forces and the civil service and ruled that government contracts could not be given to companies which refused to employ black workers.

In 1946 Truman set up a civil rights committee which recommended anti-lynching laws, voting rights, an end to discrimination in interstate travel, a Fair Employment Board and a permanent Commission on Civil Rights. Truman also made a number of speeches supporting civil rights, but his good will did not translate into significant changes in the status of black people.

By contrast, President Dwight Eisenhower (1953–61) seemed less committed to civil rights. On his election team he employed only one black worker, who was given minor jobs (such as arranging parking lots).

Nevertheless, Eisenhower introduced civil rights bills in 1957 and again in 1960.

Eisenhower's bills made it illegal to obstruct school **desegregation** and illegal to stop black voters from voting. However, they increased the number of black voters by only 3 per cent.

Brown v. Topeka

The key breakthrough in black civil rights, however, came not from the government but from the NAACP, through the courts.

In 1954 the NAACP fought the Board of Education of Topeka, Kansas, in the Supreme Court. NAACP lawyers asserted the right of a black church minister named Oliver Brown to send his daughter to the nearby white school, rather than a black school far away. In a landmark ruling, Chief Justice Warren stated that the concept 'separate but equal' was unconstitutional and that segregated schools were psychologically harmful to children.

A group of black American students walk past supporters of segregation in Baltimore, Maryland.

The backlash

The Brown case brought the Ku Klux Klan back to life. It was led by Robert Shelton and the 'White Knights of the Ku Klux Klan'. Shelton declared desegregation 'communist', thus linking two fears held by white southerners – the third being that black men might violate white women.

The Klan received passive support from southern whites, especially Protestant churches. Klan ceremonies – in which members dressed in long white robes and hoods – were mocked in the media, but the organisation was racist and violent. Murders and bombings increased.

Klansmen who did these things were often protected by police officers who were themselves members of the Klan. In addition, juries made up of white people were often reluctant to find people guilty of Klan activities.

In 1955 Emmett Till, a 14-year-old black boy from Chicago, was murdered when, during a visit to his great-uncle in Mississippi, he whistled at a white female shopkeeper. Three days later, Till's body was discovered. He had been shot in the head and beaten and mutilated until he was unrecognisable. Emmett's great-uncle (bravely ignoring KKK threats) identified the woman's husband, Roy Bryant, as Emmett's abductor, but the jury took only an hour to find Bryant not guilty of murder or kidnap.

Two months after the trial, Bryant admitted the killing in an interview he gave to *Look* magazine (for which he was paid $4000), but he stayed free until his death in 1994.

SUMMARY

Was *Brown v. Topeka* the start of the Civil Rights Movement?

YES

1. Segregation was officially unconstitutional
2. Major victory for black activists – led to Little Rock, desegregation, bussing
3. NAACP had achieved legal victories, and CORE had begun to test those by direct action
4. Increased black confidence and activism

AGAINST

1. No immediate effect – ignored or resisted
2. Provoked KKK/extremist reaction/violence
3. Didn't involve Civil Rights Movement tactics – direct action, civil disobedience, mass protest
4. Black awareness had been growing since the Harlem Renaissance

A gathering of the Ku Klux Klan in the south in the 1950s. The Klan had a great deal of influence in this period.

The beginnings of change

The Montgomery Bus Boycott

In December 1955, Rosa Parks sat on a bus on her way home from work in Montgomery, Alabama. The bus was full, and when a white man boarded, the driver ordered Parks to stand up. She refused and was arrested.

Parks was a trained NAACP activist. She took her stand on purpose, after a number of incidents of rudeness and discrimination against blacks on Montgomery's buses.

Choosing a young local preacher named Martin Luther King (see pages 226–228) as their leader, the black people of Montgomery decided to boycott the buses. Thousands of black people walked to work, while the city's 210 African American taxi drivers offered seats for the cost of the bus fare. A car-pool of supporters of the boycott was also organised to get black people to work. The boycott lasted 381 days.

King and his supporters called themselves the Montgomery Improvement Association (MIA). The MIA also hired NAACP lawyers to take the case to the Supreme Court.

The MIA deliberately sought only moderate reforms – they wanted black drivers on black routes, and they wanted white bus drivers to be polite to black passengers. The MIA did not even challenge the idea of segregation, asking only that seats on city buses be allocated on a first-come-first-served basis, with black people filling up seats from the rear, white passengers from the front.

The local White Citizens' Council opposed the MIA's proposals. Its membership doubled. It ordered local officials to harass boycott leaders – King was arrested for speeding. In January 1956 his home was bombed by the KKK.

But the boycott was ruining the bus company financially, and local businesses were losing custom (local shopkeepers lost $1 million).

On 13 November the city chiefs – claiming that the car-pool was in effect a taxi service operating without a proper licence – got the car-pool stopped in the courts. The decision would have meant the defeat of the boycott, but it was rendered pointless when, that same day, the Supreme Court ruled that segregation on buses was unconstitutional.

The Montgomery Bus boycott inspired other black Americans to protest in the same way in their own towns. This photo shows a group of black women walking to their destination rather than taking the bus.

The boycott – and Rosa Parks – became an inspiration to the Civil Rights Movement. It demonstrated that when black Americans united, they could succeed, and that violent opposition only increased support.

The success of the boycott increased black confidence – when the KKK, robed and hooded, drove through the black areas of town, blacks came out and waved at them. There were copycat boycotts throughout the South.

But the success was limited. Everything else in Montgomery was still segregated. And the boycott had revealed the depth of racism and the determination of some whites. Parks and her husband lost their jobs. She received death threats, and had to move to Detroit.

Little Rock

By 1957 the Supreme Court's *Brown v. Topeka* ruling had not resulted in any immediate changes in schools. It did not order segregated schools to be abolished – it just said they were wrong. Most of the twenty segregated states simply ignored it. The government did not force them to end segregation. Where states did try to change, some schools closed rather than desegregate, and mobs gathered to stop black children going to white schools.

On 23 September 1957, nine black students tried to attend Central High School in Little Rock, Arkansas. A mob of 1,000 barred their way. Two days later, the children went into school... protected by 11,000 soldiers. The crowd shouted: '2, 4, 6, 8; we aren't going to integrate'.

In school, the black students were assaulted and abused. Back in the black community, they faced the anger of those who said the 'meddling nine' were making life harder for black people.

Little Rock is often presented in textbooks as a victory for civil rights, but in some ways it was a defeat. Few other schools dared to desegregate, and few black children wanted to face the danger. In 1964 only 3 per cent of America's black children attended desegregated schools. Little Rock itself was only fully desegregated in 1972.

Progress by 1960

By 1960 the Civil Rights Movement had begun to undermine the legal principles of segregation. The movement had its heroes and martyrs. In a TV interview in 1967, Martin Luther King said that he believed that the 1950s had created 'the new Negro', who had 'a willingness to stand up courageously for what he feels is just and what he feels he deserves on the basis of the laws of the land.'

But there was still no mass movement of black Americans, who still lacked the most basic civil rights (not least the vote). When Martin Luther King's Southern Christian Leadership Conference (SCLC) tried to organise the registration of three million new black voters in a 1957 Act, it managed to add only 160,000 more names.

Meanwhile, the movement had provoked an angry and violent white backlash. Indeed, White Citizens Councils were going through the same voters' lists and finding excuses to delete the names of black voters who were already there. 'Uppity' blacks were being fired. And a number of southern states outlawed the NAACP.

Little Rock, 23 September 1957. Black students have to be escorted to school by the National Guard.

Living standards for African Americans

Living standards for African Americans in general were improving – where 87 per cent of black Americans lived below the poverty line in 1940, that figure had fallen to 41 per cent by 1959.

However, that overall figure hid many injustices. Many black Americans had migrated from the southern states to the northern states in search of work. There, they earned more but paid high rents to live in appalling and overcrowded 'ghettos', surrounded by violence and crime. Black workers were generally trapped in low-skilled, low-paying jobs. The average black income in 1957 was only 57 per cent that of a white worker. Moreover, unemployment amongst black Americans, at 11 per cent, was double that of whites.

By the end of the 1950s, there had been little or no change in the everyday experience of blacks, who were still segregated and discriminated against socially, economically and politically.

SUMMARY

Had much progress had been made by 1960?

YES
1. Legal successes – e.g. *Brown v. Topeka*
2. Government action – Truman and Eisenhower
3. Bus boycott – first mass protest/direct action
4. Growing confidence – 'New Negro'

NO
1. Little change (voter registration/ segregation)
2. Opposition – KKK/Till/Parks sacked
3. 'New Negro' only in Harlem Renaissance

2.7b How effective were the methods used by the Civil Rights Movement, 1961–68?

Martin Luther King

In 1954 Martin Luther King was the young Baptist minister of a 'rich folks' church' in Montgomery, Alabama. His vision was to follow the example of the Indian Mahatma Gandhi, who led a non-violent campaign of passive resistance against British rule in India in the 1940s. King first came to public notice in 1955 when – as leader of the Montgomery Bus Boycott – his house was bombed, but he declared: 'We must meet violence with non-violence'.

Martin Luther King rose to be the hero and figurehead of the Civil Rights Movement, but it is worth remembering that in the 1960s there were a number of different black organisations campaigning for black rights.

The NAACP had already achieved a number of legal successes by the time King started his campaign. Indeed, after King's success in the Montgomery bus boycott, the NAACP leader Thurgood Marshall simply remarked: 'All that walking for nothing'. The boycott had not secured the end of segregation on Montgomery's buses, whereas the NAACP had, through the Supreme Court.

Meanwhile, CORE (see page 221) had been campaigning since the Second World War.

King founded the Southern Christian Leadership Conference (SCLC) in 1957. But the SCLC was poorly organised, and the male, educated Church ministers who ran it were pompous and quarrelsome.

The sit-ins

The first Civil Rights successes did not come from the SCLC at all. In 1960, in Greensboro, North Carolina, four college students went to the local Woolworths store and sat down at the white section of the lunch counter. The first day they were simply ignored, so they returned the following day with 30 students; this time they got in the local newspaper. Next day there were 66 black students, and after a week of escalating trouble – including a bomb threat – the store was forced to close.

The protest immediately spawned copycat sit-ins all over the South, involving perhaps 50,000 students in all.

The protesters were humiliated and assaulted. Not all of them managed not to fight back.

In fact Greensboro had an effective NAACP organisation, had managed to register large numbers of black voters, and had even got black Councillors elected. But as a minority on the Council, the black councillors found that not only could they not reform segregation in Greensboro, their presence on the Council simply made it look as though they supported the Council's segregation policies.

The sit-ins were therefore a new tactic for civil rights – they were 'direct action' to challenge segregation. At the end of the sit-ins, the Student Nonviolent Coordinating Committee, or SNCC ('Snick'), was formed.

King had nothing to do with organising the sit-ins, and he generally disapproved – he was only persuaded to join one in October 1960 (after which he was arrested and sentenced to four months of hard labour).

The students had chosen to highlight racial inequality because 1960 was a presidential election year. One of the reasons John F. Kennedy won a close vote was his protest about the imprisonment of Martin Luther King. Kennedy had won over large numbers of black voters. The increase in the number of black voters was becoming something that the US government had to take into account.

A group of black students take part in a sit-in at a diner.

Freedom Rides

The following year, events again ran ahead of King. In May 1961 James Farmer of CORE organised the 'Freedom Rides', during which young blacks tried to exercise their legal right to travel on segregated interstate buses. It was an act of calculated martyrdom – the riders knew they would be attacked. When a first bus reached Alabama, the tyres were slashed and the bus set on fire; the mob tried to hold the doors shut so that the passengers would be burned alive. When a second bus reached Birmingham, Alabama, the police and KKK attacked the riders with clubs and chains as they left the bus. White Freedom Riders were especially badly beaten by the mob.

In all, there were 60 Freedom Rides, involving 450 very brave people. Most were beaten and/or imprisoned. While they waited for connections, the Freedom Riders would also go and break the rules in segregated restaurants and hotels.

Many SNCC students participated in the rides, which King supported. CORE, SNCC and SCLC all ignored the government's request to stop the Freedom Rides because they were causing civil unrest, and in the end Attorney General Robert Kennedy had to act to enforce the Supreme Court's decision that segregation on interstate travel was illegal.

Violence against blacks on a Freedom Ride in 1961.

Failure at Albany

In 1961, SNCC students began a campaign against desegregation in Albany, Georgia, including sit-ins and Freedom Rides. Older civil rights leaders in the city invited King, who – much to the annoyance of the SNCC – led a march and met the City Council.

The police refused to use violence and simply arrested and fined 1000 protestors. Eventually King ran out of supporters prepared to be jailed. Instead of desegregating its amenities, the Council closed parks, sold the swimming pool and took all the seats out of the library.

King left believing that Albany was a failure. However, after he left, a Black Voter Registration campaign was very successful, and in 1962 the city desegregated all its facilities.

The civil rights marches

In 1957 – against the advice of other black leaders – King had organised a votes-for-all march in Washington in support of Eisenhower's Civil Rights Bill. The March on Washington, attended by 20,000 people, had been regarded as a success.

Now he and his supporters used civil rights marches to publicise the cause of civil rights. The first 'freedom march' had been organised by Rev C.T. Vivian and the Nashville Christian Leadership Conference (an affiliate of the SCLC) in 1961.

SUMMARY

Why was the Civil Rights Movement so successful in the early years of the 1960s?

1. The NAACP had established the fact that blacks were legally in the right
2. 'New Negro' attitude made it a mass protest
3. Figurehead leadership of Martin Luther King
4. Right principle (non-violence) and tactics (direct action/single issues) to gain public support
5. Government support – prepared to enforce laws
6. KKK/violence created public support
7. TV publicity created public awareness

Success at Birmingham

In 1963, King decided to use the tactic of large marches at Birmingham, Alabama. He chose Birmingham because of its reputation for racism (it had even banned a book which showed black and white rabbits), and because the town's police chief 'Bull' Connor was known to be hot-headed. King called it 'the most segregated city in America'. He demanded the desegregation of eating places and the employment of black sales staff.

Although King (as always) insisted on non-violence, his campaign was named 'Project C' – and the 'C' stood for confrontation. The demonstrations began with sit-ins at lunch counters in downtown stores and with a succession of marches, during one of which King was arrested.

Actually, initial support for King in Birmingham was poor, so on 3 May he recruited a thousand school children to join one of the marches. As expected, the police attacked with water hoses, dogs and batons. There was a media outcry. King was thrown into solitary confinement, and the KKK bombed his motel room (shortly after the state troopers guarding it mysteriously left).

Blacks rioted, and the government was forced to step in. The city authorities gave in and desegregated the restaurants; soon after, they desegregated all Council facilities.

Most of all, TV images of brave, non-violent protestors being attacked by the police and racists created a huge groundswell of middle-class support.

The Washington Freedom March

In August 1963 King decided to make use of this support. He organised a march that drew a quarter of a million people (including at least 75,000 white supporters), all of whom heard his brilliant 'I have a dream' speech in front of the Lincoln Memorial in Washington. Watched by millions live on television, to the cheers of the crowd, he finished by looking forward to the time when black Americans, in the words of the Negro spiritual, would be 'Free at last! Free at last! Thank God Almighty, we are free at last!'

By the end of 1963, King had become the leader of the Civil Rights Movement. He had proved he could manipulate the media and was the most famous civil rights campaigner. Furthermore, the government supported him, because it realised he was more moderate than other campaigners.

Selma

In 1965 King went to Selma Alabama. Again, he chose it because its sheriff, Jim Clark, could be relied on to get violent. King knew that non-violent protests 'make people inflict violence on you'. As a result they gain bad publicity and destroy their own case; so King intentionally provoked violence. On 'Bloody Sunday', 7 March 1965, brutality against the marchers was such that there was national outrage when it was shown on television. The public outcry was one of the reasons why President Lyndon Johnson's Voting Rights Act passed through Congress in August of that year.

Martin Luther King salutes the crowds on the Washington Freedom March, 28 August 1963.

Increasing Radicalisation

Black American movements which were much more radical and violent emerged during the 1960s.

The ghetto riots

Martin Luther King and his civil rights successes in the south seemed irrelevant to blacks living in the poor areas of American cities – where poverty, deprivation and unemployment were rife. In Chicago's ghettos, some 70 per cent of black youths were unemployed. Poor housing led to violence and crime. Only 32 per cent of ghetto children finished high school. The ghettos were a powder-keg waiting to explode.

In 1965, a clumsy and brutal attempt by police to arrest a black drunk-driver led to riots in the Watts area of Los Angeles. Between 1964 and 1968, there were 238 riots in more than 200 US cities. These riots resulted in 250 deaths (many from police shootings) and billions of dollars worth of damage.

The middle-class campaigners of the SCLC and the NAACP knew little of this ghetto world. But black activists were working in the ghettos. After 1964, CORE workers rented **'freedom houses'** in the northern ghettos, from which they distributed information on education, employment, health and housing. And in 1966 the SNCC mounted the Atlanta Project, in which a group of SNCC students cleared waste areas, published a newsletter called *Nitty-Gritty* to denounce 'white lies' in the press, and persuaded local blacks to vote in elections.

Nation of Islam and Malcolm X

Nation of Islam (NoI) was a black Muslim movement formed in 1930. It was nationalist and separatist, and its solution to the problems of black Americans was either a return to Africa or a separate black American state in the southern USA. King labelled NoI 'a hate group', and NAACP leader Thurgood Marshall called them 'a bunch of thugs', but NoI had about 250,000 members by 1970 – the most famous being Muhammad Ali, the world champion boxer, and Malcolm X, the black activist.

Malcolm X was a vigorous and aggressive man who joined the NoI while in prison for drug-dealing. He presented himself as 'the alternative to Dr King', whom he branded a 'fool'. He rejected King's 'turn the other cheek' non-violence and argued that white policies often left black Americans with no alternative but violence. After a 1959 TV documentary, *The Hate that Hate Produced*, Malcolm X became famous.

In 1964 Malcolm X was suspended from NoI after appearing to welcome the assassination of President Kennedy. As a result, he renounced NoI. His New York home was fire-bombed in 1964, and in 1965 he was assassinated by a NoI gunman. Although he never established a lasting organisation, Malcolm X:

- became a role model for angry young blacks
- forced America's black leaders to re-focus their attention away from civil and legal rights and instead on social and economic conditions
- introduced the idea of violence as a legitimate tactic.

Malcolm X making a speech advocating increased radicalisation.

Black Power

As CORE and SNCC worked in the ghettos, both became more radicalised – their politics became more left wing/socialist, and their tactics became more racially charged and violent.

In 1966 SNCC chose Stokely Carmichael as its leader and expelled all white members. Carmichael rejected non-violence and instead advocated self-defence. He brought the phrase 'Black Power' to the public's attention when he shouted it out at a speech in Greenwood, Mississippi, after the Meredith March (see page 232). Next year, Carmichael was succeeded by H. 'Rap' Brown, who encouraged poor black people to seize white shops and thus directly caused a number of ghetto riots later that year.

Meanwhile, in 1966 the radical Floyd McKissick took over CORE, which expelled its white members in 1968. McKissick, too, rejected non-violence.

The most famous expression of Black Power came during the 1968 Mexico City Olympics, when medal winners Tommie Smith and John Carlos raised their fists in a Black Power salute. Smith wore a black scarf to symbolise black pride; Carlos wore beads in memory of black slaves and black victims of lynchings.

The athletes were members of the Olympic Project for Human Rights, an organisation founded in 1967 to protest against discrimination against blacks in sport.

Black Panthers

Huey Newton formed the Black Panther Party in 1966 as a response to police brutality in the Watts Riots. The Party had a ten-point programme; its demands included 'Land, Bread, Housing, Education, Clothing, Justice and Peace'. At its height it had 5,000 members organised into 30 'chapters'. In 1968–69, the Black Panthers temporarily merged with the SNCC.

The organisation forged links with communist freedom fighters all over the world. In Los Angeles, it set up health clinics and an ambulance and gave free breakfasts to ghetto children. It also attacked the police. Black Panther patrols would shadow police patrols. If the police started harassing black Americans, the Panthers would help the blacks. A number of Black Panthers were shot, notably in a gun battle that followed the ambush of a police patrol in 1968.

In response, California decided that it would recruit policemen in proportion to the size of the black and white population in the state.

The FBI labelled the Black Panthers a 'black nationalist hate group'. Its leaders were targeted and jailed, and the movement had fizzled out by 1970.

Black American sprinters Tommie Smith and John Carlos give the Black Power salute as they receive their medals at the 1963 Olympics.

2.7c How important was Martin Luther King in the fight for Civil Rights?

Protest Organiser, 1955–63

It is arguable that King was initially a failure. He faced opposition on every side. Black extremists accused him of being the white man's lackey, white people claimed that he was advocating anarchy, and NAACP leader Roy Wilkins accused him of pride. The early successes of the Civil Rights Movement were achieved by CORE, SNCC and the NAACP, and where King did intervene – as in Albany – he was often less than successful.

By 1963, however, King had learned his lessons. He had developed the tactics of mass protests, civil disobedience and direct action. Albany taught him the importance of unity and of a single clear goal. He also realised that it was useless negotiating with the white authorities.

In 1963 – after his successes at Birmingham and in the Washington Freedom March – King was at the height of his influence, and in 1964 he won the Nobel Peace Prize for his fight against racial discrimination.

However, he had little in common with the radical black movements that grew up after 1966, and by 1968, when he was assassinated, King had come to believe that he had failed and that 'the day of violence is here'.

In 1983 the third Monday in January became Martin Luther King Day, a national holiday in the United States.

Towards a Civil Rights Act

Partly as a result of their respect for Martin Luther King, President Kennedy and his brother Robert became committed to civil rights. As attorney-general, Robert Kennedy was in the forefront of the action.

- In 1962 the government introduced an act to reduce discrimination in housing.
- Also in 1962, Robert Kennedy sent 500 federal marshals to help James Meredith, a black student, enrol at the University of Mississippi.
- In 1963, federal marshals forced state governor George Wallace to desegregate the University of Alabama.

Finally, the Kennedys introduced the Civil Rights Bill, which became law after President Kennedy's assassination.

Martin Luther King meeting with Robert Kennedy.

GradeStudio

Describe how Martin Luther King helped the cause of Civil Rights.

Led Montgomery Bus Boycott/SCLC ☐

Did not negotiate – confronted prejudice ☐

Principle of non-violence ☐

Control of media – speeches ☐

Influence with the Kennedys ☐

The Civil Rights Act, 1964

The Civil Rights Act of 1964 was part of the 'Great Society' programme, which the new president, Lyndon Johnson, had designed to bring 'an end to poverty and injustice'. The act outlawed racial segregation in schools, public places and employment and set up an Equal Opportunities Commission to enforce this ruling. Johnson directed funding to those states which made fastest progress on desegregation, and so states were encouraged to work harder.

In 1964, after the murder of two young Civil Rights workers, Johnson ordered the FBI to hunt down the killers: 19 KKK men, including a sheriff and deputy, were arrested. Next year, Johnson passed the Voting Rights Act (1965), which ended the literacy tests and other tricks by which whites had stopped blacks registering to vote – now every person had a vote, as of right. In 1965 an Education Act provided funding for public schools; black students gained significantly, and the number of black pupils leaving with high school diplomas increased.

Affirmative Action

Johnson's vision went further than simply civil equality, however. As early as 1962, James Farmer had recommended what he called 'Compulsory Preferential Treatment' – giving black people extra help to allow them to compete with more advantaged whites. Johnson adopted this idea, calling it: '**affirmative action**'. A Higher Education Act (1965) gave aid to black colleges. In 1968, the Civil Rights Act (also called the 'Fair Housing' Act) banned discrimination in housing. It was designed to allow black Americans, if they wished, to move into areas where white Americans lived.

However, Johnson's 'Great Society' programme was overtaken by the Vietnam War. The government no longer had the money to spend on an ambitious programme of social reform. By 1967 the average black person's income had risen, but only to 62 per cent of the average white person's income. And by this time, black politics had radicalised, amongst the riots of 1964–68.

King and Black Power

After the Watts riots of 1965, King visited the area and was horrified at the 'economic deprivation, social isolation, inadequate housing, and general despair'. In 1966, he went to live in the ghettos of Chicago to see how he might help.

King was not particularly successful in Chicago. He quarrelled with the mayor and was not well liked by the local black people. In the hot summer, the 'fire hydrant riots' broke out when police shut down a fire hydrant black youths had been playing in. The mayor blamed King for the riots.

In 1966 King joined an SNCC march in Memphis. Known as the 'Meredith March', it was held in support of James Meredith, who had intended to march on his own but had been shot and wounded on the second day. It was not a happy event. King argued with Stokely Carmichael (the new SNCC leader) about whether the march should be blacks-only. On the march, SNCC members sang: 'Oh what fun it is to blast/a trooper man away', and Carmichael used the event as a platform from which to preach Black Power.

King had little in common with the new Black Power leaders, most of whom despised him personally. He did not like talk of Black Power because he feared it would frighten his white supporters and provoke racial conflict. He said that he wanted 'striped power', in which black and white would share equally. Most of all, he was horrified by the Black Power movement's open advocacy of violent protest.

SUMMARY

How different was MLK from the Black Power leaders?

VERY DIFFERENT

1. They advocated violence / MLK was non-violent
2. Black Power expelled white members / MLK wanted 'striped power' and had white supporters
3. They were nationalist (NoI) or wanted social action / MLK concentrated on civil rights
4. CORE 'freedom houses' and Atlanta Project / MLK was not welcome or successful in Chicago
5. King believed he had failed ('Day of Violence')
6. King clashed with Carmichael on the Meredith March
7. Malcolm X called King a 'fool' (MLK called NoI a 'hate group')

NOT SO DIFFERENT

1. MLK was horrified by the deprivation in Watts
2. MLK went to live in Chicago in 1966
3. *Where Do We Go From Here?* advocated affirmative social action
4. MLK opposed the Vietnam War
5. MLK was anti-retaliation, but he provoked violence (Project 'C' in Birmingham/Selma).

Changing opinions

Despite his differences with the Black Power leaders, towards the end of his life, King realised that – now that desegregation and voting legislation was in place – what was needed was social action. The Civil Rights Movement had secured legal equality, but – as one writer puts it – this only gave black Americans 'an opportunity, not a deliverance'.

In his book *Where Do We Go From Here?* (1967), King took up the idea of affirmative action. Giving black Americans the vote had cost white America nothing; now it was time for social and economic action.

As a result of his new left-wing political views, in 1967 King began to speak out against the Vietnam War, declaring that it was immoral on social grounds: 'It costs half a million dollars to kill a Vietcong soldier; but we are only spending $53 on every poor American back at home', he said.

His assassination in 1968 cut short this stage in his career.

After Martin Luther King

In the event, successive American governments have failed to deliver significant improvements in social or economic equality.

The years since 1964 have seen black Americans achieve an impressive string of 'firsts' – the first black mayor, the first black general, the first black U.S. Ambassador to the United Nations, the first black space shuttle commander, the first black secretary of state. And in 2008 a black man, Barack Obama, achieved what a generation earlier had been utterly unthinkable: he was elected president of the United States. It might be argued that Martin Luther King's dream is beginning to come true.

Yet many black Americans still do not share in the American Dream. The census of 1992, for instance, showed that the average black income was about 62 per cent of the average white income – exactly what it had been 25 years earlier. A third of all black males aged 20–29 were in prison, on parole or on probation (a black American was seven times more likely than a white American to be in jail). While unemployment in the black population stood at 14 per cent generally (double the figure for white Americans), in some of the inner-city ghettoes it was as high as 63 per cent.

Despite its achievements in the field of civil rights, America has a long way to go before it becomes a colour-blind society.

SUMMARY

Did Martin Luther King make a major contribution to the Civil Rights Movement?

YES

1. Leadership/a figurehead
2. Set up the SCLC, which organised protest
3. Achieved high profile successes – Montgomery, Birmingham, Selma
4. Set the principles of the early movement – non-violence, mass protest, direct action
5. Developed the tactics – single issue/provoke violent reaction
6. Spectacle – 'I have a dream' speech

NO

1. Others: sit-ins and freedom rides initiated by COPE/SNCC; NAACP's legal breakthroughs
2. King's principles/tactics were inappropriate for the ghettos
3. After 1965 new leaders, new tactics (self-defence and riots), new principle (Black Power)
4. Achieved political, not social or economic rights

With the growth of civil rights, bussing encouraged black children to attend schools previously dominated by white children.

Racial discrimination and violence continues. In 1991 Los Angeles police were filmed giving Rodney King 'a monkey-slapping' (as one of the officers described it); when a jury acquitted the officers in 1992, black protesters rioted for six days. During the Rodney King riots, 53 people died and one billion dollars of damage was done.

Preparation - 'Describe'

- the attitude to black people in the southern states during the 1950s and 1960s
- the Montgomery Bus Boycott
- what civil rights campaigners did to try to win equal rights, 1960–63
- the Civil Rights Act of 1964
- the Black Power movements of the late 1960s
- Martin Luther King's role as a protest organiser
- the ghetto riots of 1965–66
- attempts at affirmative action

Using this textbook, an encyclopaedia or the internet, make sure you know enough to write at least TWO detailed descriptions of each item in the list above.

Preparation - names and specialist terms

- NAACP
- CORE
- KKK
- MIA
- SCLC
- SNCC
- FBI
- lynching
- ghettos
- sit-ins

- Jim Crow Laws
- segregation
- 'new Negro'
- *Brown v. Topeka*
- Freedom Rides
- Freedom Marches
- Watts riots
- Atlanta Project
- Meredith March
- Black Panthers

- Black Power
- fire hydrant riots
- Charles Houston
- James Farmer
- President Truman
- President Eisenhower
- Robert Shelton
- Emmett Till
- Rosa Parks
- Thurgood Marshall

- Martin Luther King
- Robert Kennedy
- Rev C.T. Vivian
- 'Bull' Connor
- Malcolm X
- Muhammad Ali
- Stokely Carmichael
- H. 'Rap' Brown
- Floyd McKissick
- Huey Newton

Using this textbook, an encyclopaedia or the internet, make sure you know about each of the above so that you can include them in your exam answers.

Preparation - 'Why?'

WHY...

- did many white Americans resent black people?
- did the Montgomery Bus Boycott take place?
- did King try to provoke and confront white leaders?
- did many black leaders oppose King?
- was King successful in gaining black civil rights?

Working in a small group, think of TWO reasons for each situation in the list above.

Preparation - 'How?'

HOW did this...

- World War II...
- *Brown v. Topeka* ...
- *Brown v. Topeka* ...
- Freedom Rides...
- Freedom Marches...
- civil rights action...
- Black Power...
- Martin Luther King...

cause this?

- black civil rights agitation
- Little Rock
- the death of Emmett Till
- attacks on the Freedom Riders
- police violence (e.g. Birmingham, 1963)
- the Civil Rights Act of 1964
- *Where Do We Go From Here?*
- Barack Obama

Working as a whole class, think of TWO ways in which each factor on the left led to the outcome on the right.

'Martin Luther King had nothing in common with the Black Power leaders of the late 1960s.'
Do you agree? Explain your answer.   (12 marks)

Full sample answer

Comments

There is an argument that Martin Luther King had nothing in common with the Black Power leaders of the late 1960s – they seem different in many ways.

Defend the null hypothesis.

Firstly, the Black Power leaders advocated violence, whereas King tried to follow the non-violent passive resistance methods of Gandhi.

Secondly, the Black Power leaders of SNCC (Carmichael, 1966) and CORE (McKissick, 1966) expelled their white members, but King was afraid of alienating his white supporters – he said he wanted 'striped power' not black power.

These are all basic clashes of principle, and meant that King had little in common with the Black Power leaders – King clashed with Carmichael on the Meredith March and Malcolm X called King a 'fool' (and King called NoI a 'hate group'). Certainly, in 1968 King believed he had failed to adapt to the new ideas, saying sadly that he feared 'the day of Violence is here'.

> At least TWO reasons why the null hypothesis IS true. EXPLAIN HOW the null hypothesis is true. Include FACTS.

Argue that the null hypothesis is not true.

However, it could be argued that King was not as far away from the Black Power leaders as it might seem at first.

King was horrified by the 'economic deprivation, social isolation, inadequate housing and general despair' which he said had caused the Watts Riots, and as a result went to live in Chicago in 1966 to experience ghetto life for himself. This shows that he was not solely a middle-class black man preaching to the middle class.

Also, it is clear that King – like the Black Power leaders – saw the need for social action in the ghettos. His 1967 book: <u>Where Do We Go From Here?</u> took up the ideas of affirmative social action, and in 1967 King spoke up against the Vietnam War because it was taking money away from social spending on 'every poor American back at home'. So it is clear that King was not only concerned for civil rights.

> Begin the second section with a connective of comparison. At least TWO reasons why the the null hypothesis IS NOT true. EXPLAIN HOW the null hypothesis is not true. Include FACTS.

Reach a conclusion.

Therefore, it seems that – although King in the early 1960s was far from the radical social and nationalist campaigner that the Black Power leaders were in the later 1960s – it is true to say that, by the end of the 1960s, King had come round much more to their way of thinking. And even though he always said that he rejected their violent methods, it is worth remembering that by 'passive resistance' King meant 'non-retaliation' – King was not afraid of violence, and he often knowingly provoked violence (for example, by his Project 'C' – 'Confrontation' – in Birmingham in 1963, and on the march at Selma in 1965).

> Begin the third section with a connective of comparison. EXPLAIN HOW you reached your judgement. Include FACTS.

2.8 The USA and Vietnam: Failure Abroad and at Home, 1964–1975

2.8a How effective were guerrilla tactics during the Vietnam War?

The theory of guerrilla warfare

In 1937, when he was trying to drive the Japanese out of China, the Chinese communist leader Mao Zedong wrote a little pamphlet called *On Guerrilla Warfare*.

Guerrilla warfare, he said, was the way a smaller, weaker force could resist a larger, more powerful invader.

Mao identified three phases of a guerrilla war: FIRST, getting the support of the people, SECOND harrassing and weakening the enemy, and THIRD, driving the enemy out by conventional means. It is the second phase that most people think of when they talk about 'guerrilla warfare' – the goal, in Mao's words, is 'to exterminate small forces of the enemy; to harass and weaken large forces; to attack enemy lines of communications; to establish bases capable of supporting independent operations in the enemy's rear, to force the enemy to disperse his strength'.

The only rule about guerrilla warfare, said Mao, is that it has no rules.

During the Vietnam War, 1964–75, the North Vietnamese military leader Vo Nguyen Giap

Guerilla warfare was used by the Vietnamese against more conventional American tactics, such as bombing.

followed Mao's theory, although he had to adapt the tactics to Vietnam's situation (see page 239), and it became clear as time went on that the facts did not quite fit the theory.

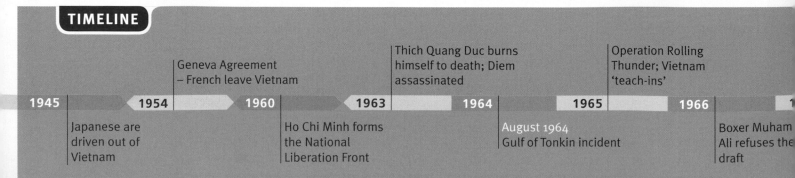

TIMELINE

1945	1954	1960	1963	1964	1965	1966	
	Geneva Agreement – French leave Vietnam		Thich Quang Duc burns himself to death; Diem assassinated		Operation Rolling Thunder; Vietnam 'teach-ins'		
Japanese are driven out of Vietnam		Ho Chi Minh forms the National Liberation Front		August 1964 Gulf of Tonkin incident		Boxer Muham Ali refuses the draft	

Background

Before the Second World War, Vietnam was part of the French colony of Indo-China. In 1941, however, the French were driven out by the Japanese. The Japanese were resisted by nationalist Vietnamese freedom fighters – the Viet Minh – led by a former schoolteacher called Ho Chi Minh. At the end of the war, Ho Chi Minh declared Vietnam an independent republic (2 September 1945).

The French tried to re-impose colonial rule. This was the time of the Cold War, and Ho Chi Minh was known to be a communist, so the Americans supported the French with $3 billion of financial aid, 1949–1954. In March 1954, however, the Viet Minh destroyed the French army at Dien Bien Phu, and in July 1954 the Geneva Agreement gave Vietnam independence. Vietnam was divided between a communist north (under Ho Chi Minh) and a 'democratic' south. The new leader of South Vietnam was a Vietnamese nationalist called Ngo Dinh Diem, who had been in exile in a Catholic seminary in New Jersey. Diem had the support of the US, who saw in him someone who would prevent the spread of communism.

Ho Chi Minh, however, did not accept the division of Vietnam, and in 1954 he set up the National Liberation Front (NLF), a patriotic movement to reunite Vietnam. Diem scornfully called the NLF the 'Vietcong' ('Vietnamese Commies'), but the South Vietnamese army (ARVN) was unable to defeat them. Instead, to counter NLF terrorism, Diem started the 'Agroville Program' (later called the 'Strategic Hamlets' program). Under this scheme hundreds of thousands of peasants who lived in Vietcong-controlled areas were moved to live in 'safe' villages (which were, in effect, concentration camps).

Diem's Government

The Americans did not like their new ally, but they were stuck with him, and the US funded the Saigon Military Mission – a unit of about 1000 military advisers sent to Vietnam to train the ARVN in guerrilla warfare.

In 1963, however, Diem's government lost US support altogether. On 8 May 1963 – Buddha's birthday – Buddhist monks in the town of Hue asked permission to fly Buddhist flags. Diem refused. When the Buddhists demonstrated, the ARVN attacked them with hand grenades and put Hue under military control. In protest, on 11 June 1963 a Buddhist monk named Thich Quang Duc burned himself to death. The event provoked a worldwide outcry. The Americans' patience with their repressive ally ran out.

In November 1963 the CIA arranged a government coup (military takeover), and Diem was assassinated.

SUMMARY

Why did the USA get involved in Vietnam?
1. Because the French had been driven out
2. Initially, to support the Diem government against the Buddhist/popular uprising
3. To stop the communists
4. To stop further communist successes (domino theory)
5. Gulf of Tonkin incident
6. Once they had become involved, the Americans had to keep escalating the war to try to defeat the Vietcong

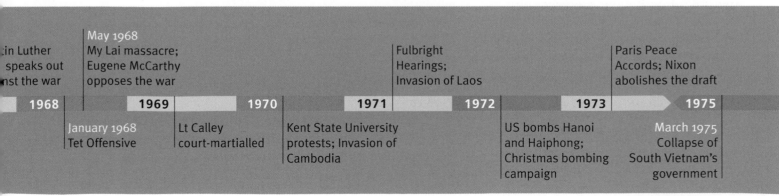

...in Luther speaks out ...nst the war	May 1968 My Lai massacre; Eugene McCarthy opposes the war			Fulbright Hearings; Invasion of Laos		Paris Peace Accords; Nixon abolishes the draft
1968	**1969**	**1970**	**1971**	**1972**	**1973**	**1975**
	January 1968 Tet Offensive	Lt Calley court-martialled	Kent State University protests; Invasion of Cambodia		US bombs Hanoi and Haiphong; Christmas bombing campaign	March 1975 Collapse of South Vietnam's government

Gulf of Tonkin Incident

The American president, Lyndon Johnson, believed in the domino theory – the theory that if one country fell to communism, others would follow. He believed that if the communist takeover of Vietnam was not stopped, communism would spread throughout south-east Asia. By 1964 Johnson was looking for an opportunity to become directly involved in the war.

That opportunity came in August 1964. At the end of July, American forces had helped the ARVN carry out raids on North Vietnamese radar stations.

After one of these operations, on 2 August 1964, in the Gulf of Tonkin, the USS *Maddox* had fired on North Vietnamese torpedo boats which had come too close. On the night of 3/4 August, sailors on the *Maddox* panicked, fearing they were under renewed attack.

Johnson never believed that the North Vietnamese had attacked the *Maddox*. In his words, 'those dumb stupid sailors were just shooting at flying fish'. However, he told Congress that the North Vietnamese 'had conducted deliberate attacks against US naval vessels'.

On 7 August 1964, Congress authorised him to escalate (increase) US involvement. Johnson immediately ordered bombing raids and sent more troops to Vietnam.

The Gulf of Tonkin Resolution was a major turning point in US legal history, since it gave the president the power to wage war without a declaration of war by Congress. (One of the results of the failure of the war was the War Powers Resolution 1973, which took this power away from the president.)

The Americans knew that the war could be won only on the ground. They sent 2.8 million soldiers to Vietnam, 1964–75.

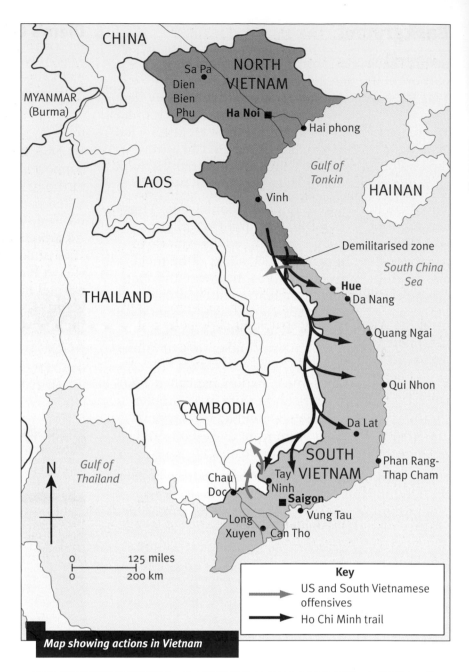

Map showing actions in Vietnam

GradeStudio

Describe how the USA became involved in the Vietnam War

Wanted to stop the spread of Communism in South-East Asia ☐

$3 billion financial aid to the French, 1949–54 ☐

Supported Diem for leadership in 1954 ☐

Set up the Saigon Military Mission in 1954 – military advisors sent to train the AVRN ☐

Arranged the assassination of Diep in 1963 ☐

Domino theory – by 1964 President Johnson was looking for an opportunity to go to war ☐

Gulf of Tonkin incident and resolution, August 1964 ☐

Operation Rolling Thunder after attacks on US helicopter base, February 1965 ☐

Military actions in Vietnam – Guerrilla Warfare 1964–68

The NVA and the Vietcong

Neither the North Vietnamese Army (NVA) nor the Vietcong (VC) in the south could defeat the Americans in a direct fight, so they fought a guerrilla war. It was to some extent a war of tactics against technology. The key Vietcong tactic was called staying 'close to the belt' – Vietcong guerrillas launched hit-and-run raids and always stayed as close as possible to the American troops to make it difficult for US planes to bomb them.

The Vietcong relied on ambush, using small arms fire (many of the guerrillas' weapons were bought from the ARVN). They struck quickly – often at great personal risk – and killed the 'point' soldiers (on watch for the enemy), command officers and radio operator as quickly as possible. In all, 58,000 American troops died in Vietnam.

The guerrillas carried little, so they could run at a moment's notice. They wore the simple black pyjamas of peasants, so that they could mingle with the population; ordinary people generally supported the VC, but the VC also threatened to murder anyone who cooperated with the Americans. The entire area around Saigon was a network of tunnels, and VC soldiers could disappear down one and reappear miles away.

Tunnels and tracks were booby-trapped with poisoned bamboo sticks and landmines; the worst landmine, called 'bouncing Betty', leapt into the air and exploded at hip level.

Weapons and supplies were brought south from North Vietnam to the VC guerrillas by truck, cart and even bicycle, down thousands of miles of forest tracks called collectively the Ho Chi Minh Trail. Many of the tracks did not even run through Vietnam but instead through nearby Laos and Cambodia.

SUMMARY

'The Americans fought a high-tech conventional war; the Vietcong fought a low-tech guerrilla war.'
Do you agree?

YES
1. USA used: warships; B52s; Operation Rolling Thunder and Nixon bombing; cluster bombs; helicopters; napalm; Agent Orange
2. Vietcong used: hit-and-run; staying 'close to the belt'; tunnels; bicycles; small arms; bamboo stakes

NO
1. USA used: 'search and destroy' missions; Zippo raids
2. North Vietnamese/Vietcong had: torpedo boats; radar systems; SAM guided missiles; MiG fighter planes; 'bouncing Betty' mines; and fought Tet Offensive

Vietnamese guerilla tactics used small groups of soldiers in 'hit and run' tactics.

The USA in Vietnam

Operation Rolling Thunder

In February 1965 the NLF destroyed a US helicopter base and destroyed 10 planes. On 13 February President Johnson launched Operation Rolling Thunder, a massive bombing campaign in North Vietnam. At first, US bombers attacked identified targets, such as bridges, radar systems and weapons dumps. After 1965, American planes simply flew over North Vietnam looking for targets.

In addition to conventional bombs, US planes dropped napalm (a petrol jelly that sticks to the skin and burns) and cluster bombs (which burst in mid-air, spreading 600 'baby bombs' that explode into shrapnel pellets). Later, cluster bombs exploded into fibre-glass fragments, which could not be found in the body by X-ray.

American planes also dropped Agent Orange, a defoliant which stripped the leaves off the trees, so NLF soldiers would find it harder to hide. The North Vietnamese fought back, using Soviet-supplied anti-aircraft guns, SAM guided missiles and MiG fighter planes.

The Americans did not bomb Hanoi or – surprisingly – the port of Haiphong (which was the entry route to North Vietnam for supplies from the USSR).

In the three years of the operation, the US made 153,784 raids, dropping 864,000 tonnes of bombs, causing $370 million of damage and 90,000 casualties, with the loss of 922 planes. In November 1968, the US Joint Chiefs admitted that Operation Rolling Thunder had not worked, and President Johnson called it off.

Hearts and Minds

Johnson always insisted that victory would come only if the USA won the 'hearts and minds' of the Vietnamese people – on one occasion he defined it as a policy of 'hope and electricity'. The Americans built schools, roads and sewers and provided medical aid.

However, the Strategic Hamlets program, and unrestrained killing by the US forces in Vietnam, undid any good work this might have achieved.

Search and destroy: The US army in action in Vietnam in the 1960s.

The US strategy

The American strategy was to launch 'search and destroy missions' – small groups of soldiers would go out looking for VC units. Essentially, they were bait – they would wander about until attacked, whereupon they would call in the airforce to napalm the enemy.

American commanders measured success in terms of 'body count' – the number of VC killed.

The chances of being killed for an American combat soldier was one in five. The worst casualties were amongst the 'cherries' (new, inexperienced soldiers) who were a danger not only to themselves but to every man in the unit. But the US policy of one-year tours of duty meant that most men were cherries.

Eventually, morale collapsed. By 1971 the *New York Times* was reporting soldiers 'questioning orders, deserting, smoking marijuana, shooting heroin, stealing from their buddies and hurling racial abuse and rocks at their brothers'. In 1970, 18 per cent of soldiers had gone **AWOL** and there had been 425 cases of 'fragging' (shooting an officer). There had been many more cases of 'working it out' – a process by which a unit would simply refuse to do as told, so the officer had to negotiate a safer course of action with his men.

The My Lai Massacre

For the young American soldiers – average age 19 – the 'search and destroy' missions were terrifying and morale-destroying. They became trigger-happy and cruel – US troops called the missions 'Zippo Raids', after the cheap lighters they used to set fire to Vietnamese homes. Many came to regard the Vietnamese as sub-human, as the people responsible for the deaths of friends.

In January 1968 the North Vietnamese had launched the Tet Offensive (see page 246). During that offensive, the 48th VC Battalion had retreated to the village of Son My in the north of South Vietnam, and was believed to be hiding there. The whole area was a known Vietcong 'fortress', and leaflets had been dropped warning all non-Vietcong to flee.

On 16 March 1968, Charlie Company of the 23rd Infantry Division was ordered to 'press forward aggressively and eliminate the 48th Battalion'. The commanders were assured that most of the population of the area were 'VC or VC sympathizers', and that any civilians would have left for market by 7am. They were told to burn the houses, kill the livestock, destroy foodstuffs and close the wells.

Son My consisted of four hamlets, called My Lai 1, 2, 3 and 4. The assault began about 8 am, when First Platoon, led by Second Lieutenant William 'Rusty' Calley, attacked My Lai 4.

The Americans met no opposition and quickly entered the village, where they went berserk, burning houses and killing the inhabitants (almost exclusively old men, women, and children). Women were gang raped. Some victims were mutilated, with the words 'C Company' carved into the chest. Between 70 and 80 Vietnamese were taken to a ditch and shot.

Similar killings took place throughout the village. When one soldier refused to kill the Vietnamese, Calley took his gun and shot them for him.

In the end, Calley was the only soldier found responsible for the massacre, but members of the 2nd Platoon were doing the same in the northern part of the village, and the 3rd Platoon later rounded up and killed everybody 1st and 2nd Platoons had missed. Officially 147, actually perhaps 500 people, were killed. Later that day, soldiers from another battalion similarly attacked the village of My Khe, throwing grenades into the houses and shooting women and children.

The My Lai incident was witnessed by an American helicopter pilot, Hugh Thompson, who tried to persuade Calley to stop the killings and rescued a number of villagers. He reported the killings, but his report was dismissed as exaggeration. Instead, in April 1969 the event was reported as a victory, with 128 Vietcong dead and 22 civilians killed 'inadvertently'.

SUMMARY

Why did 1st Platoon massacre the villagers of My Lai?

1. Unclear orders which emphasised killing
2. They were told only VC would be there
3. Racist attitudes towards Vietnamese people
4. Desire for revenge for fallen friends
5. Frustration because they could not find an enemy to fight
6. Poor officers – Calley was a college dropout
7. Poor leadership, who 'turned a blind eye' and tried to cover up problems
8. Emphasis on body count to show success
9. Inability to communicate with the villagers
10. Vietnam was a brutal and brutalising war of mass-killing and destruction

2.8b How did the coverage of the Vietnam War in the USA lead to demands for peace?

TV and media coverage

Vietnam was the first war which appeared on TV the next day. It was the first 'living room war', extensively reported in the newspapers and on television – without censorship. Media coverage had a decisive effect on public opinion.

Early Representations

In the early years of the war, the American media was generally supportive. In 1962, for example, *Time* magazine praised the war as 'a remarkable US military effort.'

The American soldier in Vietnam – especially if he was a 'Green Beret' – was singled out for praise. An article in *Time* in 1961 idolised him as a man who 'can remove an appendix, fire an obsolete gun, sweet-talk some bread out of a native in his own language, fashion explosives out of chemical fertilizer, cut an enemy's throat, live off the land…' In his 1965 novel *The Green Berets*, Robin Moore (who claimed, allegedly untruthfully, to have fought with the Special Forces) glamorised his subjects as down-to-earth heroes, there to help the Vietnamese and set them free. South Vietnamese soldiers, however, were not portrayed so favourably – Moore called them 'lousy little dirty bug-outs'.

In 1968 John Wayne starred in *The Green Berets*, a film made with the full cooperation of the Johnson government. After showing American Special Forces supervising humanitarian aid and giving sweets to local children, the film focuses on the brutality of the Vietcong. The story involves the mission of Colonel Mike Kirby to capture a top NVA officer, who lives a life of luxury while his people go hungry.

Changing views

Even as it was shown however, people had realised that Wayne's portrayal of Vietnam as another 'Wild West' to be tamed by good and decent heroes was – in the words of one critic – 'the way Vietnam ought to be', not the way it was. In 1965 CBS had shown American soldiers firing the thatched roofs of Vietnamese houses with Zippo lighters; 1968 was the year of the Tet offensive, and Americans had to face up to what was really happening in the Vietnam War.

In February 1968, the journalist John Wheeler wrote an article called 'Life in the V Ring'. It was a description of a day during the Battle of Hamburger Hill (as it became known). Wheeler's account concentrated on the fears and bitterness of the soldiers who were having to fight.

One famous image of the Tet offensive, ARVN Colonel Nguyen Ngoc Loan killing a Vietcong captive in Saigon, was shown on NBC. The Vietcong had just murdered the entire family of one of Loan's most trusted officers. This photo shows the captive just before execution.

That same month, the TV news presenter Walter Cronkite made his crucial 'We Are Mired in Stalemate' broadcast. He summed up the growing mood of defeatism. Cronkite, who was admired for his moderate and realistic views, reported that he had 'no confidence in the Vietnamese government', was 'disappointed by the American leaders' and concluded: 'the only rational way out will be to negotiate, not as victors, but as an honourable people who… did the best they could.'

Public reactions to My Lai

Defeatism turned to horror as details of the My Lai massacre leaked out. Vietnamese propaganda reports of the massacre and the complaints of a number of soldiers were ignored or covered up for 18 months, and only in November 1969 did the journalist Seymour Hersch break the story. As well as soldiers' testimony, there were photographs taken by Ron Haeberle, the official US army photographer who – in addition to the black and white photos he had given to the military – had also taken graphic colour photos on a secret second camera.

Calley was court-martialled for murder in March 1971. He claimed he was just following orders but was sentenced to life imprisonment. Three days later President Nixon transferred him from prison to house arrest. His sentence was reduced to 20, then to 10 years, and in the end he was freed after serving little more than 3 years.

Nobody else was convicted for the massacre or for covering it up.

Given the accepted theory that media coverage horrified the US public and turned them against the war, the reaction of Americans to My Lai was surprising: 79 per cent disapproved of Calley's court-martial, and 20 per cent refused to accept that what he had done was wrong.

Even so, the massacre completely destroyed any vestige of 'moral right' that Americans might have felt about the war. The US public was confused and distressed – how had so many good American boys been able to do such a thing? Returning Vietnam soldiers no longer came back as heroes, but now found themselves stigmatised as 'baby killers'.

The effect of media coverage

It is sometimes claimed that media coverage directed public opinion by horrifying the public about the war. Yet only a quarter of reports contained images of dead bodies, and before 1968 most news reports were pro-American.

TV reporting of the war became hostile only after public opinion began to turn against the war. So it may be that TV reporting followed rather than led public opinion. But it has to be remembered that public opinion had been substantially formed by the images and reports the public had been seeing for the previous four years. Americans had watched TV and made up their own minds.

Television continued to produce pictures which showed the true horror of war. This 1972 image shows innocent villagers fleeing from a napalm attack launched in error on a 'friendly' village. The little girl in the centre has had her clothes burnt off.

Protest movements

As the war progressed, opposition to the war increased.

Student opposition

The first protests against the war occurred in 1964 and were made by students.

In 1965 a student group called the Vietnam Day Committee organised a 36-hour 'teach-in' against the war at the University of California. It was attended by 30,000 students, and dozens of leading pacifists gave talks. Later that year, University of California students were the first people to burn their **draft cards**, and in November Norman Morrison, a 31-year-old pacifist, set himself on fire under the office window of Secretary of Defense Robert McNamara.

In 1967 the anti-Vietnam protest movement began to grow, but it still had a 'hippy' feel to it. A 'Human Be-in' in San Francisco included protests about the Vietnam War. Christian groups also registered their opposition, and in October 100,000 anti-war protesters marched to the Lincoln Memorial in Washington, DC. The protesters were attacked by police, and there were 647 arrests.

Civil Rights protesters

By this time, the movement had been joined by Civil Rights protesters. In 1964 President Johnson had promised Americans a 'Great Society' programme of state welfare and good homes. With the war costing $20 billion a year, he had been forced to cancel it. Many young people questioned this choice, saying that the war was a waste of money.

The Muslim group Nation of Islam asked why black Americans should fight for a country which would not grant them equal rights (page 229). In 1966 Muhammad Ali, the world heavyweight boxing champion, had refused to be drafted.

By contrast, the black leader Martin Luther King at first hesitated to criticise the war because he wanted the government to support his civil rights campaign (see pages 226–228). In 1967, however, King spoke out. King declared the war immoral on social grounds: 'It costs half a million dollars to kill a Vietcong soldier; but we are only spending $53 on every poor American back at home'. He also opposed it on racial grounds. Black Americans were less likely to be able to 'dodge the draft' (refuse their call-up for the army). They were more likely to be sent on active duty and twice as likely to be killed as white Americans. As Muhammad Ali commented: 'No Vietcong ever called me nigger'.

Other Americans began to dodge the draft. In all, 600,000 young men evaded the call-up. Famous draft-dodgers included two later presidents, Bill Clinton and George W. Bush. Some people publicly burned their draft papers and were arrested. Rich people simply went abroad until they were too old to be called up. 170,000 Americans received official **conscientious objector** status.

Students burning Vietnam draft cards.

SUMMARY

Why did some Americans oppose the war in Vietnam?

1. Saw it on TV – saw failures and atrocities – saw how awful the South Vietnam government was
2. Hippies wanted to 'make love not war'
3. Draft dodgers didn't want to fight
4. It seemed a waste of money when there was need for Johnson's Great Society programme against poverty
5. It was a civil rights issue – young black men fought and died disproportionately
6. Some genuine conscientious objectors
7. Vietnamese **veterans** against the war – ashamed of atrocities
8. When the marches were attacked by the police it gave the movement more determination
9. National loss of confidence in America's moral right to impose its democracy on others

Other voices

It was not only students and civil rights protesters who were questioning the war.

In 1968 the Democratic presidential candidate Eugene McCarthy campaigned on an anti-war platform.

Later that year, Secretary of Defense Robert McNamara admitted in public that Operation Rolling Thunder was not working.

Congress was also beginning to question the war. In April–May 1971, the Senate Foreign Relations Committee held a series of 22 hearings (called the Fulbright Hearings) for proposals to withdraw from Vietnam. The Committee Chairman, William Fulbright, openly opposed American involvement, and he started the proceedings by criticising the 'fraudulent Gulf of Tonkin episode', which had taken responsibility for the war away from Congress. Fulbright said that the purpose of the hearings was 'positive congressional action to end American participation in the war'.

Other voices against the war were those of the returning veterans. In 1971 John Kerry, a returning war hero, complained on the veterans' behalf to the Fulbright Hearings about a war they had been *told* was a war against communism, but which turned out to be a civil war waged by people fighting for their freedom while their country was ravaged by American bombs. In 1971 war veterans led an anti-war march that attracted half a million people; veterans attending the march threw away 700 medals.

Americans who believed that the war was a mistake (Gallup Polls):

- 1965: 24 per cent
- 1966: 37 per cent
- 1967: 41 per cent
- 1968: 53 per cent
- 1969: 58 per cent
- 1970: 56 per cent

Violence

Anti-war protests became increasingly violent. In 1969, an out-of-work draftsman named Sam Melville planted a number of bombs in office buildings in protest at the war.

When students at Kent State University, in Ohio, demonstrated on 4 May 1970 against the US bombing of Cambodia, the state's governor turned out the National Guard, who shot four students dead.

In response, 100,000 demonstrators marched on Washington, and more than four million students went on a National Student Strike. Anti-war protesters set fire to 30 Reserve Officers Training Corps (ROTC) buildings, and in August a van filled with 907 kilograms of ammonium nitrate was blown up at the University of Wisconsin–Madison.

Nixon tried to reduce the opposition to the war by saying that he agreed with the anti-war movement's aims but opposed the violence they used. In 1969 he made the draft fairer by choosing names on a lottery basis (in 1973 he abolished the draft altogether). And in 1971 he set up the President's Commission on Campus Unrest to address student opposition to the war.

It is worth noting that not all Americans were opposed to the war. Opinion polls after the Kent State shootings showed that half those polled agreed with the invasion of Cambodia, and 58 per cent thought that the students' deaths were their own fault. And on 20 May 1970, 100,000 New Yorkers marched through the city in support of the war.

This march against the war in Washington attracted 100,000 demonstrators.

2.8c Why did the USA lose the Vietnam War?

The Tet Offensive

Historians do not really know why the North decided to mount a direct military attack on the South in 1968. One theory suggests the Hanoi government had become convinced that (according to Mao's theory of guerrilla warfare) the ARVN was unable to resist, and that the Americans were so unpopular that the peasants were ready to rise up and drive them out. Another theory suggests it was a desperate last-ditch attack, because American bombing of North Vietnam had convinced the Hanoi government that it was about to lose the war. A third theory suggests that it was the Hanoi government's way of getting rid of the South Vietnamese Vietcong and taking over control of the war effort.

The Americans were not – as is sometimes stated – taken completely by surprise. Noticing the Vietcong build-up, General Westmorland had withdrawn 15 US battalions from the country to defend Saigon. However, the North Vietnamese had offered a truce for the Vietnamese New Year, or Tet holiday (27 January to 3 February) and so – despite the fact that on 28 January a number of Vietcong were caught in Saigon with taped appeals to people to rise up against the Americans – half the ARVN were allowed to go on leave.

On 31 January 1968, 84,000 Vietcong troops attacked a hundred towns and cities.

The Vietcong had some spectacular successes. A 15-man suicide squad captured the American embassy in Saigon and held out for six hours. The northern town of Hue was captured and – allegedly – hundreds of South Vietnamese 'collaborators' were executed. It took American soldiers 25 days to recapture the town; at least 3000 civilians died in the American re-occupation, and 75 per cent of the town's houses were wrecked. Many towns were the same – 'we had to destroy the town to save it', said the American commander at one town.

The Vietcong offensives were defeated with heavy losses. The ARVN did not crumble, and the peasants did not rise up. Nevertheless, the Vietcong made two further direct military pushes, in May and again in August.

US forces fight to recapture North Saigon street by street.

Results of the offensive

The Tet Offensive is famous as the only military action that both sides lost.

The results, initially, appeared disastrous for the North Vietnamese, who suffered, in the first phase, at least 45,000 losses. Their most experienced guerrilla fighters had been killed, and much equipment had been lost. Morale fell, soldiers deserted, and for a time the North Vietnamese considered surrendering. In April 1969, the North Vietnamese issued Directive 55: 'Never again are we going to risk our entire military force.'

However, the Tet Offensive was also a setback for the South Vietnamese – 14,300 civilians were killed, 70,000 homes were destroyed and there were 627,000 refugees.

And for the Americans, the Tet Offensive was also a disaster. President Johnson, realising he had lost the confidence of the public, decided not to stand for the presidency again. The media turned against the government. A **credibility gap** opened up between what the government was telling people, and what they believed to be true. Things weren't helped when the North Vietnamese realised what was happening and started boasting that they had defeated the Americans. An attitude grew up in America that the war was unwinnable.

SUMMARY

Who won the Tet Offensive?

The NVA?

1. Three major offensives, January, May and August
2. ARVN taken by surprise
3. American embassy in Saigon captured
4. Hue captured and held for 25 days
5. President Johnson did not stand for re-election
6. The US public lost faith in the war
7. Large-scale destruction in South Vietnam

The Americans?

1. 45,000 NVA and VC soldiers killed
2. Vietcong destroyed in South Vietnam
3. North Vietnamese morale fell – soldiers deserted/considered surrendering
4. The ARVN did not crumble
5. The peasants did not rise up in support of the NVA

Damage done in the Cholon (Chinatown) market area of Vietnam's capital city Saigon, during the Tet Offensive. The NVA 8th Division had set up its headquarters there.

President Nixon

In 1969 Richard Nixon became president. In November, he told the American people his plan to end the war.

Nixon said that he wanted to bring the troops home, but he could not abandon Vietnam. The massacres in Hue in 1968 had shown what would happen if the North Vietnamese won the war. He also felt obliged to maintain America's position as a world power. Nixon asked the 'silent majority' of Americans to support him as he continued to try 'to end the war in a way that we could win the peace'.

A new policy

In fact, Nixon had no intention of stopping the war at all; all he wanted to do was to make its continuance palatable to the American people. The main way he did that was by what he called 'Vietnamisation'. It was the job of the ARVN to defend South Vietnam, said Nixon. American forces were 'foreign' and should not be there. So he gradually 'brought the boys home'. This policy made him popular.

In Vietnam, he continued to prosecute the war by financing the ARVN and bombing North Vietnam. This suited the public too; people couldn't SEE the war coming home in a body bag – it wasn't hurting *them*.

Madman in the White House

The early 1970s were the years of 'Détente' in the Cold War (see pages 100–106). Nixon visited both Russia and China – there had never been such an ideal opportunity to end the war. Henry Kissinger, Nixon's National Security Adviser, began secret peace talks with the North Vietnamese.

One of Nixon's privately expressed theories was what he called the 'Madman Theory' – the belief that if the North Vietnamese thought he was ready to do anything (even use the nuclear bomb), he could frighten Hanoi into a negotiated agreement.

He was certainly not frightened to escalate the war to try to undermine the North Vietnamese war effort and to force them to negotiate. The NVA – at the invitation of the Cambodian government – used bases in neighbouring Cambodia to assemble its forces. The Americans – in 'Operation Menu' – had been secretly bombing NVA supply bases in Cambodia since 1969. In 1970, however, Nixon decided to 'go for broke', and 100,000 US and South Vietnamese forces invaded Cambodia to attack the

North Vietnamese presence in the country. The operation captured huge amounts of NVA weapons and supplies.

In nearby Laos, communist forces (the 'Pathet Lao') were trying to take over the country. They were supported by the NVA, who used Pathet Lao-controlled areas to store supplies for their guerrilla forces. In 1971 the ARVN mounted a major attack on Laos (Operation Lam Son 719), supported by a massive US bombing campaign against NVA stockpiles and the Ho Chi Minh trail. The ARVN were defeated and driven out, but the operation may have prevented a planned VC attack on South Vietnam.

In 1972 Nixon bombed Hanoi and Haiphong and mined North Vietnamese harbours.

SUMMARY

Did the USA lose, or did the Vietcong win?

UNITED STATES LOST

1. Failure of US army to defeat Vietcong guerrillas – 'search and destroy'/body count tactics
2. Young, inexperienced troops/low morale
3. South Vietnam government corrupt and weak
4. Opposition at home

VIETCONG WON

1. The peasants supported and hid the Vietcong, who wore ordinary black peasants' pyjamas
2. Vietcong guerrilla ambush tactics, close to the belt, using knowledge of area/tunnels
3. Supplied from China and Russia
4. Bravery of North Vietnamese fighters

GradeStudio

Describe how the USA defeated in Vietnam, 1969-75.

1965–75 Growing opposition at home	☐
Military stalemate in Vietnam	☐
1968 Tet Offensive damaged US confidence	☐
1972 Massive Christmas bombing campaign	☐
1973 Paris Peace Accords/US troops left	☐
1974 US Congress reduced aid to Thieu	☐
1975 Thieu government fell to NVA	☐

US Withdrawal

Throughout Nixon's very public escalations of the war, however, secret peace negotiations continued, and in October 1972 Kissinger announced that 'peace was at hand' in Vietnam.

Suddenly, there was confusion. Negotiations stalled. South Vietnamese leader Nguyen Van Thieu refused to accept the terms of the ceasefire (his position was the 'policy of the Four NOs' – no talks, no shared government, no reforms, no surrender). The North Vietnamese also left the negotiating table, blaming the Americans for trying to change the agreed terms.

Over Christmas 1972, Nixon conducted a massive bombing campaign over North Vietnam, dropping more bombs in 11 days than in all the years 1969–71. At the same time he placed pressure on Thieu, telling him that America was signing with or without him, but promising financial support for the South Vietnamese government.

Negotiations resumed, and the Paris Peace Accords were signed on 27 January 1973. The treaty established a ceasefire and the withdrawal of US forces, along with the return of all prisoners of war, after which direct talks would be held between North and South Vietnam for a political settlement.

The last American troops left Vietnam on 29 March 1973.

Thieu immediately renounced his promises to the Hanoi government – or Provisional Revolutionary Government (PRG), as it was now called – and began to try to drive PRG forces out of South Vietnam.

By contrast, the Hanoi government, fearful of provoking an American retaliation, issued its commanders the 'Five Forbids' – don't attack, don't resist enemy attacks, don't surround enemy positions, don't shell enemy positions, don't construct defences. Local PRG commanders ignored Hanoi, and 1973–74 were the years of the 'Cease-fire War' in South Vietnam; in these years, 56,000 ARVN and 100,000 PRG soldiers died.

The Fall of Saigon

Thieu's problem was not military – the Americans provided unlimited armaments. It was economic. Whilst they had been stationed in South Vietnam, American forces had pumped $2 billion into the local economy. Now they had gone, the South Vietnamese economy collapsed. In April 1974, Thieu asked for more economic aid – instead the US Congress reduced it. The South Vietnamese were on their own.

In March 1975, the North Vietnamese government decided to invade South Vietnam. The ARVN collapsed; the NVA found it difficult to advance as quickly as the ARVN was retreating. Thieu resigned, and on 30 April 1975 communist troops marched victoriously into Saigon as the last Americans were frantically helicoptered out.

The North Vietnamese took their revenge. According to reports, 60,000 supporters of Thieu's government were killed, and another 300,000 sent for 're-education'. In the next 15 years, one and a half million 'boat people' tried to leave Vietnam on rafts or in small boats. Many drowned. A million South Vietnamese went to live in America or France. Vietnam was ruined and for the next 20 years was one of the poorest countries in the world.

The last remaining members of the US embassy staff are air lifted from the roof of the embassy.

GradeStudio

Preparation - 'Describe'

- Vietcong guerrilla tactics in Vietnam
- US army tactics in Vietnam
- how the US came to enter the war, 1963–65
- opposition to the war in the US
- the Tet Offensive, 1968
- the My Lai massacre, 1968
- TV and media coverage of the war
- the attacks on Laos and Cambodia, 1970–71
- President Nixon's policy towards Vietnam
- how peace came, 1969–73
- how Saigon fell

Using this textbook, an encyclopaedia or the internet, make sure you know enough to write at least TWO detailed descriptions of each item in the list above.

Preparation - names and specialist terms

- NLF
- ARVN
- NVA
- AWOL
- VC
- ROTC
- PRG
- Tet
- draft
- guerrilla

- Indo-China
- Viet-minh
- Napalm
- Agent Orange
- cluster bombs
- hearts and minds
- body count
- 'fragging'
- 'cherries'
- Vietnamisation

- 'credibility gap'
- strategic hamlets
- USS Maddox
- My Lai
- 'close to the belt'
- Ho Chi Minh Trail
- Zippo Raids
- bouncing Betty mines
- Fulbright Hearings
- Madman Theory

- Martin Luther King
- Vo Nguyen Giap
- Ho Chi Minh
- Thich Quang Duc
- Ngo Dinh Diem
- Eugene McCarthy
- Muhammad Ali
- Henry Kissinger
- Pathet Lao
- Operation Lam Son

Using this textbook, an encyclopaedia or the internet, make sure you know about each of the above so that you can include them in your exam answers.

Preparation - 'Why?'

WHY...
- did the US government get involved in Vietnam?
- did Johnson order Operation Rolling Thunder?
- did US soldiers sometimes 'frag' their officers?
- did the Vietcong Tet Offensive fail?
- did opposition to the war grow in the USA?
- did the USA lose the war?

Working in a small group, think of TWO reasons for each situation in the list above.

Preparation - 'How?'

HOW did this...	cause this?
- Mao Zedong...	- defeat of USA in Vietnam
- the Gulf of Tonkin incident...	- US involvement in the war
- TV...	- opposition to the war in the USA
- the Tet Offensive...	- opposition to the war in the USA
- opposition to the war in the USA...	- US withdrawal from Vietnam
- the election of Nixon...	- US withdrawal from Vietnam

Working as a whole class, think of TWO ways in which each factor on the left led to the outcome on the right.

Grade Studio

'Vietcong guerrilla tactics were the main reason why the US lost the war.' Do you agree? Explain your answer.   (12 marks)

Full sample answer

Comments

Defend the null hypothesis.

There is an argument that VC guerrilla tactics were the main reason why the US lost the war. The VC ambushed and killed American troops, and murdered anyone who co-operated with them. They set traps and mines. They stayed 'close to the belt' so they could not be napalmed. They wore peasant pyjamas and dug a network of tunnels so they could escape and re-appear elsewhere.

At least TWO reasons why the null hypothesis IS true. EXPLAIN HOW the null hypothesis is true. Include FACTS.

This worked directly, by killing US forces (in all 58,000 Americans died). But it also worked indirectly by destroying US morale – search and destroy missions were essentially bait, and by 1971 the US solders were 'questioning orders, deserting, smoking marijuana, shooting heroin, stealing and hurling racial abuse'. They went AWOL and 'fragged' their officers. Lt Calley and his troops massacred the civilians in My Lai. By the 1970s, it was clear that US draft 'cherries' were not going to win the war.

Argue that the null hypothesis is not true.

However, it is also possible to argue that guerrilla tactics were NOT an important reason why the US lost the war. The VC did not drive the US out of Vietnam. The US army chose to go – so it is arguable that factors other than VC tactics defeated the US.

Begin the second section with a connective of comparison. At least TWO reasons why the the null hypothesis IS NOT true. EXPLAIN HOW the null hypothesis is not true. Include FACTS.

One of these was public opinion in the United States. Gallup Polls showed the growing percentage of people who opposed the war, and protests (especially student protests such as that at Kent University in 1970) became more violent (e.g. the Wisconsin-Madison bomb, August 1970). It is arguable that public opinion forced the US to withdraw.

Another important factor taking the US out of Vietnam was President Nixon. He tried to frighten the North Vietnamese to make peace by convincing them that he was ready to do anything. His policy of Vietnamisation – by taking US soldiers out of the firing line – stopped the protests in the US. His Secretary of State Henry Kissinger negotiated the peace accords in 1973.

Reach a conclusion.

Nevertheless, there is a strong argument that VC guerrilla tactics were the main reason why the USA lost the Vietnam War. One of the reasons why the US public came to oppose the war was the military failure, which the public could see on the TV every day. The US army defeated the Tet Offensive, but the NVA's success – especially the 'spectaculars' (e.g. the capture of the US embassy) – shocked public opinion, and opened up a 'credibility gap'.

Begin the third section with a connective of comparison. EXPLAIN HOW you reached your judgement. Include FACTS.

251

2.9 Britain: The Challenge in Northern Ireland, 1960–1986

2.9a How far did political and economic inequalities lead to the Troubles?

Background

Northern Ireland's 'Troubles' date back to as early as 1171, when Henry II of England invaded Ireland. Relations between England (later, Britain) and Ireland were for a long time soured by resentment for past repressions and rebellions. This resentment gained a religious dimension in the 16th century, when England became a **Protestant** country while Ireland remained Catholic and when the English then began to establish Protestant 'plantations' in the north of Ireland.

Were the Troubles a 'War of Religion'?

Although historians commonly talk about Catholics versus Protestants in Northern Ireland, religion was only one of many issues dividing the two sides in the Troubles. In fact, it is more helpful to think of the two sides as races and of the Troubles as a race war.

In 1961, about 1.4 million people lived in Northern Ireland, of which 500,000 (35 per cent) were Catholics. Many Catholics were nationalists (who wanted independence from England) and republicans (who rejected the British monarchy). Some Catholics supported Sinn Fein (the political party which campaigns for independence) and the Irish Republican Army, or IRA (the terrorist organisation which aimed to drive out the British by force).

In 1970 the Social and Democratic Labour Party (SDLP) was formed as a moderate Catholic alternative to Sinn Fein. The SDLP was prepared to co-operate with the British and sought to unite Ireland by peaceful means. Catholics were nicknamed 'Micks' or 'Taigs' by Protestants, or sometimes 'Fenians' (after a 19th-century Catholic terrorist organisation) or 'Papists' (that is, followers of the Pope).

By contrast, most of the 900,000 (65 per cent) Protestants were Unionists (or Loyalists) who wanted Northern Ireland to remain part of the United Kingdom. Some Protestants were members of the Orange Order, which is sworn to defend the Protestant faith and the Union with England. The Official Unionist Party (OUP) held power until 1972, but a more extreme Protestant party – the Democratic Unionist Party (DUP) – was formed in 1971. Protestant terrorist groups include the Ulster Volunteer Force (UVF), the Ulster Defence Association (UDA) and the Ulster Freedom Fighters (UFF).

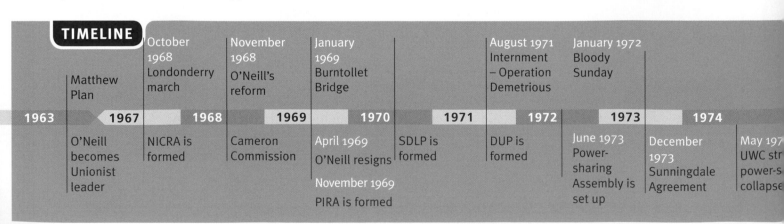

TIMELINE

1963	1967	1968	1969	1970	1971	1972	1973	1974
Matthew Plan		October 1968 Londonderry march	November 1968 O'Neill's reform	January 1969 Burntollet Bridge		August 1971 Internment – Operation Demetrious	January 1972 Bloody Sunday	
	O'Neill becomes Unionist leader	NICRA is formed	Cameron Commission	April 1969 O'Neill resigns / November 1969 PIRA is formed	SDLP is formed	DUP is formed	June 1973 Power-sharing Assembly is set up	December 1973 Sunningdale Agreement / May 197 UWC str power-s collapse

A Protestant statelet

In the early years of the 20th century, Britain still occupied the island of Ireland. However, the British were beginning to lose control. In 1905 Irish nationalists formed the political party Sinn Fein to campaign for independence, while the Irish Republican Army (IRA) waged a guerrilla war. In **Ulster** (the northern six counties of Ireland), however, the Unionists also armed themselves and threatened to fight if Britain agreed to Irish independence.

Consequently, when the Irish Free State (Eire) finally broke free from Britain in 1921, Northern Ireland remained part of the United Kingdom but with its own government and parliament.

The new government of Northern Ireland found itself under attack. There was considerable tension between Ulster and the Irish Free State, whose constitution claimed sovereignty over the whole of Ireland. Meanwhile, the IRA continued the terrorist war. In May 1922 the group attacked police barracks and ambushed police patrols, shot Protestants and burned down factories and country houses. An IRA unit invaded West Fermanagh. The IRA's intention was to destroy the new state and unite it by war with the Irish Free State. The Protestants in Northern Ireland quickly developed a 'siege mentality'.

In response, the Ulster government set up several forces of armed Special Constables, so that by 1922 one in five Protestants owned a gun. There were three categories of Specials – A-Specials (full-time), B-Specials (part-time volunteers, but paid), and C-Specials (unpaid reservists). The Specials were regarded by Protestants as 'decent' men, defenders of the community; but they developed a reputation for attacking Catholics. On 'Bloody Sunday', 10 July 1921, Specials attacked the Catholic areas of Belfast, killing 10 Catholics and burning 161 Catholic homes.

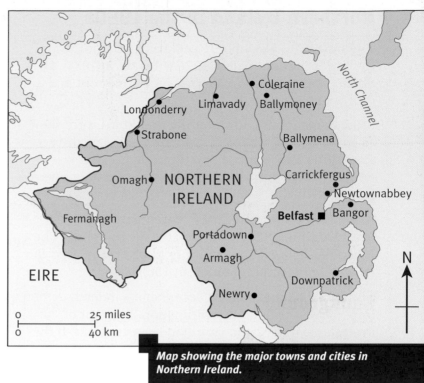

Map showing the major towns and cities in Northern Ireland.

In the two years 1920–22, loyalist mobs attacked Catholic areas on a number of occasions, looting and burning houses. **Sectarian** killings (killings on the basis of religion) increased. One extremist Protestant group had as its aim 'the extermination of Catholics by any and every means'.

As an additional security measure, in 1922 the Ulster government passed the Special Powers Act, which gave the police the right to imprison IRA suspects without trial (this kind of imprisonment was called **internment**). By August 1922 the IRA campaign had failed; Ulster had survived.

(In 1926, the A-Specials were incorporated into the Royal Ulster Constabulary (RUC), and the C-Specials were disbanded, leaving the B-Specials as a reserve force.)

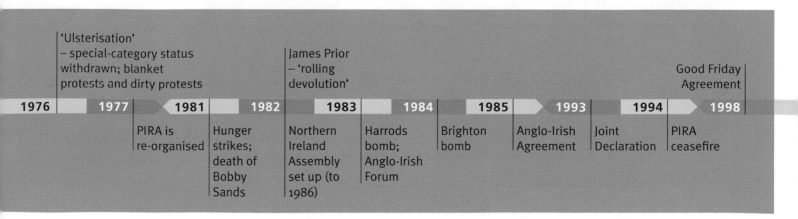

1976	1977	1981	1982	1983	1984	1985	1993	1994	1998
'Ulsterisation' – special-category status withdrawn; blanket protests and dirty protests				James Prior – 'rolling devolution'					Good Friday Agreement
		PIRA is re-organised	Hunger strikes; death of Bobby Sands	Northern Ireland Assembly set up (to 1986)	Harrods bomb; Anglo-Irish Forum	Brighton bomb	Anglo-Irish Agreement	Joint Declaration	PIRA ceasefire

Northern Ireland in the 1960s

The new state was openly sectarian – James Craig, the first prime minister (1921–40) said in 1934, 'all I boast is that we are a Protestant Parliament and a Protestant State'.

Protestants (godly, law-abiding and kind) were seen as superior to Catholics (superstitious, lazy, dirty drunkards and rebels). The Catholic religion was not only 'Popish trash', but devilish – Catholics were going to Hell.

Also, Protestants genuinely feared that Catholics would 'outbreed' them and take over the state. 'They breed like rabbits and multiply like vermin', said Ian Paisley, a Protestant leader, in 1969.

Thinking like this made it acceptable – indeed imperative – to build discrimination in favour of Protestants into Northern Ireland's institutions. If the Catholics lost, they could fight again; if the Protestants lost, the Catholics would take Ulster into the Irish Free State, and Northern Ireland would be lost for ever.

Economic inequality

Most businesses in Northern Ireland were owned by Protestants, and business owners made sure that Protestants were preferred for jobs. Of 8,000 workers at the huge Harland and Wolff shipyard in Belfast in 1972, fewer than 500 were Catholic. Adverts generally stipulated 'Protestant preferred', and poorly qualified Protestants regularly gained jobs over much more highly qualified Catholics.

Owing to disadvantage in the jobs market, Catholic families were usually poorer than their Protestant counterparts. Catholics also found it harder to get houses. To give a person a house was to give him a vote, so Londonderry Corporation never gave a Catholic a house in North Ward or Waterside Ward, and it discouraged new housing in South Ward. Consequently, Catholics' living conditions were generally worse.

A young Ian Paisley is held aloft by a large crowd of Orange marchers.

Political inequality

The people of Northern Ireland had three levels of government after 1921. They elected MPs who sat in the United Kingdom Parliament in Westminster. They also elected members to a Northern Ireland Parliament, which dealt with such matters as industry, transport and laws of the province. Finally, they elected councillors to local councils, which dealt with local matters – council housing and dustbins, for example. At every level, the system discriminated against Catholics.

Ulster council elections were not based on 'one-man-one-vote'. Only ratepayers could vote in local elections; they were given votes according to how much property they owned, up to a maximum of seven – in Londonderry, for example, wealthy Protestant factory owners might have seven votes, but 21,644 Catholics (who were not ratepayers) had no vote at all.

But the Protestants went further. In 1923, Craig set up a Boundaries Commission which re-organised the different ward boundaries to '**gerrymander**' an artificial Unionist majority even in places where Catholics outnumbered Protestants. Thus, in Londonderry in 1969, for example, there were 14,835 Catholics and only 8,781 Protestants. The city, however, was divided into three wards. The boundaries of South Ward were drawn so as to include all the Catholic areas of Creggan and the Bogside; 10,047 of the city's Catholics lived there (and only 1,138 Protestants). South Ward, therefore, regularly returned 8 nationalist councillors. But that left Protestant majorities in the smaller North Ward (8 seats) and Waterside Ward (4 seats) – so the Protestants always controlled the Corporation by a margin of 12 to 8.

The 1921 Government of Ireland Act had introduced a 'proportional voting' system, according to which councillors were selected in proportion to the number of votes cast for each party. In 1929 the Ulster government replaced this with a 'first-past-the-post' system. As a result, the Protestant always won, and the Catholic minority was always un-represented.

A change of attitude amongst Catholics

Discrimination was built into all the political institutions. In the 1930s, if a Nationalist tried to speak in the Northern Ireland Parliament in Stormont, the Unionists simply got up and walked out. And the Cameron Commission (1968) found 'abundant evidence' of discrimination in the RUC (the Ulster police force), which it said was guilty of 'misjudgements' and 'misconduct' towards Catholics. For more than 40 years, the only hope Catholics had of improving their position was that, somehow, Northern Ireland would become part of the Republic of Ireland.

Catholics in Northern Ireland were often given poor quality, rundown housing.

Nevertheless, Catholic attitudes began to change after the Second World War, when the British Labour Government brought in the welfare state. The National Health Service (NHS), free secondary education, and unemployment benefit were not available south of the border. This meant that – even though they suffered embedded discrimination – most Catholics would be worse off in a united Ireland.

At the same time, in 1959 Sean Lemass, the Irish Taoiseach (prime minister) encouraged Ulster Catholics to get involved in life in the province. As a result, support for nationalism fell. In the 1961 election, Sinn Fein won only 15 per cent of the vote. An IRA campaign in 1956–62 fizzled out; instead the IRA rejected armed conflict and advocated a gradualist, communist ideology.

Another healing influence came in 1964, when the Roman Catholic Church publicly accepted that Protestantism contained 'elements of truth' and that Protestants were 'joined in many ways' to the Catholic Church.

In January 1965 Lemass went to Belfast to visit Ulster's prime minister, Terence O'Neill, and O'Neill returned the visit the next month. This led to a series of meetings, which – for a while – gave hope that relations between Northern Ireland and the Republic might improve.

O'Neill's failure

At the same time, there was a softening in the Unionist position. A (very) few Unionists even suggested allowing Catholics to join the Unionist Party. In 1963 Terence O'Neill became the Unionists' leader. At the time, he seemed conciliatory – now it is clearer how dreadfully patronising he was: 'If you give Roman Catholics a good job they will live like Protestants... in spite of their religion.'

The O'Neill government believed that prosperity would solve Northern Ireland's problems. The Matthew Plan of 1963 set up a Ministry of Development, which – using £450 million pumped into the Ulster economy by the British government – built council houses, motorways, a new airport and a new port, and attracted 'modern' industries, including a tyre factory, a gramophone factory and an oil refinery. A total of 29,000 new jobs were created.

All these developments led to a hope, in the 1960s, that there might be a healing of the divisions in Ulster. The British government, aware of how outdated the Ulster government was, encouraged O'Neill to introduce reforms.

But even as his reforms brought hope of an improvement in community relations, they stirred up opposition among some Protestants. Their leader was Ian Paisley, an angry preacher with links to the Protestant terrorist Ulster Volunteer Force (UVF). Paisley accused O'Neill of being 'soft on Rome'. The new jobs, he claimed, were going to Catholics, not Protestants. Paisley stirred up rioting in Belfast in 1964 and threw snowballs at Sean Lemass's car when the Irish Taoiseach visited Belfast in 1965. In 1966 a UVF member, 'Gusty' Spence, killed a Catholic barman.

At the same time as he was angering the Protestants, however, O'Neill was irritating the Catholics. His actions didn't match his words. When Catholic leaders urged him to introduce reforms, he publicly criticised the Catholic Church. A new industrial estate was put in a Protestant area and called 'Craigavon' (after Ulster's first prime minister). The new university was sited in a Protestant area, not in Londonderry, as the Catholics there had expected. When O'Neill set up new boards for Youth Employment, Hospitals and Health Services, they included only seven Catholics among 79 members.

And when O'Neill finally announced the promised reform programme in 1968, it only scratched the surface – a points system for council houses, abolition of multiple votes in local elections, and a review of the Special Powers Act. O'Neill had raised expectations but had failed to reduce the political and economic discrimination faced by Catholics.

Terence O'Neill, Unionist Leader from 1963.

SUMMARY

Did the situation in Ulster improve during the time of the O'Neill government, 1963–69?

YES

1. Welfare state/economic growth made staying in the UK worthwhile for Catholics
2. Sean Lemass urged Catholics to get involved
3. IRA/nationalism was declining
4. Unionists were slightly more tolerant

NO

1. What he said revealed his underlying prejudice
2. Industry (called 'Craigavon) and new university sited in Protestant areas
3. His November 1968 programme failed to satisfy the growing call for civil rights:
   - Offered a points system, not reform of housing
   - Did not establish one-man-one-vote or abolish gerrymandering
   - Offered to review the Special Powers Act not abolish the B-Specials

Civil rights movements

The first civil rights group in Northern Ireland was the Dungannon Homeless Citizens League, formed in 1963 to protest against the local council's discriminatory housing policy. Patricia McCluskey – a local doctor's wife who had joined the group – became aware of discrimination in many other areas of Ulster life. In 1964 she formed the Campaign for Social Justice and lobbied the British government to force reforms on Ulster.

In 1967 a number of different groups – including trade unionists, communists and nationalists – came together to form the Northern Ireland Civil Rights Association (NICRA). Its members were politically aware, and they condensed the general discontent into four political demands: one-man-one-vote; the end of gerrymandering; an end to discrimination in jobs and housing; and the disbanding of the B-Specials.

All these early civil rights organisations were non-sectarian, but apart from a few idealistic Protestant students, the membership was mainly Catholic – *they* were the ones who lacked these civil rights. It is also true that every one of the NICRA demands struck at the bases of Protestant power in Ulster – they were a direct challenge to the Protestant ascendancy.

Londonderry, 5 October 1968

NICRA modelled itself on the Civil Rights Movement in the USA (see pages 222–228). It used what it called 'direct action' – squatting in council houses and disrupting traffic and council meetings.

On Saturday 5 October 1968, civil rights protesters held a march in Londonderry itself. Traditionally, only Protestants marched within the city walls, and the RUC had banned the march. On the day, only about 2,000 marchers turned up. But the TV cameras were there, and horrified television viewers watched the police club men and women to the ground.

Burntollet, 4 January 1969

Before October 1968, civil rights had been something for activists; the 5 October march turned it into a mass movement. A march along the same route in November attracted 15,000 people. When, on 22 November, O'Neill announced his package of reforms (see facing page), his appeal for calm had no effect.

Four days after the Londonderry march, a group of young socialists had come together to form People's Democracy. They wanted more radical, confrontational action. In January 1969 they organised a four-day march from Belfast to Londonderry, through some of the most fiercely loyalist areas in Northern Ireland.

It was a calculated act of martyrdom, designed to show the depth of sectarian hatred in Ulster. At Burntollet Bridge, on 4 January 1969, the marchers walked – knowingly – into a Protestant ambush and were stoned and beaten up. Many of the attackers were off-duty B-Specials. The RUC either ran away or watched approvingly; some members even joined in. When the march arrived in Londonderry, Catholics fought the RUC in the streets.

Police attacking marchers on 4 January 1969 at Burntollet Bridge in the aftermath of the march.

GradeStudio

Describe how discontent turned into violence in Northern Ireland, 1960–69.

Background of sectarian killings, religious discrimination, and economic and political inequality	❑
1965 Sean Lemass visited O'Neill	❑
1966 Protestant protests; Gusty Spence killed a Catholic barman	❑
1967 NICRA formed	❑
1968 O'Neill's reforms were inadequate	❑
1968 Londonderry and Burntollet – Protestants attacked NICRA marches	❑
August 1969 Apprentice Boys march and Battle of the Bogside – British troops entered Northern Ireland	❑
November 1969 PIRA formed	❑

2.9b Why was it difficult to find a solution to the Troubles?

The British in Northern Ireland

O'Neill resigned in April 1969, and the government introduced one-man-one-vote, but by this time events were out of control. When a group of youths escaped from RUC officers by running through the house of a local Catholic named Samuel Devenny, the angry and frustrated officers beat Devenny unconscious. He died three days later. That same month, a Protestant paramilitary group called the Ulster Volunteer Force (UVF) planted a number of bombs in public buildings, in protest at what it saw as O'Neill's surrender to the Catholics.

Tension grew. When, on 12 August, the Protestant Apprentice Boys Parade in Londonderry passed by the Bogside, Catholics rioted. When the RUC went in to restore order, the Catholics organised the Derry Citizens Defence Association and drove them back. The 'Battle of the Bogside' went on for two days, and rioting spread throughout Ulster. Law and order had clearly collapsed. On 14 August the British government sent the first troops to Northern Ireland. At first, many Catholics welcomed them – they felt the army had come to protect them from the loyalist militias.

At first, the British government tried to do exactly that. In October 1969 the Hunt Report recommended disbanding the B-Specials, and Arthur Young, commissioner of the City of London Police, was appointed head of the RUC. A Ministry for Community Relations was set up, and so too, was a Commissioner for Complaints. In 1970, the Macrory Report recommended local government reforms, and in 1971 a Housing Executive was set up to reform housing. The first riots against the British presence (October 1969) were by Loyalists, not Catholics.

However, British soldiers also protected Protestant marches, and in June 1970 they used **CS gas** on Catholics who were protesting an Orange march in Belfast. They also imposed a curfew on the Catholics areas of Belfast and conducted house-to-house searches for guns in Catholic areas (110,000 Protestant members of 'rifle clubs' were legally allowed to keep their firearms). Catholics increasingly came to regard the British soldiers as 'the enemy'.

The Provisionals

Meanwhile, changes had been happening in the IRA. In November 1969 a group calling itself the Provisional IRA (PIRA), dedicated to violent terrorism, broke away from the IRA. The 'Provos', as they came to be called, started out by bombing shops, banks and electricity stations.

On 6 February 1971 the first British soldier was shot in Northern Ireland, and in March three Scottish soldiers were lured from a Belfast pub and executed. Meanwhile, the bombing campaign got worse – there were 37 bombings in April 1971, 47 in May, 50 in June, 91 in July.

One of the traditional roles of the IRA was to protect the Catholic community against attack by loyalist mobs. As well as defending Catholic areas, the PIRA acted as the law-and-order force. It beat up petty criminals, such as shoplifters, and **kneecapped** or even killed serious criminals, such as rapists or drug pushers. Provos also collected funds, ran protection and drug rackets, and '**tarred and feathered**' people who helped the British.

SUMMARY

Were the PIRA the main cause of the outbreak of the Troubles in 1969?

YES
1. Sectarian violence angered Protestants and drove them to support extremist politics
2. Murder of British soldiers angered the British
3. Defenders of Catholics – encouraged revolt
4. Led to internment/Bloody Sunday, etc

NO
1. 900 Years of troubles and sectarian hatred
2. Discrimination against Catholics – political and economic – enflamed by NICRA
3. Institutional discrimination in the police
4. O'Neill's failures
5. British reforms failed

Internment

Events in Northern Ireland were being driven by events on the streets. When Brian Faulkner became Ulster's prime minister in March 1971, he tried to take back some of the political initiative.

John Hume, one of the civil rights leaders who had become an Ulster MP, condemned the violence of the PIRA nationalists. In 1970 Hume had helped to form the Social Democratic and Labour Party (SDLP) as a party for Catholics who did not want a war against the British. In June Faulkner approached Hume, and the two tried to set up a system which would give Catholic moderates control over two of three new committees – on social services, industry and the environment – which Faulkner proposed to set up. It was a very early attempt at a kind of power-sharing.

In July, however, two unarmed youths in Hume's constituency were shot dead by the army, and Hume turned against the government. At the same time, Faulkner was under pressure from his own party to pursue a tougher line. The committee idea failed.

Instead, in August 1971, Faulkner telephoned Ted Heath, the new British prime minister, and asked him for permission to introduce internment. The deaths of British soldiers in Northern Ireland had led to pressure on Heath himself to take firm action.

Consequences of internment

At 4:15 am on Monday 9 August 1971, in 'Operation Demetrious', 3000 troops moved into Catholic areas and arrested 342 people.

Internment was a disaster from the start. A 'dry-run' (practice) exercise a fortnight before had warned the Provos what was about to happen, and most of them evaded capture. The lists were out of date (some of those arrested had been troublemakers in 1921). Of the 342 people arrested, 116 turned out to be totally innocent and were released the same day.

Internment turned the international community against the British government. Army internment methods – such as hooding, deprivation of sleep and food, high-pitched noises and wall-standing – were condemned as acts of torture in the European Court of Human Rights. Funds flooded in to the PIRA from the Irish Republic and the USA. Recruitment to the PIRA increased.

The consequences in Northern Ireland were extreme. In all, 1981 people were interned. Only 107 were loyalists. The result was 1874 Catholic families who were outraged and for ever after hostile towards the British.

The PIRA increased its bombing campaign. In August it exploded 100 bombs. Up to internment, 92 people had died in the troubles, 1969–July 1971. Between August 1971 and the end of 1972, 587 people died.

Interned Catholic prisoners are marched around an exercise yard in prison.

Bloody Sunday

One of the consequences of internment had been 'Free Derry' – the Catholics of Londonderry had erected barricades and made the Creggan and Bogside areas of the town a 'no-go' area for the army. In Free Derry, the PIRA organised a bombing campaign and sniped at British soldiers; according to one estimate, in the last five months of 1971, snipers fired some 2,000 bullets at British soldiers, killing seven.

The Faulkner government had banned all marches in August 1971, but the Civil Rights Association organised a number of anti-internment marches in spite of the ban. On Sunday 30 January 1972, it organised a march in Londonderry to protest against internment. Both the official IRA and the PIRA promised to suspend action for the day of the march.

The army decided to keep the march in the Catholic Bogside area; they put up barriers and ordered the tough First Battalion of the Parachute Regiment to go in and conduct 'a scoop-up' operation to arrest as many hooligans and rioters as possible.

The marchers – estimated numbers range from 3000 (British) to 30,000 (NICRA) – reached Free Derry Corner and started to hold a rally. Some youths started throwing stones at the soldiers manning the barriers.

The Paras moved into the Bogside. In the next half-hour, they fired 108 rounds, killing 13 people and wounding 13 more.

Major Hubert O'Neill, the Londonderry City Coroner, declared that 'the army ran amok that day... shooting innocent people. It was sheer unadulterated murder'.

Father Daly waves a white handkerchief as a group of people carry Jackie Duddy (aged 17), who had been shot while unarmed and allegedly running away.

After Bloody Sunday

The soldiers, on the other hand, insisted they had been fired at first. Some soldiers even believed they had killed *more* than 13 people – it was unlikely that 80 of the rounds fired had missed – and claimed that the IRA had removed all the PIRA victims, leaving only the innocent.

In 1972 the Widgery Report accepted the soldiers' version of events. It found that all the dead were wholly innocent of handling a gun or a bomb when shot, but suggested that some of them *might* have done so earlier in the day. Catholics dismissed the report as a cover up; in 1997 the Saville Inquiry was set up to re-investigate the killings. Publication of the inquiry's report is now planned for 2010.

After Bloody Sunday, there were riots, strikes and sectarian killings throughout Northern Ireland. In February 1972 the PIRA planted a bomb at the Paras' headquarters in Aldershot which killed seven civilians, and the British Embassy in Dublin was burned to the ground. On the other hand, the Protestant leader William Craig formed the Vanguard Party, which demanded the 'liquidation' of the IRA and the repeal of all reforms made so far (see page 256).

Responding to the crisis, on 24 March 1972, Ted Heath announced that the Northern Ireland Parliament was suspended. Direct rule from London was established.

SUMMARY

To what extent had the British effort in Northern Ireland failed by February 1972?

POSITIVES

1. Catholics welcomed British troops at first
2. Reforms – Hunt report, Ministry for Community relations, Macrory Report, Housing Executive
3. SDLP formed 1970 to campaign peacefully for nationalism

NEGATIVES

1. Alienation of loyalists – riots of 1969, formation of Vanguard Party
2. Alienation of Catholics (by curfews, protection of Orange marches, gun searches, use of CS gas)
3. PIRA formed (resulting in their bombing campaign, including Aldershot bomb, killings of British soliders)
4. Internment fails
5. Bloody Sunday causes outrage

British troops take cover behind the doors of armoured cars, Bloody Sunday, 30 January 1972.

The Ulster Workers' Strike, May 1974.

From direct rule to power sharing

Northern Ireland was now the British government's problem, and the British began to seek a solution. A White Paper of 20 March 1973 proposed first, a council of Ireland at which southern and northern politicians could talk about Ulster affairs; and second, the idea of 'power sharing' – a government in which both Catholic and Protestant politicians would have an equal say.

An election was held on 28 June 1973 – with voting by proportional representation – and a coalition SDLP–Official Unionist government was formed. Ministerial posts were shared between the Official Unionist Party and the SDLP. Brian Faulkner of the OUP became chief executive; Gerry Fitt of the SDLP became deputy; and John Hume was minister for commerce. In December 1973, at Sunningdale in Berkshire, a Britain-Ulster-Irish Republic Conference set up a Council for Ireland to discuss issues of joint interest.

All this struck extreme Protestants as just the first steps towards a united Ireland. They reacted. There was a string of horrific murders of Catholics. In May 1974, loyalist extremists set up the Ulster Workers' Council and called a general strike to destroy the power-sharing Executive. The strike – enforced by a loyalist terrorist group called the Ulster Defence Association (UDA) – lasted a fortnight and brought life in the province to a halt.

The strike was widely believed to have taken Ulster to the brink of anarchy – normal government all but collapsed. Power cuts halted industry and threatened to close the pumping stations which alone prevented large areas of Belfast from being flooded with sewage. All the petrol stations closed, and all travel and transport came to a halt – doctors, social workers and bakers queued to get 'essential petrol' tokens from UDA terrorists. There were rumours that the Army had warned that it would refuse orders to break the strike.

On 28 May 1974, Faulkner admitted that the Executive had failed, and he resigned.

A second attempt at shared power in 1974–76 – the Ulster Convention – never got off the drawing board.

SUMMARY

Why did the Sunningdale Agreement fail?

1. Background of the Troubles/sectarian violence had inflamed both sides of the community
2. Extremists in both communities could inflame sectarian hatred by terrorist acts
3. The UWC mobilised Unionist support against the Agreement; the strike forced the power-sharing government to resign
4. Traditional mistrust of Unionists towards cross-border co-operation with the Republic of Ireland
5. The Agreement did not take enough care to allay Unionist fears

2.9c How far from peace was Ulster in 1986?

Continuing terrorism

Throughout the 1970s and 1980s, sectarian terrorism continued.

Terrorism was not only an attempt by Republicans to wear down the British and force them out of Northern Ireland. It was used by extremists on both sides as a political weapon.

Terrorism created hatred, and it provoked reprisals. So whenever the British government tried to draw together moderates on different sides of the community, the extremists on either side knew that they could wreck any initiatives simply with a few high-profile incidents.

The 1970s and 1980s, therefore, can be represented as an endless series of terrorist atrocities. PIRA actions tended to be high-profile and indiscriminate – civilian casualties were often high, and the PIRA had to apologise on a number of occasions. Protestant terrorism, by contrast, was often more sectarian and more personal in nature – in one typical incident, Protestant terrorists covered a mother in a sack, and made her children watch as they clubbed her to death with a baseball bat. The UFF carried out 259 killings during the troubles.

As time went on, however, the security forces got better at counter-terrorism – particularly as a result of better surveillance. Using paid informers and blackmail, and even giving details of suspects to loyalist assassination groups, were other ways the security forces combated the IRA.

One problem was the way the PIRA was organised, with a structure of command – so that once a member was caught, he could identify all his leaders. In 1977, therefore, the PIRA re-organised itself into 'Active Service Units' – small independent units whose members knew only the other members of their group. The problem with this arrangement was that groups sometimes acted foolishly – for instance, by bombing a Remembrance Day Parade in 1987.

Nationalist terrorist atrocities

- February 1974: IRA bomb attack on a British Army coach on the M62 in England (12 killed).
- June 1974: IRA bomb in Parliament.
- November 1974: IRA bombs in pubs in Birmingham, England (20 British civilians killed).
- February 1978: IRA fire bomb attack on the La Mon House restaurant in County Down (12 Protestant civilians killed).
- March 1979: Irish National Liberation Army (INLA) bomb kills British MP Airey Neave (shadow secretary of state for Northern Ireland) as he leaves Parliament.
- August 1979: IRA bomb attack on a British Army post near Warrenpoint, County Down (18 killed).
- August 1979: IRA bomb blows up the boat of Earl Mountbatten (the uncle of Prince Philip, the queen's husband), who was on holiday in the Republic.
- October 1981: IRA nail bomb near the Chelsea Barracks, London (2 killed).
- July 1982: IRA bomb attacks in London (11 British soldiers killed).
- December 1982: INLA bomb at the Droppin' Well bar in Ballykelly, County Derry (17 killed).
- December 1983: IRA bombs Harrods.
- October 1984: IRA bombs the Conservative Party conference at the Grand Hotel, Brighton.
- February 1985: IRA mortar bomb in Newry, County Down (9 RUC officers killed).
- November 1987: IRA bomb during the Remembrance Day Ceremony in Enniskillen (11 killed).

Loyalist terrorist atrocities

- May 1974: UVF car bombs in Dublin city centre and in Monaghan (33 killed).
- July 1975: UVF murders three members of 'The Miami Showband', whom they stop at a fake checkpoint on their way back to the Republic.
- 1975–77: A UVF gang known as the Shankill Butchers carries out a series of brutal killings in Belfast (at least 19 killed).
- January 1976: Six Catholics die in attacks by Loyalists.

Preparation - 'Describe'

- how Catholics were discriminated against before 1969
- the impact of Terence O'Neill
- the civil rights marches, 1968–69
- internment 1970–71
- Bloody Sunday, 1972

- the power-sharing experiment, 1973
- Provisional IRA terrorism
- the hunger strikes, 1980–81
- the Northern Ireland Assembly, 1982–86
- the impact of John Hume
- the Anglo-Irish Agreement, 1985

Using this textbook, an encyclopaedia or the internet, make sure you know enough to write at least TWO detailed descriptions of each item in the list above.

Preparation - names and specialist terms

- SDLP
- Sinn Fein
- IRA
- PIRA
- OUP
- DUP
- UDA
- UFF
- UVF
- RUC
- NICRA
- UWC
- Taoiseach

- Orangemen
- Nationalists
- B-Specials
- gerrymandering
- Cameron Commission
- People's Democracy
- internment
- Operation Demetrious
- Free Derry
- Widgery Report
- Vanguard Party
- power sharing

- Sunningdale Agreement
- Active Service Units
- Ulsterisation
- blanket protest
- dirty protest
- hunger strike
- Alliance Party
- Anglo-Irish Forum
- Northern Ireland Assembly
- Anglo-Irish Agreement
- Good Friday Agreement

- James Craig
- Terence O'Neill
- 'Gusty' Spence
- Major Hubert O'Neill
- Gerry Adams
- Roy Mason
- Garrett Fitzgerald
- John Hume
- Brian Faulkner
- Margaret Thatcher
- Albert Reynolds
- James Prior

Using this textbook, an encyclopaedia or the internet, make sure you know about each of the above so that you can include them in your exam answers.

Preparation - 'Why?'

WHY...

- did violence erupt in 1969?
- was it difficult to find a solution to the Troubles?

- did power-sharing fail in 1973?
- did Margaret Thatcher sign the Anglo-Irish Agreement in 1985?

Working in a small group, think of TWO reasons for each situation in the list above.

Preparation - 'How?'

HOW did this...	cause this?
- B-Specials...	- increasing anger in the Catholic community
- O'Neill's reforms...	- increasing anger in the Catholic community
- Battle of the Bogside...	- British troops in Northern Ireland
- internment...	- an increase in violence
- Anglo-Irish Agreement...	- an eventual end to the Troubles

Working as a whole class, think of TWO ways in which each factor on the left led to the outcome on the right.

'The failures of the government of Terence O'Neill, 1963–1969, were the main reason why the Troubles broke out in 1969.' Do you agree? Explain your answer. (12 marks)

Full sample answer

Comments

There is an argument that the failure of Terence O'Neill in 1963–69 was the main reason that the Troubles broke out in Northern Ireland in 1969. Terence O'Neill seemed conciliatory. He encouraged economic growth, and promised reforms.

Defend the null hypothesis.

However, his reforms angered some Protestants, who thought he was 'soft on Rome'. Their leader Ian Paisley stirred up rioting in Belfast in 1964, and in 1966 a UVF member, 'Gusty' Spence, killed a Catholic barman. This added to the sectarian tension.

At the same time, O'Neill irritated the Catholics. He publicly criticised the Catholic Church. A new industrial estate (called, confrontationally, 'Craigavon') and a new University were built in Protestant areas. And the promised reform programme (1968) only scratched the surface – a points system for Council Houses, abolition of multiple votes in local elections, and a review of the Special Powers Act. O'Neill had raised expectations, but had failed to improve the political and economic discrimination faced by Catholics – his actions merely aggravated Catholic grievances, which led to NICRA, rioting and, eventually, the outbreak of the Troubles.

Argue that the null hypothesis is not true.

However, there were many other reasons why the Troubles broke out.

Firstly, Irish nationalist grievances went back to 1171, and to economic and political discrimination (such as internment and gerrymandering, and discrimination in the job market and housing allocation) since 1921. This led to NICRA, and the Londonderry March of 1968, and so directly created the Troubles.

Secondly, since the 1920s, the B-Specials had terrorised Catholics, and in January 1969, helped by the RUC, they viciously attacked the People's Democracy March at Burntollet Bridge. This increased Catholic anger, and led them to turn to the PIRA.

Reach a conclusion.

All these factors suggest that O'Neill's failure was just one small factor amongst a mass of grievances which caused the Troubles.

Nevertheless, there is a strong argument that O'Neill's failure was paramount because it came at a time when there was a chance of peace. The early 1960s marked a low point in nationalist fortunes. The welfare state, not available in the Republic, meant that Catholics would be worse off in a united Ireland. An IRA campaign had fizzled out by 1962, and the Pope had accepted that the Protestant faith contained 'elements of truth'. The Irish Taoiseach Sean Lemass had visited Ulster.

It is undeniable that a string of British reforms in 1969 – one-man-one-vote, disbanding the B-Specials, and housing reform – came too late and did not satisfy Catholic anger. Maybe if O'Neill had done more, sooner, he could have nipped the Troubles in the bud.

At least TWO reasons why the null hypothesis IS true. EXPLAIN HOW the null hypothesis is true. Include FACTS.

Begin the second section with a connective of comparison. At least TWO reasons why the the null hypothesis IS NOT true. EXPLAIN HOW the null hypothesis is not true. Include FACTS.

Begin the third section with a connective of comparison. EXPLAIN HOW you reached your judgement. Include FACTS.

2.10 The Middle East, 1956–1979

2.10a How far did the years 1956–1967 show how difficult it was to find a solution to the Middle East problem?

Background

The word **diaspora**, which means 'scattering', refers to the worldwide community of Jewish people. The Jews were exiled from the land of Palestine in ancient times. Through the centuries they have been persecuted, forced to live in ghettos, and made victims of wholesale **pogroms** to drive them away. Hatred of the Jews simply because of their race is called **anti-Semitism**.

Faced with constant persecution, many Jews dreamed of a national homeland in Zion (Jerusalem). After 1882 increasing numbers of **Zionist** Jews began to go to Palestine. There they bought land, turned off the people who lived there, and began to settle in large numbers. By 1914, 60,000 Jews lived in Palestine.

The problem with Palestine is that TWO peoples believe absolutely that it is 'their' land. Palestine was conquered and settled by Muslim Arabs in AD 638. Later these Arabs fought centuries of war to stop the **Crusaders** from conquering Palestine. So, when large numbers of Jewish people turned up and started turning them off their land, the Arabs objected strongly.

The British Mandate

During the First World War – when British and Arab troops fought on the same side – the British promised the Arabs that after the war they could have an independent Arab state. However, after the war, the British took over Palestine as a **mandate** (that is, they administered the country on behalf of the League of Nations). One of the problems they faced was Arab riots in protest at the growing number of Jews.

TIMELINE

	April 1948 Deir Yassin atrocity					January 19 PLO is set Fatah bon
Arab League	14 May 1948 Declaration of the state of Israel	Law of Return	July 1954 Lavon Affair	July 1956 Suez Crisis		National V Carrier
1947	**1948** **1949** **1950**	**1953** **1954**	**1955** **1956**	**1957**	**1964**	
	November 1947 UN Resolution 181	15 May 1948– January 1949 Arab invasion of Israel	October 1953 Qibya raid	Baghdad Pact	Fatah formed	

The Jews had an advantage in their relations with the British, because every pupil in the Christian world was taught that God gave Palestine to the Jews as their 'promised land'. In 1917 the British foreign secretary Lord Balfour had stated that Britain wanted 'the establishment in Palestine of a national home for the Jews' (his statement is called the Balfour Declaration). The British not only firmly put down the Arab riots, they trained a Jewish defence force called the Haganah, so that the Jews would be able to defend themselves. During the inter-war period, Jews continued to emigrate to Palestine. By 1939 there were 430,000 Jewish people living there.

The Second World War and Partition

The **Holocaust** – the attempted genocide of the Jews by the Nazis during the Second World War (see pages 202–203) – created sympathy for the Jews, especially in the USA. In 1942 American Zionists announced their 'Biltmore Program', which demanded a Jewish state in Palestine.

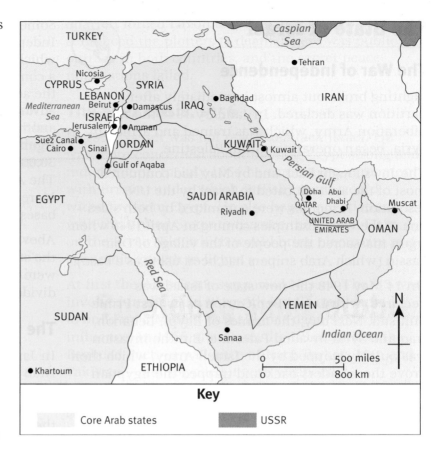

Key

Core Arab states   USSR

At the same time, the Holocaust created an angry determination among young Jews in the Middle East. Led by David Ben-Gurion, they demanded an independent Jewish state in Palestine. They regarded the British as their enemies, and in 1946 Irgun, a Jewish terrorist group led by Menachem Begin, began terrorist attacks on the British.

In February 1947 the British gave in and asked the United Nations to solve the Palestinian problem. In November 1947, UN Resolution 181 partitioned Palestine into two independent states. The division was based on the balance of population in each area (although the Jewish population did not own the majority of the land in any part of Palestine).

Among the 13 countries which voted against the resolution were the Arab nations of Egypt, Iraq, Lebanon, Saudi Arabia and Syria. In 1945 they had joined together to form the Arab League; one of its members – even though it was not yet an independent state – was the Arab state of Palestine.

Israeli army attacks Karameh base, Jordan

September 1972 Munich Olympics

February 1974 Israel-Egypt Disengagement Accord

20 November 1977 Sadat speaks to the Knesset

March 1979 Israel-Egypt Peace Agreement

| 1968 | 1970 | 1972 | 1973 | 1974 | 1975 | 1977 | 1978 | 1979 | 1993 |

o July 1967 Day War

September 1970 Black September

6 September–24 October 1973 Yom Kippur War

17 October 1973 Oil Ban

December 1973 Geneva Talks fail

UN Resolution 3379

March 1978 Operation Litani

17 September 1978 Camp David Accords

9 September 1993 Yasser Arafat and the Palestinian Authority recognise Israel

ember 1967 Resolution 242

2.10b How close to victory were the Arabs in the 1970s?

The PLO, 1965–70

The defeat of the Arab nations in the Six Day War increased the importance of the PLO – it was now the main Arab organisation carrying on the war against Israel.

The main source of recruitment for the PLO was the Palestinian refugees. After the 1948–49 War, the Arab states had made little effort to absorb the Palestinian refugees into their countries; they left them in the refugee camps which the United Nations set up. When the British journalist Jonathan Dimbleby visited in 1979, many Palestinians were still living in tents – and dying of disease and starvation. These refugees had nothing to live for but the defeat of Israel and the return to their homes – many passed down, from father to son, the keys to a long-lost family home in what was now Israel.

The PLO established bases in Jordan, Syria and the Lebanon. In 1968, when the Israelis attacked a PLO base at Karameh, in Jordan, the PLO fought back, killing 28 Israeli soldiers and knocking out several Israeli tanks. Although the base was destroyed, it made the PLO the heroes of the Palestinian refugees.

In 1968 Yasser Arafat became the leader of the PLO. There was a growth of Palestinian nationalism and pride. Fatah terrorists attacked Israeli buses, markets, football matches and tourist resorts – the randomness of it all made it all the more terrifying. Fatah hijacked and attacked two dozen planes, 1967–71. In the most famous incident, the terrorists hijacked three separate planes and flew them to Dawson's Field in Jordan (a former British RAF airbase), where they blew them up on the runway (September 1970).

The blowing up of the planes was an embarrassment to King Hussein of Jordan. The PLO had become a 'state within a state' which threatened his power. During 'Black September' in 1970, he drove the PLO out of Jordan.

Munich 1972

In 1972 eight Fatah terrorists – all from Palestinian refugee camps – attacked the Munich Olympics. Calling themselves 'Black September', and armed with AK-47 assault rifles, pistols and grenades, they entered the Israeli quarters in the Olympic Village early in the morning of 5 September 1972. Two Israelis – wrestling coach Moshe Weinberg and weightlifter Yossef Romano – tried to fight the terrorists to let their colleagues escape, but they were killed.

The terrorists took nine hostages. Then they demanded the release of 236 Arab prisoners in Israeli and German jails. Two Germans allowed into the apartment reported that the hostages had been beaten up and one had been wounded. The hostages behaved with dignity and appeared resigned.

Late that night, the Germans took the terrorists, with their hostages, to a local air base in two helicopters. A plan to rescue the hostages was bungled; sensing a trap, the Palestinians set off a grenade in one helicopter, killing all aboard, and then shot all the Israeli hostages in the second helicopter.

Three terrorists were arrested but released when other Fatah terrorists hijacked a German plane. After the massacre, Mossad, the Israeli Secret Service, mounted a seven-year secret operation (called the 'Wrath of God') to kill the terrorists.

A PLO terrorist looks out during the Munich siege in 1972.

The Yom Kippur War, 1973

Anwar Sadat had become president of Egypt in 1970. He had an 'Egypt-first' policy and was determined to restore Egypt's pride and reputation – by force if necessary. The early 1970s, however, were the years of Détente between the USA and the USSR (see pages 100–106), and Sadat found that the Russians were stopping him attacking the Israelis. So in 1972, Sadat expelled 15,000 Soviet 'advisers'. The West completely misunderstood this action – they thought it was a move towards peace.

Early in 1973 the Russians gave way and sent Sadat the latest SCUD surface-to-air missiles.

On 6 October 1973 the Egyptians attacked the Israelis across the Suez Canal, whilst the Syrians attacked from the Golan Heights. The Israelis were completely taken by surprise. The Israelis had believed themselves safe behind the natural barriers gained in 1967 and thought the Egyptians would not dare to go to war. Moreover, since it was **Yom Kippur**, the holiest day of the Jewish year, many Israeli soldiers were on leave.

The Israelis were driven back. A counter-attack failed. They were in danger of running out of ammunition. The Israelis had nuclear weapons, and for a time, the government seriously debated using them. Golda Meir, the Israeli prime minister, phoned the American president, Richard Nixon, every day begging for help.

Finally, American aid arrived. The tide turned. The Israelis drove back the Syrians and marched on Damascus. They trapped an entire Egyptian army in Sinai, crossed the Suez canal and marched towards Cairo.

Then two things happened. On 17 October Saudi Arabia and the Arab oil-producing nations (OPEC), banned oil shipments to the USA. Also, sensing a total Arab defeat, the USSR threatened to send troops to fight; since the Americans would then have had to send troops to help Israel, the war suddenly threatened to turn into a third world war between the superpowers.

The effect of these two developments was immediate. The USA put pressure on Israel to stop its advance, and on 24 October the United Nations organised a ceasefire.

The balance sheet

Some historians regard Yom Kippur as a great Israeli victory. The Egyptian army had been totally defeated. The Americans had been forced to step in to save Israel from destruction. Most important, the defeat of 1973 was the beginning of the end for the united Arab attempt to destroy Israel.

However, the Arabs made significant gains. They had shown that Arab armies could co-operate and defeat the Israeli army. Israeli losses in the war (2838 killed, 840 tanks destroyed) had been lower than Egyptian losses (5000 dead, 1100 tanks destroyed). Yet the war had shown that Israel was not invincible. Israel's confidence was badly shaken. Israeli intelligence had utterly failed to see the attack coming, and the Israeli army had failed to defend Israeli territory; when the official report into the war was published in April 1974, the entire Israeli government resigned.

Also, the Russians – faced with the alternative of seeing their influence in the Middle East wiped out altogether by an Israeli victory – had been forced to step in and support the Arabs, even though they had not wanted to; this was a huge diplomatic victory for Sadat.

An Israeli tank tows another from the front lines during the Yom Kippur War.

The failure of peace after Yom Kippur

In December 1973 US Secretary of State Henry Kissinger persuaded Israel, Jordan and Egypt to meet for talks at Geneva in Switzerland. It was an achievement even to get the parties into the same room. But the conference lasted only a day. It made no progress towards peace.

Kissinger travelled to and fro, talking first to the Egyptians, then to the Israelis (a process known as 'shuttle diplomacy'). In January and February 1974 he managed to negotiate a Disengagement Accord between Israel and Egypt – both sides agreed to withdraw their armies and accept a UN 'buffer zone'. In May 1974 he achieved a similar Golan Heights Disengagement Accord between Syria and Israel. In 1975 Kissinger persuaded the Israelis to pull back even further from the Suez Canal, but after that, all other attempts at peace failed.

The Oil Wars

The most important outcome of the Yom Kippur War was the use of oil as a weapon. The oil boycott during the war cost the USA $15 billion and put half a million people out of work. The economy of the West was severely damaged and entered a period of 'stagflation' – economic stagnation coupled with rising prices. The western economies of the time found this impossible to stop; pumping money into the economy to cure the stagnation set inflation running out of control, but restricting the money supply to hold back inflation just threw the economy into recession. In Britain, economic pressures also led to strikes and industrial unrest.

Consequently, the Arab nations found that the ability to withhold oil empowered them as nothing else before had done.

Suddenly, everybody supported the Arabs. The United Nations declared the right of Palestinians to self-determination. The European nations urged Israel to return the territories captured in 1967. France supplied nuclear technology to Iraq. The high-point of 'oil diplomacy' came in 1975, when the UN passed Resolution 3379, which stated 'that Zionism is a form of racism'.

The PLO prospers

PLO policy before 1974 demanded the destruction of the state of Israel, and the destruction of all 'reactionary' Arab governments (such as that of King Hussein of Jordan) who were prepared to talk to the Israelis. In 1974, to undermine Kissinger's disengagement agreements, PLO extremists made a number of terrorist attacks; the worst being an attack on a nursery in the Israeli village of Ma'alot, where Palestinian terrorists took 90 children hostage and killed 20 of them.

Meanwhile, however, at the twelfth meeting of the Palestine National Council in June 1974, Arafat and other moderates in the PLO suggested that they would be prepared to accept a Palestinian state comprising the West Bank and the Gaza Strip.

As Palestinian terrorism increased and Kissinger's diplomacy failed, the UN General Council held a debate on 'the Palestinian Question'. On 13 November 1974, Arafat came to New York and spoke to the General Assembly of the UN.

Arafat appeared before the United Nations carrying an olive branch and wearing a gun holster. He said: 'Today I have come bearing an olive branch and a freedom fighter's gun. Do not let the olive branch fall from my hand.'

2.10c How close to peace was the Middle East by the end of the 1970s?

Sadat visits Israel

In 1977 Menachem Begin and his hard-line Likud party won elections in Israel; it seemed that peace was further away than ever.

Yet suddenly, during 1977, Israel and Egypt began to move towards peace. One factor was the election of a new American President, Jimmy Carter; Carter wanted to make a difference in the Middle East and was prepared to take risks to do so – in March he advocated the idea of a 'Palestinian homeland', and in October he made a joint statement with the Soviets which called for Israeli withdrawal from the occupied territories and upheld 'the legitimate rights of the Palestinian people'.

Attitudes were softening, also, in Egypt and Israel. In July the Israeli government warned Sadat of a Libyan plot to assassinate him. For his part, in September, Sadat opened secret peace talks with Israeli officials. Sadat wanted to widen the Suez Canal, and he wanted peace so that he could free up funds to pay for it. Peace would also free him from reliance on Soviet military aid.

In November 1977 Sadat declared that he was prepared to go to Israel to discuss peace. Taken by surprise, Begin agreed to see him. Sadat went, and he spoke to the Knesset: 'I declare to the whole world that we are prepared to live with you in permanent peace based on justice', he said. Begin replied that, although the flight from Cairo to Jerusalem was only short, Sadat had covered a distance that was 'almost infinite'.

The Camp David Accords

The US seized on Sadat's initiative, and in 1978 President Carter invited Sadat and Begin to Camp David, the president's mountain retreat in Maryland. On 17 September 1978, after 12 days of negotiations (during which Carter first cut all aid to Israel, and then promised an extra $3 billion) the two sides agreed peace. Israel agreed to withdraw from Sinai, and Egypt recognised Israel.

Disagreements broke out immediately – over practical details such as the timetable for Israeli withdrawal, but also because both Begin and Sadat came under immense pressure from their own people not to make any concessions. However, after Carter had personally visited both countries, the Camp David Accords were finally ratified by a peace treaty which was signed at the White House in March 1979.

Camp David and the Peace of 1979 marked the end of the Arab-Israeli conflict as an international problem. The united Arab front against Israel was destroyed – without Egypt, there could never be a united Arab war to destroy Israel, as there had been in 1967.

SUMMARY

Was Anwar Sadat responsible for the Camp David peace agreement of 1978?

YES

1. He broke with the Russians in 1973
2. Visit to Israel 'out of the blue'
3. Nothing was happening prior to his initiative
   - Failure of Kissinger's 'shuttle diplomacy'
   - Begin and Likud in control in Israel

NO

1. Détente – Russia allowed him to act on his own
2. The Yom Kippur War had failed to defeat Israel
3. Egypt needed peace – expense of war
4. Success of Oil Wars – Israel was isolated internationally and was open to peace
5. Begin wanted to settle the occupied territories
6. America wanted peace/was willing to broker a peace deal

The Occupied Territories

Why had Menachem Begin – a hard-line former-terrorist – made peace with Egypt? One reason was American pressure, of course, but Begin had other motives. Making peace with Egypt freed up Begin to address the Palestinian problem; many Arabs were angry with Sadat because they said he had abandoned the Palestinians.

After the 1967 War, Israel had taken control of the Gaza Strip and the West Bank. More than a million Arabs lived there. The West Bank was a problem for Israel. Despite massive immigration of Jews into Israel during the 1970s and 1980s, the Arab population in Israel had increased as quickly as the Jewish population because Arab families tended to have more children. The Jews called this factor 'the population time-bomb'; there was a time coming when Arabs would outnumber Jews in Israel.

Arab workers on the West Bank got jobs in the Israeli economy. The Israelis organised electricity and water supplies and provided welfare services. This made the Arab population much better off. However, it made them economically dependent on Israel, and it meant that every day hundreds of Arabs crossed from the West Bank to go to work in Israel – this created a security problem.

Israeli security on the West Bank was aggressive. The area was placed under the control of military governors. PLO members were beaten, imprisoned or deported; sometimes their homes were blown up, leaving their families homeless. Israeli security was based on reprisal; after any incident, Israeli security forces would use disproportionate force to attack those whom they felt were guilty.

The Arabs did not become citizens with political rights, but they had to obey Israeli laws.

Meanwhile, a Jewish organisation called *Gush Emunim* ('Bloc of the Faithful') called for the occupation of all of 'Eretz Israel' ('the land of Israel' – that is the Judea and Samaria of biblical times). Religious Israelis took over land on the West Bank and built settlements there. These settlements were often provocatively placed in prominent locations – on hilltops, for example, or in the middle of Arab towns like Hebron. By the year 2000, a quarter of a million Israelis were living in the Occupied Territories. The government supported these settlements. It renamed the West Bank 'Judea and Samaria', gave settlers building grants and low taxes, and provided soldiers to defend them.

In 1977 Jordan complained to the United Nations that this situation was 'creeping annexation' – the taking over of Palestinian land bit by bit.

The Jewish settlements on the West Bank have proved a significant barrier to a peace settlement.

A Palestinian settler on the West Bank looks out over the Israeli settlement in the hills.

How close was the Middle East to Peace in 1979?

After Camp David, Carter was disappointed that peace between Israel and Egypt did not lead to general peace in the Middle East.

Instead, the other Arab nations were furious, and they threw Egypt out of the Arab League. Even 'moderate' Arab nations such as Jordan and Saudi Arabia rejected the peace, and the PLO, Syria and some organisations in Egypt attacked Sadat for making peace.

In some ways, the accord between Egypt and Israel might even have *delayed* peace. Peace with Sadat freed the Israelis to deal with the Palestinian problem; they continued building settlements in the Occupied Territories.

Lebanon and the PLO

After Black September 1970, the PLO set up in Lebanon, where the government was too weak and divided to stop them. PLO terrorist attacks on Israel increased after Sadat's visit to Israel in 1977, and after a particularly bloody attack on a bus in March 1978, the Israeli Army mounted Operation Litani: the invasion of south Lebanon. They attacked PLO villages and established a 14-kilometre 'security zone' along the border with Lebanon.

When this did not stop PLO attacks, in 1982 the Israelis mounted another, larger, invasion of Lebanon and drove the PLO out altogether.

Arafat re-located to Tunisia, but many Palestinians accused him of being too soft on the Israelis. Other anti-Jewish terrorist groups grew up – Hezbollah in Lebanon (organised by Iran), Islamic Jihad (organised in Egypt by Dr Fathi Shqaqi), and Hamas (organised in Gaza by Sheik Ahmad Yassin).

International settlements...

In December 1987 the Palestinian population in the Occupied Territories rebelled. The Palestinians – especially young Palestinians – rioted and threw stones at Israeli soldiers. This was called the Intifada (a word that means 'shaking off'). Three years later the Israelis were still facing riots and attacks.

At the same time, the USA was placing great pressure on the Israelis to settle the Palestinian problem. In Oslo, Norway, on 9 September 1993, Arafat formally recognised the state of Israel. In return, the Israelis agreed to allow a Palestinian Authority to run the West Bank and Gaza and promised to withdraw its troops from Gaza and Jericho. Shortly after, King Hussein of Jordan also signed a peace treaty with Israel.

... but still no peace

However, although the Oslo Peace Agreement signalled the end of international conflict over Israel, it did not settle the Palestinian problem, particularly after January 2006, when the terrorist group Hamas won elections for the Palestinian Parliament. Instead, Israel returned to traditional ways of combating the terrorists – for example, re-invading South Lebanon in 2006 to attack Hezbollah and invading Gaza in 2009 to attack Hamas.

It seemed as though a settlement of the 'Palestinian problem' was as far off as ever.

In 2002, rather than withdraw from the Occupied Territories, Israel began Operation Defensive Shield. It built a huge wall to cut Israel off from the West Bank, but the wall also brought large areas of occupied land under Israeli control.

GradeStudio

Preparation - 'Describe'

- the foundation of Israel, 1948
- the Suez Crisis, 1956
- the founding of the PLO, 1964
- the Six Day War, 1967
- the Munich Olympics, 1972

- the Yom Kippur War, 1973
- the Oil War, 1973
- Israeli settlement of the West Bank and Gaza
- the Israeli invasion of Lebanon, 1978
- the peace process, 1977–79

Using this textbook, an encyclopaedia or the internet, make sure you know enough to write at least TWO detailed descriptions of each item in the list above.

Preparation - names and specialist terms

- Zionism
- *fedayeen*
- Knesset
- Haganah
- Irgun
- kibbutzim
- Fatah
- PLO
- Mossad
- *Gush Emunim*
- 'Intifada'

- Hamas
- Hezbollah
- Arab League
- Baghdad Pact
- Balfour Declaration
- Biltmore Program
- 12th Palestine National Council
- pre-emptive counter-strike
- Disengagement Accords
- Camp David Accords

- Qibya raid
- Deir Yassin atrocity
- Ma'alot atrocity
- Law of Return
- Lavon Affair
- Three No's
- 'Wrath of God'
- National Water Carrier
- Arab Liberation Army
- Black September
- Operation Litani

- UN Resolution 181
- UN Resolution 242
- UN Resolution 3379
- David Ben-Gurion
- Menachem Begin
- Gamal Abdul Nasser
- Yasser Arafat
- King Hussein
- Anwar Sadat
- Golda Meir
- Jimmy Carter

Using this textbook, an encyclopaedia or the internet, make sure you know about each of the above so that you can include them in your exam answers.

Preparation - 'Why?'

WHY...
- did the Arab nations want to destroy Israel?
- did Israel invade Egypt on 29 October 1956?
- did Israel invade Egypt on 5 June 1967?

- did Israel win the Yom Kippur War?
- did Anwar Sadat go to speak to the Knesset in November 1977?

Working in a small group, think of TWO reasons for each situation in the list above.

Preparation - 'How?'

HOW did this...
- the War of Independence...
- the Suez Crisis...
- the founding of the PLO...
- 'Egypt First'...
- the Oil War...
- *Gush Emunim*...

cause this?
- the *fedayeen*
- the end of British influence in the Middle East
- increased tension in the Middle East
- the Yom Kippur War
- Arafat's speech to the UN on 13 November 1974
- continuation of the conflict

Working as a whole class, think of TWO ways in which each factor on the left led to the outcome on the right.

'Anwar Sadat was the main reason for the progress of peace in the Middle East, 1977–1979.' Do you agree? Explain your answer. **(12 marks)**

Full sample answer

Comments

Defend the null hypothesis.

There is an argument that Anwar Sadat brought peace to the Middle East 1977–79. It was he who – out of the blue – declared that he was prepared to go to Israel to discuss peace, and surprised Begin into inviting him. He told the Knesset that 'we are prepared to live with you in permanent peace', and Begin admitted that Sadat had covered an 'almost infinite' distance. Out of that visit – apparently – came the Camp David Accords and the Peace Treaty of 1979.

Sadat was important also, because his 'Egypt-First' policy led him to expel 15,000 Russian 'advisers' in 1973. Up to that point, the Middle East had become part of the Cold War – Russia supporting the Arabs, the US supporting Israel. Sadat broke this link, which helped set up the chance of a Middle East peace.

Argue that the null hypothesis is not true.

However, there were many other reasons why peace came in 1977–79.

Firstly, both Egypt and Israel needed peace in 1977. Egypt had lost the Yom Kippur War, and Sadat wanted a period of peace so that he could pay for the widening of the Suez Canal. On their part, the Israelis were prepared to make an international peace agreement with Egypt, because that freed them up to get on with settling in the occupied Palestinian territories conquered in the 1967 war.

A second factor was the success of the 'Oil War' in damaging the West economically (especially in a time of 'stagflation' in the western economies). Worried by this, the western powers had begun to abandon Israel – they had invited Arafat to the UN in 1974 – and Israel was isolated internationally, and willing to accept an offer of peace. Connected to this, was the fact that President Carter of America – Israel's main supporter – had started talking of a 'Palestinian homeland' and was keen to broker a peace.

Reach a conclusion.

Therefore, although, there is a strong argument that Sadat helped bring peace in 1977–79, all these factors suggest that Sadat's initiative was just one small factor amongst a mass of causes. His initiative only worked because the world was ready for peace in 1977.

And the biggest argument proving this is the fact that, in the end – even after Sadat's initiative, and all the factors causing pressure for peace, Carter first had to cut all aid to Israel, and then promise an extra $3billion to persuade Begin to agree the Camp David Accords. In the end it was money, not gestures, which brought peace in 1979.

Comment boxes:

At least TWO reasons why the null hypothesis IS true. EXPLAIN HOW the null hypothesis is true. Include FACTS.

Begin the second section with a connective of comparison. At least TWO reasons why the null hypothesis IS NOT true. EXPLAIN HOW the null hypothesis is not true. Include FACTS.

Begin the third section with a connective of comparison. EXPLAIN HOW you reached your judgement. Include FACTS.

Historical Enquiry

How should I plan for the controlled assessment?

Unit 3 in the AQA History Specification B GCSE lists four topics:

1. The British People in War (that is, life on the Home Front during the First and Second World Wars)
2. Britain at War (in the two world wars)
3. Britain and the Aftermath of War (that is, how life in Britain changed in the years immediately following the two wars)
4. The Changing Role and Status of Women in Britain since 1900

Your teacher will choose one topic from this list for you to study. You will have to answer two questions on the topic. Unit 3 carries a quarter of the total marks for your History GCSE.

The Unit 3 examination works a little differently from the other two. It is called a controlled assessment. You will be told what the two questions are in advance. You will then be given time in lessons (plus as much homework time as you need) to research and plan your two answers. You must keep a record of all your notes and research in a 'diary'. You will be allowed to take this diary, containing all of your planning and preparation work, into the exam with you.

You will write your two answers in 'controlled conditions' – you will supervised, just as you are when taking a normal exam. You will be allowed up to four hours.

Every year the board will set new questions on different aspects of the topic. Your teacher will select some initial sources to get you started, and then you will have to research the topic for yourself. You will be expected to find some sources of your own. You will also be expected to discover relevant facts and theories about the topic to help you answer the two questions.

This chapter contains notes on each of the Unit 3 topics. These notes are not intended to tell you all you need to know in order to answer your two questions. They simply provide a brief, matter-of-fact overview of the whole topic. You should read the overview first and then begin your own detailed research into the particular aspect of the topic covered by the two questions.

There are two kinds of questions in this unit:

1. A 'Usefulness' question (15 marks)

This is the same kind of question that appears in Unit 2A (see pages 116–119). The difference here is that you have to evaluate the usefulness of FIVE sources, not just one.

2. A 'How far' question (25 marks)

This kind of question combines elements of two questions in previous units: the 'Analysis and explanation' question in Unit 2B (see pages 171–172), and the 'Interpretations' question in Unit 1 (see pages 2–4). Again, you have to refer to a large number of sources (more than six).

GradeStudio

Before you start this unit, go through the relevant section (of the four topics on pages 287–303) and make a list of all the 'specialist terms' you can find. For each, make sure you know the historical context, know what it is and what it means. When you write your controlled assessments, try and get all these specialist terms in your answers.

How do I approach a 'Usefulness' question?

As in Unit 2A, the first controlled assessment question asks you evaluate the usefulness of a source. It is worth 15 marks. The question will probably look something like this:

Select FIVE sources. Explain how useful these sources have been in informing you in your inquiry.

You will have about an hour and a half to write your answer, and you will be expected to write about 800 words. In an electronic document with 2.54 centimetre margins, this number of words will fill about two pages of typing in double-spaced Times New Roman font size 12. In the average person's handwriting, 800 words will fill about two-and-a-half sides of paper. Your writing may be larger or smaller than average, so it is a good idea to work out how much paper 800 words will fill in your writing.

When dealing with this part of the exam, you should be looking at the source and asking yourself, 'How might this information be useful to a historian?' Keep this question in the forefront of your mind all the time you are writing your answer. And remember that your answer must draw attention to two aspects of each source:

1. The provenance
The first issue is the source's provenance. Where does the source come from? What kind of source is it? Who wrote it, drew it or said it? Why? Is that person a reliable witness whose opinions might be USEFUL?

2. The content
The second issue is the source's content. What is its message? How does its message relate to what you know of the events and time-period it refers to? How might the information it holds be USEFUL to historians?

The difference between this question and the 'Usefulness' question in Unit 2A is that you will have FIVE sources to evaluate, not just one. You will be asked how useful five selected sources have been in pursuing your inquiry.

A good way to approach this question is to divide the five sources into two groups: those that are useful and those that are not. Then you can structure your answer as follows:

First Section: Not useful
First write about the sources that ARE NOT useful. Explain WHY each source is not useful, making sure you refer to the provenance and content of each source. Go into as much depth as possible.

Second Section: Useful
Next, write about the sources that ARE useful. Explain WHY each source is useful, making sure you refer to the provenance and content of each source. Go into as much depth as possible.

Conclusion
Write a conclusion, drawing together your ideas and making some general points. What made the useful sources useful? What were the shortcomings of the sources which were less useful? Which were the most useful and the least useful of all? Are there any limits on your ability to assess the usefulness of any of the sources?

GradeStudio

Writing a conclusion

Remember: a conclusion does not just repeat the points you made in the first two sections of your essay. You must come up with some new ideas – if you do not make any new points, you will not get any more marks.

BE A HISTORIAN!

- Search through a range of books and internet sites and try to find places where other historians have used the same sources as you are using. How have those other historians used them?

- Does this information affect your judgement of how useful they are as historical sources?

On the other hand, there is also evidence of significant improvements in the situation of women during the 1920s and 1930s.

The 1920s was the decade of 'flappers' (see page 160), who broke with social convention.

Birth control became more freely available, thanks largely to the work of Marie Stopes. The ability to decide when to become pregnant improved women's health and longevity. With family sizes reduced, the housewife's job became much easier.

At the same time, the increased availability of gadgets, such as vacuum cleaners and cookers, saved housewives work, while radio expanded their experience. It is worth noting that these developments did not get women 'out of the house' – if anything, they made women more home-oriented (as is shown by the appearance of magazines such as *Woman's Own*).

The 'new' industries of the 1930s (electronics and plastics, for example) preferred female workers. Women could handle the work just as well and were cheaper.

Although there were only a few female MPs, historians have noted that they had a huge effect on legislation. In 1923–25 laws were passed which allowed women to seek divorce on grounds of adultery, gave women the same property rights as men, and introduced widows' pensions and a number of improvements in childcare.

The feminist campaign during this period is sometimes called the 'new feminism'. In the 1920s and 1930s Eleanor Rathbone renamed the NUWSS the 'National Union of Societies for Equal Citizenship' and campaigned for wages to be paid to mothers for bringing up the nation's children.

The Second World War

In the Second World War as in the first, there was an increase of women drafted into the workforce to compensate for the men who were conscripted into the armed forces. The Essential Work Order (1941) allowed the conscription of women aged 20–24 into industry. Many went to work in munitions and engineering factories. Others joined the armed forces and worked on ack-ack guns or as nurses, ferry pilots or in the Women's Land Army (see pages 287–289). Many others joined the Women's Voluntary Society or the Women's Institute and did voluntary work. It has been pointed out that it was women who bore most of the burden of evacuation (by looking after other women's children).

With many men in the armed forces (and even if a man was not in the armed forces, his wife was still regarded as the homemaker), the stress of rationing and air raids fell almost exclusively on the nation's women. For many women, the war brought stress, tiredness and breakdown.

Once again, many of the women who went to work in industry were resented by their male colleagues. This was especially true because the government had trained the women properly for the job. Some women were far better workers than men who had done the job for years.

There were some advances in the position of women during the war:

- The number of female trade unionists increased.
- The Extended Employment of Women agreement (1940) gave skilled women workers the right to move onto equal pay to men over time.
- The Women's Parliament was formed in 1940 to campaign on matters of interest to women – one of its greatest successes was to win compensation for air raid victims.
- In 1943 the Equal Pay Committee gave equal pay to female and male teachers.
- Many women felt liberated and empowered – one effect of the war was greater sexual freedom.

Nevertheless, by the end of the war, women still earned on average only half as much as men, and the Restoration of Pre-War Practices Act (1942) made it clear that the employment of female workers was a temporary measure that would remain in place only until the end of the war.

After the Second World War

Again, if the war had secured any advances for women, it could be argued that they all evaporated after the war. Two million women left work. The new Welfare State (see page 298) discriminated against women, who got lower sickness and unemployment benefit and a lower pension. Beveridge openly said that the true role of a woman was as a 'housewife and mother'. In 1946, though, a Royal Commission on Equal Pay decided that this restriction was a bad idea.

The number of married women in work increased and continued to increase from 10 per cent in 1931 to 21 per cent in 1951 and 47 per cent in 1972. But this development merely added to a woman's workload. Having worked all day, many were still then expected to come home and do the housework. Some took evening shift work so that they could still do the housework during the day.

New gadgets and labour-saving devices may have made housework easier, but they helped create an image of a person whose life was made worthwhile by a new cooker. Some historians have argued that regard for women actually fell during this period. During the 1930s, the mother had been the linchpin of family survival. During the 1950s, the housewife became 'the little woman' whose job was to make the home 'a haven for a tired man when he returns from work'.

Little changed during the 1960s. The drugs and free love of the swinging sixties did not make women into feminists. Many feminists complained that most women did not even realise they were oppressed.

After the 1960s

The 1970s saw the birth of 'second-wave feminism'. The Women's Liberation Movement was set up in 1970. Its members invented phrases such as 'sexism' and 'male chauvinist pig'. 'Revolutionary feminists' came to see men as the enemy. They burned their bras, protested at Miss World contests and campaigned for equality. The National Abortion Campaign (1975) supported 'a woman's right to choose', and WAVAW (Women Against Violence Against Women) campaigned against domestic violence.

Acts of Parliament gave women new legal rights:

- The Equal Pay Act (1970)
- The Sex Discrimination Act (1975) – which set up the Equal Opportunities Commission
- The Employment Protection Act (1975) – which created maternity leave.

It is debatable whether the equality of women in law has led to the social, political and economic equality of women. Women are still generally paid less than men and are still under-represented in parliament and in the higher positions in industry and commerce. Easier divorce has left many women as single-parent providers. Surveys still report plenty of 'passive husbands' who 'let' their wives do the housework.

Nevertheless, there are indications that the last quarter of the century has seen a number of improvements in the position of women. In the 1990s the Labour Party introduced women-only shortlists for parliamentary elections. This policy has led to an increase in the number of female MPs. Slowly, the pay gap between men and women is narrowing, and the number of female managers and executives is increasing – as is the number of female home owners. In education, girls are now outperforming boys at every level except A-level. Another example of increasing equality is the emergence of 'laddettes' who go binge drinking 'just like the boys'.

Issues and historiography

There are many issues of debate:

- Did the suffragettes help or harm the campaign for women's suffrage?
- Did the First World War give women the vote?
- Did the two world wars permanently change the status of women, or were the effects only temporary?
- What part have women played in the improvement of women's status: was legal equality taken by women or given by men?
- There have been huge changes in the role of women, but have these changes led to any significant improvement in the status of women?
- Have the changes in women's lives resulted mainly from changes in technology, society and wealth that have affected everybody?
- Has the improved position of women been caused by changes in women's views of what it is to be 'feminine', or by changes in men's views of what it is to be 'masculine'?

BE A HISTORIAN!

Use the information on pages 300–303 to consider these questions:

1. How did women achieve a greater equality of status throughout the 20th century?
2. What impact did the two world wars have on the status of women in Britain?

ExamCafé

Tools and Tips

Right, now you are ready to take your GCSE History exam.

Or are you? What do you need to do to prepare?

In order to do well in the exam, you will need to show that you have certain skills as a historian. Exam Café will help you focus on those skills. There is also a CD-ROM with specific advice for each of the units you will have studied. Look out for this logo. If you have used Grade Studio throughout the course, you will already have practised some of the key skills that are vital in revision and in the final exam.

Exam Café

Getting started

Remember that revision has two main purposes. The first is to understand the content of all the topics you have studied. The second is to practise presenting your knowledge in the right way in the exam.

Revision may seem like a daunting task, but these hints and tips will make it seem much simpler.

- Organise your notes before you start and make sure that you have everything you need.

- Know what you will be tested on in each exam. Checklists on the CD-ROM will help you work out what you need to know for each paper.

- Plan a realistic revision timetable. History is not the only subject you will need to revise, and you are still allowed to have a social life as well! On the CD-ROM there are examples of revision timetables to help you organise yours.

- When revising, make sure you are in a calm and organised environment. If your desk is messy, you won't be as focused.

- Set yourself realistic targets and divide your time into small sections of about half an hour. Give yourself lots of breaks and rewards.

- Some people find it helps to revise with a friend and test each other.

- Try not to cram too much in. Pick out key points and summarise the main ideas and events. See your CD-ROM for useful hints on how to summarise.

- Find a revision style that suits you. Everyone is different, so don't worry if your friends are revising in a different way from you. If your way works, stick to it.

- Don't leave everything until the last minute!

There are lots of ways to revise, and it is important to find one that suits you. Here are some examples of techniques that you might find useful.

Revision techniques

Mind maps

A mind map is a diagram on which key ideas branch out from a central key word

Try to use colour, images and short snappy phrases (rather than lots of writing) on your mind map. If you make it look good you are more likely to remember what is on it.

Flash cards

Flash cards are a good way of remembering important facts and figures.

Write a question or a clue on one side and all the information you need to remember on the other.

What did FDR do during the 100 days?

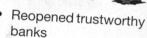

- Fireside chats
- Closed banks
- Reopened trustworthy banks
- Given emergency powers by Congress
- Repealed Prohibition
- Started Alphabet Agencies (The New Deal)

Try to use images, bullet points and mnemonics on your flash card, as these will help you remember what is on it.

Mnemonics

A mnemonic is a word or phrase made up of the first letter of other words.

Here is an example:

Saar plebiscite
Conscription and re-armament
Rhineland
Austria
Munich
Czechoslovakia
USSR/Nazi Pact
Poland

Helps you remember some of the key events your will need to know about in the build-up to the Second World War (Saar plebiscite, Conscription and re-armament, Rhineland, Austria, Munich, Czechoslovakia, USSR/Nazi Pact, Poland).

You could also add images to a mnemonic. Visual clues can sometimes make it easier to remember ideas in an exam. Images may spring to your mind more quickly than words (this process is called visualising).

Timelines

A timeline will help you see the 'big picture'. By putting all your ideas together in a chronological list, you will be able to see how historical events are connected to each other.

1939	The Second World War.
1942	Bevin suggests a free NHS
1945	War ends, soldiers return injured. Labour win the election
1948	First day of the NHS

On timelines you can mark turning points and measure progress or change.

To help you memorise your timelines, you could choose different colours for all the events that are related to a particular topic (this process is called colour-coding). You could also add images (visual cues).

ExamCafé

Revision

Lesson One: International Relations, Part 1-3

In this lesson you will:

- Consolidate your knowledge of International Relations, Parts 1–3
- Learn how to summarise your ideas using a timeline.

Getting Started

What can you remember about this topic?

Write down ten facts that you can recall from any of the following International Relations topics:

1. The Origins of the First World War
2. Peacemaking 1918–19 and the League of Nations.
3. Hitler's foreign policy and the origins of the Second World War.

The first step of your revision should be to organise your notes. You will not be able to remember everything you have made notes about, so don't try to do so. Instead, go through your notes and work out which notes you will need to learn and which you can manage without.

There are lots of handy hints on summarising key ideas on the CD-ROM.

Activities

One way to summarise your ideas is by creating a timeline. A timeline will help you to place events in their wider context.

Look at the charts opposite. Your job is to organise the boxes onto a timeline. The blue boxes are events. You need to look through your notes and work out the date on which each event occurred.

The yellow boxes are dates. You need to look through your notes and work out what event happened on this date. Make sure you add detail about what happened on this day to your timeline.

You should complete your timeline using the events from each of the topics that you have studied. Remember, you may not have studied all three of the topics.

1. The Origins of the First World War

The Schlieffen Plan is drawn up.	Kaiser Wilhelm visits Tangiers in Morocco.	March 1911	March 1905
Russia and France sign an agreement to help each other if attacked.	Revolution breaks out in Turkey, the 'sick man of Europe'.	28 June 1914	July 1911
Britain joins the Triple Entente.	Britain launches the first Dreadnought.	23 July 1914	2 August, 1914

2. Peacemaking 1918–19 and the League of Nations

The First World War ended.	Greece and Bulgaria come into conflict.	11 November, 1918	November 1935
The League of Nations is created.	The Lytton Report is published	28 June 1919	October 1925
Reparations are set at £6,600 million.	The Hoare-Laval Pact is drawn up.	January 1921	October 1932

3. Hitler's foreign policy and the origins of the Second World War

Nazi's invade Czechoslovakia.	Chamberlain and Hitler meet at Bad Godesberg.	October 1933	March 1938
Britain and France declare war on Germany.	The Anglo-German Naval Treaty is signed.	October 1933	1 September 1939
The Rome-Berlin Axis is formed.	Germany re-occupies the Rhineland.	March 1939	March 1935

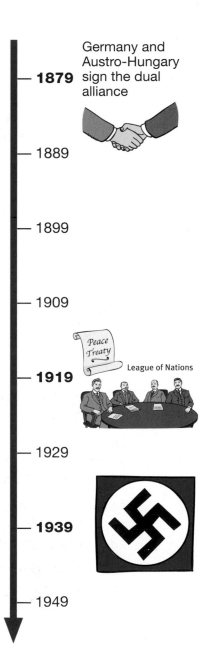

Timeline:

1879 — Germany and Austro-Hungary sign the dual alliance

1889

1899

1909

1919 — Peace Treaty — League of Nations

1929

1939

1949

Extension Task

1. Is there anything missing from your timeline? Add any other key events that you can think of.

2. Adding images to your revision notes is a good way to help remember key ideas, as your brain often remembers images better than it remembers text. Try adding images to your timeline.

Revision

Lesson Two: International Relations, Parts 4–6

Getting Started

Can you identify the key figures in each of the cartoons below?

The AQA History Specification B GCSE divides the Cold War, 1945–91, into three topics. You may have studied one or more of the following subjects:

The Origins of the Cold War 1945–1955
Crises of the Cold War 1955–1970
Failure of Détente and the Collapse of Communism, 1970–1991

During the course you will have learnt about a number of key figures. It is important that you are familiar with the role each individual played in the events that you have studied.

In this lesson you are going to consolidate your knowledge of the Cold War topic or topics you have studied. You will do so by completing a table that summarises information about the key figures who influenced events in this era.

Don't forget that there is further guidance on summarising your notes on the CD-ROM which accompanies this book.

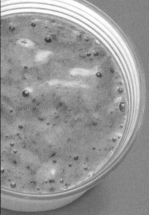

Activity

Copy and complete the table below, using the notes that you have made on Chapters 4, 5 and 6 of Unit 1.

Do not include in your chart any of the key figures you have not studied.

Name	Nationality	Job/position	Key beliefs	Events associated with this figure
Harry S. Truman				
General Douglas MacArthur				
Joseph Stalin				
Nikita Khrushchev				
John F. Kennedy				
Fidel Castro				
Jimmy Carter				
Ronald Reagan				
Imre Nagy				
Alexander Dubcek				
Lech Walesa				
Mikhail Gorbachev				

Have you studied any other key figures who you think should be added to this chart?

Activity

Now that you have revised the key figures associated with this topic, have a go at memorising your ideas.

There are a number of methods you could use to help you. Pick one of the following:

- Mnemonics
- Flash cards
- Multiple choice quizzes

If you decide to use flash cards or multiple choice quizzes, there are resources on the CD-ROM that will help you revise.

Exam Café

Exam Café

Revision

Lesson Three: 20th Century Depth Studies (Section A)

In this lesson you will:

- Consolidate your knowledge of the topic you have studied in Unit 2A.
- Organise your revision using a mind map.

Getting Started

Answer one of the following questions, which follow the style of those set in Paper 2, Section A:

From Tsardom to Communism: Russia, 1914–1924

In August 1914 Russia became involved in the First World War.
Explain why Nicholas II became increasingly unpopular during this war. (6 marks)

Weimar Germany, 1919–1929

Explain what Stresemann did to help the German economy recover in the years 1924–1929 (6 marks)

The Roaring 20s: USA, 1919–1929

Explain the consequences of Prohibition for the USA in the 1920s. (6 marks)

Activity

Create a mind map to summarise your understanding of the topic that you have studied.

A mind map is a diagram that mirrors the way your brain works by making links from one idea to another. Look at the example shown.

To draw your mind map, take a piece of plain paper and turn it so that it is wider than it is tall (landscape layout).

Write the topic you have studied in the middle of your page.

From this central title, draw branches. Add key events, figures, words and theories from your topic to these branches.

You should include lots of colour and images – your brain remembers these visual cues more easily than it remembers text.

Use the following summaries to help you focus your ideas.

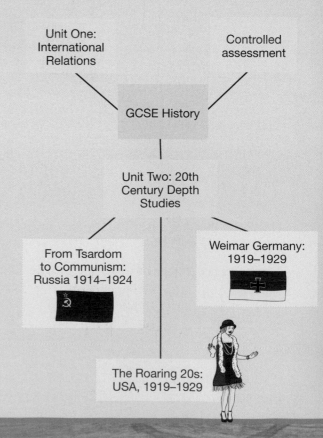

From Tsardom to Communism: Russia, 1914–1924

Use the following key questions as your main branches. Each of these branches should have smaller branches leading off it. On these smaller branches write details of specific events, individuals, words and beliefs.

1. Why did the rule of the tsar collapse in February/March 1917?
2. Why were the Bolsheviks able to seize power in October/November 1917?
3. How successful was Lenin in creating a new society in Russia?

Weimar Germany, 1919–1929

Use the following key questions as your main branches. Each of these branches should have smaller branches leading off it. On these smaller branches write details of specific events, individuals, words and beliefs.

1. How far do the early problems of the Weimar Republic suggest that it was doomed from the start?
2. How far did the Weimar Republic recover under Stresemann?
3. How far did the Nazi Party develop its ideas and organisation up to 1929?

The Roaring 20s: USA, 1919–1929

Use the following key questions as your main branches. Each of these branches should have smaller branches leading off it. On these smaller branches write details of specific events, individuals, words and beliefs.

1. How and why did the USA achieve prosperity in the 1920s?
2. How far was the USA a divided society in the 1920s?
3. Why did the US Stock Exchange collapse in 1929?

ExamCafé

Revision

Lesson Four: 20th Century Depth Studies (Section B)

Getting Started

Before you sit your final examination, you should practise a key skill: developing a description into an explanation. Many students find this task difficult.

Here is a task to help you develop this skill. Look at the picture below and have a go at answering the questions.

1. Describe what the fireman is wearing.
2. Explain why the fireman is wearing a hat.
3. Explain why the fireman is wearing boots.

Section B:

Your Unit 2 assessment is split into two sections. In Section B you will be assessed on one of the following topics. You can find revision content for all of these topics on the CD ROM.

- Stalin's Dictatorship: USSR, 1924–1941
- Hitler's Germany, 1929–1939
- Depression and the New Deal: The USA, 1929–1941
- Race Relations in the USA, 1955–1968
- The USA and Vietnam: Failure Abroad and at Home, 1964–1975
- Britain: The Challenge in Northern Ireland, 1960–1986
- The Middle East, 1956–1979

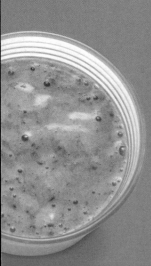

Activities

1. Practise answering an exam-style question that asks you to explain how far you agree with a statement by considering two sides of an argument.

   Can you put the following mark scheme into the correct order, by matching the level and mark to the description?

Level:	Description:	Mark:
1		0-3
2		4-6
3		6-7
4		

A	EITHER Identifies several reasons OR Explains one reason using knowledge and understanding
B	An analytical, linked, multi-causal answer clearly focused on the question. To achieve this level the candidate must have reached, supported and explained a final judgment.
C	Explains more than one reason
D	Simple descriptive comment and/or identifies one reason.

2. Chose one of the following questions to answer. Use the mark scheme you created during the Getting Started activity in order to help you develop your answer.

1	**Stalin's Dictatorship: USSR, 1924–1941**	'Stalin became sole ruler of the USSR by 1928 because he had been able to use his position as general secretary at the time of Lenin's death.' Do you agree? Explain your answer.
2	**Hitler's Germany, 1929–1939**	'The Nazis' use of threats and violence was the main reason why Hitler became chancellor of Germany in 1933.' Do you agree? Explain your answer.
3	**Depression and the New Deal: The USA, 1929–1941**	'The New Deal led to the economic recovery of the USA in the 1930s.' Do you agree? Explain your answer.
4	**Race Relations in the USA, 1955–1968**	'Without Martin Luther King the fight for civil rights in the USA would not have made progress in the 1950s and 1960s.' Do you agree? Explain your answer.
5	**The USA and Vietnam: Failure Abroad and at Home, 1964–1975**	'The Tet Offensive in 1968 was the main reason why the USA lost the Vietnam War.' Do you agree? Explain your answer.
6	**Britain: The Challenge in Northern Ireland, 1960–1986**	'Poverty and economic inequality were the main reasons for the Troubles in Northern Ireland in the 1960s and 1970s.' Do you agree? Explain your answer.
7	**The Middle East, 1956–1979**	'The signing of the treaty between Egypt and Israel in March 1979 brought peace to the Middle East at the end of the 1970s.' Do you agree? Explain your answer.

To get full marks you need to explain evidence from both sides of the argument and reach, support and explain a final judgment.

Glossary

abdicate – when a king or monarch, like the Tsar or the Kaiser, voluntarily gives up the throne.

affirmative action – President Johnson's policy of giving black people more support to complete with more well-off white people.

agitki – short propaganda newsreels shown in the countryside of the USSR.

agitprop – a combination of agitation and propaganda, used by Stalin to strengthen his control over Russia.

alliances – agreements between nations, often based on mutual defence.

amendment – in American politics, a change made to a part of the Constitution by the Government.

anarchists – people who believe there should be no form of government.

Anderson shelter – a air raid shelter in the Second World War, named after Sir John Anderson, the minister in charge of air raid protection.

annex – the seizing of a land from one country by another country.

anti-Semitism – an irrational hatred of Jewish people.

apparatchiki – the roughly 20,000 government officials of the USSR, beneath the *nomenklatura* (q.v.).

appeasement – Neville Chamberlain's policy of agreeing to some of Hitler's demands in order to pacify him.

armistice – an agreement between two sides in a war to stop fighting for a period of time.

arms race – a competition between two nations who want to build more military equipment and weapons than the other.

assassins – killers hired or trained to kill a public figure.

assembly line – an industrial method pioneered by Henry Ford in which a product is assembled a piece at a time on a conveyor belt by a team of workers.

atom bomb – the original nuclear weapon (q.v.), this type of weapon was dropped on Hiroshima and Nagasaki by the American Airforce at the end of World War Two.

autarky – the name given to Hitler's policy of self-sufficiency (q.v.).

autocrat – a monarch who has absolute power in their kingdom.

AWOL – Absent Without Leave; soldiers leaving their post without permission.

besieged – surrounded a place with military forces in order to capture it.

bill of rights – a law that gives the population civil and legal rights, such as freedom of speech.

black market – an illegal market for goods that are hard to get hold of.

blitzkrieg – 'lightening war'; the name given to the German tactic of using faster troops to cut through enemy defences and advance far behind enemy lines, used at the start of the Second World War.

blockade – sealing off a location to prevent goods and people from entering.

Bolsheviks – one of the factions formed from the split of the Russian Social Democratic Labour Party at its London Conference in 1903. The Bolsheviks followed Lenin, and became the government of Russia after the October Revolution.

bootleggers – people who smuggled alcohol into America during Prohibition (q.v.).

capitalism – a society that encourages private ownership of companies aiming to increase their wealth in a free market.

capitulation – ending all opposition to an opponent and giving in to their demands.

caricature – a cartoon-style image of a person, which stresses their key features.

censorship – government control over the media, preventing anything unacceptable to the government from being printed.

civil liberties – the legal rights and freedoms of the people, designed to protect them from the Government (such as freedom of speech, right of privacy, right to fair trial etc.).

coalition government – a government made up of several different parties working together.

collectivisation – an economic policy introduced by Stalin in 1929 that combined Russian farms into collectives run by committees, who produced a set amount of grain.

colony – a land that is established and ruled by another country.

common market – also known as the European Economic Community (EEC), this was an international organisation founded in 1957 to bring about economic integration between member European states.

commonwealth – a group of countries who work together for a common well-being.

Commissars – Soviet government officials, who hold authority over political and military decisions.

communism – a form of Marxism that calls for a classless society with common ownership and shared decision making.

compensate – to give someone something, often money, to make up for a loss or injury.

Congress – the name given to the parliament of the United States, including both the House of Representatives and the US Senate.

conscientious objector – a person who refuses to fight in a war for moral reasons.

conscription – a policy of compulsory military service for a fixed number of years.

constitution – a set of written rules and principles that guide the government of a country.

contraceptive – a device or medicine designed to prevent pregnancy.

cosmonauts – the name of the Russian astronauts.

covenant – a formal agreement which binds the parties involved to a specific action.

credibility gap – the difference between what the government tells people and what those people believe.

cruise missile – a guided, jet-powered explosive missile.

Crusaders – a group of Christians in the middle ages who had tried to conquer the holy land.

CS gas – also known as 'tear gas'; police often use this riots.

Dambusters – the name given to the British pilots who destroyed a series of German dams in a bombing raid on 17 May 1943.

decadent – a term used to describe a period or person which is in a state of moral or cultural decline.

decommission – to put material out of use.

decree – a government order that has become law.

demilitarised zone – an area between two countries, where no troops are allowed.

democracy – a form of government where the people elect their representatives.

depression – an economic downturn that leads to a reduced value of money, higher unemployment, bankruptcies and a fall in trade.

desegregation – the policy of ending the deliberate separation of black and white Americans in the 1950s and 1960s.

destabilised – this situation occurs when an action damages the status quo between two groups.

Détente – a political term for the easing of tension between the USSR and the Western Powers.

devolution – the granting of power from central government to a regional or local one.

Diplock courts – courts without a jury, used against IRA suspects in the 1970s.

diplomacy – the discussion and creation of agreements between countries.

disarm – to reduce the number of a country's armed forces and weapons.

Dissidents – people who disagree with the government over issues.

domino theory – the theory that one country turning communist would lead to all its neighbouring countries turning communist as well.

Doodlebug – the name given by the population of London to the German V1 flying bomb during the Second World War.

draft cards – a card held by men of military service age in America in the 1960s and 1970s. The card entered men into a lottery for service in Vietnam.

Dreadnought – the name given to a type of warship, named after the *HMS Dreadnought,* launched in 1906. Building these ships was a key part of the arms race between Britain and Germany before the First World War.

Duma – the Russian parliament introduced by the Tsar in 1905.

dust bowl – the name given to the effect of drought in the South and Midwest states of America in the 1930s which turned the soil to dust.

Eastern Front – the battlefields East of Germany during the First and Second World Wars.

economies of scale – the money saved by buying products in bulk rather than one at a time.

empire – a group of countries across the world that is ruled by another country.

Enabling Law – a law introduced by Hitler on 23 March 1933 which allowed him to pass law without consulting the Reichstag or President.

Entente Cordiale – an agreement between Great Britain and France to remain on good terms and not quarrel over colonies, signed in 1904.

evacuated – the movement of people from a dangerous location to a safer one.

exiled – banned from a country for political reasons.

famine – a terrible shortage of food that leaves a population starving.

Fascism – a strongly nationalist political theory that aims to make a country stronger at the expense of other nations. Nazism is a type of Facism.

fedayeen – 'those who sacrifice themselves', the name given to a group of Palestinian terrorists who attacked Israelis in the 1950s.

Fourteen Points – the key aims of President Woodrow Wilson after the First World War, which included self-determination and the League of Nations.

freedom houses – houses rented by CORE workers, from where they distributed information on education, employment, health and housing.

fundamentalist – a person with an extremely traditional religious viewpoint.

GNP – Gross National Product; the value of all goods produced by a country in one year.

genocide – a deliberate attempt to destroy a whole race of people.

gerrymander – to fix election boundaries to guarantee Protestant majorities in Catholic areas.

ghettos – areas in which certain groups are housed, with poor, crowded housing, violence and high crime.

Gold standard – the link between the exchange rate value of a country's currency and the amount of gold that country holds.

grammar school – selective schools post-1944 that provided free secondary education for those who passed the 'Eleven plus' exam.

Great Depression – the name given to the economic downturn (recession) in America in the 1930s, caused by the Wall Street Crash.

Gregorian calendar – the name for the internationally accepted calendar.

guerrilla warfare – a type of warfare where a smaller force uses stealth and hit-and-run tactics to fight a much larger, better-supplied force.

gulag – the system of labour camps in the USSR

haemophilia – a medical condition, where the blood can not clot, meaning the body can not stop bleeding when cut.

hire purchase – a buyer buys something but pays for it in installments over a period of time.

Hitler Youth – the name given to the Nazi organisation for boys.

hobos – unemployed people, often travelling from place to place looking for work.

Holocaust – the attempted Nazi genocide (q.v.) of the Jewish people.

Home Defence – groups and systems established in Britain during World War Two to help protect from a possible German invasion.

Home Guard – Local Defence Volunteers in Britain during the Second World War, on duty during air raids and on the look-out for a possible German invasion.

Hoovervilles – the name given to homeless communities in America during the Great Depression (q.v.) as an insult to President Hoover.

hyperinflation – a financial crisis where the value of money becomes so low that it is virtually worthless.

ideology – a set of beliefs and viewpoints that form a political theory.

immigrants – people who move to live in another country, often for financial or political reasons.

imperialism – the belief in building a country's power by conquering over countries.

indoctrination – the process of programming a group of people to believe a certain set of ideas or values.

industrialisation – the process of introducing machines into a country's industry.

internment – the imprisonment of IRA suspects without trial.

interpretation – an individual's viewpoint.

Iron Curtain – the phrase invented by Winston Churchill to describe the division in Europe between the Western powers and the Soviet Union and its allies.

isolationism – a belief that your country should not get involved in the events in other countries.

khozyain – 'father figure'; Stalin was known as this after the 1924 Party Congress.

kibbutzin – co-operative farms in Israel.

kneecapped – shooting someone in both kneecaps.

Knesset – the Israeli Parliament

Kulak – a group of well-off peasants in 1920s Soviet Russia. Stalin later purged this group in the 1930s, blaming them for food shortages.

labour camps – a type of prison where the inmates are forced to carry out physical labour. Stalin used labour camps, called gulags, for many of his political opponents.

laissez-faire – 'leave things be'; a policy of leaving things to take their own course without interference.

Lebensraum – 'living space'; one of Hitler's main policies was Germany's right to more land or living space, to be taken from their neighbouring countries.

looting – the stealing of goods from damaged or deserted areas during war.

mandate – a licence given by the League of Nations or United Nations to one country, allowing it to govern another.

Marxism – a theory that sees class differences, caused by economics, as central to political change.

means test – a test in 1930's Britain designed to make sure that an unemployed man had no way of raising money other than by going on the dole.

megatons – a measurement of the explosive force of a nuclear weapon.

Mensheviks – one of the factions formed from the split of the Russian Social Democratic Labour Party at its London Conference in 1903. The Mensheviks sided with the Provisional Government and were outlawed in 1921.

militarism – a belief in the importance of a strong and well prepared army.

mobilisation – placing armies on alert and preparing them for combat.

Mujaheddin – an Islamic term for a Muslim fighting in a religious war.

munitionettes – women recruited to work in the armaments industry during the First World War.

MX missile – this missile has a nuclear warhead and can be fired from a range of smaller locations, making it easier to launch than a bomb.

nationalisation – making an industry government-owned and run.

nationalism – a powerful love and loyalty for your own country and all its actions.

neutral – not taking a side in an argument.

Neutron bomb – a type of nuclear weapon, with a smaller explosion than a standard nuclear weapon, designed to release radiation into the atmosphere. It can kill more people than a standard nuclear weapon but destroy much less property.

nomenklatura – the name given to the top 5000 Communist Party officials in the USSR.

nuclear weapons – weapons that use the energy from reactions between small amounts of two different types of material to create a much larger explosion.

oppressed – a term used to describe a people whose rights are denied by their government.

OGPU – the Russian Secret Police, which later became known as the KGB.

pact – a formal agreement between two countries.

Pan-German League – an organisation in Germany that promoted the idea of a Central Europe dominated by a strong German state, including all German-speaking peoples.

pacifist – a person who does not believe in violence.

passive resistance – a non-violent form of resistance, usually involving non-co-operation.

paternalism – treating others as children who need to taken care of.

Peaceful Co-existence – a new policy introduced by Khrushchev, where the USSR would recognise the Western powers' right to exist.

phonograph – an early 1920's record player.

plebiscite – a vote in which the population is asked what they want to do on a single issue.

pograms – a violent riot focused against a particular group.

Politburo – the group of Commissars who ran the day-to-day government business of the USSR.

pre-emptive strike – an attack that is launched by one side before the other side can attack.

prefabs – prefabricated houses, where all the parts of house are pre-built then assembled on site.

Proletariat – a term, often used by socialists, to describe the lower classes.

Prohibition – the period between 1919 and 1933 when alcohol was illegal in America.

proportional representation – the awarding of seats in parliament according to the number of votes received nationwide, giving every group representation.

protection rackets – schemes under which criminal organisations demand money from businesses to protect them from criminal action against them.

protectionism – the policy of putting tariffs on imported goods, making them more expensive and encouraging people to buy domestic goods instead.

Protestant – a branch of Christianity which began in opposition to the Catholic church

provenance – where something comes from.

province – an administrative area controlled by a central government.

puppet government – a government that is in fact controlled by the government of another country.

putsch – a German word for coup; Hitler attempted a Putsch against the German government in Munich in 1923.

radar – a system that uses electromagnetic waves to calculate the range, direction, speed and altitude of approaching objects.

ratify – to confirm an agreement, such as a treaty.

rationed – a fixed amount of something, usually food, that each person is allowed in a time of shortage.

raw materials – materials from nature that can be used for industry or construction, such as iron or oil.

re-armament – increasing the strength of the army in a nation and increasing the production of weapons.

rebellion – a violent attack against a government.

renegade – a person who abandons an organisation or set of ideas and acts on their own authority.

reparations – the payments made by Germany to the rest of Europe, especially France, after the First World War to pay for war damage.

repressive – term used to describe a government that puts restraints on personal freedoms.

Russification – the Soviet policy of enforcing Russian culture onto other communities.

sabotage – deliberate damage to machines or tools to prevent them working.

sanctions – restrictions placed on a country, usually on trade, to force that country to agree to an international agreement.

satellite states – countries that are independent but follow the lead of another, more powerful country.

sectarian – discrimination and prejudice due to differences in a group, such as religious differences in Ireland

segregation – the policy of keeping two different groups completely separate, e.g. blacks and whites in America in the early 20th century.

self-determination – the right of people of a single national group to rule themselves, introduced by President Woodrow Wilson after the First World War.

self-sufficient – being able to produce all the foods and raw materials you need yourself.

Socialism – a political ideology that calls for state ownership of the economy and a distribution of goods by need.

sonar – an underwater system that uses sound waves to locate other objects and navigate around them.

Soviet – a worker's council and later used by the Bolsheviks (q.v.) as the basis of their government in the Soviet Union.

spats – a cloth cover for the ankle and instep of a shoe, popular in 1920's America.

speakeasies – illegal bars which sold alcohol during Prohibition (q.v.).

speculators – people who risk their money by buying and selling shares on the stock exchange.

sphere of interest – a country or area that another country has power, but not direct authority, over.

Stakhanovites – workers in the USSR who achieved more than their quota, named after a famous coal miner, Stakhanov.

stalemate – a draw where neither side can make a move without losing an advantage.

stock exchange – the market where stocks and shares are bought and sold.

stocks and shares – the names given to the 'shares' of ownership in companies that are traded on the stock exchange.

subsistence farming – a farming system in which people only grow what they need to survive.

summit – an international meeting between two or more national leaders.

surplus – the goods left over once a requirement has been met.

swastika – the symbol of the Nazi party.

tariffs – taxes, or duties, put on goods imported from other countries.

tarred and feathered – name given to mob justice aiming to humiliate and hurt, which came from the practice of covering people with tar then feathers.

Third Reich – the name given to the government of Nazi Germany.

time and motion – a study looking at making each worker's task as quick as possible.

totalitarian – term used to describe a government that is undemocratic and ruled by a single person or party.

treaty – a formal agreement made between states, which can be about anything from trade to ending a war.

trench foot – a First World War foot condition caused by standing in wet mud in the trenches.

Triple Alliance – the military alliance formed between Germany, Austro-Hungary and Italy in 1882.

Triple Entente – the agreement reached between Great Britain, France and Russia in 1907.

Troika – this was the name given to the anti-Trotsky alliance of Stalin, Kamenev and Zinoviev.

tyranny – term used to describe the rule of a government that is cruel and oppressive.

tyrant – a person who rules a country in a cruel and oppressive way.

Ulster – the northern six counties of Ireland, later becoming Northern Ireland.

Ulsterisation – the British policy of withdrawing British soldiers from Northern Ireland and removing political status from IRA prisoners.

USSR – the Union of Soviet Socialist Republics, or Soviet Union; the name given to Russia and a number of smaller countries by the Communists.

utility clothing – a fashion during the Second World War which encouraged use of less cloth in the making of clothes.

Vozhd – Russian for leader of Boss; Stalin was often called this.

Wall Street Crash – a devastating financial crash on the US stock market on 29 October 1929, which led to a world wide depression.

Warlords – the strong military figures who ruled different areas of China.

Welfare state – introduced in Britain after the Second World War, this provided a free Health Service, unemployment support, council housing, free secondary education and full employment.

Western Front – the battlefields to the West of Germany in both the First and Second World Wars.

Yom kippur – the holiest day of the Jewish Calendar.

zeppelins – German airships filled with hydrogen or helium.

zionism – a Jewish political belief which argued for a Jewish State.

Index

Single User Licence Agreement: AQA B GCSE Modern World History ActiveBook CD-ROM

WARNING:

This is a legally binding agreement between You (the user or purchasing institution) and Pearson Education Limited of Edinburgh Gate, Harlow, Essex, CM20 2JE, United Kingdom ('PEL').

By retaining this Licence, any software media or accompanying written materials or carrying out any of the permitted activities You are agreeing to be bound by the terms and conditions of this Licence. If You do not agree to the terms and conditions of this Licence, do not continue to use the AQA B GCSE Modern World History ActiveBook CD-ROM and promptly return the entire publication (this Licence and all software, written materials, packaging and any other component received with it) with Your sales receipt to Your supplier for a full refund.

Intellectual Property Rights:

This AQA B GCSE Modern World History ActiveBook CD-ROM consists of copyright software and data. All intellectual property rights, including the copyright is owned by PEL or its licensors and shall remain vested in them at all times. You only own the disk on which the software is supplied. If You do not continue to do only what You are allowed to do as contained in this Licence you will be in breach of the Licence and PEL shall have the right to terminate this Licence by written notice and take action to recover from you any damages suffered by PEL as a result of your breach.

The PEL name, PEL logo and all other trademarks appearing on the software and AQA B GCSE Modern World History ActiveBook CD-ROM are trademarks of PEL. You shall not utilise any such trademarks for any purpose whatsoever other than as they appear on the software and AQA B GCSE Modern World History ActiveBook CD-ROM.

Yes, You can:

1. use this AQA B GCSE Modern World History ActiveBook CD-ROM on Your own personal computer as a single individual user. You may make a copy of the AQA B GCSE Modern World History ActiveBook CD-ROM in machine readable form for backup purposes only. The backup copy must include all copyright information contained in the original.

No, You cannot:

1. copy this AQA B GCSE Modern World History ActiveBook CD-ROM (other than making one copy for back-up purposes as set out in the Yes, You can table above);

2. alter, disassemble, or modify this AQA B GCSE Modern World History ActiveBook CD-ROM, or in any way reverse engineer, decompile or create a derivative product from the contents of the database or any software included in it;

3. include any materials or software data from the AQA B GCSE Modern World History ActiveBook CD-ROM in any other product or software materials;

4. rent, hire, lend, sub-licence or sell the AQA B GCSE Modern World History ActiveBook CD-ROM;

5. copy any part of the documentation except where specifically indicated otherwise;

6. use the software in any way not specified above without the prior written consent of PEL;

7. subject the software, AQA B GCSE Modern World History ActiveBook CD-ROM or any PEL content to any derogatory treatment or use them in such a way that would bring PEL into disrepute or cause PEL to incur liability to any third party.

Grant of Licence:

PEL grants You, provided You only do what is allowed under the 'Yes, You can' table above, and do nothing under the 'No, You cannot' table above, a non-exclusive, non-transferable Licence to use this AQA B GCSE Modern World History ActiveBook CD-ROM.

The terms and conditions of this Licence become operative when using this AQA B GCSE Modern World History ActiveBook CD-ROM.

Limited Warranty:

PEL warrants that the disk or CD-ROM on which the software is supplied is free from defects in material and workmanship in normal use for ninety (90) days from the date You receive it. This warranty is limited to You and is not transferable.

This limited warranty is void if any damage has resulted from accident, abuse, misapplication, service or modification by someone other than PEL. In no event shall PEL be liable for any damages whatsoever arising out of installation of the software, even if advised of the possibility of such damages. PEL will not be liable for any loss or damage of any nature suffered by any party as a result of reliance upon or reproduction of any errors in the content of the publication.

PEL does not warrant that the functions of the software meet Your requirements or that the media is compatible with any computer system on which it is used or that the operation of the software will be unlimited or error free. You assume responsibility for selecting the software to achieve Your intended results and for the installation of, the use of and the results obtained from the software.

PEL shall not be liable for any loss or damage of any kind (except for personal injury or death) arising from the use of this AQA B GCSE Modern World History ActiveBook CD-ROM or from errors, deficiencies or faults therein, whether such loss or damage is caused by negligence or otherwise.

The entire liability of PEL and your only remedy shall be replacement free of charge of the components that do not meet this warranty.

No information or advice (oral, written or otherwise) given by PEL or PEL's agents shall create a warranty or in any way increase the scope of this warranty.

To the extent the law permits, PEL disclaims all other warranties, either express or implied, including by way of example and not limitation, warranties of merchantability and fitness for a particular purpose in respect of this AQA B GCSE Modern World History ActiveBook CD-ROM.

Termination:

This Licence shall automatically terminate without notice from PEL if You fail to comply with any of its provisions or the purchasing institution becomes insolvent or subject to receivership, liquidation or similar external administration. PEL may also terminate this Licence by notice in writing. Upon termination for whatever reason You agree to destroy the AQA B GCSE Modern World History ActiveBook CD-ROM and any back-up copies and delete any part of the AQA B GCSE Modern World History ActiveBook CD-ROM stored on your computer.

Governing Law:

This Licence will be governed by and construed in accordance with English law.

© Pearson Education Limited 2009